Imperial Citizens

Imperial Citizens

Koreans and Race from Seoul to LA

Nadia Y. Kim

Stanford University Press
Stanford, California

Stanford University Press
Stanford, California

Printed in the United States of America on acid-free, archival-quality paper

Library of Congress Cataloging-in-Publication Data

Kim, Nadia Y.
    Imperial citizens : Koreans and race from Seoul to LA / Nadia Y. Kim.
        p. cm.
    Includes bibliographical references and index.
    ISBN 978-0-8047-5886-4 (cloth : alk. paper)—ISBN 978-0-8047-5887-1 (pbk. : alk. paper)
    1. Korean Americans—Race identity—Case studies.   2. Korean Americans—Social conditions—Case studies.   3. Immigrants—United States—Social conditions—Case studies.
4. Racism—United States—Case studies.   5. Imperialism—Social aspects—United States—Case studies.   6. United States—Race relations—Case studies.   7. Korean Americans—California—Los Angeles—Social conditions.   8. Koreans—Korea (South)—Seoul—Social conditions.   9. Los Angeles (Calif.)—Race relations.   10. Seoul (Korea)—Race relations.
I. Title.
    E184.K6K486 2008
    305.895'707979494—dc22   2007049983

Typeset by Westchester Book Group in 10/14 Minion

To my dad,
for a love that outlives your Time. Your dreams
wake me up every day.

To Ty,
for selflessly guiding us here when the
world had other plans.

There is a hole to escape through even when the sky collapses on us.

—Korean proverb

Contents

Illustrations

Figures

Tables

Note on Terminology

IN THIS BOOK I EMPLOY THE TERMS "Asian American" and "Korean American" and, for the sake of brevity, use these interchangeably with "Asian" and "Korean," respectively. Precisely for the reasons that I analyze in this book, however, the "American" locution is problematic insofar as it belies the fact that Asians in the United States are denied an authentic American status. "Asian American" also tends to normalize some Asian ethnics and elide others. Although mindful of these concerns, the lack of a better term leaves me little choice but to use it. I address the authenticity issue by using the term alongside the qualified moniker "White American" and the like. I also employ the term based on its all-inclusive definition, referring to East, South, and Southeast Asian groups (unless I specify otherwise), without suggesting that there are no important differences between these groups. Specific to Koreans, at times I use "Korean immigrant" and "Korean American" interchangeably unless I qualify otherwise. I am guided by the notion that, irrespective of citizenship, Koreans who intend to live in the United States for a long period are "Korean Americans." For Koreans in Seoul I use "South Koreans," "Seoul residents," or "nonmigrants."

Also for the sake of brevity I use "White" and "White American" interchangeably. I eschew the word "Caucasian" except in interviews when I borrow the terminology of my respondents. As far as I am aware, "Caucasian" refers to Whites' origins in the "Caucasus" region, one from which some scholars have alleged a "superior 'race'" originated. In addition, I use "Black," "Black American," and "African American" interchangeably, but I find "Black"/"Black American" to be the most inclusive as it captures diverse ethnics whom U.S.

society would deem phenotypically "Black": Africans, West Indians, and Latinos in addition to the native born. In this study I refer mostly to Mexican and Central Americans but sometimes (though sparingly) use "Latinos" interchangeably and do my best to specify when I am referring to the national Latino population.

With regard to the key concepts of my book, I define "race" as a sociohistorical construction based on biological (heritable) phenomena that is externally imposed yet contested. Whenever possible, I denote the socially constructed character of "race" by placing quotations around the word and employing the term "racialized." Relative to "race," I conceptualize "ethnicity" as a category that is more volitional, more internally defined, and more rooted in historical-cultural criteria (e.g., national origins, language, religion, folk traditions; Cornell and Hartmann 1998). When I use "ethnonationality" in this book I refer to an essentialist construction whereby the nation is seen to share blood ancestry and constitute a family (see Balibar 1991). By "color" I borrow from Thomas Guglielmo (2003) who deems it a *socially defined* descriptor of "race," one's skin tone; yet the social basis of color can be evidenced by the fact that those labeled "White" may be of darker skin tone than those labeled "Black." Although I note the conceptual differences between the above categories, I also recognize that "race," ethnicity, ethnonationality, and color overlap, intersect, and interact.

On other terminology, I acknowledge that "America" is also a problematic term, because the United States is certainly not the only America. Yet, because many of the respondents themselves used the term, it typically fit better than the cumbersome "United States (of America)" or "USA," and as few alternatives exist, I found little choice but to use it. I do my best, however, to make clear when I use the term to invoke the hegemonic glorification that is "America"; I do so by putting quotes around the word. When referring to South Korea I also use the term "home country," not because I do not conceive of the United States as Koreans' home, but because I am usually conceptualizing it from the ethnonationalist vantage point of the Koreans themselves. Last but not least, I draw on the McCune-Reischauer romanized spelling of the Korean language in this text, except in the case of mainstream newspaper names.

Acknowledgments

I ALWAYS ENJOY THIS EXERCISE. Acknowledgments displace our American penchant for individualism and the cult of personality. I'm humbled by how many people have walked with me. Sadly, space issues preclude me from naming everyone and doing justice to those I do name. First, I thank all the Korean participants who made this possible. They opened up their homes, spent time with me in the field, and let me take them to an inevitably emotional place. *Komapssŭmnida.*

As a graduate student at the University of Michigan (UM) I had the great fortune of working with Sonya Rose. Her keen acumen, skilled mentoring, and empathy helped me finish on my feet. I must thank her and my readers, John Lie and Al Young, for commenting on the entire book manuscript some years later—I'm grateful for their minds and unfailing support. I thank my other sharp, stellar readers, Mark Chesler and Amy Stillman, and I thank Eduardo Bonilla-Silva, Silvia Pedraza, Don Deskins (Seoul!), Mayer Zald, Renee Anspach, and Tony Chen for reading chapters or seeing me through. I thank the grants and fellowships that helped me move toward the book: the American Sociological Association Minority Fellowship, the Northeast Consortium Dissertation Fellowship, the Center for Comparative Immigration Studies (CCIS) Research Fellowship, and UM and Brandeis University awards.

I must thank those who helped someone they didn't have to: In-Jin Yoon was instrumental in Seoul, Kyeyoung Park was instrumental in Los Angeles (I also thank her for her feedback). Others who generously gave comments at various stages are Amílcar Barreto, Prudence Carter, CCIS writers, Reg Daniel (who groomed me into a sociologist), Shilpa Davé, Yen Espiritu, Joe Feagin,

Wolverines Tom Guglielmo and Moon-Kie Jung, Debby Kaufman, David Lopez, Laura Miller, Michael Omi, Rhacel S. Parreñas, Bandana Purkayastha, Karen Pyke, Kerry Ann Rockquemore, John Skrentny, and Gaku Tsuda. Thanks to Sharmila Rudrappa for commenting on the whole manuscript.

Research assistants do not get enough credit. Without Heejin Choi, the Seoul fieldwork would have crashed on takeoff. I am also indebted to Omari Jackson, Jun Choi, Monica Kang, Ashley Rondini, Cristen Powell, Janice Yoo, and all the persevering transcriptionists.

My deep gratitude to Kate Wahl—I couldn't have asked for a better editor. I thank Dick Flacks, John Foran, and Diane Fujino for first seeing my potential; my UM graduate student family of sweet, brilliant peers (and Academics for Affirmative Action and Social Justice!); and those who offered scholarly insights and resources for this project: Tyrone Forman, Amanda Lewis, Barb Kim, Sherri-Ann Butterfield, Ed Chang, Luis Falcón, Kathrin Zippel, Cassandra Jackson, Regine Jackson, Mina Yoo, the Romeros, Jen Guglielmo, Sue Lanser, Sarah Lamb, Anita Hill, David Cunningham, Ed Park, Loyola Marymount University Sociology and Bellarmine College, Ewha University, and Evergreen Church. Thanks to those who constantly checked up on me or gave me shelter in the field (you know who you are). Extra thanks to Kŭn Gomo, Kŭn Gomobu, Oppa Kyuho, Tarak Bang Hasuk, Samchon, Nick Rattray, and the Sasakis.

My mother was my solace and strength through car accidents, maladies, and fatigue in the field. My triumphs are hers. I thank Doc; "sibs" Mike, Jeff, Mina, Dave; and my various in-laws, with special thanks to Poh Poh Tran for her kindness and to Julie, lil' Ethan, and lil' Jordie for reminding me how just the world could be if we learned to see it through children's eyes.

I owe all my friends and family time, but the tab for Dan Han is the biggest. Dan, without your generosity almost to a fault, I could never have finished. I marvel every day at how you listen to your heart, and most importantly, how you *are* your heart. More than my work, I dedicate to you—my everyday miracle—my life.

I must end by recognizing the individuals who devote their existence to fighting for justice and uplifting others. I admire nobody more. To the "freedom fighters" who march on and beyond for all of us, may the world fall in step.

1 Introduction

Imperial Racialization

GROWING UP, I often heard my mother recount how she had loved watching *Gone with the Wind, Wuthering Heights,* and other classic American motion pictures back in South Korea. She also told me that she had witnessed "real Americans" walking around near her hometown of Pusan, soldiers who were not just American but also Black. As a child I was too young to appreciate how much my mother knew about the United States and its people long before she immigrated there from South Korea in 1969. Indeed, it took some years before I could appreciate how intimately aware my mother and her friends were of President John F. Kennedy and his Camelot, seeing as how they cried when news of his death crossed the Pacific. Soon, however, my intellectual curiosity was roused by her stories. Simpler questions—What other American mass media had she engaged? What were her views of White and Black soldiers during the Korean War—translated into my curiosity about how she had generally constructed "Americanness" and her own countrypeople before emigrating.

My unanswered questions came to trouble me viscerally, however, as I watched Koreatown and other parts of Los Angeles aflame in 1992 purportedly because of Black-Korean racial conflicts, not then knowing how racially sensationalized the event was (Abelmann and Lie 1995). I could not help wondering whether Korean immigrants had taken cues from Whites' racism toward Blacks in their Korean homeland and in that way helped fuel LA's fires. Perhaps Koreans had seen too many *Gone with the Wind* mammy stereotypes or interpreted Black soldiers' second-class American status as reflective of a natural order, perhaps embracing the Confucianist ethos that deemed inequality as natural? On the other side of the divide, had U.S. stereotypes of Asian Americans as "model minorities" or racial "foreigners" fostered anti-Asian stereotypes among Blacks? Did Blacks target Korean ethnics for imposing on "real" Americans?

Indeed, the foreignness of Korean Americans jumped off the television screens and newspaper pages, whether the media depictions were of model minority ghetto merchants or of immigrant outsiders (Palumbo-Liu 1994), another source of my deep disquiet. It seemed impossible for even the most well-intentioned person not to stereotype Koreans in these binary ways. I cringed at the recycled repertoire of images of Koreans crying and shrieking in the "un-American" Korean language, as hard-working, innocent model minority immigrants wronged by Black and Latino hoodlums, or as AK-47–toting vigilantes atop store rooftops who didn't seem to follow normal American customs of calling the police. To be sure, none of these sensationalist sound bites could capture the complexity of Korean America.

Upon combing articles and books and enrolling in numerous courses on "race" and ethnicity as a means to understand the chaos around me, I realized that most of the classic tools and theories I was given, such as various assimilation accounts, seemed to simplify the Asian immigrant experience by predicting that Koreans, as model minorities, would assimilate along most societal lines and "whiten." Unsatisfied, I began to harvest the fruits of my longtime intellectual curiosity and desire for social change. I returned to my mother's stories and peered beyond Los Angeles and the United States to ask other questions. For instance, did Koreans' history of being subjugated by U.S. imperial rule and their exposure to American racial hierarchies in their ethnic homeland not matter in any way? Did the U.S. government's lack of regard for Korean Americans and South Korea have anything to do with its inaction when Koreatown was burning for days, in contrast to its swift troop movement once Beverly Hills was *potentially* threatened (Cho 1993; E. Kim 1993)? Did the racial ideology[1] of Asian Americans as foreigners in the United States play no role, a notion that seemed to originate with U.S. imperialism? I realized that the classic social scientific literature could not help me fully understand such tragedies as the 1992 unrest. For one, the literature started and stopped its analyses within U.S. boundaries. If most Koreans (and other Asian Americans) had been arriving in the United States since 1970, however, I knew that the previous decades of U.S. dominance or influence in their home country had already been grounded in racial hierarchies. As Yen Le Espiritu (2003:210; see A. Ong 1996) aptly remarks in the case of Filipinos in the United States, their lives—and I believe Koreans' lives—are "shaped not only by the social location of their group within the

United States but also by the position of their home country within the global racial order." In other words, a consideration of racialization[2] *across borders* (Espiritu 2003) and through *multiple and related lines of inequality* (C. Kim 1999) begs reevaluation of the assimilating, whitening Asian model minority and of U.S. "race" inequality more broadly. By way of a global and multiracial framework, this book pursues a cross-border analysis of "imperialist racial formations" in South Korea and in the United States (Omi and Winant 1994). That is, I analyze the hegemonic link between the U.S. state and social movements, the backbone of American "race" dynamics in both countries, in a context of American imperialism. I do so from the vantage of the margins because macro social structures often do not reveal as much about the nature of power as those who are marginalized, who live the contradictions (Glick Schiller 2005). I draw primarily, then, on interviews with Koreans in Los Angeles County, California, and Seoul, South Korea (Republic of Korea or ROK), and I draw secondarily on ethnographic observations in Seoul, informal observations in Los Angeles, and archival newspaper research. Conducting multisite fieldwork rather than practicing what Andreas Wimmer and Nina Glick Schiller (2003) call "methodological nationalism" allows me to capture the nature of American racial dominance in South Korea and its links to "race" within its own borders, as well as the cross-border lenses that immigrants use to navigate U.S. color and citizenship lines.

Informed by renewed inquiries into empire (e.g., Hardt and Negri 2000; Harvey 2003), I focus on the role of U.S. imperialism in shaping immigrants' transnational understandings of "race" and their related identities, thus departing from the American-centered framework of the field of U.S. immigration. Models of incorporation and assimilation in the United States have thus dominated, such as the segmented assimilation thesis (Portes and Zhou 1993) and, in more recent years, a well-received (neo)institutional theory by Richard Alba and Victor Nee (2003). Segmented assimilation, Alejandro Portes and Min Zhou (1993) theorize, is a segmented process of immigrant incorporation that departs from the unilinear trajectory of classic models, which is the theory's strength. In this framework, immigrants, the second generation in particular, navigate the modes of incorporation that greet them (e.g., policies, prejudices) and in the process follow three different pathways. One is "growing acculturation and parallel integration into the White middle-class; a second leads straight in the opposite direction to permanent poverty and assimilation into the underclass; still a third associates rapid economic advancement with deliberate preservation of the immigrant community's values and tight solidarity" (Portes and Zhou 1993:82; see Gibson 1988). Laudably, the theory emphasizes the effects of color and integrates meaning-making within the processes that shape immigrants' fates. Yet, as all the pathways unfold in linear fashion in the United States, the model does not consider the fact that, for many groups, their choices and cultural mores, as well as the barriers they face, are tied to a history of Western dominance over their home countries. On this issue with reference to Asian Americans, Kenyon S. Chan and Shirley Hune (1995:213) aptly state that "throughout U.S. history each Asian American community continued to have its image and well-being defined not by its activities in the United States but by a racial order that was both domestic and international. No other American immigrant community has had its domestic relations with the U.S. government so determined by the nation's foreign policies with homeland states." In forging their lives in the United States, then, Asian immigrants are always reminded of and affected by these foreign relations.

Another major model, (neo)institutional theory (Alba and Nee 2003), laudably treats assimilation not as inevitable but as the unintended consequence of immigrants' working toward everyday goals of getting a good job, an education, and so on within institutional structures. Moreover, the theory avoids the presumption that immigrants are the only ones who change from assimilation processes because it posits that institutional structures themselves are changed by the immigrants. Despite the model's insightful correctives for the problems that have plagued more traditional assimilation models, it focuses only on what happens to the immigrants in institutions within the bounded United States. And in somewhat of a contrast to Portes and Zhou (1993), Alba and Nee do not consider institutionalized discrimination to be a barrier (anymore) for Asian Americans in the United States. Argued thus, the model leaves no room for the impact of Western racial hierarchies and ideologies in the immigrants' home countries. My study finds, however, that U.S. society conflates Asians in Asia and Asians in the United States in large part because of its historical and dominant relationship to both.

In considering segmented and (neo)institutional assimilation, I also depart from the primacy these accounts give to social class mobility as a determinant of immigrants' increased equality. Immigrants are said to assimilate in large part through movement up the social class ladder. What my study shows, however, is that social class is neither the only key axis of assimilation nor a ticket out of institutionalized and everyday racial barriers. To be certain, Korean Americans, including the second generation, do selectively assimilate by expressing strong ethnic identification and relying on ethnic networks to move up socioeconomically. But, again, social class is but one mark of social inequality. There are myriad factors that preclude full membership in the mainstream United States culture and the national identity. For instance, as long as Asian Americans continue to be associated with Asia, they do not escape racial bias simply because they have made it into the White American middle class. That is, no matter their command of English, high rates of female intermarriage with White men, Harvard degrees, and Beverly Hills homes, Asian Americans have still been treated as unassimilable "forever foreigners," in the words of Mia Tuan (1998). To be certain, Asian Americans (of mostly Eastern or Southern Asian backgrounds) have been valorized for their socioeconomic successes relative to presumably underclass Black Americans. As a result, Asian Americans can and do benefit from their "model minoritized bodies" at the expense of Blacks, especially in light of Whites' greater willingness to live beside and marry Asian Americans (C. Kim 2000). Yet, the fact that model minority acclaim has not been enough to confer authentic American status onto Asian ethnics yields a sort of fraternal twin in Black Americans' experiences of class. That is, just as a high class profile has not spared Black Americans from both institutionalized and everyday racism (e.g., S. Collins 1997; Cose 1993; Feagin and Sikes 1994; Williams 1991), class status has not spared, and in fact often exacerbates, nativistic racism toward Asian Americans. This link between the model minority and the yellow peril / foreigner makes apparent that the two ideologies are not discrete but part of a continuum of racialization. As Gary Okihiro (1994:142) aptly states, the model minority and the yellow peril are not poles but "form a circular relationship that moves in either direction." That is, although Asian Americans' success can incite anti–yellow peril discrimination (see Ancheta 1998; Newman 1993), the (feminized) model minority image can assuage fears of a (masculinized) yellow peril, enabling the representations to exist side by side (Okihiro 1994; see Espiritu 1997). The limits of social class upward mobility for undoing criminal notions of Blacks and forever foreigner conceptions of Asian Americans throw into relief the operation of racial dominance. In other words, through elites' frequent emphasis on "race" above social class and pitting of groups of color against one another, the larger racial order goes unquestioned and, more important, unchanged.

By incorporating Asian Americans' struggles with "race" and its citizenship dimensions, I critique sociological scholarship that predicts that Asian Americans (and Latinos/as) are "whitening," or racially assimilating, with Whites in some fashion (Bonilla-Silva 2002; Gans 1999; J. Lee and Bean 2004; Warren and Twine 1997; Yancey 2003). Although these "Asian racial assimilation theses," as I call them, are stimulating, provocative, and work from different points of interest, my study problematizes the question itself. Can scholars categorically say that Asian Americans will "become" White or converge with Whites if "American citizen" and "White" continue to be hegemonically equated, with little sign of abatement (Lipsitz 1998; see Barrett and Roediger 1997)? This question and the related Asian American "foreigner" concept underscores the need for a new framework, one that captures racialization processes specific to Asians as a group (as well as Latinos). Namely, this framework would not simply impose concepts derived from the traditional White-Black color line onto Asian Americans (see Ancheta 1998; C. Kim 1999; T. Lee 2000; Okihiro 1994). Apt here is Cherríe Moraga's (1981:29) oft-quoted observation of men of color's activist focus on "race"/nation at the expense of gender, "the danger lies in failing to acknowledge the specificity of the oppression" (Moya 1996). Aside from not analyzing the *specificity* of "race" and Asian Americans, on an empirical level the whitening predictions do not talk to or systematically observe the group (or Latinos) in the United States, nor do they draw on data from representative surveys that pursue questions specific to "race" and citizenship (Committee of 100 Survey 2001; see T. Lee 2000).[3] Additionally, these authors do not engage the convincing evidence that the White American "fathers" of the Chicago School in fact popularized Orientalist notions of Asian groups and contributed to the very foreigner racialization (H. Yu 2002) that today's sociologists of whitening either do not acknowledge or dismiss as relatively unimportant.

In a move beyond these racial assimilation theses, which do not account for racial barriers or the global inequalities that foster them, I examine in this book one of the key sources of racialization of Asian ethnics: U.S. imperialism in Asia since World War II (Espiritu 2003; Lowe 1996). Although a universalist analysis of United States–led racial formations in Asia has yet to be done and is beyond the scope of this study, I contend that the U.S. occupational forces and mass media culture are most pivotal in spreading American racial ideologies and forging White superiority over Koreans and Black Americans simultaneously.[4] This racial triangle of Koreans, White Americans, and Black Americans along multiple, unequal lines constitutes the imperialist racial formation in South Korea. Although the military occupation and mass media culture play primary roles, I demonstrate that American racialization would not enjoy its level of potency were it not for complementary ideologies in South Korea and those channeled through Japan.

U.S. Imperialism and Global Racial Ideology

Scholarship on empire and imperialism has enjoyed a renaissance (e.g., Hardt and Negri 2000; Harvey 2003), further buoyed in recent years by the U.S. "War on Terror." Contemporary imperialism since World War II has involved a state's intervention into another by way of military armament and restructuring of capital, the military side of which cannot be overstated (Glick Schiller 2005:453). Without military force, the presence and profitable aims of capital are often not secured.

Despite a U.S. military occupation and subsequent capital investment in South Korea since World War II, insufficient attention has been paid to the U.S. empire here, rendering the "Forgotten War" and the overall Korean–United States history even more forgettable. Fixed attention on the Koreas, however, reveals that the U.S. intervention was part of the larger World War II project to realize global hegemony, especially over Japan (Lowe 1996:17). The United States was therefore not in Korea (or Vietnam) simply to stave off Communism or to capitalize on economic resources. It sought to use Asia as a "brutal theater" on which to "perform its technological modernity and military force in relation to the Asiatic world, a process legitimated by the emergence of the Soviet Union's and China's global influences" (Lowe 1996:17). To lay this postwar groundwork, the United States "liberated" Korea from Japan in 1945 and spared certain Japanese colonial institutions and agents in order to secure imperialist domination of the peninsula (Abelmann and Lie 1995). Since that time, an apex of 37,000 to 40,000 troops has been stationed in South Korea and has stood ready at the thirty-eighth parallel, the dividing line recklessly drawn across a map by U.S. and Soviet officials. This line, however, has remained the most militarized zone in the world.

Even with the sword, imperialist rule has needed racial ideologies in order to sustain itself. The growing scholarship on global racism has examined the spread of Euro-American ideologies of White racial superiority (Batur-VanderLippe and Feagin 1999; Bonilla-Silva 2000; Goldberg 2002; Smedley 1993; Winant 2001; see Hardt and Negri 2000). Despite growing apace, this generative field has said less about the history and nature of Western racial ideologies in (East/Southeast) Asia. Students of cultural studies, however, have documented U.S. imperialists' Orientalist ideologies of Asia and Asians as exotic, feminine, Other—a foil for White (masculine) superiority (see Lowe 1996:101; Said 1979)—in order to justify imperialist ventures in Asia. The United States premised its war against Japan on "race," that is, against the "colored" yellow people seeking to take over Whites' global reign (for Japan, it was also a "race" war; Dower 1986; see Lipsitz 1997). The Vietnam War also fomented the foreigner racialization of the poor, third world, Communist "gook." Yet, even Asia's rapid economic growth into "Asian Tigers," one of the contradictions of U.S. imperialism (A. Ong 1999), has not necessarily fostered more positive racializations. Rather, Asian nations' eventual global investment in the United States and other advanced Western nations has served to *reinforce* the racial subordination of Asians and Asian Americans. That is, Japanese purchases of choice American real estate and popular cultural icons, Chinese campaign contributor John Huang's influence on President Bill Clinton, and Korean conglomerates buying up parts of the United States and Europe have morphed model minority Asians into the yellow peril (A. Ong 1999:174–80). Because the larger public typically cannot distinguish among Asian groups, all groups are vulnerable to antiforeigner backlash intended for other ethnics.

"Race" is also central insofar as U.S. rule abroad has relied on a military that, on balance, has positioned Whites over Blacks. In countries populated by mostly Asians, then, the physical differences between White and Black Americans tend to be the most apparent. By way of its White-Black order, the United States racially "Americanizes" other countries.

As further testament to this fact, I will show that South Koreans were acutely aware of the White-Black "face" of the military yet were largely unable to identify Latinos as another group stationed in their country. Not only was this blind spot the product of stark White-Black phenotypic differences and of initial Jim Crow segregation, it was also the effect of Koreans' weaker familiarity with the Latino/Hispanic category. Also important has been the lack of South Koreans' local conflicts with Latinos as a collective. Although the U.S. occupational forces have familiarized the Republic of Korea (ROK) to ideologies of White superiority *as they relate to* Black inferiority, the lines of hierarchy are complicated by Black Americans' role in U.S. imperialism over a non-White country like South Korea.

Broadly conceived, U.S. imperialism has extended to non-White countries a version of racial formation, one that need be differentiated, however, from racial formation in the United States (Omi and Winant 1994; see Goldberg 2002). One difference is U.S. imperialism's noted reliance on one group of color to help subordinate another group of color in a lesser country, thereby creating multiple and complex lines of inequality. Additionally, in subordinated nations such as South Korea, people are not solely fighting against imposed *racial* categories as fashioned in and by the United States, but for the ability to determine their *national* status, albeit racialized, in the global economic order. From their nationalist vantage point, then, sovereignty and positive recognition in this global order would elevate Koreans' racialized place in the United States and, thereby, the world. To be certain, those Koreans who have immigrated tend to favor "America" and its modernity more than those who did not leave (Abelmann and Lie 1995:68–81). Even immigrants who sense an imperialist edge to the U.S. military "ally's" so-called benevolence—a celebrated view among some in the ROK—themselves emigrate with an idealized view of "America" as the land where all their dreams will come true (see Glick Schiller 2005:455). In this way, consent to White American superiority or to Korean or Black inferiority resides right along with resistance to these ideologies.

However, I should caution against American readers imposing U.S. discourses[5] of antiracism and social desirable "race" talk onto South Koreans. Without excusing or dismissing learned prejudices, it needs to be said that South Korea is a near-homogenous nation with few Black American civilians in its midst. Its slave system, which had ended by the late 1800s, oppressed its own or those of similar phenotype across kingdom factions (Peterson 2000:4), standing in stark contrast to White Americans' enslavement of Africans. The fact that "race" per se has not been at the center of South Korean systems diverges from Americans' profound conditioning by antiracist social movements and norms of social desirability since slavery. I also follow Tyrone Forman's (forthcoming) contention that institutions and dominant ideologies are "racist" while individuals are "prejudiced." Rather than racist, I would thus describe Koreans as racially prejudiced, just as I would not describe Black Americans who reiterate anti-Korean or anti-Asian stereotypes to be racist but prejudiced.[6]

The Global Culture of "Race"

Globalization involves not just the spread of military, capital, and goods but also the flows of images and ideas. In addition to the indelible impact of the U.S. armed forces, South Koreans have been profoundly affected by U.S. mass media saturation, whether in the form of pro-military programs on American

Forces Korea Network, *Gone with the Wind,* commercials for Uncle Ben's rice, *Mission Impossible III, Peyton Place,* or CNN's coverage of the 1992 LA unrest. In fact, Koreans often interpret the superpower status of White America through cultural tropes in U.S. mass media. As Darnell Hunt (1997:144) argues, it is people's concrete situations through which race-as-representation in media texts acts as "an immediate social force." For instance, impoverished South Korean children who gleefully receive chocolate from smiling White American soldiers would likely have little problem making sense of media imagery of White Americans as powerful, rich, and happy (see Appadurai 1990).

In defining the globalization of culture, John Tomlinson (1999:1) makes clear that globalization and its economic and political dimensions are not *reducible* to culture (see also Featherstone 1990; A. Ong 1999). At the same time, he contends that "the huge transformative processes of our time that globalization describes cannot be properly understood until they are grasped through the conceptual vocabulary of culture; likewise . . . these transformations change the very fabric of cultural experience and, indeed, affect our sense of what culture actually is in the modern world."

As paralleled in the GIs and chocolate bar example, Tomlinson (1999) conveys that people within the proverbial global village are not motivated simply by global political-economic structures. They require a cultural repertoire that affords an interpretation of these structures. Nina Eliasoph and Paul Lichterman (1999) explain further that the way in which people *talk* about social phenomena, such as globalization, dictates their behaviors; for instance, if political discussions are constrained by norms of polite conversation or if people believe that all major social problems are rooted in the family, most will not be galvanized into action against the injustices of the World Bank. On the nature of global culture, Tomlinson also notes that changes wrought by a world with more porous nation-state lines transform the very cultural repertoire from which people draw. As a final note, Hall (1991:28) makes the important point that local differences are in part sustained even with the major homogenizing shifts brought on by global culture. In other words, South Korea is not becoming another "America," but its cultural system certainly has folded in, and defines itself against, an "American conception of the world" (Hall 1991:28).

What happens, then, when this conception of the world involves *racial* messages? In a piece on racist ideologies and the mass media, Stuart Hall (2003:90) contends that mass media are particularly important for spreading ideologies as "they are, by definition, part of the dominant means of *ideological* production." He specifies that the media, "amongst other kinds of ideological labour . . . construct for us a definition of what 'race' is, what meaning the imagery of 'race' carries, and what the 'problem of race' is understood to be. They help to classify out the world in terms of the categories of 'race.' "

The media's teaching of "race" is also forceful because "race" has been "one of the most profoundly 'naturalised' of existing ideologies" (Hall 2003:90). South Koreans therefore come to take American racial inequalities for granted, such as the "normativity" of White America and the "inferiority" of Black America. This naturalized order serves their own ends as well, such as the need to be better than others, like Black Americans, as part of their resistance to the U.S. occupation and to compensate for their own internalized inferiority[7] at the hands of Japan and the White West. At the same time, the U.S. mass media's classification of the United States into White and Black highlights Korean and Asian Americans' outsiderness relative to Blacks. Asian groups (and, for that matter, indigenous peoples and Latinos) are less "American" in the United States and, by extension, have little visibility in the United States–led *global* order.

Imperialist ends are also served by convergences between mass media culture and the military institution. The armed forces' transmission of its television station (AFKN) across the peninsula can—through both military-specific and regular American programs—inculcate into Koreans justifications for the U.S. presence, a positive image of the U.S. military, and a White American–centered perspective on the world. In addition, military media can be situated within the larger historical context of Euro-American commodity racism (McClintock 1995). Since the late nineteenth century, White racial superiority over dark-skinned Others has been validated by images of military conquest on packages of soap, in advertisements for beef extract, and on boxes of bleach. Not only did these representations enjoy a global reach (McClintock 1995), contemporary forms have prevailed as well. For instance, the post-1945 U.S. military occupation of Japan and the subsequent anti-Black ideologies propagated by White soldiers sparked Japanese commodity racism: a market of blackface or "darky" products (Russell 1991).[8] The export of these products to South Korea could only reify U.S. military and mass media ideologies. To be sure, media texts have also fomented resistance to White American racisms, as has been the case in South Korea.

Significantly, none of the cultural representations would carry the force that they do unless they made sense within South Korean cultural logics. As an example, South Koreans were primed for American racial exports by their own category of ethnonationality, in other words, the nation as blood family. This key unit of social difference in South Korean (and Japanese) society shares parallels with the American notion of "race," one being the naturalization of inequality. Other congruent cultural lenses are Koreans' longstanding valorization of the color white over that of black and the related agrarian hierarchy of light-skinned nobility over tanned or dark-skinned peasants, an agrarian system that the postwar U.S. presence, incidentally, would unravel (Lie 1998), all but its skin color hierarchy.

"Race" and Transnationalism

Nina Glick Schiller (2005:443) laments the tendency of transnational scholars to presume the lack of inequality between states, that is, to excise the role of power from scholarly analyses of transnationalism. She contends that the lacunae can be prevented by fusing the scholarship on imperialism and transnational social fields, a marriage that has not come soon enough. Within this marriage, she also exhorts for greater attention to the way in which everyday actors are implicated in imperialist projects. My study addresses all of these gaps by analyzing how the imperialist United States racializes many of its immigrants both before and after arrival and how Koreans, though not transmigrants, negotiate this transnational racialization.

The process itself reveals that globalization projects (imperialism) spark exchanges of transnational ideologies, imaginaries, and personal correspondence. Although in this sense global and transnational processes are interrelated, I also draw and build on Michael Kearney's (1995) distinction of global processes as *not* tied to national territories but transnational processes as thus tied. For instance, capitalist development can be considered global insofar as it did not develop in a single state or between states but, as Nina Glick Schiller (1999:96) writes, "by various emerging European bourgeois classes utilizing resources, accumulated wealth, and labor throughout the world." In contrast, transnational processes are both anchored in and extend beyond the borders of nation-states (Glick Schiller 1999:96). I would add to this definition that "transnational" connotes directionality—the immigrant leaves a home country, goes to a new country, relates back to the home country, and so on. Global processes, in contrast, are less anchored in *specific* directions of flows. Finally, "transnational" tends to connote flows across *two* nation-states (e.g., the United States going back and forth to South Korea), although global processes need not. Yet, as noted, Korean immigrants in this study are not "transmigrants," or those who partake in a "process of movement and settlement across international borders in which individuals maintain or build multiple networks of connection to their country of origin while at the same time settling in a new country" (Fouron and Glick Schiller 2002:171). Rather, the informants in this study, and I believe most Korean immigrants in the United States, have settled for good (see Espiritu 2003:3–4). Although some Korean Americans send economic remittances, participate in home country politics, and maintain two sorts of households in both countries, they by and large consider the United States their place of residence.

In this light, I conceptualize transnationalism among the Korean immigrants as rooted in imagining, in other words, drawing on cultural frames of reference, as well as interpersonal exchange (see Parreñas 2001). In addition to this micro-level process, I conceptualize transnationalism as involving top-down ideological processes (e.g., racialization by the U.S. state in the ROK; ROK's "export" of nationalism to U.S. Koreans). However, whether transnational racialization processes have been at the institutional or interpersonal level, they have been understudied in general,[9] even when imperialism and transnationalism are fused. If "race" is incorporated into transnational studies at all, it is usually to address how immigrants embrace their home country identities in response to racism in the United States (e.g., Foner 2000; Glick Schiller 1999; Kasinitz 1992; Waters 1999). Although such a response among immigrants is certainly common, as the Koreans in this book will bear out, a focus on this process alone overlooks how immigrants from American-dominated countries have been subordinated by White racism there. Moreover, while a number of studies examine how immigrants, namely of West Indian origin, negotiate the distinct racial structures of their home country and the United States (Charles 1992; Vickerman 1999; Waters 1999)—an impressive endeavor—these works undervalue the force of global racial ideologies in the sending societies. To be sure, Mary Waters (1999:38) touches on it in her description of the growing "Americanization of the Caribbean," yet these studies do not empirically pursue the impact of U.S. racialized dominance on sending societies and on the emigrants who go to the United States.

This book pursues precisely these issues. It asks how U.S. immigrants are transnationally racialized and how they draw on cultural notions from both societies to navigate the U.S. racial landscape. Further, I investigate immigrants' "social remittances" (Levitt 2001) and any transnational media about "race" that could make a potential mark on South Korea. In pursuing these questions, I argue that one of the central axes of inequality that these immigrants navigate across borders is social citizenship.

Social Citizenship: Visible Foreigners, Invisible Subjects

U.S. history reveals that citizenship was initially the province of White men of property (Glenn 2002). Not until the 1950s were the last laws barring the naturalization of Asian Americans lifted. Despite the fact that subordinated groups like Asian Americans had fought for and secured the right of legal citizenship, they have continued to be denied its more crucial promise of civilized existence and membership in the nation, that is, *social* citizenship (see Marshall 1973; L. Park 2005). At the same time, Yen Espiritu (2003) makes clear that marginalized groups like Asian Americans have never been *fully* excluded. Rather, she believes that U.S. groups of color have undergone "differential inclusion" at the hands of elite White America. By differential inclusion she refers to "the process whereby a group of people is deemed integral to the nation's economy, culture, identity, and power—but integral only or precisely because of their designated subordinate standing" (47). This concept moves beyond notions of outright exclusion toward a recognition of how Asian Americans and other groups have been both removed from, and incorporated into, the U.S. nation (Espiritu 2003:47).

"Nativistic racism" is the mechanism through which Asian Americans have been outcast from the nation (Ancheta 1998:11). This form of racism has relied on several ideologies and stereotypes: economic competitor, organized criminal, "illegal alien," unwelcome immigrant (Ancheta 1998:11), and military enemy (i.e., "yellow peril"). Historically, White Americans' resentment of alleged economic competition from the "yellow hordes" led to the exclusion acts against Chinese, Japanese, and Korean Americans in the late nineteenth and early twentieth centuries. In addition, the alarmist "yellow peril" ideology, often couched as "American patriotism," has been an especially egregious form of nativistic racism. It emerged from the U.S. war against Japan during World War II and crystallized through the conflict with Koreans and Chinese in the Korean War, with the Vietnamese during the Vietnam War, and with most of these countries during the Cold War. Arguably, the U.S. racial state's most pernicious form of anti-Asian racism on American soil was the World War II mass incarceration of Japanese Americans, a group that was comprised predominantly of U.S. citizens. Because of Franklin Roosevelt's Executive Order 9066 against Japanese Americans, the general Asian population continues to annually suffer intimidation, violence, and other hate crimes on December 7, the anniversary of Japan's bombing of Pearl Harbor (Ancheta 1998:12).

Racial Triangulation Theory

This history of subjugating the Asian foreigner is generally omitted or downplayed in sociologists' analyses of "race" in the United States and in projections of the racial future. Although Patricia Hill Collins (2000) noted Asian American women's experiences in her groundbreaking *Black Feminist Thought*, she excises Asian Americans from her racial triangulation account of the U.S. nation (P. Collins 2001). Her otherwise deft account proffers a racial triangle in which Whites—the dominant, normative citizens—and two groups of second-class citizens—indigenous peoples and African Americans—are positioned relative to one another in the construction of the nation and national belonging. Here she overlooks the fact that the denial of citizenship to Asian groups has been at the center of the definition and policing of the nation's racial and literal borders (in fact, whenever the article mentions people of color, Asian Americans are not included). To be sure, one of the strengths of Collins's theory is her move beyond conceptualizing the U.S. racial hierarchy as simply the White-over-Black color line. As George Lipsitz (1997:347–48) writes, "race relations in the United States have always involved more than one outcast group at a time acting in an atomized fashion against a homogeneous 'white' center . . . Communities of color are mutually constitutive of one another, not just competitive and/or cooperative." Political scientist Claire Jean Kim (1999) also conceptualizes thus, but unlike Collins, makes central in her model of racial triangulation the ever-foreign status of Asian Americans relative to White and Black America (though she could be faulted for omitting other groups). In this way, the line I call "citizenship" (or that Taeku Lee [2005] calls "nation") coexists and interrelates with the color line.

Kim (1999:106) grounds racial triangulation in a Foucaultian understanding of power. She contends that "public discourse about racial groups and their relative status generates a field of racial positions . . . in a given time and place." Kim (1999:107) also states the following:

> Since the field of racial positions consists of a plane defined by at least two axes—superior/inferior and insider/foreigner—it emphasizes both that groups become racialized in comparison with one another and that they are differently racialized. As a normative blueprint for who should get what, this field of racial positions profoundly shapes the opportunities, constraints, and possibilities

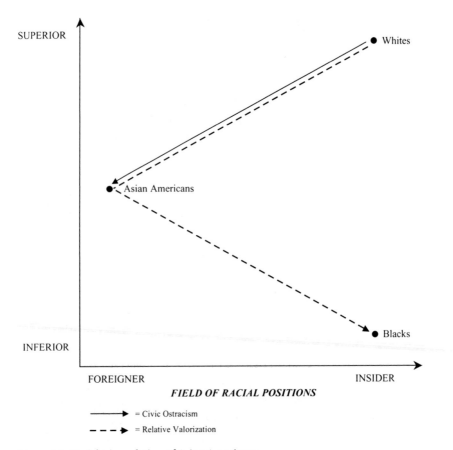

Figure 1.1 Racial triangulation of Asian Americans

SOURCE: Claire J. Kim, The racial triangulation of Asian Americans, *Politics and Society* 27(1) (1999):105–38.

with which subordinate groups must contend, ultimately serving to reinforce White dominance and privilege.

She describes that Asian Americans are "racially triangulated" vis-à-vis Whites and Blacks (positioned with reference to these two groups) by means of two types of processes (see Figure 1.1). The first process is "relative valorization" whereby dominant Whites valorize Asian Americans relative to Blacks in order to dominate both, but especially Blacks. Second is "civic ostracism" whereby Whites construct Asian Americans as "immutably foreign and unassimilable with Whites in order to ostracize them from the body politic and civic membership" (Kim 1999:107). Kim's positioning of racial/ethnic groups along these binaries aligns with Jeffrey Alexander's (1992:290) trenchant argument that "there is no civil discourse that does not conceptualize the world into those who deserve inclusion and those who do not."

In the pages that follow, I borrow from this incisive multiracial model while also critically assessing it. I find racial triangulation to be a brilliant account of the multiple *and* related ways in which U.S. groups are racialized. The model, however, in some sense falls prey to the common tendency of American-centered thought. To be sure, Kim acknowledges that Asian Americans are presumed to be foreign because they are conflated with Asians abroad. Yet, I argue that many Asian immigrants are not suddenly racially triangulated once they get to the United States.[10] Rather, U.S. militarist, capitalist, and/or cultural dominance in their home countries means that Asians experienced a version of the racial triangle before coming to the United States, one that is woven into dominant ideologies on American soil. By overlooking the process by which Asian immigrants are racialized by the United States abroad and how the immigrants respond, Kim, like others, does not consider the cross-border dimensions of Asian American racialization.

Rather than apply the full theory in the United States (though I apply a closer version of it in South Korea), I borrow Kim's (1999, 2000) multiple axes of racialization, what I deem the "color line" and the "citizenship line." These axes are useful for examining Korean immigrants' pre- and postmigration views of their social location vis-à-vis Whites and Blacks in a transnational racial landscape. In addition to Koreans and the White-Black order, both racialization axes bode well for the multiracial/multiethnic *reality* of "America's" (particularly California's) demography. Given the conspicuous presence and importance of Latinos, namely Mexicans and Central Americans, in California, I consider how Korean Americans understand their social location vis-à-vis another racialized group.

Finally, in this book I contend that White America does not render Asian Americans foreigners solely by *civically ostracizing* them. The dominant group also "foreignizes" Asian groups by not being familiar with or concerned with them, relegating them to the status of invisibility or partial presence (Espiritu 2003:47). In other words, I contend that Asian Americans' social citizenship can also be denied by people's (especially dominant group's) lack of familiarity with the group. Being an unrecognized, and thus insignificant and ignored, subject is especially devastating inasmuch as identities themselves do not exist outside of recognition of them (see Gutmann 1994). It is especially damning in a society and world organized around different identities and the allocation of resources on the basis of those differences (e.g., Espiritu 1992). I argue, then, that Asian Americans' racialized status as foreigners goes beyond being *visibly* different from the norm, an assumption that underpins most analyses of the subordination of Asian Americans as foreigners. Rather, it also involves being nonexistent on the national radar, in other words, invisible or almost so.

To be certain, being visibly foreign as well as invisible overlap and can be mutually constitutive. Given Asian Americans' greatest *visibility* in U.S. racial discourse as model minorities (Kim 1993), for instance, they are perceived as not experiencing any discrimination and thus become justifiably *invisible* in the discourse on who is harmed by racism in the United States (S. Lee 1996). Espiritu's (2003:47) concept of differential inclusion also captures the salience of invisibility or partial visibility to the dominant group's power when she invokes Edward Said's (1993) claim that "outcast populations . . . are valuable precisely because they are not fully present."

In focusing on the ways Korean Americans suffer from their invisibility (or weak visibility), I complicate Kim's (2000) claims about Korean immigrant entrepreneurs' categorical advantage as a middle group in the U.S. racial order. She argues that Korean Americans, in response to racial strife with Blacks during the 1990 Red Apple boycotts in New York, were mainly "protecting their collective position within the racial order and thereby the order itself" (158). In this study, however, I find that Korean immigrants also seek to *disrupt* their foreigner position and thereby *alter* the racial order. They do so in part by working to overturn their invisibility and foreignness. As her own data show, Korean American merchants sought to familiarize Blacks and the mainstream writ large to the plight of otherwise unknown Korean Americans and South Korea. Jung Sun Park's (1999) study of Chicago Korean Americans' responses to the 1992 LA unrest reveals similar struggles to disrupt the foreigner stigma. Park found that this community countered its racialization as foreigners, which pervaded media texts on the uprising, by no longer proclaiming themselves "Koreans" but rather "Korean *Americans*." In their process of claiming American membership, they began to shed notions of themselves as mere South Korean political subjects. Had Kim (1999) interviewed Korean merchants in her study, perhaps she would have identified these sentiments of racial resistance.[11]

In summary, I employ a derivation of racial triangulation theory to analyze South Korean society, yet only borrow the racialization axes—the color line and citizenship line—in my analysis of U.S. society. Generally, I build on the model by examining these axes in transnational perspective, the overlap between the axes, and the ways in which social citizenship concerns are tied to invisibility as much as to processes of civic ostracism. Throughout, I also pay attention to how nation, ethnicity, gender, and social class figure centrally in Korean Americans' navigation of "race," as "race" does not always act alone but relationally with other oppressions in a "matrix of domination" (P. Collins 2000).

Studying Korean Americans in Los Angeles and Seoul

Data Collection

To pursue this study I draw on open-ended, in-depth interviews with first-generation[12] Korean immigrants and on various interviewing methods with South Korean nonmigrants (virtually all interviews were conducted in the Korean language). I draw secondarily on ethnographic observations in Seoul, informal observations in Los Angeles, and on archival newspaper research. By way of these methods, I seek to show that we cannot fully and accurately grasp the U.S. immigrant experience without a multisite methodology, one that is informed by a global and transnational perspective.

The history of U.S. involvement in South Korea makes Korean immigrants a fitting case study. South Korea has been occupied by the U.S. military and dependent on its capital for over sixty years. Historically, U.S. influence began in this country with a 1945 World War II agreement that granted the United States and the then-Soviet Union, respectively, trusteeship possession of the southern and northern portions. Only a matter of days after Japan's fall in 1945 did the U.S. military march into the south, soon after introducing its goods, culture, and racial ideologies. The advent of the U.S. military's television station in 1957 (then American Forces Korea Network [AFKN], now AFN Korea) along with other global U.S. mass media have had extensive cultural influence on this "Asian Tiger," such as inspiring in the first place out-migration to the land of milk and honey (Abelmann and Lie 1995). Such a "return" to the imperial center (Lowe 1996:16) is propitious for capturing how immigrants are shaped by U.S. ideologies in their Asian nation and by eventual life as "Asian Americans" in the U.S. center itself.

In this vein, the multisite research design allows for analysis of the distinct transnational vantage of Korean immigrants in the United States. To capture as best I could these immigrants' premigrant understandings as well as their transnational imaginaries and interpersonal exchanges, I interviewed Koreans who had just come to the United States, as early as two months before. I refer to this group as "newcomers" throughout the book. To capture the sending context I also interviewed residents in Seoul, South Korea, drew on archival data from the highest-circulation South Korean newspapers, and conducted ethnographic observation for six months in 2000. Finally, I interviewed Korean Americans who had lived in the United States for a long period of time and drew on my lifelong observations of Korean immigrant communities there. These "old-timers" were typically best able to speak about U.S. immigrant life and transnational connections and comparisons over time.

Research Sites

On a number of counts Los Angeles County is a fitting research site. Aside from being the second-largest Korean city outside of the two Koreas, Los Angeles is nested within the state that boasts the nation's largest Korean American and Asian American populace. In 2000, one in six Korean Americans lived in Los Angeles County alone (E. Yu 2003). This demography enables me to see whether or not "Asian foreigner" ideologies matter to Koreans who live amongst such high concentrations of coethnics and who enjoy the most well-established Koreatown (and other Asian enclaves) in the country. Los Angeles County also boasts a conspicuously multiracial/multiethnic demography in which Korean Americans interact not only with Whites and Blacks, but with Latinos (44.6 percent of Los Angeles County) as well as other Asian Americans (see Table 1.1).

Los Angeles therefore allows an analysis of how Koreans have been racialized *in relation* to Whites and Blacks, as well as in relation to other groups such as Latinos. Finally, the county is the site of the 1992 LA uprising in which Korean Americans sustained almost half of the one billion dollars in property damage in the wake of the acquittal of the White police officers who beat Black motorist Rodney King. This watershed moment transformed the perceptions of Korean Los Angelenos and Koreans everywhere about their group's and Blacks' plight within the U.S. racial system. Going to the source of that historical moment was important for documenting its impact on Korean Americans' consciousness of, and responses to, their racialization.

As noted, I argue that Korean immigrants start to understand themselves in relation to White Americans and to White-over-Black America in their originating context of Seoul, South Korea. In the early 1990s about one in every four

Table 1.1 Composition of select racial/ethnic groups in Los Angeles County

Ethnic group	Population	% of population
Anglo	2,959,614	31.09
Latino	4,242,213	44.6
Black	920,957	9.8
Chinese	329,352	3.5
Korean	186,350	2.0
Japanese	111,349	1.2

SOURCE: Data from U.S. Census Bureau, Census 2000.

South Koreans lived in Seoul (that ratio approaches one in two if we count those who live within commuting distance). It is therefore not surprising that most of the post-1965 Korean immigrants—largely of urban, college-educated, and professional middle-class origins—originate from the capital of Seoul. Seoul is also appropriate because it stands not just as the literal but the symbolic capital of South Korea and boasts an unmistakable American capitalist and cultural presence. Moreover, the U.S. military bases amidst the urban hustle and bustle of Seoul allow for some contact, even if fleeting, between Americans and middle-class South Korean society. For further discussion of the methodology, please see the Appendix.

Outline of Book

In the following pages, this book examines the impact of transnational racialization processes forged by U.S. imperialism on an immigrant group's racial ideologies and identities. Chapter 2 provides vital background information on South Koreans' primary cultural frames of ethnonationality and nationalism, those that underpin the interpretations of the informants throughout and thus orient the reader's understanding. I focus especially on these South Korean, Euro-American, and Japanese dynamics that have primed Koreans for the U.S. imperialist racial formation in their country. Chapter 3, which is the first of a two-part installment on the nature of U.S. racialization in South Korea, analyzes American military and cultural forms of dominance in a context of White superiority. How South Koreans have consented, resisted, and contradicted these processes is the focus. Chapter 4, the second installment, examines United States–propagated ideologies of White superiority and Black inferiority and how Koreans have positioned themselves vis-à-vis the two. I conceptualize the relationship as a racial triangle along not just the color line, but that of national and U.S./global citizenship. Chapter 5 is the first of the chapters based in the United States. It focuses on how Korean immigrants affirm, challenge, and/or add to their premigrant understandings in light of experiences in a newer racial terrain, including greater attention to "Asianness" (despite intraracial issues) and Latino groups. Chapter 6 is central, one in which I examine how the immigrants respond to their racialized positions as model minorities and foreigners in light of Korean and American hierarchical ideologies in the home country and within a U.S. social context of Whites, Blacks, and Latinos. While Chapter 6 focuses on the invisible dimensions of foreignness, Chapter 7 pays more attention to Korean immigrants' everyday struggles as *visible* foreigners. Also explored is the confluence of both dimensions in the 1992 unrest (e.g., "foreign model minorityhood") as well as Koreans' general political responses. I feature in Chapter 8 successful second-generation Korean Americans' battles with "foreign model minorityhood" to show that the struggle is in no way limited to the first generation. Chapter 9 examines the transnational feedback loop: what Korean immigrants share with South Koreans about the group's racialized status along multiple lines in the United States, especially with those who are considering emigration. I assess the potential for these messages to ripple within home country understandings and discuss some early signs. Chapter 10 ties the themes together, the implications of the findings, and implications for future research and for the future.

2

Ethnonationality, "Race," and Color
The Foundation

I asked Father why we had come to a place [the United States] where we were not wanted. He replied that we deserved what we got because that was the same kind of treatment that Koreans had given to the first American missionaries in Korea . . . [But] they showed by their action and good works that they were just as good as or even better than those who laughed at them.

—Mary Paik Lee, *Quiet Odyssey*

THIS CHAPTER IS INDISPENSABLE TO THE BOOK. Without a grasp of South Koreans' own cultural system it is impossible to see through their eyes the way they interpret American racialization of South Korean society and take part in imperialist racial formation. Simply put, the ideologies may be American, but much of the cultural toolkit used to interpret them is not. Here I demonstrate that in South Korean society ethnonationality, not pan-nationality (American "race"), is the key unit of Korean racial understanding. At the same time, the construct of nation, especially as it concerns "blood" origins, complements U.S. racial ideologies such that émigrés were primed for a sense of inferiority to the White West and for White American dominance over Black Americans.

In this chapter I chart the construction of the Korean nation and ethnic nationalism and then turn to the related significance of Japanese and Korean color and Confucian hierarchies. I also describe incipient influences under Japanese colonialism that primed Koreans for "White America" and "White-over-Black America." Although I argue in the book that transnational media and personal stories have been crucial in spreading tropes about U.S. "race" dynamics among Koreans, in this chapter, unlike in others, I focus on the historic period just before the 1970s' major emigration waves.

Nation and Ethnic Nationalism
As John Lie (2004) argues in *Modern Peoplehood*, state-building, spearheaded by Europe, gave rise to "the nation" and, in turn, the twentieth-century

constructs of peoplehood and nationalism. The case of Korea certainly bears this out. From 1895 to 1905 when Korea faced the threat of a new external power, Japan supplanting China in that role, Korea's Patriotic Enlightenment Movement (*Aeguk kyemong undong*) began (Schmid 2002:3). In response to nationalist efforts aimed at protecting newly won independence from China and regaining rights once Japan assumed power in 1905 (Schmid 2002:3), this *sui generis* movement was the first in Korea's history to grapple with the subject of "the nation." This diverse group of thinkers documented their anti-establishment ideas in newspapers, journals, and textbooks. Around the same time, commoners were forging their own nationalist movement (Robinson 1988), peasants who were aggrieved by Korea's opening of its erstwhile closed doors to Japan in 1876, the first modern treaty with another nation. The eventual peasant-led Tonghak ("Eastern Learning") Rebellion in 1894 (also against corrupt Korean politicking) marked the arrival of nationalism among the masses (Schmid 2002:3).

The elite and commoner strains formed the bedrock of modern Korean nationalism (Schmid 2002:14). In fact, Michael Robinson (1988:53) contends that "modern Korean culture flourished within the new press . . . in short, daily reading of . . . newspaper[s] was de rigueur for any informed citizen of the colony." Primary to the construction of the Korean "nation" was a 1908 piece by editorial writer Sin Chaeho in which he resolves debates about Korea's national identity and sovereignty by unearthing an old foundation myth about Grandfather Tangun (a mythic figure). Based on a masculinized construction of the nation as patrilineal family, writer Sin sanctified Tangun as the originator, the bloodline, of the Korean nation. These ideologies, linked as they were to the social Darwinist frame of "survival of the fittest 'races' " spreading in East Asia, supported "an organic, almost biological view of the *minjok*" (Robinson 1988:183). More importantly, Sin's idea of the ethnic nation, *minjok*, took. In one newspaper, readers had regularly written about Tangun and, in Darwinist fashion, had even proffered that the country's most urgent task was to preserve his bloodline in a time of world struggle (*Sŏbuk hakhoe wŏlbo*, December 7, 1908). Koreans' beloved trope of *tanil minjok*—"the single ethnic nation"— would soon come into its own (see Shin 1998).

The centrality of blood has been revived in more current times as well. Korea as a colony had been subject to Japan's notion of itself as a homogenous, monoethnic "race"/nation—one that was superior to the rest of Asia and the West—in the period leading up to and during World War II. Japan's declaration of itself as the superior Yamato "race" (per its dominant Yamato group) was not sui generis but had taken cues from Western intellectual influences and Western pressures (Dower 1986:265), such as Germany. Although Japan never adopted Nazi genocidal policy, it did adopt Nazi slogans of "blood and soil" and the culturally similar trope of an "organic" racially bonded community, the "Volk" (Dower 1986:265–66). To be sure, the Japanese state did not believe that blood determined all innate capabilities. At the same time, state officials' fixation on a " 'race' war" returned to the trope of Yamato blood purity— "unsurpassed in the world," they would say—and to admonitions against over-seas Japanese marrying colonial subjects lest they destroy the Yamato "national spirit" (Dower 1986:269, 277). Such emphasis on blood purity accounts for why the Japanese generally deemed themselves to have few or no blood ties to Kore-ans despite the colonial assimilation policy for Koreans (bearing in mind that this policy served to legitimate the empire; Brooker 1991:217). Moreover, the murderous brutality with which colonial Japan repressed Korean dissidents (and everyday people) betrayed a belief in the subjects' inferiority to the "heaven-descended Japanese family nation" (Brooker 1991:217). Among many others, the contradiction of Koreans' purported inclusion in the Japanese na-tion and Japan's procrustean abuses of power could only foment the modern Korean nationalist movement and celebration of its own blood. As with most anticolonial movements, however, Korean nationalism was birthed alongside its twin, a shared sense of collective inferiority to their oppressor.

In the postwar era of the late 1960s and early 1970s, President Park Chung Hee sought to legitimate his authoritarian rule by capitalizing on Koreans' na-tional shame over the invasions and colonization and on the Koreans' related ethnocentrism and suspicion of outgroups (see I. Kim 1981; H. Lee 1993). He fomented heightened nationalism by way of an ideology of racial purity. As part of this campaign, he "nationalized" the Korean language by pressuring schools to discontinue the study of *Hancha*, the Korean language system rooted in Chinese characters, as well as forcing out the Chinese people within (see All Empires History Forum 2007).[1] Owing to the primacy of blood in Koreans' construction of Tangun / the nation and ethnic nationalism, today's citizens continue to conflate the nation's characteristics—for example, strong or weak, fast- or slow-paced—and the people's blood (e.g., "Koreans are born impatient, that's why our society's so fast-paced").

The continued force of Korean blood purity was evinced by the respondents in my study, as in longtime immigrant Mr. Jung's[2] response to my question of why he always supported Korea in sporting competitions: "That's, I think, blood." Even more telling was his lack of explanation for his answer, as if I, a Korean, knew precisely what he meant. In another instance when I asked recent émigré Ms. Kim to explain her statement that second-generation Korean Americans could never be treated as if they were White, she replied: "Most of all, appearance. Yes, in addition to appearance, you know, the blood. That's important . . . Because of the blood of a single ethnonational people (*tanil min-jok*), you can't completely be changed even though you live here." During my fieldwork in Seoul I was queried many times by young adult Koreans, "What is your blood type?" They needed this piece of information to know if we were truly compatible as friends. Lucky for me, my blood type meant that I did not have the worst friendship potential (such as the most difficult or disloyal personality) so I spared myself the sudden loss of my friends. Although my portending such a loss may be a slight exaggeration, the power that Koreans vest in blood cannot be overstated. Indeed, not only do Koreans use blood type to assess whom they should have as friends but to determine whom to date and marry—or not. Such a nationalist power of biology means that, rather than culture, personality traits such as romanticism, disloyalty, and evil pointed to nature, to the encoding in one's blood. It is thus not surprising that South Koreans do not see themselves as sharing the same blood as the Chinese or Japanese and certainly not, say, the Vietnamese. In countries like the United States that do not share one blood ancestry, Koreans have racialized these nations based on their majority or ruling group: Americans are thus Whites (see Lie 2001:145).

At the same time, under the 1930s' state policy of the "Greater East Asia Co-Prosperity Sphere," colonial Japan ushered in a pan-national ideology. The policy sought to promulgate a pan-Asian identity by justifying empire under the guise of Japan liberating its Asian neighbors from Western imperialism (Palumbo-Liu 1999:32–33). Despite the noted contradiction of Koreans as both "one of us" and "not one of us," Japan's pan-Asian banner seemed to have worked from some kind of precedent. For instance, editorials from the magazine *Kaebyŏk* (Creation), the leading and longest-lived intellectual forum of the previous decade (1920s), identified racial inequality as among the three fundamental problems plaguing Korea in particular and humanity in general. Bracketing for the moment Japan's racialized oppression of Korea, the *Kaebyŏk* editors employed a pan-national lens to claim that "the world was filled with inequality, injustice, and oppression characterized by the domination of 'superior peo-

relationship (handwritten annotation)

ples' (*udŭng injong*, i.e., white, European) over 'inferior peoples' (*yŏldŭng injong*, i.e., other races)" (Robinson 1988:59).

Learning "Race," Learning Color—East Asia and the Western Powers

Japan's colonial rule in part normalized to Koreans the later authority of the United States, notwithstanding committed forms of resistance in both instances. On the level of "race," South Korea was also primed for the U.S. White-Black order by Japan's and its own hierarchies of color. Because Korea had positively signified white/light and attached negative meanings to black/dark long before the first century, color has been critical. As Malcolm X's (X and Haley 1965) acclaimed autobiography shows, hierarchical significations attached to the terms "white"/"light" and "black"/"dark" reproduce inequality.[3] In Korean culture the importance of the color white certainly cannot be overstated. The country has valorized white as representative of its people's purity and desire for peace since the Three Kingdoms Period of 57 B.C. to A.D 668. One manifestation was Koreans' primarily white clothing, earning them the moniker the "white-clad nation." Because Koreans continued to wear solely white clothing through the middle twentieth century, Western visitors would be captivated by the "enormous white waves sweeping the streets" (*Korea Now*, October 19, 2002). Although there are competing theories as to why Koreans adopted white as their clothing color of choice, the three prominent accounts are Koreans' lack of dyes, worship of a sun they considered "white," and desire to reflect their spiritual purity. More importantly, this valorization of the color corresponded with Korea's rigid status hierarchy throughout much of its pre–United States history. Under the agrarian hierarchy, nobility/elites were light skinned and the peasants who worked outside were tanned / dark skinned. Simply put, in this rigid hierarchy, light skin denoted high social status, authority, and respect, while dark skin betrayed the opposite.

In relational terms, the positive nature of white necessitates the negative nature of black, as Korean writings during the Enlightenment Movement bear out. In the middle to late 1800s when Enlightenment leaders traveled to the United States, one reformer stated upon his return to Korea that "I was born in the dark. I went out in the light, now I have returned into darkness again. I cannot yet see my way clearly but I hope I will soon" (H. Kang 1991:22). Not only does this statement valorize light as allowing people to "see clearly" while darkness shrouds vision (both physically and figuratively), lightness is further associated with the West and modernity while darkness is nonmodern third world Korea. There is also a spiritual reference there, perhaps influenced by Christian missionaries' conception of God as "light" and "the way." During my fieldwork, for instance, I noticed that most music sung in Korean churches were Korean language translations of American and European Christian songs (not surprising given Korean Christianity's origins in Western missionary work). During services I heard constant lyrical references to being "pure and white" and "evil" associated with "darkness." In a country that associates its people with the color white (clothes, sun, purity), naturalization precludes problematization.

As an external power since the late nineteenth century and a colonial ruler through much of the twentieth, Japan's own color hierarchy has influenced and corroborated Korea's own. John Russell (1991:5) contends that Japan's aesthetics before contact with Europe, such as during the Heian and Nara Period, "leave no doubt as to the value associated with white skin," especially concerning women's beauty. Japanese proverbs evidence such a valorization: "A white [skin] compensates for many deficiencies" and "In rice and women, the whiter the better." The saying *Fujisan no mieru kuni ni bijin nashii* conveys that the pale-skinned women from the overcast, snowy northern prefectures of Shimane, Niigata, and Akita are more beautiful than the darker women from warmer regions, a proverb that persists today in the coveted title *Akita bijin* (Akita beauty) (Russell 1991:5). In view of Korean society's color hierarchy, and its counterpart in Japan, it is not surprising that Korean women traditionally applied concoctions made of white rice on their faces.

The present-day commercial realms in Japan and Korea have also capitalized on this persistent beauty standard, as Korean store shelves are stocked with such products as "Pond's Double White: SPF 17+whitening" and "Mud Facial Foam: Double Brightening Effect."[4] Because Pond's is an American company, its products' whitening powers cater to and capitalize on Koreans' desire for pale skin. I have yet to see such a Pond's selling point in the United States. As Katharine Moon (1997:72) writes, "it is commonly known among Koreans that they prefer lighter skin to darker skin even among fellow Koreans and other Asians." In order to ensure pale skin, Koreans have long carried around parasols to shield themselves from the sun's darkening properties, as I witnessed daily during my fieldwork. In the instances when I myself would get quite tan from walking around summery Seoul all day, my relatives, friends, and acquaintances would comment on my being dark.

Figure 2.1 Seoul clothing store

South Korea has maintained its traditional glorification of the color white in ways beyond skin color. The ROK government honored the country's cultural attachment to white by choosing it as the background color of the national flag. The color also equated South Korea with peace and harmony. In addition, despite South Koreans' regular attire of Western clothing (they save *hanbok*, traditional clothing, mostly for special occasions), the magazine *Korea Now* (October 19, 2002) has reported that the society's reverence for white has seeped into their color choices for contemporary clothing and cars. In 2002, nearly 30 percent of the La Coste brand casual shirts sold in Korea were white (despite forty-five color choices); red came in at a distant 7 percent (*Korea Now*, October 19, 2002). As Figure 2.1 shows, "White" is a common name for Korean clothing stores, both as a throwback to Koreans' tradition of donning white clothing and an appeal to Koreans' desire for white things. The word

Nostalgia for the White

Figure 2.2 Piece of stationery, Seoul

"white" is also littered all over Seoul as names of cafes and beauty salons and is imprinted on stationery in phrases like "Nostalgia for the White" (per White Western dominance, English language phrases saturate Korea, Japan, and other Asian societies). As Figure 2.2 shows, the phrase is, perhaps not coincidentally, written next to a phenotypically White-looking person clad all in white. Finally, in 2002 Korean car makers usually offered seven or more color options for their automobiles, yet white vehicles comprised 30 percent of total sales (*Korea Now*, October 19, 2002).

Japan was also influential. By way of ambassadorial relations with the Western powers Japan came to learn, emulate, and reinterpret Euro-American racism and subsequently impart it onto the Korean colony. One should not, however, impose American lenses onto Japan and Korea and dismiss them as "racist" just like White Westerners. For one, White America continues to subordinate South Korea as well as Japan, especially Okinawa. Both countries have long had to measure themselves against the West, their "brethren" have suffered racial oppression in the United States, and their "racial" histories diverge in important ways from that of the United States (e.g., Korean vs. U.S. slave systems; Peterson 2000). The distinctive history partly explains why Japanese and Koreans do not use the word "race" in common parlance (the preferred word is "ethnonationality"). When my South Korean research assistant, a sociology doctoral student at one of the country's most eminent universities, wondered aloud, "What exact word *do* we use for " 'race?' " it bespoke a stark contrast with U.S. society's taken-for-granted use (and abuse) of the category. Unlike the United States, then, Japan and Korea have not been saturated with antiracist ideologies and socially desirable norms. A move in that direction has also been slow though apparent, due in part to the lack of non-Asian peoples until recent decades (though there are still no concentrations of African or Black residents), to U.S./Western racist ideologies, to the naturalization of rigid status hierarchies, and to norms of caricature in popular culture. In making these claims I do not mean to excuse away racialized prejudices in East Asia, just as I would not expect prejudice against Asians to be tolerable. Rather, I contend that our analytical and valuative antennae should bear in mind that the "race"-related histories, demography, and categories have been quite different in Korea and Japan than in the United States. This difference stands despite the profound impact of Western racial ideologies on Asian societies.

The caveat notwithstanding, Japanese and Korean indigenous color hierarchies have certainly corresponded with Euro-American racism. Previous to European contact, the Japanese seemed to have depicted Blacks in descriptive, nonpejorative ways. In Edo and Meiji prints White foreigners and dark-skinned or Black servants were drawn in the same Tengu style of long, narrow faces with elongated noses (Russell 1991). During the Meiji period, artist Hashimoto Sadahide sympathetically depicted African Blacks as dignified on his Yokohama Prints. To be sure, Japan also had its own indigenous color hierarchy and a Confucian racial model of a nation's "proper place"[5] (Dower 1986). Yet, Russell (1991:5) finds that after contact with Europe the Japanese did not rely solely on its own (color) orders but adopted Euro-American *racial* ideologies about groups (e.g., Blacks as racially lesser). Similarly, Korea's Confucianism has lent itself to these ideologies, a societal ethos that people are "ordered" unequally within five relationships to which all are obligated (Bodde 1953:48): between king (state) and people, parent and child, husband and wife, the older and younger, and male friends of different status (e.g., age, class, region; Min 1998:26). Although "race" is not an explicit part of this doctrine, it fits neatly into the naturalization of hierarchies that is at the heart of Confucianism and that is paralleled in Western racism.

Through such a lens, Korea was influenced by Japan's desire for Western-style modernity, prompting emulation not just of Euro-American political-economic development but of "Western values and racial paradigms, imported along with Dutch learning and Western science" (Russell 1991:5). In the 1500s to 1600s, Russell (1991:5) finds that Japan's initial contacts in its port cities with Portuguese and Dutch traders as well as the African and East Indians who served them gave rise to Japanese metaphors of Blacks as racially lesser. In another example of Western powers' culpability, U.S. Naval Commodore Matthew Perry celebrated the 1854 treaty that opened Japan to U.S. trade with an "Ethiopian" minstrel show performed by White crew members in blackface, arguably the earliest introduction of the stereotypical Black comic jester and natural entertainer to Japan (Russell 1991:10). The diaries of the White crew members documented what they considered the Japanese people's delight by the comical "serenade of pseudo-darkies" (Barr 1965:37; Heine 1990:169; see Russell 1991:10). As further testament to Western culpability, Sambo-esque visual exaggerations of Black features were not standardized in Japan until they were popularized in advanced Western countries at the turn of the century (Russell 1991:18).

It is telling that when Japanese delegates ventured to the United States in 1860 to forge ambassadorial relations, they were not completely shocked by the U.S. institution of Black enslavement; they in fact likened Africans to the ethnically subordinate *burakumin* on their own soil (Miyamoto 1979; Wagatsuma and Yoneyama 1980; see Russell 1991:6). The Japanese delegates' diaries point, as well, to the influence of the White guides on their trip: "The faces of these natives are black, as if painted with ink and resemble those of monkeys. According to the Americans, they are the incarnation of apes" (Wagatsuma and Yoneyama 1980:64; see Russell 1991:6). Around the same period, reformers in Japan's next-door neighbor of China had also begun ordering humankind into a racial hierarchy of biological groups (Dikoetter 1994:407). A Chinese writer at the time wrote that "yellow and white are wise, red and black are stupid; yellow and white are rulers, red and black are slaves" (Dikoetter 1994:407). Chinese and Japanese ideas likely cross-pollinated, as Chinese intellectuals often studied in Japan and then went to Korea.[6]

Japan's alliance with and respect for Germany leading up to and during World War II would leave a lasting mark on Korea in the postbellum era. Although Korea did not adopt anti-Semitism (*Hangyŭrae* March 2, 2007), its respect for Germany was nested within a broader cast of postwar idealization of the Western hegemons (e.g., noble Britain, elite France, superpower "America"). Several examples include Korea's modeling of its legal system after that of

Korea ⟷ Germany *(handwritten annotation)*

Germany, German as one of the languages of choice in Korean schools, and many students trekking to Germany to study, spurring chain student migrations and remitted transnational stories of Germany's many strengths and achievements.[7]

Early Encounters with White America

After suffering invasions from all sides in the early 1600s, Korea sealed itself off from the rest of the world for two and one-half centuries, earning itself the moniker "the hermit kingdom" (S. Chan 1990:xxiii). Staying true to its name, Korea had successfully defended itself from Western domination by driving back French warships in 1866 and five American vessels in 1871 (S. Chan 1990:xxiii). The Korean government had also opposed the migrating Euro-American missionaries, even executing some of the French Catholic priests who began slipping into the country in the 1830s. Korean converts were also persecuted, 2,000 of whom were killed in 1866 alone (S. Chan 1990:xxxiii). However, due to pressures to modernize, King Kojong signed the 1882 treaty with the United States that would open Korea's doors westward for the first time in its history. On the relations that ensued in the wake of the treaty, Hyon-du Kang (1991:19) writes: "No group of foreigners ever enjoyed greater intimacy at the court of an Asian state than did the Americans [in Korea] during the last quarter of the nineteenth century." Many of the Americans who were intimate with the court were missionaries. Although under formal imperialist domination missionaries traditionally had functioned to enforce and legitimate empire, American missionaries—unlike their French counterparts—made a much more favorable, though complex, mark on Korea under the Japanese empire. In fact, the American Protestants who proliferated from the 1880s onward were such successful proselytizers that Korea became known as one of the best mission fields in Asia, and has remained so. One of the key reasons for this was the coincidence of the spread of Christianity and the rise of Japanese colonization (hence, Korean nationalism). Owing to the fact that Koreans were under a colonial *Asian*, not Western, power, they did not associate Christianity with Western imperialism in the ways potential converts elsewhere had. Rather, they eventually "indigenized" Christianity by taking over the churches and practicing a religion that felt like their own (S. Chan 1990:xxxv).

Central to Koreans' general respect and admiration was the missionaries' support, sometimes at their own peril, of Korea's anti-Japanese movements. Despite an officially neutral stance on the colonial regime, individual missionaries were among the few non-Koreans to protest against the most egregious acts of the administration. At times they harbored activists, protected King Kojong, and notified the U.S. government of the atrocities (S. Chan 1990:xxxii). One stain on the United States, however, was the fact that it ignored the king's repeated requests for American advisors to prevent a Japanese takeover. Yet, the American missionaries were always there to offer counsel to the king, even if the issues were much beyond their expertise (S. Chan 1990:xxxiv–xxxv). Koreans also needed the vital services that the Americans provided, from medical to educational services. The first missionaries translated the Bible into *hangŭl* (a language script that had previously been shunned by the *yangban* [noblemen]). Both because of *hangŭl*'s simplicity—it is one of the world's simplest writing systems—and the fact that the scriptures were among the first written materials given to the masses, Sucheng Chan (1990:xxxv) writes that "studying the Bible became synonymous with acquiring literacy—a skill that hitherto only the *yangban* and the *chungin* (middle people [professionals] . . .) had possessed." Korea's status today as one of the most literate societies in the world therefore traces back to these missionaries. Relatedly, Presbyterians Horace Allen and Horace Underwood helped found medical schools and colleges that would become the nation's second-highest ranking Yonsei University, while Methodist Mary Scranton would establish Ewha Haktang, later the country's highest-ranking women's university. Among contemporary Koreans, this is no small gesture, as the population values education fiercely owing to years of study for government examinations, merciless standards for entrance into the top three schools (the only three that afford the highest-ranking jobs: Seoul, Korea, and Yonsei Universities [SKY]), and little chance at a middle-class life without a college degree from a relatively respectable school. As such, Koreans to this day are extremely grateful to the White Americans who educated them and modernized their society, as the busts and other markers valorizing these figures on college campuses attest.

Korean women (and liberal-minded men) also hold the missionaries in high regard. Women in particular were attracted to Christianity given the social freedoms and educational opportunities afforded them as well as the parallels it shared with shamanism (S. Chan 1990:xxxvi). That Ms. Scranton founded the first school for girls and women (in her home) in Korea's history attests to the watershed influence she has had on women in the society and on the society writ large (incidentally, I frequently walked by her bust on the Ewha campus; S. Chan 1990:xxxv–xxxvi). Although the Yi Dynasty had mandated

Confucianist patriarchy in a draconian manner, American missionaries like Ms. Scranton gave the women opportunities to walk around spreading the gospel and even to travel, all during the daytime, acts prohibited under Yi rule. Women of low status earned wages, even if meager, and were given public roles and a general purpose in social life.

In addition to the favor that the Americans curried among the populace, it is likely that Koreans' longtime association of whiteness/lightness with peace, purity, and noble status translated into a reverence for the White Americans (notwithstanding initial backlash). The Enlightenment admiration for U.S./Western modernity, and the desire to "be like them," was also part and parcel of the relationship to the missionaries. As well, Koreans must have been taken with Americans' wealth, as exhibited in their medical supplies, doctors, funds for building entire hospitals and colleges, their high level of education, and the like. It is not surprising that cultural nationalists in the 1920s praised, and sought to emulate, the capitalist and middle-class models of England and the United States (as well as Japan; Robinson 1988:75).

At the same time, the Americans planted, and even harvested, some imperialist seeds. Former missionary Horace Allen served as secretary of the U.S. Legation in Seoul for seven years. A conduit between the two governments, he gained several coveted resources for the United States, such as the Unsan gold mines, the most productive ever in the country. He was also a conduit between his friends and the Korean people, securing various franchises for the former. Indeed, at the behest of Hawaiian corporate growers who sought to supplant the ever more militant Japanese laborers, Allen convinced his friend King Kojong to allow Koreans to migrate. Allen thus played a direct hand in the first wave, albeit small, of Koreans who went to the "Christian land" (S. Chan 1990:xli), or "the Beautiful Country," the literal translation of the Korean word for "America," *miguk*. Despite the fact that, by dint of this move, Allen was supporting the oppressive practices of the Hawaiian companies, hurting the cause of the Japanese strikers, and sending Koreans to the most exploitative of jobs, he is typically remembered for giving Koreans the American dream. The meager wages in the United States were often better than what little they could eke out in Korea. This close and generative relationship between Korea and the U.S. missionaries, however, would be rived by colonial Japan's aggressive expansionist policy in the 1930s.

Scattered Encounters with Euro-American (and Japanese) Racism

As I argue that U.S. imperial rule is the most potent source of relational White-Black *racial* ideologies (as opposed to notions of color) in Korea, it is important to chart the ways in which such rule has relied on merging military and mass cultural forces. Historically under imperial capitalism, this merger has yielded "commodity racism," that is, capitalists created desire for consumer products by affirming White racial superiority over "vanquished" darker-skinned peoples on their products and advertisements. As Anne McClintock (1995:209) shows of Victorian-era Britain, commodity racism marked a watershed insofar as it stretched much past the propertied, literate elite to touch the masses like never before. Says McClintock (1995:209), "Imperial kitsch as consumer spectacle . . . could package, market and distribute evolutionary racism on a hitherto unimagined scale." Soap was often at the center of such commodity spectacle, bringing not just "race" but gender, the cult of domesticity, into the national imaginary (McClintock 1995:209). The infamous 1899 advertisement for the British Pears' Soap in *McClure's Magazine* featured as its commercial jingle the theme of Rudyard Kipling's "The White Man's Burden," a poem on the U.S. conquest of the Philippines and other former Spanish colonies. It read: "The first step towards lightening The White Man's Burden is through teaching the virtues of cleanliness. Pears' Soap is a potent factor in brightening the dark corners of the earth as civilization advances." Above the jingle is an all-white-clad White male officer washing his hands with the soap in a clean modern bathroom, a drawing flanked by side images of colonial conquest: ships and shipyards, a colonizer "purifying" a "native," and the like.

A more contemporary illustration of the merger between military rule and cultural representation is the blackface/"darky" commodity racism in Japan in the post–World War II era. Parallel to its impact on South Korea, the U.S. occupation of Japan (which ended, at least formally, in 1952) brought in Black American soldiers as well as the anti-Black racism of the military (Russell 1991; see Chapter 4). But there were smaller kernels of commodity racism before that, sparked by the popularity of blackface minstrelsy in the United States in the period between the 1820s and the 1950s. Britain, for example, took a cue in 1895 from its former colony by adopting author Florence Kate Upton's "darky" Golliwog character. Britain later sold the "Golly" doll across the globe (Museum of Public Relations 2006). The West therefore first introduced to Asian countries caricatured and dehumanizing portraits of Blacks. Capitalizing on the trend, one of Japan's most recognizable and longest-lasting images was a primitive African man (*kuronbo*), an image designed by German artist Otto Dünkelsbühler. In Russell's (1991:10) words, the image bespoke "European modernism's fascination with 'Negro primitivism.' " As *kuronbo* graced the beverages of Japan's Calpis company from 1923 until 1989, Koreans who lived in Japan, and perhaps outside, consumed it. There were also examples, however, of Japanese support for the Black American struggle. Before the war, some nationals in the United States organized disillusioned Black Americans in the name of uniting all non-Whites under Imperial Japan (Allen 1994:19, 26). There was also evidence of respectful treatment of Black soldiers by the Japanese in the occupation era (Lipsitz 1995:63). After the war, however, a United States–occupied Japan witnessed a market of blackface/"darky" products grow apace *for export to the United States*, a process bearing the contradictions common to all oppressions. The U.S. occupations of both countries lay bare the fact that globalized armament never travels alone. It is always accompanied by its travel partner: global mass culture.

The overall discussion reveals that Koreans were primed racially for the White-over-Black order and an acceptance of it by a host of interrelated factors. In brief, they include (1) Korean and Japanese color hierarchies, (2) Confucianist notions of groups' proper places, (3) blood-based constructions of the nation since the Enlightenment Movement, (4) previous encounters with elite Whites, (5) colonial Japan's scattered introduction of Euro-American racial ideologies, and (6) a lack of *antiracist* movement history and discourse (notwithstanding racialized national oppressions). More precisely, it is the congruence and overlap between these dimensions through which Korea's early relations with the United States / West and the eventual occupation should be understood.

In Marches America

Koreans have negotiated Euro-American power and influence within the logic of color and ethnonational (blood) categories, often in reference to national rankings in the global order. As the remaining chapters will show, the U.S. occupation itself taught Koreans many new and complementary lessons.

The United States entered World War II in part to stem the tide of Japan's ascent in Asia and the world. In the postbellum era, the United States sought to acquire extractive economies, stave off Communism, and establish global hegemony from the Asian stage (Lowe 1996). In a World War II treaty, the U.S.

and Soviet superpowers arbitrarily divided Korea at the thirty-eighth parallel and, in so doing, divided the lives of Korean families, friends, and lovers—most of whom have been separated and estranged ever since. Immediately after signing the pact in 1945, the U.S. occupational forces marched into the country and have been there ever since. Today the thirty-eighth parallel, also known as the demilitarized zone (DMZ), remains the most heavily armed region in the world. Many expansive bases have been built to accommodate both the soldiers and complex military objectives.

Whether South Koreans in the postwar period have wanted to believe it or not, the United States' sense of racial and national superiority has, even if subtly, shown its face. The military drew on historic racism toward Korea, as propagated by American journalist Frederick Palmer. In a 1929 *Chosun Ilbo* article (December 18, 1929:2) the author condemned Palmer's depiction of Koreans as a lice-infested people "without exception" in *Liberty Magazine*, then America's second-most popular general interest periodical. Palmer adds insult to injury by comparing lice-headed Koreans with the "very clean" Japanese who he insists could not consort with their colonial subjects, "the dirtiest group of people in the world." Koreans did not take such fighting words sitting down, however. Although the South Korean newspaper bitterly chastised Palmer, Korean Americans from the U.S. Chosun Students Association sent letters to the magazine to protest the prejudicial insult. Despite Palmer's differentiation of Japanese and Koreans, another example of U.S. racial dominance involved conflating the two. In World War II the United States and Allied powers subsumed the Chosun people under the Japanese enemy and deemed Korean immigrants in the United States "enemy aliens" (L. Kim 2001).

Along with U.S. military prowess in South Korea, American mass media and commodities have been a powerful marker of modernity, inspiring "American Fever" and subsequent emigration to the United States (Abelmann and Lie 1995:64; K. Park 1997). Beyond exports of imperialist commodity racism to Asia, the influence of both the U.S. military and mass media culture on Korean society converges in the form of American Forces Korea Network (AFKN). In 1957 the United States began this military television and radio broadcasting network for its soldiers and, by extension, introduced it to South Koreans (in 1997 AFKN became AFN Korea). The local South Korean population's access to the military network has been unique owing to the technical problems that usually preclude it. AFN Korea, however, has long transmitted throughout Seoul and in most areas where American soldiers are deployed. Moreover, the

general South Korean population has been privy to all the media texts that
Americans watch in the United States: movies,[8] soap operas, and a heavy dose
of professional sports and prime-time programming (*Washington Post*, November 15, 1986). Though I could not locate statistics on demographics of view-
ership in South Korea (and sources claimed that they did not exist), many
South Koreans remarked that students and professionals who desire to learn
English, or those who simply adore American culture, tend to watch AFN ⟨
Korea regularly (see J. Kang and Morgan 1988). Perhaps some Koreans simply
found this programming "more interesting." My midthirties male cousin used
to come home late each night after work and watch all sorts of dubbed Hollywood films; he would also do so on the weekends. If the larger audience also
watches any of the military-specific programs, they could be influenced by a
hegemonic perspective on the occupation, as AFN Korea's mission statement
reads: "We take our motto 'Here For You' seriously. It's not enough just to provide our audience with TV and radio programming from the United States. We
also provide them with a range of services designed to keep them informed on
important issues and events concerning US Forces Korea, as well as help make
local events more meaningful and entertaining"/ (AFN Korea 2005).

In the wake of AFKN's arrival in 1957, South Korea's own popular broadcasting stations arrived with a bang. Two of the country's three main television
networks began during this decade: Korea Broadcasting Service (KBS) and
Munhwa Broadcasting Co. (MBC). The country's third major station, Seoul
Broadcasting System (SBS), emerged much later in 1990. In addition to the big
three, South Koreans today receive a number of local television stations and
can subscribe to many cable stations and a digital satellite service (Skylife), to-
taling more than sixty channels of domestic and foreign broadcasting (BBC,
June 3, 2005).

Since the 1960s, popular cultural consumption has risen so dramatically
(H. Kang 1991) and citizens have received so much media feed that the country
has earned the moniker "media dependent society" (K. Lee 1999). In 1963 there
were 35,000 television receivers in South Korea (likely owned by the more affluent); the number skyrocketed to over 5 million, or two-thirds of all households, some sixteen years later (H. Kang 1991:131). The same study also found
that about 4 percent of households subscribed to cable television despite cable's
arrival only two years prior in 1995 (H. Kang 1991). It is not surprising, then,
that South Koreans are known to depend on television programming for information as well as leisure.[9] According to a 1997 Korean Broadcasting Co. study,

South Koreans watch about 184 minutes of television during weekdays and 276 minutes on weekend days (higher among women than men; K. Lee 1999).

A mid-1990s study revealed that the United States was the world's leading exporter of television programs to other countries, between 100,000 to 200,000 hours each year (*Hollywood Reporter*, January 3, 1995). Currently, many of Korea's cable channels are also American corporate broadcasters. One venture between Turner International and Yonhap Television news, a 24-hour Korean channel, has provided access and dubbing rights to CNN International's programs and breaking news.[10] Furthermore, because the United States enjoys some of its largest movie markets in Asian countries like South Korea, cable channels have fought to increase their importation of films and programs from the United States (the largest source at 70 percent) as well as from Japan, France, the United Kingdom, and Germany. In fact, more films from these countries have been imported for South Korean television than for theater release; in 1996 the three major networks allotted 8–18 percent of their programming to imported films. To be certain, the Korean Wave (*hanryu*) of movies, soap operas, and music that has taken much of Asia by storm (e.g., Japan, China, Taiwan, Vietnam, Singapore, Malaysia) and garnered the attention of some Western audiences has, along with other examples (Bollywood), begun to change the tide of global culture.

As of yet, however, American movie imports for regular theater release have not ebbed in South Korea. The country typically has been the second largest and the tenth most lucrative for Hollywood outside of North America (Groves 1998). American films accounted for almost 75 percent of box office receipts in 1998 (M. J. Lee 1999). Some of the country's biggest box office hits have been, to name only a few, *Ghost, Forrest Gump, Titanic, The Gladiator*, and *Mission Impossible*. Although the United States no longer owns and produces most globalized media, the actual texts and the cultural "look" of such media are largely American (Ang 1996; Hall 1991). Because the mass media have been deemed the most powerful influence on the shape of contemporary culture (Bauman 1992:31), the "Americanness" of such imagery is no small matter.

In broad terms, U.S. military and "cultural" imperialism throughout Asia has imported structural racism in two key ways: by ruling over a non-White country (e.g., South Korea) and by introducing a White-over-Black order.[11]

Koreans Go "Back" to "America"

As noted, White Western missionaries and labor recruiters were behind the first wave of Koreans to the United States. In addition to political and economic shifts and changes in immigration laws in both countries, Koreans have continued to make the trans-Pacific journey toward modernity, such as national and individual prosperity, an advanced democracy, a Christian country, and a "modern" family structure and gender relations (Abelmann and Lie 1995:66). Moreover, individuals' desires, emotions, and personal circumstances matter as much as structural factors in inspiring people to leave (Espiritu 2003:36).

By way of Horace Allen's personal contacts and negotiating skills, the first wave consisting of some 7,000 Koreans, mostly bachelors, arrived between 1903 and 1905 to labor in Hawaii's plantations in the wake of anti-Chinese exclusion laws and Japanese American labor strikes.[12] Another contemporaneous group of Koreans were students and political exiles, many of whom were important leaders in the pre–World War II community, such as eventual first president of South Korea, Rhee Syngman, and political activist Ahn Chang Ho. In addition, some 1,100 "picture brides" entered the United States before the immigration laws in 1924 completely excluded Koreans and most other Asians (in 1945 the law began to change). These Korean picture brides were by and large better educated than the men, brought their husbands to cities and to the U.S. mainland, and were active in church activities and independence movements that helped free Korea from Japan.

In fact, much of the post-1965 Korean immigrant community in the United States is traceable to the women who came as military wives and then sponsored kin through the family reunification clause. The Korean American population is therefore a population formed in large part by women-centered kin migration (K. Park 1997). The history of this migration network began with U.S. intervention in the Korean War of 1950–1953. U.S. soldiers came home with their Korean wives, arranged adoption of war orphans, and sponsored students to the United States (E. Yu 2003). My own father was one of those sponsored students. A GI he befriended while working small jobs on the U.S. military base agreed to help him get to "America" and my father suddenly found himself in Wisconsin in 1954, shortly after the war's truce had been called. He was in the United States amidst the 6,500 military brides who entered between 1951 and 1964, a relatively large number for a short span; today, there are more than 100,000 military brides living in the United States (E. Yu 2003:58).

After the Hart-Cellar act was passed in 1965 to overturn the racially discriminatory immigration quotas of 1924, these military wives along with student immigrants (most of whom had become U.S. professionals) petitioned for their parents, siblings, and/or spouses. Immigrant kin soon composed the majority of immigrants to the United States (E. Yu 2003). Of note is that 1970s migration cohorts were considerably more educated and of higher class standing than the overall South Korean population. Christians are also overrepresented among Korean immigrants, because the middle class and the upper class are disproportionately of this faith (Abelmann and Lie 1995:69). If they were not Christians when they left, however, they often became so in the United States; or at least became active in the Korean church for the assistance, social networking, and solidarity that it affords immigrants (Min 2000). I intentionally mirrored these demographic trends to construct my sample for this study: most hailed from Seoul and/or other urban centers and from middle-class or higher class backgrounds. I should note that although a small minority of my sample came from less advantaged backgrounds than the majority, I did not find a clear difference along class lines as regards racialized/national perceptions and ideologies. And perhaps because of a coincidence between middle-class status and Christianity, I did not find distinct racialized perceptions between those who were Christian or church-attending and those who were not. Racialized notions tend to transcend these lines, from what my research shows, because Korean ethnic nationalism is common across the classes and because church attendance could serve to cement or liberalize people's views (see Chapter 5). I did notice the more frequent discourse of "God made all people equal, so no one should be racist," or a close variant thereof, among Christians. Yet, non-Christians would say the same, just without the reference to God.

A final note on Korean immigrant demography: recent trends reveal that annual admittance has declined in the 1990s (E. Yu 2003) likely due to South Korea's economic growth (except around the period of the 1997 International Monetary Fund crisis) (*Chosun Ilbo*, August 23, 1995:39). Although the impact of the 1992 LA unrest is hard to measure, it stands to reason that it also weighed heavily on the minds of would-be immigrants. Still, Eui-Young Yu (2003) finds that a steady and substantially large in-migration accounted for the 35 percent increase in the Korean population from 1990 to 2000. This increase is notwithstanding the slow growth in the total U.S. population at 13 percent. The continuing growth of the Korean American population, and the even larger growth rates of most other Asian ethnics, proves that the Asian first generation will continue its stream into the United States and will define the Asian American community for years to come (see Massey 1995). These statistics belie some scholars' claims that the first generation is largely inconsequential for the "fate" of Asian Americans and that only successive generations will matter. This view in and of itself is based on the Southern and Eastern European immigrant model and on the unprecedented conditions under which they sealed their fates in "America" (Massey 1995).

To put it simply, the immigration trends of Asian ethnic groups are impressive. Between 1990 and 2000 the entire Asian American population grew 48 percent, second only to Latinos, who grew 58 percent. In contrast, the White population grew at one of the lowest rates, 6 percent (E. Yu 2003). In addition, the effects of Asian immigration have been most conspicuous in the state of California where the Asian population has roughly tripled since 1980. The racial demography of the United States writ large is also changing. Whereas prior to 1965 Blacks comprised the vast majority of non-Whites in the United States, Latinos now outnumber Blacks at 12.6 percent versus 12.3 percent, according to the 2000 Census. What is more, Black Americans themselves have become a more ethnically diverse population in light of recent decades of immigration, especially from the Caribbean and Africa. Yet these ethnic differences are elided by a U.S. categorization system that deems Black one group (Mittelberg and Waters 1992; Waters 1999), and are thus lost on most people, including Koreans. Such is the power of "race" to collapse ethnic and national differences, especially for groups like Blacks who have been in the United States in large numbers for a long time.

In this book I examine in depth how Koreans themselves understood the subordination of their people and that of Blacks at the hands of dominant White America. In the following chapter, I venture to where "America" first migrated.

Racialization in South Korea, Part I

Koreans and White America

*I looked for myself on the screen wooed by Gable and Brando and McQueen
on the tube selling Colgate or Camay or Kotex or Crisco . . . I meet myself
pigeon toed and shuffling, tongue twisted, chop chop / sing song / giggle / rots of
ruck / bucktoothed / cokebottle eyeglassed / cartoon camera carrying foreigner
who is invisible on America's pages.*

—Janice Mirikitani, "Looking for America"

AFTER LISTENING TO OTHER KOREANS NARRATE THEIR LIVES, it became clear that my
mother was not the only one who had come to idealize "America" through
Hollywood movies and pro-U.S. ideology. Narratives abounded of "America"
rescuing Korea from a near inexorable fate (read: Communism, poverty)
thanks to their benevolent intervention in the Korean War, U.S. generosity
with humanitarian aid and military protection to boot, the beauty of Clark
Gable, and so on. Situated within the context of Japanese colonization and
U.S. dominance over the home country, I examine here South Koreans' and
immigrants' sense of inferiority to (masculine) White America and, of course,
resistance to the perennial complex. In line with "imperialist racial formation,"
Koreans' adoption of their own inferiority was a response to the White-led U.S.
military state and congruent representations channeled through American
mass media culture (see Abelmann and Lie 1995). As the U.S. intervention
spurred mass Korean migration to the United States and thus gave rise to
media and immigrants' reports on "America," these transnational sources have
further reinforced the collective sense of inferiority. For instance, imprinting
itself on South Korean society was the 1992 LA unrest. For recent cohorts to the
United States especially, the historic unrest was instructive for its display of
White dominance and racism, Black "criminality" and political power, as well
as Koreans' racial problems and invisibility. Initiated by the occupation and
largely understood within the logic of Koreans' cultural categories (see Sahlins
1981), White American power has saddled the occupied people with the plight

of invisibility and foreignness long before they ever leave for the United States. Although key differences such as time of emigration matter, the pattern of Koreans' simultaneous conformity and resistance to American racial ideologies cuts across the Korean cohorts.

In this chapter, I discuss first the cultural context in which South Koreans' sense of inferiority to the United States was obtained, namely one of ongoing inferiority to a Japan that they revere and hate, the antinomic products of colonial subjugation. Thereafter I examine Koreans' adoption and rejection of ideologies instantiated by (White) American militarist and cultural imperialism, transnational exchanges, and—among newer immigrants—the 1992 LA unrest.

The Colonizer and the Inferior Within

In their own national imaginary, Koreans lament and censure their proscribed self-determination at the hands of external powers: China, Japan, and, most recently, the United States. As with all oppressions, the subjugated must navigate a world in which they are constantly reminded of their inferiority, in which their devalued difference is the proverbial water they swim in. In modern history, most Koreans categorically condemn Japan as evildoers, as those who poisoned their water. Many of the middle-aged and elderly Koreans whom I queried about Japan conveyed dejection, torment, and/or bitter hatred, especially in reference to Japan's refusal to apologize for its war crimes (e.g., "comfort" women) and continuing claims on the Tokto Islands despite Korean control. Although diplomatic relations and the people's sentiments have varied since liberation, it is normative to hear in Seoul the ire of a middle-aged person such as Ms. Oh: "Why do we think Japan's better than us? How could they be? What they did was horrible. Anyway, I really hate Japan." Although young adult Koreans tend to be more uneven in their outlook, they expressed similar sentiments despite not having been direct colonial victims of Japan (except through their families). Mr. Chun, a college student who described himself as less nationalistic than most Koreans, conceded that "when I think about how Japan ruled over us for thirty-six years, I get pissed off. And when they say Tokto Island is theirs, I also get pissed off!" Other young adults admitted more explicitly the sentiment that undergirded much of the angst over Japan: a sense of inferiority.

Ms. Park: Even when we have bad feelings about Japan, when it comes to technology we recognize their . . . (pause)

I: We become jealous?

Ms. Joo: We have a sense of inferiority or something like that, we think that they're superior.

Ms. Park: Yeah.

Others noted the paradox that usually attends a sense of inferiority to the colonizer:

Ms. Jung: We have this incredible animosity towards Japan, it doesn't matter what the situation is, we just have to beat Japan in everything.

Mr. Jun: But we only buy Japanese products (laughs)!

Ms. Jung: That's a problem, yeah, of course. We can only try to stop . . .

Mr. Jun: But most of all, let's beat them in the world cup next year (laughs)!

Ms. Jung: (laughing) That's right!

"We've got to beat Japan" is a persistent refrain on the peninsula. In a jointly hosted 2002 World Cup with Japan after cautious negotiations, "Korea Republic" would indeed outperform Japan by a wide margin, beat Italy, and reach the highest stage of any Asian nation in the history of the sport: the semifinals. Even segments of the world audience that had thought little about Korea could not help but note its people's coordinated, vociferous, sea-of-red patriotism. As Mr. Jun points out, however, Korean patriotism has been more uneven under "buy only Korean" campaigns despite the people's immense pride in (successful) Korean products. Japan's economic superiority has militated against such nationalist pressure because Koreans clamor for the ostensibly shinier, better, and status-raising Japanese products.

The potent sense of inferiority to Japan still fifty-five years after liberation, with little sign of abatement, is a powerful indicator of how domination by the United States has opened up old wounds and caused new ones, saddling further Koreans' sense of national worth. Notwithstanding the dualist sentiments that render the United States a savior to be admired and an imperialist to be ousted, the South Koreans of all generations with whom I spoke admitted, or alluded to, a sense of inferiority. Mr. Suh, sixty-one years old, repeated to me the common adage, "America is a great country; we dream of getting to their level." Even university students who have been at the helm of anti-American movements lamented the travesty that has been South Koreans' genuflection to the United States. Ms. Kim, twenty-one years old, responded thus to the question, "What do you think Korean society thinks of the Americans?": "It's a sad story, really. Our nature of being flunkeys toward China in the old times is what we transfer to the Whites, like the U.S."

This tendency to "submit to the strong," as Koreans are wont to call it, manifested itself in the way that I, a Korean American, was treated in South Korea. Although I had grown accustomed to my South Korean relatives celebrating me like a prodigal daughter whenever I visited, it was not until I befriended stranger after stranger over the years that I realized how much my American status conferred privilege onto me. To be sure, many Koreans enacted the anti-American side of their duality and mistreated me for precisely the same status (see Appendix), but I was given special advantages nonetheless. To illustrate, whenever a group of my South Korean friends and I went out to restaurants they always instructed me to ask for things that they themselves wanted. They explained, "Because you're from America, they'll definitely give what *you* ask; they'll give you bigger servings, too." They were right. My housemates would also ask me to do the same with our boarding house mother and, despite my discomfort, she indeed gave me better quality and bigger servings of food; in general, I noticed that she was nicer to me than to them. In another instance when I was hanging out with my middle-class, elite Yonsei-attending, normatively attractive friend Joon who seemed to have everything going for him (he was also in a pretty good cover band), he staunchly dismissed Korea as lacking and undeveloped in so many ways compared to the United States (incidentally, his female friend who was with us retorted, "C'mon, Korea's not that bad!"). On another day during my fieldwork I had to venture to the state records office to extend my visa. A gentleman requested that I prove my family ties to the Korean relatives I was visiting. I was bewildered and helpless; how could I prove my relations to them—album pictures? In the United States, we had no state offices devoted to family registry and Americans did not carry around family paperwork for state identification (recall that in Korea, as with much of Asia, the social unit is not the individual but the family). When I asked the gentleman if he could just look up my family registry information on the computer, he flatly said that that was not possible. I replied, "Oh, you don't have these records on computer?" Looking at me with eyes partly cast down, he said matter-of-factly, "You come from a powerful country that can do that, but we're a weak country." As my mind was nowhere in the realm of national comparisons, I was startled into an apology for an ideological judgment that I never intended to make. His response speaks volumes, however, about how such a subordinate national position was precisely what has weighed on his and other South Koreans' minds during much of their lifetimes.

If my being from the United States meant that I enjoyed higher status, it is necessary to examine the history of South Koreans' perceptions and treatment of *White* Americans in the context of U.S. power.

"American" Is White

With little exception, Koreans conform to White America's hegemonic construction of itself as the racialized reference point (see Lipsitz 1998). This self-representation of Whiteness[1] accords with Koreans' association of a nation with its "owners" or majority group. As well, much of Koreans' interactions with Americans since the 1880s have been with *White* Americans (diplomats, missionaries). The most potent indicator of the persistence of this racialization today is Koreans' use of *miguk saram* ("American person") to denote a White person. Koreans also frequently use "foreigner" (*oeguk saram*) to denote a White person unless they specify otherwise, demonstrating that White Westerners are the reference point for anyone not Korean. Across the immigrant cohorts, Koreans would stipulate the identities of non-White Americans (e.g., "Asian," not "American," "foreigner" versus "Thai foreigner"). Upon my asking old-timer Ms. Pak to specify whom she meant when she used the term "American," she replied in a somewhat surprised tone, "I mean Whites when I say Americans. When I say foreigners, I mean White people, same thing." New immigrant Ms. Kong also shares a telling narrative about how she and her friends in South Korea deemed anyone with a White phenotype "American": "In the past when I was on the street and I saw a White person walking by, my friends and I would say, 'Oh! That's an American!' Because in Korea everyone knows about the U.S. and hears about it all the time, so rather than thinking that that person was British, Italian, European, we'd say that that person was American!" Most Koreans took the Whiteness or White Americanness of "foreigners" for granted and were thus jolted out of their assumptions when I asked them whom they meant by "Americans" or foreigners.

Beyond a perception of the country's racial reference point, Koreans were primed for White American dominance over their country by their own cultural valorization of the color white and light skin as well as the Confucianist naturalization of hierarchy. In light of the Confucianist demand that people respect and subordinate themselves to the state (those in authority), Koreans, despite fierce resistance, have had to engage this ethos in some way both with regard to Japan and the United States. Furthermore, Koreans had already subscribed to White American benevolence since the missionaries began caring for medically, educating, schooling, and Christianizing Korean society, as well as assisting the anti-Japanese movement and sending Koreans to the United States. In this way, Koreans' ideologies of White Americans had been underway for some time before the advent of the occupational forces in 1945. What differed, however, was the arrival of American institutionalized and armed dominance over South Korea. This stark inequality between the two nations corresponded with, and deepened, a sense of inferiority that had begun germinating under the missionaries. In addition, the U.S. occupation stirred the oppositional side of Koreans' duality concerning "America": resentment, condemnation, and heightened desire for sovereignty. Because "imperialist racial formations" often beget dualism from the margins such as antinomic love and hate (e.g., Japan), I start here by focusing on how Koreans' reverence for (White) America was intensified and textured by the U.S. military intervention, especially through the 1970s.

U.S. Military: Might and White

Although Japanese colonization had helped shore up Koreans' sense of oneness as a blood nation, postliberation Koreans were still fragmented along several lines when the U.S. occupational forces arrived: class, region, dialect, ideology, and so on. By virtue of the mass arrival of White and Black people, Koreans' sense of their group as a uniform collectivity in relation to the two emerged.[2] In addition, American "race" categories collapsed the ethnic/national differences *within* the White and Black groupings, differences that were usually at the center of Koreans' orientation. Thus understood, one of the facets of racialization was underway.

Despite tensions and disagreements between the U.S. and ROK (Republic of Korea) governments, on balance, the South Korean state and its citizens have been pro–American from the 1950s through much of the 1970s (Moon 1997). Within this vein, South Korean society has largely directed its passionate gratitude to White America, a continuation of their deep sense of indebtedness toward the Protestants. The U.S. military has also shored up the American reference point of Whiteness (see Lipsitz 1998). General Douglas MacArthur, for instance, has served as the icon of U.S. military humanitarianism in the Korean War and continues to be valorized in South Korean history textbooks. In the country's popular culture, Hyon-du Kang (1991) notes that Korean characters set in the immediate wake of 1945 expressed intense gratitude to "Americans" for "liberating" their nation from the Japanese. In this content analysis of popular Korean short stories and books from 1945 to 1975, Kang (1991) found descriptions of "big nose" Westerners with "golden hair and blue eyes" (while Blacks were referred to as "Blacks" and were written about less often). Against this contextual backdrop both older and newer immigrants, along with those who had never left, conformed to hegemonic idealizations of White America as Korea's savior. Such admiration for the United States also reveals the fissures and contradictions in Koreans' fervent ethnic nationalism.

In response to questions about the U.S. military intervention in particular, older immigrants who had endured the Korean War often expressed deep gratitude and depicted Korea as "helpless" without American aid. Because this generation lived through the U.S. withdrawal of all active troops a year before North Korea attacked in 1950, their sense of debt also stems from the fear of what Korea would have become (i.e., Communist) had the United States not reintervened in 1950. The role of the ROK state in such a reckoning cannot be overstated. It has officially labeled the United States an "ally," endorsed the military presence, and expended painstaking efforts over the years to maintain it. Aside from contributing its best 50,000 troops for the Vietnam War effort in an act of reciprocal goodwill (Lyman 1968), the ROK government actively tried to prevent the reduction of U.S. troops proposed by President Nixon under the 1970s "Nixon Doctrine." This policy sought a gradual full-scale withdrawal from South Korea to transfer troops and resources to the Vietnam effort. The ROK government, however, tried to stop the doctrine at all costs (Moon 1997:58). In light of the government's apparent dependence on U.S. troops and the ever-present stain of the Korean War (and Japanese colonialism), it is not surprising that older generations of Koreans tend to support a continued U.S. military presence while younger generations generally do not (*Chosun Ilbo*, September 17, 1990). The older generations also vividly remember the United States bringing material luxuries to a starving Korea, especially food items hitherto unseen like Taster's Choice coffee, Spam, Oscar Mayer hot dogs, butter, peanut butter, cheese, Oreo cookies, Ritz crackers, Jello pudding, the signature Hershey's chocolate, and much more (Yuh 2002:34). Ji-Yeon Yuh (2002:34) writes, "An army ration staple that GIs often tossed to Korean children, chocolate symbolized the abundance and generosity of America. Not only was America so rich that it could provide its soldiers with a candy like chocolate, but

Americans were so generous that they simply gave it away to the children they saw. Given the power of chocolate giveaways to symbolize modernity and to "win hearts and minds," it is no surprise that the U.S. military gives away the same almost sixty years later to Iraqi and Afghani children. More mundane than handouts, however, American wealth was evident simply in the sheer amounts of food the military could waste (see Abelmann and Lie 1995:61–62). Just before and during the Korean War, my father would wait every day outside of the mess hall amidst the many Koreans also clamoring for a possible job on base and for whatever food scraps—bones, extra fat, uneaten Spam—the GIs would throw out so that they and their families could eat. When he brought back something new one day, cheese, his parents and siblings gathered around and marveled at its bright color, putting the curious substance in their hungry mouths with excited trepidation.

Longtime transmigrant[3] Ms. Yi was among the older guard who tended to be grateful to "America" for its military assistance. She said, "America helped us so much, what would we have done if they hadn't? We wouldn't have been able to make it . . . Even now, Americans are living in Korea, which is how the South is stable because at any moment something could happen from the North."

A recent émigré, middle-aged Ms. Kim (7 months in United States), invoked the White American masculine icon of U.S. aid, General Douglas MacArthur, to express her Christian-inspired gratitude.

K: To this day, I think America is our ally.

N: Who?

K: Americans (*miguk saram*). Yes, yes, our friendly ally (chuckles). They helped us during the Korean War—you know, people like General MacArthur. Of course it was all done by the will of the Lord, but anyway we received a lot of help from America . . . I don't know about each individual, but anyway, I still think people in America are good and are good to Korea.

Even more flattering for the White-led military is Ms. Kim's perception that God had preordained the United States to assist South Korea in the war effort through Douglas MacArthur. She thus implicates White Americans in God's plan of "divine intervention." Although the male respondents were as grateful as Ms. Yi and Ms. Kim, they tended to be more inclined to express their gratitude through positive relations with White American men, especially soldiers and veterans. For instance, Mr. Chun, an eleven-year immigrant, had given a White male client of his LA textile manufacturing company a substantial discount for being a veteran who "helped us [Koreans] during the war." In his interview he repeatedly stressed that this male client was a "good friend," a point of apparent pride for him. Another longtime immigrant, Mr. Koh, responded to my query on whether he had met any Americans while in South Korea by boasting about his friendships with White soldiers while he served in the Korean army.

> K: I even *trained* with foreigners in the military.
> N: Were you with Whites or other racial groups, or . . . ?
> K: They were American army men. I had spoken with them from time to time, but we often just joked around with each other or would just say "Hi," just to that extent. I also learned a little English from them . . . in the American army ESL classes. At that time, Americans were school teachers [and] tutors for conversation.
> N: Did you like them or no?
> K: They were nice. All of them were nice.

Mr. Koh's ability to work and play with White American men in the institution that represented America's unmatched power (the masculine military) was a source of pride for him. He also took pains to depict Koreans and Whites as mutually respectful and friendly, implying a more egalitarian relationship. As he lamented during his interview his spiral down the U.S. class ladder into blue-collar work, I was not surprised that he proudly pulled out pictures of his days in the Korean military, an affirmation of his more masculine middle-class days.

Despite the persistence of potent anti-American sentiment since the 1980s, especially among student activists, the hegemonic hold of (White) American benevolence has persisted among some members of the younger generations. The university students and young professionals whom I interviewed often cited having "friendly feelings towards the United States." Some were pro-American in ways that served a Korean nationalistic purpose. Student Ms. Jung, for instance, conveyed that "I have always liked Americans since the Korean War because they gave us food and stuff . . . Whites seem much more advanced than us so if we want to improve ourselves as a nation, I feel like we have to associate with them." Her hope for her nation also invokes South Koreans' self-conscious desire to realize itself in terms of White Western modernity.

The U.S. military indeed doled out not just food but "stuff." The stuff included a public relations program wherein the military offered free reconstructive surgery to Korean war victims as well as plastic surgery, namely the double eyelid procedure in which a fold is cut into the eyelid (Palumbo-Liu 1999:95). Although the eyelid surgery flourished in postwar Japan in response to military brides' efforts to "fit into" their receiving countries, it actually enjoyed its high point in South Korea in the wake of the 1950–53 Korean War (Palumbo-Liu 1999:95). As such, the massive and booming plastic surgery industry in Korea (and Asia), especially for the double eyelid and other European features, can be traced in part to the U.S. occupational forces in South Korea. David Palumbo-Liu's (1999:95) analysis of a 1955 essay by one of these army surgeons, D. Ralph Millard, reveals the doctor's sense of racial/national superiority over "Orientals" and the propagandist belief that the United States was only in Korea for humanitarian reasons. The doctor remarks, "We can be relatively certain that after each deformity was corrected or improved and the Korean returned home, America had won the heart of the patient, his family and possibly even part of the village" (Millard 1955:319). Consider also the case of one male patient, in the words of Millard: "A slant-eyed Korean interpreter, speaking excellent English, came in requesting to be made into a 'round-eye.' His future lies in his relation with the west and he felt that because of the squint in his slant eyes, Americans could not tell what he was thinking and consequently did not trust him. As this was partly true, I consented to do what I could." Dr. Millard proceeded to give the interpreter a double eyelid and extra nose cartilage, rendering him in such a way that others mistook him for Mexican or Italian. With pride, the doctor went on to say that his patient, a Christian, could now go to the United States to study for the ministry.[4]

Nowhere does Millard acknowledge, however, that the U.S. military and he himself were crystallizing Koreans' sense of inferiority to their White racial bodies. For instance, his consent to do the surgeries at all legitimates to Koreans the very sense of shame over their appearance that motivated them to see Millard in the first place. As the "good doctor" admits, he consented to the surgery because it was "partly true" that the interpreter's "squint in his slant eyes" cast him in an untrustworthy light. Indeed, Koreans' sense of aesthetic inferiority would only grow, as "Western-style whiteness and facial features became the Korean ideal" in the wake of the Korean War (Jo 1992:403). Besides wanting double eyelids, Koreans desired to be as tall as the "Americans." Men desired to emulate White American masculinity while women desired to emulate White

American femininity.[5] As one example, Lie (1998:143) found that South Korean politicians began to change their names to "improbable" American ones, like Patrick Henry Shinicky (*Sin Ik-hŭi*) and John M. Chang (*Chang Myŏn*). South Koreans, then, have been made to feel inferior not just by virtue of their reliance on a superior U.S. military, but by the *racial ideologies* of the military itself, those of Dr. Millard representing one of many examples. In fact, had Koreans not internalized—that is, believed in—their inferiority vis-à-vis White America, they likely would have identified and resisted earlier the imperialist dimensions of the military intervention (notwithstanding the anti-U.S. movements that would be submerged until about the 1980s).

The U.S. military was not unique in its fostering of such ideological inequalities. White Americans' racial bias against Koreans had shown itself long before, as in *Liberty Magazine*'s depiction of Koreans in the 1920s as the world's "dirtiest people," full of lice, and much lower than the Japanese (*Chosun Ilbo*, December 18, 1929:2). Although during World War II the United States had deemed the Japanese as racially inferior, inhuman savages with a penchant for sadism—a view they often transferred onto the North Koreans (Dower 1986:14)—the U.S. "liberating" army in Korea seemed to unearth a secret respect for Japan, perhaps inspired by the lower status of Koreans to both powerhouses. The U.S. military continued to use Japanese colonial officers and worked with them in disturbing shows of camaraderie (Cumings 1981:138). Certainly, both sides could simply have been relieved that the war was over. Yet this early partnership was significant, as it ushered in anti-Korean prejudices that would prevail throughout the occupation (Cumings 1981:138). Bruce Cumings (1981:138–39) contends that the Americans seemed to like the Japanese better than the Koreans: "The Japanese were viewed as cooperative, orderly, and docile, while the Koreans were seen as headstrong, unruly, and obstreperous. These characterizations cropped up repeatedly in the literature and probably had their origin in initial American responses to Korea in the fall of 1945." Even after Koreans expressed their displeasure over U.S.-Japanese camaraderie, prompting the dismissal of the colonial officers, the occupational forces still called on the Japanese as unofficial advisors (Cumings 1981:138–39) and/or drew on Korean colluders. Also alarmed by the use of repressive colonial rightists and by American paranoia over Communism, *Chicago Sun* correspondent Mark Gayn drew on his eyewitness account in the fall of 1946, a year after the troops arrived, to conclude, "We appear uncertain whether we had come to liberate or to occupy" (Gayn 1981:352).

The American officers were also, at times, ambivalent toward their former enemy. For one, the U.S. forces were also occupying Japan (under the leadership of General Douglas MacArthur) in large part to strip down Japan and bury any chance of future military prowess.[6] Members of the military also racialized all Asians, Japanese included, as foreign, strange, exotic, and "gookish." General Hodge, the U.S. commander in the ROK remarked that Koreans "are the same breed of cats as the Japanese" (Lauterbach 1947:201). In addition, Gayn (1981:349) identified racism among the U.S. officers, citing one lieutenant who deemed Koreans "dirty and treacherous" and that "psychological warfare [is] the only way to show these gooks we won't stand for any monkey business." In another instance, Alfred Crofts (1960:544), a member of the U.S. military government in South Korea, criticized his colleagues for turning the buildings reserved for Seoul National University into U.S. military barracks. He described how a Colonel Blimp rejoined: "These Gooks don't need colleges! Let's close the places up and train them to be coolies." Not only does he stand in stark contrast to the early missionaries who built the colleges, Colonel Blimp's statement brings to light the U.S. *racial* ideology, which collapses Asians and Asian Americans ("coolies") as well as Chinese and Korean ethnics. Indeed, the blurred interface between "Oriental" and "Orient" had been popularized by the Chicago School in the United States (H. Yu 2002) by the time the military officials arrived at the end of World War II to "liberate" Korea.

In summary, racialized biases and injustices against the Korean population since 1945 have evidenced Americans' view of the dependent Koreans as "dirty," "lice-headed," and "don't need colleges" (read: the inferior third world); "gooks," "unruly," and "treacherous" (read: inscrutable foreigner, yellow peril); and "same breed of cats" and "coolies" (read: all Asians are the same). Even into the 1990s, it was common for U.S. soldiers to refer to Koreans as "gooks" or worse (Lie 1998:144). However, in front of the Korean state and the masses, the U.S. military has hegemonically defined and lauded itself as a "liberator" and "ally."

Whites/Heroes in American Mass Media

The above ideologies betray the cooperation between the U.S. militarist state and dominant representations, a relationship on which imperialist racial formations depend (McClintock 1995; see Omi and Winant 1994:56). One example brings us back to military surgeon Dr. Millard. His map of Korea rendered the entire northern portion "Goonyland" (Millard 1955). Such a reckoning yields no acknowledgment of the fact that North Korea was an arbitrary construction of his Stars and Stripes and the Hammer and Sickle a mere decade prior. He shows no sensitivity to the fact that the arbitrary division prevented *South* Korean families and friends who happened to fall on the wrong side of the line from perhaps ever seeing each other again. In a similar vein, his medical chart comparing two sets of eyes, the "Occidental look" above the "Oriental look," legitimated that Occidental eyelids were superior and that Korean patients should be willing to mutilate their bodies to approximate them. True to Orientalist form, Millard conformed to Edward Said's (1978:55) contention that those in power ensure that "something foreign and distant acquires . . . a status more rather than less familiar." Along the lines of mass mediated representations, the American military and U.S. mass culture converge in the form of American Forces Korea Network (AFKN). Now dubbed AFN Korea, South Korean residents have been exposed to the same U.S. military propaganda and pro-American representations that have saturated the bases since 1957. As South Koreans have been inculcated with ideologies of the United States as a savior and have witnessed what they consider U.S. heroism and material abundance, "America" has become synonymous with "utopia" (Yuh 2002:35). Koreans' literal encounters with the U.S. military are informed by, and inform, the images of White Americans they have watched on television or in movie houses. Darnell Hunt (1997:144) characterizes these experiences as the concrete situations through which race-as-representation acts as "an immediate social force," a force that has accompanied "America" wherever it has traveled. In the case of South Korea, this link between the state and dominant representations has forged the superiority and normativity of White America and, in relation, the inferiority and Otherness of Korea and its people. Many Koreans' surgical alteration of their eyelids is just one example.

America, the Vast Cowboy Frontier

First, it cannot be overstated that all the respondents in my study had engaged American media in South Korea in one form or another irrespective of time of emigration, age, social class, region in which they grew up, or gender. Although Koreans who have immigrated to the United States since the late 1980s / early 1990s have had the greatest and most diverse access to American television, movies, music, and print journalism, U.S. popular culture has been an integral part of South Korean life for the past forty years (H. Kang 1991). Not to be taken lightly, American material and popular culture has been a driving force behind Koreans' longing for and migration to "America" (Abelmann and Lie 1995:64). In this setting, even those who left the country around 1970, the first year of mass Korean exodus to the United States, reported having watched a great deal of American movies and television programs.

One pattern was middle-aged Korean men's proclivity for the film genre of westerns while living in South Korea. Mr. Bae, a fifteen-year immigrant, was one such fan.

> You know, lots of American culture has been imported to Korea, for example, movies like the western movies . . . such as the John Wayne movies. At that time [watching them], I thought that America was really big.

Mr. Bae's exposure to John Wayne's contemplative and action-packed journeys through the vast terrain of the West painted a picture for him of an "America" larger than life. This characterization was especially salient for a people who share the common adage, "our small country," and frequently attribute short-comings, even Koreans' narrow-mindedness, to small size (recall that Koreans believe that people "embody" their nations). In another example, old-timer Mr. Koh (age 54) had watched his share of westerns and other films on the U.S. military station AFKN, about which he seemed to boast when he spoke with me.

> K: I watched a lot of American movies! . . . Since I was young, I've watched a lot of American movies, westerns . . . There was John Wayne, Gary Cooper, Cary Grant. I watched a lot of movies, not only love stories but many different kinds because lots of American movies are shown in Korea. You can even say that I've been watching it since I was ten years old . . . There's also the TV channel AFKN; uh (pause), what is the title of that program in Texas? What's that program dealing with Texas oil?
>
> N: Oh, *Dallas*?
>
> K: *Dallas*, like that drama. Those were much more interesting than Korean dramas!

His impulse to show off his knowledge of American mass media, including John Wayne films, seemed to flow from the same pride he derived from training with and befriending White GIs, that is, of being associated with White America. His familiarity with hegemonically masculine icons like John Wayne, Gary Cooper, Cary Grant and the Ewing brothers brought him closer to their racially and nationally dominant status.

"Americans" Are Richer Than Us

Koreans selectively drew on these media texts—namely the wealthier, more powerful, and more beautiful White reference point—to construct "America" as ideal. For instance, none of the men mentioned the Native American sidekicks or enemies in the westerns and, in general, Koreans did not invoke depictions of the poor from any of the texts. Focusing instead on American wealth, South Koreans interpret it within a formidable class logic that naturalizes the superiority of the rich. They idealize White Americans for their innate talents that begot the wealthiest country in the world. It is not surprising, then, that the immigrants' recollections and South Koreans' interpretations tended to highlight the White middle-class (or upper-class) norm in U.S. media texts (see Ehrenreich 1995). As noted, the U.S. occupational forces had already alerted Koreans to American wealth. Chocolate giveaways and bountiful PXes (multipurpose stores for the military) spawned stories of how Americans were so rich that they had meat at every meal, each with a huge serving (Yuh 2002:34). The fact that even rank-and-file soldiers could enjoy such culinary abundance gave rise to the belief that American common folk were richer than the Korean upper class (Yuh 2002:35). Their views were affirmed by the military bases themselves, such as the U.S. Forces in Korea (USFK) headquarters in Yongsan (Seoul) replete with golf courses, bowling lanes, movie theaters, swimming pools, restaurants, and a mini-suburban America complete with houses, vast lawns, schools, parks, sports leagues, and Parent-Teacher Associations (Yuh 2002:35). Even after South Korea arrived as an "Asian Tiger" economy, American foods like Spam remained luxury items sold as gourmet delicacies in upscale department stores. Foods from U.S. military PXes such as Oreo cookies, Cheese Whiz, and Kraft singles continue to be sold in Korean markets (Yuh 2002:34–35). I also noticed during my fieldwork how middle-class housewives would show off expensive American items like Pringles in their homes by making them visible or by using them as storage containers after the chips were gone.

In a less-developed Korea, however, old-timers like middle-aged Ms. Go recalled gleaning America's more "modern" lifestyle from the first U.S. prime-time soap opera, *Peyton Place* (1964–69), which chronicled the lives of an upper-crust New England White American family. It starred Mia Farrow and Ryan O'Neal.

Like we watched TV, like the American drama and there's more modern living and . . . we can "catch" America from there, you know? Yeah, *Peyton Place*, that kind of thing . . . I think at that time we had cars, but *each* family didn't own a car at that time, you know? Only really rich people had a car and like a TV, even. Yeah, we [would think], "Oh, that country's like really more sophisticated-looking." [modified][7]

Ms. Go's narrative makes salient the power of material trappings and other cultural symbols in establishing the "superiority" of one "race"/nation (White America) over another (Korea/Koreans). Although other informants had a more difficult time pinpointing specific media texts, they reached similar conclusions when recollecting their premigration views. Mr. Han (age 65), a former film director in South Korea who has lived in the United States for twenty-five years, focused on the theme of Western abundance.

> H: Because of my job, I watched a lot of movies, not just American, but French ones, etc. . . . From there, in terms of work, I thought, it [United States] was rich and well-developed, better than Korea, and I wanted to come to a bigger country to do lots of things.
> N: You mean the things that you couldn't easily do in Korea?
> H: Right.

Recent immigrants like Ms. Yoon (age 48) tended to echo social class stereotypes about White American wealth. "I'm sure most Koreans thought like me. Before I got here, I thought Whites were high-classed people who lived in luxury and wealth just like in the movies . . . I'm sure it's not just me but about fifty to sixty percent of all Koreans think that way about Whites." South Koreans concurred with the recent immigrants. In a focus group exchange, students and young professionals evoked a similar naturalization of White American affluence:

> MR. HAN: When I think of Whites, the picture in my head is of people wearing tuxedos at a party and walking around holding champagne.
> Ms. JUNG: When I was young, although I don't really think that way now, I thought all Whites were rich. Like when I watched Hollywood movies, I thought even the beggars looked stylish!
> Ms. LEE: Well, I still think that way now (laughs). If they're White then I think that they're rich!

These U.S. media representations of White middle-class and upper-class life convey to a people who essentialize national development and social class status that White Americans are richer because of their natural talents. By contrast, Koreans were poorer because they as a people had been unable to move their nation up the global ladder. For the early 1970s immigrants "watching" from a comparatively less-developed Korea, the sense of inferiority stung that much worse.

"Americans" Are Happier, Nicer, and Freer Than Us

During their interviews, Koreans of both genders readily conjured up the classic American films they had seen, the vast majority of which featured and were exclusively about White Americans.

> I saw a lot, you know, like *Breakfast at Tiffany's*. (Ms. Song, age 28, 3½ years in United States)

> Mʀ. Juɴɢ: [*26 years in United States*] *Titanic*, yeah! . . . there was also another
> one (pause). I don't remember much, uh, gosh, *Roma Holiday* . . . ?
> N: Oh, *Roman Holiday*?
> Mʀ. Juɴɢ: *Roman Holiday*? With Audrey Hepburn? [Nadia nods] . . . yeah,
> that one I watched.

Needless to say, Whites are the reference point in these and earlier-mentioned texts (incidentally, with an overrepresentation of Audrey Hepburn, a household name in South Korea). And in the television series *Dallas*, an internationally renowned drama about a wealthy Texas oil family, the Ewings certainly had no recurring friends or relatives of color of which to speak. Attractive and typically well-off Whites (especially relative to a developing Korea) are also the protagonists of *Roman Holiday, Breakfast at Tiffany's*,[8] and the old (and new) *Titanic*. Extending from tropes on the kindness of early missionaries, and even more widespread, U.S. benevolence during the Korean War, the respondents gleaned from mass media texts the happier, nicer, and more liberated "Americans." To reach such a conclusion, Koreans did not simply characterize Whites as happy and liberated because they got to enjoy "America's" wealth and democracy. They also understood White Americans within the logic of Korea's cultural norms, such as not engaging in the following with strangers: smiling, making eye contact, being extroverted, and sharing deep emotions. They noticed, however, that these norms were more common amongst White Americans themselves (to be sure, South Koreans have incorporated some of these norms in recent years). Invoking this frame, Mr. Jung, who immigrated in the 1970s, recollects how he came to understand White Americans through a famous Korean folktale about optimism and pessimism. Akin to the half-full, half-empty glass adage in the United States, both characters in the Korean tale look at the same moon, yet one sees it as good and is happy while the other sees it as bad and is melancholic. Mr. Jung remarks that movies like *Roman Holiday* taught him that Whites were the happy optimists: "*Itaebaegi* is always saying happy things . . . American people are *Itaebaegi* [and have] optimism (chuckles)." Elderly Mr. Sohn, who had also consumed a good amount of American popular culture before immigrating in 1983, had a similar perception but stressed White Americans' liberation from the Confucian collectivist norms that he was used to as a Korean (e.g., not sticking out of a crowd, going along to get along).

> S: The images I had was that they had more freedom, that they were more outgoing and expressed themselves more and were more open-minded than Koreans, acted freely. I had these kinds of images and thoughts about them.
>
> N: You mean all the White Americans?
>
> S: Yeah, all of them. They were outgoing, energetic.

He conveys their more "liberated" tendencies by using words associated with individualism: "outgoing," "open-minded," "expressed themselves," and "acted freely." In contrast, Koreans were generally not these things, a fact he would lament later in the interview.

More recent immigrants described Whites similarly but also revealed their increased exposure to sensationalistic news broadcasts compared to that of earlier immigrants. In recent years, South Koreans have been much abuzz about school shootings in the United States, as such a phenomenon is virtually incomprehensible and wholly bewildering within a society in which civilian gun use is illegal and not practiced. There is little to no cultural context for guns in everyday South Korean life.

> P: I thought that if I became friends with those people [White Americans] in the U.S., then I thought they'd be good people.
>
> N: Why?
>
> P: I thought of them as very understanding and friendly to others.
>
> N: You thought that before you came?
>
> P: Yeah, from looking at movies, books, they seemed very kind. But one thing that scared me was kids carrying guns to school and kids dying, getting injured . . . So although I was scared of that, the typical people seem like they are kind . . . As long as you don't offend any of them, they seem to be kind, more so than Koreans are, if you know them for awhile.

Although Ms. Paik, like Mr. Sohn earlier, believed Whites were generally more pleasant people than Koreans, she echoed the sentiments of South Koreans who questioned the integrity of White Americans. How could White students shoot and kill one another and themselves in their classrooms, such as in Columbine? In fact, in a society in which schooling is so paramount that students during some parts of the year go to school from 6 A.M. to midnight or 6 A.M. to 10 P.M. and then off to supplementary tutoring schools (hagwŏn) until 1 A.M., South Koreans often base their decision against immigrating on the alarming U.S. phenomenon of student murderers. Such incidents prompted Ms. Paik to qualify that typical Whites were nice as long as "you don't offend any of them."

"Americans" Are Better Looking Than Us

Koreans' valorization of White Americans is not surprising in light of "mere exposure effect" studies that find people's familiarity with a sign to beget greater liking for it (Bornstein 1989). The familiarity of Whites' physical aesthetic from the missionaries to the post-1945 American forces and mass media has secured Koreans' noted sense of aesthetic inferiority. For instance, advertisements for Western products, especially for personal care and beauty products, that proliferate in the top Korean/Asian magazines almost always use a White model (Neelankavil, Mummalaneni, and Sessions 1995). Even the widely circulated Korean (international) versions of the French fashion magazine Elle and America's Harper's Bazaar feature many models of European descent (Media Daily, July 2, 1996). Beauty is no small matter for Korean women in particular, as attracting a husband is their best chance at economic survival, and job opportunities for women are few (most middle-class women are precluded from working after marriage).[9] Whether the men explicitly stated it or not, however, both genders have succumbed to a sense of aesthetic inferiority. In fact, cosmetic surgery to Europeanize Korean features became a booming industry thanks to Korean men's and women's patronage. It is also commonplace for middle-class parents to give their daughters eyelid surgery for high school graduation presents (Toronto Star, October 4, 2001). As I showed, the European beauty standard grew out of the Korean War after which those with double eyelids and higher nose bridges became more attractive and desirable than counterparts with single eyelids and flatter, wider noses. Examples from my fieldwork are telling. The fashion models, entertainers, and beauty contestants whom Korean society hailed as the most beautiful all had double eyelids, especially in the case of women; many also boasted higher noses. On one particular day in Ewha's campus town—South Korea's premier women's, and incidentally feminist-leaning, university—I happened to be looking for a dentist and accidentally stumbled into a cosmetic surgeon's office to find several women sitting and waiting underneath posters of Europeanized Asian women. Some of the women hid behind sunglasses and low-brimmed baseball caps, perhaps recognizing the contradictions of undergoing eyelid and other cosmetic forms of surgery. Elsewhere in Seoul, I was witness to many punk rock youth of both genders with bleached blond hair, an imitation of British and American trends and perhaps related to Whiteness. I also witnessed the long-standing tradition of women carrying parasols on sunny days to remain pale.

Not surprisingly, Korean women were also more explicit than men about their internalized inferiority about appearance; this is despite men's intense exposure to hegemonic White masculinity (e.g., John Wayne, Gary Cooper, Cary Grant, the Ewing brothers). In one instance, longtime immigrant Ms. Go treats Whites' "superior" appearance as axiomatic.

G: Yeah, I thought they [Whites] were better looking.
N: . . . than Koreans?
G: (laughing softly) Of course!

Similarly, old-timer Ms. Park said the following about *Gone with the Wind*: "Yeah, yeah, when I watched that one, it was, 'Oh, that famous pretty girl [Vivien Leigh]. Wow!,' you know, sometimes I [felt] envy." Ms Song, at twenty-eight years old (three and a half years in United States), demonstrated that women in South Korea like herself had internalized White beauty standards.

S: and well, now there's the standard of being beautiful is like fixed, you know. Right?
N: It's fixed . . .
S: I mean many people think that tall, skinny, a blonde, blue eyes, you know, that kind of stereotype about beautiful ladies, right? So yeah, I think, now that I think about it, it's bad, but you know, since I watched that kind of movie from when I was very young, subconsciously, I thought that to be beautiful, you have to have like, um, blond hair or whatever, you know?

The fact that she, someone whom I considered normatively pretty, would feel inferior to blond White women was rather striking. After spotting one of the flurry of posters around Seoul of blond, light-eyed European models in a beauty salon window, another female friend from my church group interrupted our silence to ask me earnestly, "Do you think American women or Korean women are prettier?" The very fact that she asked me this question bears out the effects of all sorts of media, from movies to print advertising, on the women's racial sense of self. Beyond mass media, however, the Korean plastic surgery juggernaut itself grew out of the U.S. military and its efforts to make nice with the occupied population.

A handful of men also noted how U.S. media texts taught them that White American women were exceptionally attractive. Longtime immigrant Mr. Pak remarked on how starstruck he was by the beautiful stars of *Little Women*; he rattled off with ease "June Allyson, Janet Leigh, Elizabeth Taylor." Younger generations of recent immigrants concurred. Mr. Ryu, thirty-three years old, said that the U.S. media had taught him "that all American women are beautiful (laughs)!" When I asked him why he thought so, he replied as if stating the obvious, "Because only beautiful people appear!" Among this small group of men, however, few valorized White American women as ideal wives. Their lack of interest had mostly to do with the "traditional" wife granted them by Korean Confucian patriarchy, family pressure to adhere to obligations of patrilineage and consanguinity (i.e., carrying on the Korean family bloodline), and stereotypes of White women as too gender liberated and sexually promiscuous (see Kelsky 2001; Espiritu 2001). For instance, as images of hypersexualized and sexually promiscuous White American women abound in the U.S. media, reactions like those of my male cousin are not surprising. He and I were watching an American music video (via MTV Korea) in which a White woman flaunts her disproportionately big breasts throughout—he could not believe how brazen she was about it. These stereotypes of White women suggest that Koreans do not always idealize Whites, with mass media serving as potential fodder.

"White Men Are More Equal"

South Korean women have long expressed favor toward White Western men or, more accurately, the hegemonic White masculinity that defines them. R. W. Connell (2005:39) writes that hegemonic masculinities have globalized by way of "the economic and political expansion of European states from the fifteenth century on and by the creation of colonial empires." Such gendered hegemony has persisted through contemporary U.S. imperialism in Asia. In the context of the occupation, South Korean women have historically married

White (and Black) American servicemen in large numbers (Min 2006:46–50). In more recent years, women's perception that White men are more gender egalitarian than Korean men has motivated racial comparisons and desire for "international marriage," a trend also common in Japan (Kelsky 2001). To be sure, such a view does not mean that South Korean women cease being attracted to, or marrying, Korean men. It does account, however, for why interracial (or "international") marriages are dramatically increasing, and not just with American men. Despite some of the women's nationalist impulses and heightened concerns about White men's cultural insensitivity and despite the hankering for Korean men among women across Asia in recent years, the informants continued to racialize White men as gender egalitarian and Korean men as gender traditional. In so doing, they inadvertently reify a global hierarchy of racialized masculinity. New immigrant women tended to make these claims before they came to the United States while more old-timers often solidified such thinking *after* immigrant life (beginning in the 1970s).

A twenty-nine-year-old newcomer (6 months in United States), Ms. Um, drew on her childhood at her father's small store near an army base to invoke "men-in-uniform" masculinity notions.

U: Because when my dad had the store I thought, wow, White men looked pretty good, and even the Black men did too (chuckles)!

N: You only saw men from those two groups?

U: Yeah, the army men who walked by back and forth. So I wouldn't say that I felt that I definitely had to marry a Korean person . . . Even at that point, I didn't have any prejudice toward them whatsoever so when I was little, I used to dream about what it would be like if I married a White guy (laughs)!

Many of these women's idealization of White masculinity also drew heavily on American and European mass media images. Even women in their forties and sixties noted their idealization of White male icons like Jeremy Irons, Elvis Presley, and James Dean since their younger days in South Korea. Jeremy Irons was named several times by women of all ages, as South Korean society has long considered a British man to be the ultimate gentleman (see Robinson 1988:75). Some of the young Seoul informants named figures like Andrea Bocelli, Harrison Ford, and Keanu Reeves as highly desirable (not knowing Reeves was part Chinese); during other trips to South Korea I could not escape

Leonardo DiCaprio's face, and in more recent years, David Beckham has been all the rage.

The women, in turn, linked such idealized imagery of attractive, "modern" White men to gender egalitarianism. Young Ms. Ra (6 months in United States), for instance, recounted that she had mused over the possibility of a White husband while she was a college student in Seoul. She, like most of the women, considered a White mate in order to gain the gender reciprocity that she witnessed in American movies and that seemed unattainable within Korean marriages.

> When I was a college student I once thought about a foreigner because, *as you know*, it'd be different from being with a Korean man. The White men share the household duties with their wives equally, they know how to love their wives. You know, it's different in Korea. Even though times have changed [women are treated better], I thought that it was worth considering at that time . . . because we see them [White men] that way in the movies . . . They take good care of their wives.

Ms. Ra presents the common conception of White masculinity as more gender egalitarian ("share the household duties . . . equally"), which she then links to a proper expression of love ("know how to love their wives"). Her statement "as you know" is a dictum, one so powerful that she, like the others, was unfamiliar with White American men's general avoidance of housework (Ehrenreich 2002). Yet, Ms. Ra's romanticized view makes clear why she chose to marry a 1.5-generation Korean American (a child immigrant raised in the United States) and move to *miguk* to be with him. The Seoul informants agreed. "In a way, in Korean women's perspective, the gender roles in the West seem more fair . . . So I've never been against international marriages," said graduate student Ms. Lim. In her eyes, Korean women's marriages to Western men represented "more fair" gender practices and arrangements.

Like Ms. Ra above, the vast majority of the women claimed that they had considered marrying a White American man long before they had come to the United States. Showing that these perceptions transcend the younger generations, middle-aged Ms. Li, a seven-year immigrant, recollected that back in Seoul she had preferred a White American man over a Korean man due to more combative communication with the latter.

> L: When I was old enough to think about marriage, I thought it would be
>   much better if I married a *miguk saram* even though I couldn't communi-

cate well . . . You know how most Koreans, because of the way they talk, they fight, for example: "Why the hell do you talk to me that way? You think you can talk to me like that?" . . . Every fight begins with talking, but White Americans are not attentive to that kind of wordplay; they focus instead on behavior . . .

N: How did you know that back then?

L: That's just what I thought.

Though fewer in number, some women were shaped not just by imagery, ideologies, and second-hand stories but by the personal encounters they had with White men in South Korea. Although old-timer immigrants had fewer chances to interact with White American men, newcomers reported some, though mostly acquaintance-type, meetings with businessmen, exchange students, language teachers, and the like (recall that American GIs are mostly restricted to camptowns segregated from mainstream Korean society). Some of these women saw White men as "free-spirited," "liberal," while others had crushes. Ms. Kang (age 46, 3 years in United States), for instance, noted that seeing her cousin and her White American husband in South Korea influenced her to "always [be] open to the idea" of a White spouse, even before marrying her Korean husband. Her cousin's intermarriage had thus left a sting of envy.

K: I was so envious of her.

N: Why?

K: I don't know why. Uh, the fact that a foreigner fell in love with a Korean woman and they got to live together here—it was all so fascinating to me.

N: Do you think you would prefer Whites as a potential marriage partner, if you weren't married, that is?

K: Yes, if I wasn't married, I'd consider Whites.

N: . . . as much as you'd consider Koreans?

K: Yes, yes!

Ms. Kang's fascination with the fact that a White person would fall for a Korean also reveals a sense of racial/national inferiority. The thrill of overcoming that inferiority conjoined with the "White prince" ideal seems to guide her openness to marrying a White American. Other women, like Ms. Moon, had also learned idealized constructions of White American men through personal transnational channels, such as from girlfriends in the United States who were dating or married to White men. She noted how all her girlfriends "seemed really happy."

These interview findings are supported by data on marital preferences from Edward Chang's 1999 survey, *The Racial/Ethnic Attitudes of Korean College Students*. These nonrandom data of 1,288 students from twelve universities across distinct regions of the country revealed (assuming that all participants were truthful about their heterosexuality) that, among females, White American/European men (United States, United Kingdom, France, Germany, Italy— 57.1 percent) were a close second to Korean men (South, North, overseas—66.6 percent). The women's preferences disaggregated by nation revealed that "American" and most European countrymen (especially from Western Europe) ranked above even *North Korean* men. Although the women most prefer Korean men as an aggregate grouping, their reports reveal a gender subtext. They desire men from highly developed "modern" countries more so than they do coethnic men, pointing both to economic and "gender modernity" (see Hirsch 2003) as key criteria for their ideal spouse. In contrast, Korean men's preferences are animated by a desire for more "gender traditional" women; they preferred Koreans first, then Chinese, then Japanese before they did White American/European women (41.6 percent).

However, since about 1998 South Korean men have become idols in popular culture across Asia. The Korean Wave (*hanryu*) of popular culture that has taken much of Asia (and beyond) by storm has sparked Japanese and other Asian women's fanatical love and obsessive rituals for Korean male celebrities (*Washington Post*, August 31, 2006). Although these men, such as pop music star Rain, have become icons of hegemonic masculinity themselves, Korean women continue to associate their coethnic men with problematic gender norms. In fact, while some women take great pride in (and feel vindicated by) Japan's obsession with Korean men and Korean culture, others have not been swayed but irritated. An Internet topic entitled "Why Do Korean Women Hate Korean Men So Much?" on the popular Web site www.Naver.com (2005; see www.Joara.com 2007) finds many women writing that Korean men are self proclaimed "kings of the world" and generally "unfair," "controlling," selfish," "aggressive," and "possessive." Korean men are also known for cheating on their partners, a tendency frequently discussed on the hit program *Beauties' Talk Show* (*Minyŏdŭrŭi Suda*), a program that introduces Korean culture to beauty contestants from across the world. The women online point out that non-Korean women forget that the male characters are precisely that, characters. Indeed, Kim Ok Hyun, director of Star M, a major star management company in Seoul admits, "It's a type of character that doesn't exist much in Asian movies and television, and now it's what Asian women think Korean men are like . . . But to tell you the truth, I still haven't met a real one who fits that description" (*Washington Post,* August 31, 2006). Again, Korean women's grievances do not translate into a refusal to marry coethnic men, as the survey shows, and some rebuke those with White boyfriends who bitterly criticize Korean men online (www.empas.com 2006). The above patterns do reveal, however, that Korean women have racially idealized White American men. Yuh (2002) found the Prince Charming ideal to hold even among women who had been abused by White male GIs. Such a view should not be surprising in light of glorifications of White American masculinity in hegemonic fashion, whether as benevolent soldiers or as Hollywood heroes, that afford dismissals of abusive behavior as exceptions to the "race."

U.S. Military and Media Injustice

Korean women have also resisted hegemonic glorifications of White American men, especially as part of their anti-U.S. resistance in South Korea. Anti-American sentiment has been sparked and exacerbated by U.S. soldiers' oppressive acts against the Korean people in general and violence against and murder of Korean women in particular. These atrocities have informed South Koreans of Americans' low regard for them as weak, inferior, and unimportant. Invoking these atrocities, some of the women in Seoul and in the United States, namely newcomers, had condemned the U.S. military as a site of oppression at the intersection of nation, "race," and gender. A Seoul student named Ms. Park remarked that unlike the handsome celebrities that the women in her focus group invoked, White American servicemen immediately came to mind in reference to "Americans."

> When I think of Whites, I don't think of people from movies or TV. I immediately think of the American GIs here [*migun*] . . . especially when I think of all the controversies with Korean women or when there are Korea–U.S. problems or things like that. I think: Oh, all they believe in is the power of their country, and I bet they're nothing back in their country but here, they think they are all that; though I'm sure not every single one of them is like that.

Her words challenge other women's hegemonic constructions of White American masculinity as categorically heroic, attractive, loving, and gender egalitarian. Rather, she perceives White soldiers to be violent (including toward women), arrogant, and overly nationalistic. Recent immigrant Ms. Ra who had been in the United States seven months to begin life with her Korean American husband saw the foregoing view as widespread.

> Koreans generally think badly of American soldiers. Their basic perception of American soldiers is that they are uneducated people who come, live there for a while, take women, and then leave. And there are women who were totally deceived when they got married: the man lied that it was his first marriage when it was his third. Later, when he was killed in an accident, she found out that he hadn't reported their marriage and none of his divorces had cleared yet so she couldn't register her child's name . . . there are lots of those kinds of problems.

Although Ms. Ra was the same person whose Hollywood image of White men as gender egalitarian had prompted her to seriously consider marrying a "foreigner," she also considers White soldiers to be uneducated, antiwomen, and deceitful. Thus characterized, she introduces social class by distinguishing between this low-class, uneducated, crude White GI (subordinate masculinity) and a higher-class, refined White professional (hegemonic masculinity). Although women often racialized White men as more gender egalitarian than Korean men, in their anti-American moments they aligned with their coethnics against White American men and imperialist masculinity. Korean men are further compelled by the oppressor's "stealing of our women," a common way in which men exercise power over other men within racialized patriarchy (see P. Collins 2000; Espiritu 1997).

U.S. Military Abuses

In these ways, South Koreans' sense of inferiority to White America's military, democracy, affluence, beauty, and men did not go uncontested. In concerted ways, Koreans rejected and condemned U.S. dominance and the ideologies of Korean weakness, inferiority, and insignificance on which it depended. According to the South Korean organization Peace Korea, U.S. soldiers (and their families) have been abusing power and/or committing crimes such as assault, rape, murder, and land infractions since first arriving in 1945. In 1946, for instance, South Korean officials with the active aid of the U.S. military quelled demonstrations against the occupational forces or any activities deemed "procommunist" (Mitchell 1951). Despite major Korean protest, the U.S. military government also prohibited the merging of various Korean colleges and schools built by fellow Americans, likely out of fear of dissident movements. In the 1960s, journalist Albert Axelbank (1967:11) recounted that some 200 South

Korean soldiers attached to U.S. Army units (Katusas) had staged a hunger strike after a U.S. Army mess sergeant had stabbed a Korean in the left eye with a fork because of "too much jam on his bread." South Koreans have also had to resist U.S. land infractions waged in the name of military operations, such as the destruction of Korean villages (Yuh 2002:22–23).

A case in point is Songtan. In 1951, the U.S. Air Force bulldozed over Songtan village, built an airfield, and left homeless 1,000 families who had farmed the same plots of land for generations. Although the U.S. military had promised in writing compensation for these families (albeit at much less than the market value of the land), it reneged, prompting years of legal action from the farmers. When the ROK and the United States signed the 1966 U.S. Status of Forces Agreement (SOFA), the product of a subjected government acquiescing to a more powerful one, the United States was granted the use of any and all land necessary for its operations and at no charge. The passage of SOFA killed all of the farmers' hopes for compensation (Yuh 2002:243). It is thus not surprising that editorials in South Korea's highest-circulation newspaper, *Chosun Ilbo*, began appearing in the 1960s, around the birth of SOFA, condemning American actions and sanctioning every Korean's right to criticize the United States. The trend was inexorable, however, as SOFA would allow the U.S. military in 1992 to displace even more families for Osan Air Force Base, the largest U.S. military base in Asia (when Clark Air Force Base in the Philippines closed; Yuh 2002:23).

The SOFA stipulates U.S. military rights and privileges, the responsibilities of both governments with regard to U.S. forces, and potential jurisdiction, if any, that the ROK government has over U.S. forces and personnel who break South Korean laws (Yuh 2002:243–44). Owing to the fact that South Korea depends on the U.S. military presence to hold off North Korea and usher in U.S. investment, the SOFA essentially gives the United States some of the highest levels of legal immunity abroad. The U.S. military has thus been able to commit crimes with virtual impunity. ROK government reports of military crimes over the long stretch of 1967 to 1998 reveal that U.S. soldiers committed around 50,082 crimes, a statistic that is actually an underestimate; yet, in 1998 alone, the ROK state handled only 3.9 percent of all crimes committed by U.S. soldiers (International Action Center 2001). Historically, U.S. military crimes have been underreported by the once heavily censored South Korean media, especially in moments when the ROK state has not wished to incite or exacerbate conflict with the U.S. military (although sometimes the ROK expressed its own grievances indirectly through the newspapers; Moon 1997:185). In short, "America's" halo from past military aid, official ROK support, and underreported abuses colluded to sustain the public's pro-Americanism through much of the 1970s, the period during which half of the old-timers in this study had immigrated. As many old-timers also left between 1980 and 1983, just before or during the incipient stage of mass anti-Americanism, the horrors of the 1980s and the subsequent conflicts with the military have mostly affected those who left starting in the 1990s.

The 1980s witnessed the shift to anti-Americanism due in large part to the 1980 Kwangju Uprising (or Massacre), a prodemocracy mass student protest against the rise of a military regime under President Chun Du Hwan. The protest ended with approximately 2,000 people killed by South Korean troops (Clark 1988). The United States came to be implicated in the killings owing to its supreme command over the military hierarchy of the ROK-USA forces; the U.S. military would had to have approved such massive movement of troops, no less such specially trained ones (Yuh 2002:73, 245). Other factors confirmed the U.S. role, such as a banned book, published in 1985, detailing an eyewitness account of the massacre (widely circulated among student activists). In 1981 Ronald Reagan had invited President Chun to the White House as his first official visitor and would continue to support Chun's regime (Yuh 2002:73).[10] In this era of heightened popular protest, including sieges on and arson and bombs targeting U.S. Cultural Centers in Seoul, Kwangju, Pusan, and Taegu (*Chosun Ilbo*, May 26, 1985), a constellation of anti-U.S. movements converged to protest South Korea's capitalistic dependence on the United States and its role in the division of the country (Abelmann and Lie 1995:82). Although students were at the forefront of the movement, some of whom were killed or committed protest suicide, even moderate middle-class South Koreans began to question pro-American ideology, prompting many to join the movement around the late 1980s.[11] Throughout, the ROK government denounced the students as a small group of extremists and made efforts to assuage U.S. concerns (*Chosun Ilbo*, June 27, 1986).

For those immigrants who left South Korea after the early 1990s, such as the twenty-nine respondents in my study, other issues had long reinforced anti-Americanism. Koreans have been outraged by U.S. soldiers' numerous sexual assaults and murders of Korean women, namely those who work as waitresses-cum–sex workers at military camptown bars. Although these female workers had been staging small street protests against the sexual violence for years, the larger public was galvanized in October 1992 when Private Kenneth Markle, a White American, brutally tortured, raped, and murdered Yun Kum-Yi. Yun's body was found naked, bloody, and covered with bruises and contusions. In her uterus, Private Markle had implanted a coke bottle and about 10 inches into her rectum the trunk of an umbrella (Rainbow Center 1994). In response, thousands of noncamptown South Koreans joined the protests against the U.S. military's efforts to downplay the crime. On November 7, 1992, a large coalition of forty-six different Korean organizations wrote to the commander of the Second Infantry Division that "we the people believe that this is an example of how American soldiers treat Korean women" (Rainbow Center 1994:8). Although the United States had been in the country for forty-seven years by the time Yun was murdered, Markle, a White American, was the first U.S. soldier ever to be tried in Korean, not U.S. military, criminal courts. Although this marked a huge victory for South Korea in light of frequent U.S. military pardons and wrist slaps, U.S. officials were later able to commute Markle's sentence of life to a mere fifteen years.

Six months before Yun's murder, another incident signaled Americans' derisive and dismissive orientation toward Koreans (and, by extension, South Korea). This time it was across the ocean and was called the LA "riots." Although some South Korean media outlets tagged the unrest the "Black riots" (*hŭgin pokdong*), the coverage, even among mainstream and conservative outlets, made clear how Korean immigrants suffered tremendous losses due to the U.S. forces' protection of predominantly White and rich Beverly Hills at the expense of Koreatown (E. Kim 1993). The South Korean media also claimed that Korean Americans were scapegoats in what was ultimately a White-Black conflict, yet the U.S. media insisted on absolving Whites of blame by stressing that the unrest was a Black-Korean issue. The South Korean newspapers accused the American media of continuously airing footage of the Korean merchant, Soon Ja Du, shooting Black teenager LaTasha Harlins, and of airing scenes of Black animosity toward Koreans (*Chosun Ilbo*, May 4 and 7, 1992).

South Korean Resistance to the U.S. Military and Whiteness

Reflecting larger trends, the Korean informants in this study resisted White American dominance and the anti-Korean ideologies that justified it. Not surprisingly, such resistance was more common among the newcomers and the Seoul residents than among the old-timer immigrants who had left by the early 1980s. Although most of these immigrants had followed South Korean politics since emigration, they had become so preoccupied with survival in the United States and with adjusting to new rules, mores, and people that they had not encountered anti-Americanism as intensely as South Koreans. Generally speaking, old-timer immigrants have been much more detached from the military occupation than those who never left (N. Kim 2006b). This trend also flows from the heightened pro-Americanism among immigrants, those with a predilection for the American dream ethos.

Placing blame on White American elites rather than average citizens, middle-aged Ms. An, freshly in the United States, shared her premigration notions of White American leaders based on anti-Americanism "back home."

A: What I heard in Korea was that in terms of political relations with Korea, White people were very bad . . . White people are bad.

N: Why?

A: They are the kind of people who would use and kill any country [people] for their own advantages. They don't understand at all people who are poor, so I thought that they were very bad. But I think they are very nice now that I have met them here . . . But I don't know because I haven't met anyone in higher positions.

Ms. An makes a distinction between common White folk and White Americans in positions of power. Still, in their resistance to the U.S. state, Koreans constructed racialized notions of White Americans as potentially uneducated, tactless, violent, antiwomen, and power hungry. In the process of resistance, then, they saw themselves as *not* these things.

Mass Media and Anti-Americanism

Korean resistance has not just shone a spotlight on the occupational forces. The 1980s witnessed an emergence of nativist, though minority, movements galvanized around rejecting U.S. cultural imperialism, from consumer goods to standards of beauty to Hollywood (Abelmann and Lie 1995:83). I observed one example of the movement to resurrect indigenous Korean folk traditions at Ewha University when, around the same time every day, the traditionally dressed drumming troops would gather at the campus center to drum loud enough for Seoul to hear, overtaking the (Korean and American) bubble gum pop blaring out of the nearby CD shops. Some of these movements have also been linked to culturally nationalistic ideologies that declare Koreans' cultural superiority over White Americans (see Espiritu 2001, 2003). Koreans trumpet their over 4,000-year-old culture (relative to the youth of the United States), less individualistic selfishness, less sexual depravity, and the like (N. Kim 2003). These "counter-publics" (Habermas 1989) have lobbied to prevent youth from desiring all things American and to keep local movie industries alive,[12] a move long contested by the U.S. government and movie industry.

The larger South Korean public, often the older generations, have shown great concern with the content of American media texts. Some of the respondents here were critical of U.S. media's portrayal of White Americans as superior to non-White peoples from lesser nations. Longtime immigrant Mr. Yoo remarked how he had learned from "watching America" in South Korea that White racism existed toward all non-Whites: "Even though I can't pinpoint where exactly, you could smell the White supremacy even in the movies; not that it strongly jumped out at me, but it generally existed to a certain extent." A younger immigrant who had left much later, in 2000, Mr. Min, remarked that Hollywood had taught him the following before coming to the United States, "They [Whites] came off as arrogant and self-absorbed. It looked like they had an inflated ego, overestimating their abilities. I felt that they thought that they were somehow more cool and better than others. It looked to me like they were full of themselves in the movies."

Although the South Korean and immigrant respondents in my study had a difficult time conjuring up Hollywood images of Asians or Koreans, one movie that was met with protest in South Korea was *Falling Down*, a film about White male angst starring Michael Douglas as Bill Foster. An opening scene showcases Foster spewing nativistic racist hatred toward a Korean immigrant storeowner for overcharging for products and assuming that Foster was a thief. The Korean immigrant storeowner is generally unlikable. In chorus with one of my Seoul respondents, a 1993 *Chosun Ilbo* (February 23, 1993) article reported that "a movie called 'Falling Down' is causing a stir among Korean Americans for portraying them as 'a group of people who only care about money and are unable to speak proper English . . . Korean Americans argue that such movies plant prejudice in American society toward Koreans.' " The fact that it was not just Korean Americans but South Koreans who were affronted points to transnational resistance against stereotypic representations.

Transnational Affirmations of White America's Ugly Side

Before Koreans had come to the United States, they were heavily influenced by messages sent through immigrants about the ways in which Koreans and other non-Whites were treated in "America." As I have introduced, transnational media reporting has also had a palpable influence. As early as 1955, *Chosun Ilbo* (August 23, 1955:2) ran a story about racial discrimination against Olympic diving star Sammy Lee, a second-generation Korean American, when Lee twice attempted to buy a new home in California. The article claimed that the story was "well known not only among us [South Koreans] but also in American society." Although the article acknowledged that Vice President Nixon had gotten involved to resolve the controversy, it also stated, "It is clear that American society is still unable to get rid of its bias toward different nationalities." Continuing to track Sammy Lee's treatment by White America in the early 1980s, a *Chosun Ilbo* article (July 26, 1981) stated, "Sammy Lee argued that although he had proven through diving competitions that 'colored people' could achieve as much as Whites could, he was denied from becoming a commentator for diving competitions because of his skin color." Speaking to the same theme, the newspaper had published five years earlier an editorial from a Korean immigrant who underscored White Americans' view of him and others as foreign competitors, "The time when Americans were 'going easy' on Koreans has passed. Now, Koreans are treated as another group of competitors in America" (*Chosun Ilbo*, July 9, 1976). By the late 1980s, more reports about antiforeigner bias emerged, such as a piece on a Korea University professor's disquiet over Americans' treatment of Koreans, "Many Americans view Koreans as immigrants who destroy the American way of life" (*Chosun Ilbo*, May 10, 1987).

Beyond Korean news coverage, the respondents' exchanges with Koreans already living in the United States often affirmed the prevalence of White American racism. Although Koreans tended to idealize White Americans in media texts, they could identify the group's sense of superiority as per the occupation in the transnational messages they received about Whites. Old-timer Mr. Bae recollected, "Well, I'd heard that there was lots of racial discrimination done by Americans." Others pinpointed stories about racialized language discrimination.

Ms. Ra: [*age 25, 6 months in United States*] Ah, I'd heard this; that they despise you if you can't speak English. They don't even talk to you and don't deal with you if you can't speak.

Ms. Li: [*age 42, 7 years in United States*] When I was a senior in high school, one of my friends had immigrated to America, so from her I heard about the things that happened at school when she tried to speak English. She couldn't speak English well, so she felt she was ignored and mistreated at school.

N: Oh, by whom?

Ms. Li: By White people, so I heard she had a really hard time at school.

To some extent, however, Koreans' ethnonationalist frame prompted them to *expect* Koreans to be "outsiders" given their ideology that the United States was "owned" by Whites and that immigrants who gained entry were outsiders. Yet the above narratives, as well as those that follow, reveal that Koreans found racial prejudice to be unconscionable.

Transnational exchanges and media coverage on the LA unrest also educated recent émigrés about White American structural discrimination against Korean and Black Americans. Although many newcomers also attributed the unrest to Black-Korean mutual antipathies, newcomer Ms. Noh had gotten wind in Seoul from Korean immigrants that the unrest had erupted as a result of White racism, "They said that there was racial discrimination here. That's why the LA riot broke out, and there is the idea here that White people are superior, things like that, so I've been told many of these kinds of stories." South Korean residents affirmed these criticisms of White Americans' discrimination against Korean Americans. A university student, Mr. Chun, compared such racism to that of the KKK and neo-Nazism in Germany but also likens it to South Koreans' anti-American biases.

I sympathized with them [Korean immigrants] because of that event. What's similar to the LA riot are the White groups like the KKK and Neo Nazis. I went to Germany when my brother studied in Germany. I felt different. I felt like the Whites were going to beat up a yellow guy like me. I felt like they were looking at me in a negative way just like when we look at Whites or Blacks here.

Others in Seoul picked up on the U.S. government's treatment of Korean ethnics as invisible and unimportant. Middle-aged newcomer Ms. Kang condemned White Americans' flagrant neglect of Korean Americans' burning stores and ethnic town. In her eyes, if Whites had not been racially discriminatory, they could have easily saved Koreans' only economic lifeline.

Actually, I don't like Americans when I think of the way they handled the whole thing. They had enough manpower, police forces to deal with this situation.

When something happens it doesn't take even a minute for them to respond, the helicopter's up in the air and the whole system runs smoothly, but why did Koreans have to suffer such a great loss during the riot? When I think of this, I don't think Americans helped as much as they could have . . . To me, that's racial discrimination.

Also citing Koreans' insignificance to Whites, a student named Mr. Kim maintained, "I used to look at the U.S. in a positive way but those things build up and now I don't always look at the U.S. positively . . . The American police force got there late. I was thinking how bad they are and also sympathizing with the poor Korean people there."

Partially Present at "Home," Invisible in the World

Korean immigrants' invisibility in the United States was familiar to South Koreans given its counterpart on the peninsula. That is, not only does U.S. dominance normalize their inferiority but also their partial presence in their own home. After a long history of being reduced to a Japanese colony, Koreans had to endure U.S. land infractions, soldiers' unpunished murders of Koreans, the Kwangju Massacre, sexual violence against women, and so on. All of these acts of power have sent the message that Koreans are not fully present in their own country. Although the U.S. state depicts South Korea as an ally, connoting equality, its actions have betrayed a view of South Korea as a subordinate pawn for American gain—as bodies and land to be exploited. For one, the Yongsan Base and USFK headquarters (recall minisuburbs, golf courses, hotels, etc.) occupied one of the choicest pieces of real estate in Seoul while Koreans had to compete for high-priced housing and live in overcrowded conditions (Moon 1997:31). Adding to the myriad problems the base brings, Katharine Moon (1997:31) was told by several student activists in 1992 that the complex infrastructure (e.g., webs of underground pipes) needed to support Yongsan Base has made subway construction there impossible and thus made life very difficult for many Seoul residents.[13] In addition, South Koreans have long been restricted access to the military bases as well as to the camptowns that surround them (unless they work there or have special authorization). Camptown bars/clubs post signs above their entries that read: "Korean Nationals Prohibited: This club is registered according to the Tourism Business Law Article 21. Only UN forces and other foreigners are permitted patronage. The establishment offers tax-free liquor; Korean nationals

are therefore denied entry.—Chairman, Korea Special Tourist Association"
(Moon 1997:31). For Americans to deny Koreans access to parts of their
own country certainly shores up feelings of not being fully present in one's
own "home."

Another manifestation of the U.S. state's sense of superiority was a lack of
concern for learning or educating military personnel about South Korea. This
lack of respect in part accounts for Korea's weak visibility across the globe. In
fact, Americans who had traveled to South Korea in the wake of the U.S. military's arrival readily admitted their long-term ignorance about it. Journalist
Richard Lauterbach (1947:14) confessed, "And like most Americans, I had the
scantiest kind of information about Korea and most of it turned out to be
shockingly inaccurate." Another American named E. Grant Meade (1951:51)
wrote, "I received nine months of instruction at two military schools . . .
During this entire period [I] heard a single one-hour lecture on Korea." Despite the U.S. occupation of Korea, the specter of invisibility would continue to
haunt the people. A decade since the first shots of the Korean War, there was
only one professional Korean historian at a reputable American university and
the literature on Korean history in Western languages was almost nil (Palais
1995). In addition, the LA unrest further enlightened Korean Americans about
their weak recognition and visibility in the United States. Koreans therefore
navigate the paradox of being dominated by the United States "at home" yet
being unknown to most of the American public and the world. In other words,
although South Koreans have been told that the United States is their "ally,"
they enjoy no halo effect from this "partnership" and suffer discrimination and
invisibility in White-over-Black America. The paradox only affirmed that the
United States, also within its own boundaries, positioned Koreans as subordinates more so than "equals." Part of the reason, of course, is the U.S. state's deliberate desire to keep Korea invisible so as to cover up the imperialist dimensions of its presence in South Korea and during the "Forgotten War." In 1946,
journalist Gayn (1981:433) wrote of Korea as "the blackest, the most depressing
story I have ever covered. As an American I was ashamed of the facts that I kept
digging up . . . of the concerted effort to prevent the American people from
learning what was happening in Korea." Although the American public
could remain ignorant, the last thing South Koreans could do was "forget" the
"Forgotten War."

Owing to Japan's first world status and China's historical legacy, South Koreans have long been fixated on their weak visibility compared to that of their

East Asian neighbors. Moreover, Japanese and Chinese Americans have a longer and more established history in the United States than do Korean Americans. Some returning students from the United States affirmed this view in a 1964 *Chosun Ilbo* (August 27, 1964) article: "Americans' interest in Korea is not that big. When they see an Asian, they think China or Japan." Of course, when Seoul became the host of the 1988 Olympics, South Koreans and Korean immigrants alike were enthralled with this hallmark of the peninsula's economic arrival. On the 1988 Olympics, a Korean in the United States wrote in a newspaper editorial: "Just a few months ago, Americans used to ask Korean Americans they met if they were Japanese, the question that badly hurt Korean Americans' self-esteem. But nowadays, Americans seem to ask all Asians if they are Korean. Korea is becoming very popular in the US right now" (*Chosun Ilbo*, July 29, 1988). However, once U.S. news networks began broadcasting stories about Koreans' practice of eating dog—underscoring Koreans' "foreignness" and inciting the ire of U.S. animal rights groups—the country receded again into the shadows of the advanced West, sinking Koreans' hopes for the recognition after which they sought. As an example, transmigrant Ms. Yi echoed the voices of many immigrants who lamented Korea's weak visibility: "There are also people who've never heard of Koreans . . . Koreans became known after the Olympics but people who come from small countries don't even know about Korea." Similarly, the Seoul residents spoke at length at about how "Americans only think of Japan when they think of Asia." Ms. Che, a graduate student, bemoaned: "I think they [Americans] would recognize Japanese people because Japan is a strong country. Even though it's true that Korea got more famous because of the Olympics, I still think they would be indifferent to Korea. They wouldn't even know where it is."

Generally speaking, in their hegemonic relationship to the U.S. state and its legitimating ideologies, Koreans who immigrated before the mid-1980s tended to fall on the "consent" side of the margin. Although Koreans today struggle still with internalized inferiority, the old-timers more uniformly believed that White Americans were better than them. They left predisposed toward glorifying "America" in light of ideologies of U.S. military benevolence and, conjoined with Hollywood, of Whites as richer, better looking, nicer, and happier. Those who departed after the 1980s, however, conveyed more dualism about White America, thereby partially challenging their inferiority that the military had also propagated. The duality that began brewing among Koreans in the mid-1970s (Lim 1978) has been fomented by ongoing military abuses and the unearthing of information on past, secret forms of it. For instance, those respondents who left sometime between late 1999 and early 2001 departed in the wake of publicity on U.S. operations during the Korean War. In 1999 three AP journalists broke the story that during the war U.S. troops executed orders from their leaders to kill large groups of unarmed South Korean refugees, many women and children among them, at Nogŭnri Bridge (Hanley, Mendoza, and Choe 2002). In an early 2001 joint statement, however, the U.S. and ROK states affirmed the Pentagon's finding that no such military orders to fire on civilians existed. Although the official line on Nogŭnri would read accidental killings, the story, filled with gruesome accounts of American GIs chasing after fleeing Koreans and shooting the babies on women's backs, garnered some publicity in South Korea, especially among the anti-American student movement, and beyond.[14] Not surprisingly, a recent Korea University survey of the populace on its views of the United States revealed that 44.8 percent of Koreans supported "a gradual withdrawal of U.S. troops from South Korea" while 27 percent favored "a continued U.S. presence." Yet, as 21 percent advocated that U.S. troops remain for a *limited*, not indefinite, period, the researchers concluded that Koreans harbor ongoing anti-U.S. sentiment (also evidenced by frequent vigils, protests, and conflicts with Americans [*Hankook Ilbo*, January 9, 2003]). At the same time, these sentiments coexist with a reverence for "White America's" military prowess, wealth, size, freedom, attractiveness, and more modern men, as the Seoul residents and newcomers made clear.

In more recent decades, Koreans' simultaneous sense of inferiority and committed resistance sharpen into relief this dualist tendency. Many recent émigrés in my study, for instance, had condemned the military presence and its soldiers. As I showed, the same women who valorized White American masculinity as ideal—attractive, heroic, gender egalitarian husbands—could also deride that same masculinity as low-class, uneducated, misogynist, criminal, power-hungry soldiers. Although Koreans are forced to face their partial presence in their own country, then, they also challenge ideologies of White American superiority on which it depends. They do so in part by seeing their own group as a peaceful people who have been victimized (recall white clothing as symbolic of peace, "the hermit kingdom"). During interviews, Koreans also recited the common trope of their people as full of "brotherly love" (notwithstanding internal criticisms). In fact, resistance often grows out of resentment over having once accepted one's inferiority or continually having to struggle with it. In this way, counterhegemonic resistance does not necessarily purge a sense of inferiority, nor does it guarantee that the oppressed will not reproduce forms of inequality while resisting others. Koreans demonstrate continued struggle with the contradictions, the paradoxes, and the pain.

4 Racialization in South Korea, Part II

Koreans and White-Black America

My birthmark gleamed, an ebony light, black as Africa. Sookie held up a white jar. "Pond-su cream," she said to my face in the mirror. "Made in the U.S.A."
—**Nora Okja Keller,** *Fox Girl*

IN THE LAST CHAPTER, I demonstrated how South Koreans' experience of the U.S. racial state and congruent cultural representations have yielded a sense of racial/national inferiority and invisibility. I also showed how South Koreans resist these perennial outcomes of oppression. With both White and Black Americans in the picture here (i.e., the imperialist racial formation in toto), I show how Korean respondents draw on ideologies mainly derived from Euro-American, Japanese, and internal hierarchies to conceive of themselves as in between White and Black America. At the same time, Koreans are well aware that they are in a position subordinate to Black Americans, agents of the U.S. occupational forces. Upon examining Koreans' social locations vis-à-vis the White-Black military state and cultural landscape, I draw on and reconceptualize racial triangulation (C. Kim 1999) by underscoring hierarchies related to South Korea: those of nation-state, political recognition, and ethnonationality. The previous and present chapters establish that Korean immigrants did not suddenly experience the racial triangle in the United States but had experienced a version of it in South Korea. Similarly, they do not learn domestic racial ideologies only after they experience the United States, but engage them long before arrival.

South Korean Ideologies and the Authoritarian Personality

It is striking the manner in which Korean and American racialized ideologies have concurred, although one can always be sobered by the correspondences across all forms of inequality and oppression. A prime example of such congruence is, on the one hand, ethnonational blood tropes and a Confucian ethos of groups' inequalities and, on the other, White Americans' enslavement ideologies of Blacks. In the South Korean reckoning, Blacks' status as slaves evinces their "inferior" ethnonational blood, hence, the group's "place" beneath Whites. White Americans' dehumanization of Africans as a justification for such placement only affirms such a view.

Korean rank ordering of blood ethnonationality has also corresponded well with Western powers' nineteenth-century Darwinism of a White West, Asian middle, and African bottom (see Russell 1991:6). Although (elite) Koreans likely learned of this ranking system from Japanese colonial scholars and officials who adopted the Darwinian idea, this perception of being in between has been most forceful and popular since South Korea's own economic development. The in-between racial allegory[1] began in Japan and, with some modifications, traveled to its former colony.

As Japan's economy grew rapidly and as previously stratified classes converged, a new ideal of a middle stratum, emblematized by the *sararīman* (salary man, or white-collar worker), came into being (Lie 2001:31). Central to this middle-class construction was the late 1980s advent of low-skilled workers from less-developed Asian nations, including Korea, and from Iran. Lie (2001:32) asserts that despite many of the foreign workers' middle-class backgrounds and some shared skin tones with the Japanese, Japan constructed itself as a "whiter" and "middle-class" nation above the "blacker" and "lower-class" countries. As an illustration of this whitened/blackened divide, the Japanese added a new term to their lexicon to distinguish "blackened" foreigners (*gaikokujin rodosha*) from the "normative" foreigners, White Westerners (*gaijin*; Lie 2001:19).

In the case of South Korea, the seeds of its own postwar development were planted by Japanese colonization (Lie 1998). As an "Asian Tiger," the peninsula began borrowing Japan's racialization of the global order in the late 1980s, similarly blackening the foreign workers who would in-migrate from China, Vietnam, and South Asia (e.g., India; Lie 1998). Koreans have considered these workers' desperation for Seoul's jobs of drudgery an expression of inferior national blood, sometimes betrayed by darker skin. By contrast, South Korea is "whiter" and more "middle class" than the third world nations from which the foreign workers hail in the "world system" (Wallerstein 1974). In an example of the connection between phenotypic markers (darker skin) and class/development status, elderly Mr. Park in Seoul (who himself had only finished high school) invoked both to explain why he excluded the Vietnamese from the "Asian" category of which Koreans were part: "People from Vietnam are darker skinned than Chinese, Japanese, and us Koreans. They look different. Their country is also poorer, that's why they come and work here." In fact, Tracy, a Black American woman in her twenties studying abroad in Seoul whom I informally interviewed, noted that sometimes South Koreans mistook her for Thai because of her medium-brown skin tone, somewhat "Asian-looking nose," and her "curly hair" (which she wore as a natural, i.e., un-permed, unrelaxed, and free of fake hair).

Despite their pride, South Koreans also constantly engaged the downside of their color-class-ethnonational order: their position not on top but in the (in-visible) *middle* of the racialized, gendered global economic order. Comment-ing on Koreans' "obsession" with racial/national rankings, a student named Ms. Che remarked: "Whenever Korea assesses countries, the economic level matters in many ways. In our case, Korea seems to always think about 'rich countries, poor countries.' When our economy developed during the 1970s and 1980s, we seemed to be obsessed with wanting to be richer than other coun-tries, like we should have such and such rank in the world, you know?"

As hinted by Ms. Che, Korea's subordination to the White West (and Japan) has incited the uglier sides of nationalism, not only prejudices (I. Kim 1981; H. Lee 1993) but a submission to the powerful and mistreatment of the weak—a type of authoritarian personality (see Elms and Milgram 1966). These patterns tend to be so strong, in fact, that widely renowned public intellectuals have ex-horted the Korean people to tone down the ethnic nationalism (*minjok-ism*) and to treat more humanely those they perceive to be of lower status (www.daum .com 2005). For better or worse, Koreans themselves are quite aware of their so-ciety's collective authoritarian personality, as one focus group exchange revealed.

Ms. HA: I work at a trade company and meet foreign buyers. It's likely that the [non-Korean] Asian people will feel that Koreans are rudely honest because Koreans are a little submissive to Western people . . . Unconsciously, Koreans are submissive to the people with white color skin or yellow color hair—my co-workers are a little afraid of them—but then they disregard the people from China or Southeast Asia.

Mr. BANG: Yeah, that's right.

Ms. HA: I think the people from China or Southeast Asia would feel more that Koreans are rude.

Similarly, college student Mr. Park responded thus to the question "Who, if anyone, does Korea seem to follow?": "I hate to say the U.S. but it represents the West, the Western model . . . ; we're supposed to favor their things and follow them but we believe we should abandon or avoid the things of countries we consider far behind, like Southeast Asia or Africa."

Koreans' reverence for "the strong" and distaste for "the weak" is often made known to both parties through what Americans would consider Koreans' hypercritical and brutally frank conversational norms, such as Ms. Ha mentions. Although I myself had grown accustomed to my relatives' acute honesty about mine or others' appearances, I was struck by the words of strangers or quasi-acquaintances the more I ventured outside my circles. Some told me, "Your shoulders are really wide" or "You look scary in that picture." My male friend got, "Wow, you've gotten so fat!," while an Arab American friend of mine related that Koreans unselfconsciously talked to her about her body shape, different than their own, much to her bewilderment. Koreans are also quite aware that they do not spare their own group harsh criticism on their less nationalistic days. Ms. Lim remarked: "I think there are more Korean people who say bad things about Korean people than about anyone else." In the same light, the above narratives suggest Koreans' critical eye on their own ethnic nationalism and authoritarian personality ("obsessed with wanting to be richer," can be "rude," "hate to say" that the USA is the model). Others complained about the overwhelming pressure to buy Korean products, especially when traveling abroad, and the absurdity of "armor[ing] ourselves with the exact same identity just because we're economically inferior," in Ms. Lim's words.

Without taking anything away from the unfortunate impact of these ideologies, I find it important to caution against American readers' interpretations of these statements, norms, and behaviors from within a strictly American standpoint. From this standpoint, Koreans (and Japanese) could draw accusations of being racists (or "racist just like Whites are"). Yet, it is imperative that such a capricious temptation be avoided. Not only do I employ the distinction between "racist" *institutions/ideologies* versus "prejudiced" individuals (Forman forthcoming), I heed the distinctive histories and cultural systems of South Korea / East Asia and the United States—for one, the former's subjugation by the latter. In addition, South Koreans do not have the American cultural compass formed by Black social movements and the desirable social norms that subsequently sprung forth. To illustrate the point, although there is no doubt that stereotypes of the Black thief further animate Korean immigrants' trailing of Blacks in their stores in Los Angeles, it is actually a South Korean norm for shopkeepers and clerks to follow their customers around. They do so to track what people buy, listen in on their conversations about the products, and, at times, to answer questions and make commercial pitches. In fact, it would be rather strange if I were to shop with my South Korean friends or relatives and look behind to see no sales associates trailing us (more accurately, them, as my usual orientation was to sit my tired self in a chair and observe my companions' more earnest shopping). Because Whites' practice of following Blacks in the United States originated in anti-Black racism, Koreans are understood to be replicating the same without question of what shopping norms exist in South Korea or Korean America. Moreover, few Koreans know before coming to the United States the prosaic forms of White racism (e.g., Blacks being followed in stores, pulled over by cops, avoided on sidewalks). Korean immigrants' prejudice in the United States may be a *part* of the story, but it is not the story itself. Furthermore, as South Koreans' treatment of the "weak" and critical norms show, they are not guided by stigmas against stereotyping and discrimination that have long conditioned Americans. In mainstream Korean society, such acts are rendered acceptable within Confucianist logic (and dangerously affirmed by Euro-American racism).

Although racial prejudice should not be accepted anywhere, it is common to all oppressed groups who live in racialized systems, owing in part to internalized racism, in other words the unconscious legitimation of one's own oppression by belief in one's inferiority (Baker 1983). The "oppressor within" is thus a key individual and collective ill that must be cured for structural change to be obtained (see Fanon 1963; Lorde 1984; Moraga 1981). That said, with Black American protest turning in the direction of Japan, with increased cultural interpenetration on issues of "race," and with Korean Americans' own experiences of racism, I show that among the younger generations especially, South Koreans' sensitivity to antiracist or socially desirable discourse is beginning to ripple. As part of a broader goal to realize antiracism everywhere, I chart here the sources of racial ideologies against Blacks in South Korea, starting with globalized commodity racism.

Euro-American and Japanese Ideologies of Blacks

The U.S. military and mass media institutions often dovetail in imperialist projects, such as in the form of commodity racism. Historically, imperial capitalists used the Euro-American military conquest of darker-skinned peoples (i.e., White racial superiority) to sell products. In addition to the 1899 Pears' Soap advertisement bearing Kipling's "The White Man's Burden," the globalizing popularity of blackface minstrelsy in twentieth-century United States and Europe likely trickled in small doses into Japan and South Korea, as evidenced by the German-designed *kuronbo* image on Japanese soda cans (Russell 1991). In addition, the U.S. military occupations of Japan and South Korea likely introduced foodstuffs—sometimes through the black market—bearing "mammies" like Aunt Jemima and smiling cooks like Cream of Wheat's Rastus.

The impact of imperial militaries is also evident in the kinds of cultural representations that are sparked among the occupied populace. The United States' post-1945 occupation of Japan, for instance, brought both Black soldiers and the White military's racism to the land of the rising sun (Russell 1991:23). The military subsequently gave rise to a lucrative Japanese market of blackface minstrel/"darky" goods to be exported, in boomerang fashion, to the United States where they were hot commodities. Racism, in this way, came full circle. South Koreans likely also encountered the popular "pickaninny" illustrations in Japanese books in the 1960s, themselves inspired by the American work *The Story of Little Black Sambo.*

Although Koreans had some exposure to the pre–World War II kernels of ideas about Blacks, Japan's postwar industry of commodity racism seemed to popularize the representations across the widest of audiences. After trade relations were normalized with Japan in 1965, the Republic of Korea (ROK) began importing some of its neighbors' blackface/"darky" products. In the 1990s, for instance, the Sanrio Company's pickaninny doll was imported, at least until she was pulled from the shelves after Black Americans protested against the Hello Kitty juggernaut (Russell 1991). In response to protests and to a concern for its global image, Japan has since discontinued or modified its products, yet the "modifications" could potentially be coded versions of erstwhile commodity racism. While walking around Seoul, for instance, I was disturbed to see images on imported Japanese stationery and trinkets of what I thought were naked brown-skinned primitives with body odor (depicted by smell trails emanating from their bodies). When I brought up my frustration to my native South Korean friend, hoping she would agree with me, she replied, perplexed, "But, ŏnni,[2] these are loaves of bread." When I looked again, I realized that the figures were bread loaves and that "the smell trail" was to illustrate the heat rising from the bread. No sooner had I sighed relief and chuckled at myself that I looked again and realized that the image could possibly be new wine in old bottles, that is, a disguised way of portraying so-called primitives. With these bread people, perhaps it was just harder to tell. Even on the U.S. side of the ocean, blackface/"darky" imagery and products have survived despite fierce taboos. For instance, Grace Jones's "Slave to the Rhythm" video aired regularly on MTV in the 1980s and blackface images and actors appear prominently in Britain, the Netherlands, Spain, and so on.

Despite these modern-day manifestations, the Japanese at least have been made aware that their products are offensive. By 1990–1991 anthropologist John Russell (1991) could not gain approval from Japanese companies to reprint their blackface-inspired logos for his scholarly article; and Japanese groups against anti-Black racism have begun to sprout. Many everyday people, however, have been puzzled as to *why* exactly the images are arresting and problematic, another reminder of the dangers of imposing American cultural constructs onto Japan. Although the lack of a long and meaningful history with Blacks and antiracist movements is central, Japan's reliance on "*monomane* (comical mimicry), caricature, and stylized portraiture" is also at the heart of the confusion (Russell 1991:17). Indeed, Russell (1991:17) contends that the caricatures of Japanese celebrities common in the country would likely be deemed racist had they been drawn by someone non-Japanese; in view of such widespread caricature, he writes, "the pervasiveness of markers of pseudo-negritude has made it virtually impossible for some Japanese even to conceive of representing blacks nonstereotypically." Some of the informants in his study remarked that they would be unable to distinguish Blacks from other dark-skinned people without these markers. Korean society's wide exposure to Japanese *monomane* coupled with its own norms of frankness about (physical) appearance help explain why many of the South Korean informants themselves did not grasp the problem with Black caricatures. A memorable example from my own fieldwork throws into relief the distinct racial terrains of the two countries. During one of my observations at Young People's Church, a new prospective member had joined our small group, "Team #53," for one of our sessions. He stood out immediately, especially in comparison to the other males in the group. He was the darkest skinned and clad in urban hip-hop fashion (baggy clothes, sunglasses). I noticed that he had a keychain from which hung a small doll, a Black male in urban hip-hop fashion (baggy T-shirt, jeans, gold chain) and whose lips were disproportionately big. Not thinking clearly from sleep deprivation and thus forgetting my fieldwork hat, I asked this stranger accusingly why he had such a keychain. Startled and slightly perturbed, he asked me earnestly, "Why, you don't think he's cute?" Not satisfied with what I reckoned an unenlightened answer, I flatly said, "No" and walked away to a nearby bench. As I heard him quietly ask his friend, "Is she from around here?," I realized that my indignation at something Koreans considered benign had betrayed my nonnative status. It also jolted me into consciousness of the researcher error that I had just committed, of imposing my American lens onto a South Korean who had not been racially socialized the way I had been. In fact, he seemed to fashion himself in opposite terms: unlike ethnocentric Koreans, he liked and identified with Black people and engaged in "their culture." When he looked at his keychain he saw a "cute" Black male; when I looked at it I saw a racist caricature. To this day, I regret that I did not explain my irritation. At the same time, my reaction, no matter how undeveloped, could give him pause about the supposed benign nature of a Black male hip-hop doll with big lips.

Japan's cultural economic impact has served to corroborate the racial ideologies and institutions of the U.S. military. Although middle-class South Koreans had learned bits and pieces about Black Americans—for instance, even Harriet Beecher Stowe's 1852 novel *Uncle Tom's Cabin* enjoyed some rather posthumous popularity (H. Kang 1991)—it was not until the U.S. military occupied their country and American mass media followed on its heels that residents came to think beyond "America" as just White. Slowly, they began to receive "America" as a White-over-Black nation. Although I argue later that the U.S. mass media seared Blacks and anti-Black stereotypes more widely across the country than did the military presence, it is noteworthy that Kang's (1991) survey of 1,835 popular stories revealed Blacks' absence in Korean literature until 1961, after the military had proliferated across the peninsula.

South Korea and Black America

As noted, Koreans were primed for the White-over-Black order by an internal and Japanese valorization of the color white, distaste for the color black, and an agrarian order premised on such gradations of skin color. The other interrelated cultural lenses through which Koreans have peered include Confucianist notions of natural and obligatory inequalities between groups, biological constructions of nations since the Enlightenment Movement, previous encounters with elite Whites, a scattered introduction of Euro-American racial ideologies under Japanese rule, and a lack of *antiracist* movements in the country's history and antiracist ideologies (notwithstanding those for racialized national oppression).

Although the narratives below flow from these logics, the situational reality of Koreans' little contact with Blacks in the flesh before the U.S. military proliferation need also be considered. In this case, the fear of the unfamiliar in a predominantly Korean/Asian society should not be surprising, as Koreans were unnerved not only by Blacks' appearance but by White missionaries' alien looks. In her autobiography Mary Paik Lee (1990:12) describes how Korean children had thrown rocks at the first missionaries when they arrived, deriding them as "white devils" because of their "blue eyes and yellow or red hair." Moreover, even in a multiracial American context saturated with liberal antiracist discourse, Whites, Latinos, and Blacks alike have deemed Asian ethnics to be strange, foreign, and conniving (Committee of 100 Survey 2001; National Conference of Christians and Jews 1994; T. Lee 2000; National Conference for Community and Justice 2000, 2005).[3] Despite initial distaste among Koreans, the much earlier advent of Whites within a White-led world led to the normalization of European looks by the time Blacks arrived a century later. In addition, Koreans' negative signification of dark colors and tanned peasants meant Blacks' appearances were fear inducing. Old-timer immigrant Mr. Che affirmed, "When I first saw Black people was when they came to Korea as military personnel. Because their looks were dark, their appearance looked bad to me."

U.S. mass media representations have also fostered respondents' familiarity with, preference for, and surgical emulation of Whites' physical aesthetic. In South Korea today, predominantly White Western models grace the pages of the globally circulating *Elle* and *Vogue*, Asian/Korean versions of these, and indigenous publications (Kassarjian 1969; Y. L. Lee 1994; see Neelankavil, Mummalaneni, and Sessions 1995). As well, Whiteness is the reference point in Western television media (Hall 2003). Against this backdrop, new immigrant Ms. Min (age 26, 2 years in United States) explained why she thought White Euro-Americans were the best looking (à la Barbie) and how that standard depended on a Black antithesis.

M: I think Whites are prettier [than us] for some reason. I think it's because of the way I was manipulated in Korea.

N: You mean how you were taught that way or . . . ?

M: It's not because I was taught that way, but usually the Blacks [characters] are unattractive and somewhat overly talkative, Plus, most of the Barbie dolls are White and all the cartoon characters were White at that time. I was raised while seeing these things and hence I got more attracted to what I'd seen before.

In her statement, Ms. Min contradicts herself when she says that she was not taught a racial beauty standard yet sees dominant representations as culpable for her buying into one. Her un-self-conscious talk about Blacks is yet another example of weak Korean norms of social desirability and penchant for frankness about looks. The idealization of Whites' appearance relative to that of Blacks was also apparent in less explicit statements, as in that of newcomer Mr. Min (age 26, 1 year in United States):

> I lived in Pyong-taek. There was an American military base near my school. There were a lot of people living in Song-tan: Whites, Blacks . . . I saw little kids there. They were really pretty. White children would be standing by the road waiting for the school bus. Oh, they were so adorable! I'd seen them in movies, but . . . I saw them in the flesh for the first time in high school.

Although he speaks about how "cute" and "adorable" the White children of army families were, he makes no mention of similarly "adorable" Black children, though he grew up seeing both.

Aside from situational considerations, such as little contact with Blacks preoccupation, Koreans have adopted prejudices in an instrumentalist vein as well. Like Japan (Russell 1991), their need to position themselves above Blacks is a response to their own insecurities about their liminal position within a White-Black globe and their fear of "regressing" back into the blackened third world. Yet, although Japan has had to concern itself with the dominant White West (e.g., U.S. military; Russell 1991), South Koreans have had to contend with oppression by Japan in addition. Indeed, Korean society's very language of a "pure" bloodline and consanguinity as well as discrimination against the multiracial children serve as a symbolic point of resistance against outside powers' intrusions, cultural stripping, and pollution of Koreans' once pure blood; the more they can get rid of the evidence, the more they feel sovereign, complete, *Korean*. As a formerly colonized and presently occupied people, then, they displace their internalized inferiority in ways that foster prejudice and discrimination. This misguided search for worth revisits Koreans' earlier narratives about "lower" Southeast Asians and Koreans' collective authoritarian personality. The response, a tragically familiar one, is deftly captured by Laura Mulvey (1987:11) when she says, "It cannot be easy to move from oppression and its mythologies to resistance in history; a detour through a no-man's land or threshold area of counter-myth and symbolisation is necessary." Within a context of *multiple* hierarchies, however, South Koreans (and the margins in general) follow a more complex "detour" wherein they *reify* oppressive mythologies (e.g., prejudices) as part of their resistance to U.S. dominance and Blacks' role in it. To unravel this process, some background on the U.S. occupation is apt here.

Abelmann and Lie (1995:57) write that the "GIs carried the United States to South Korea." Carrying the United States also meant bringing in its baggage of White superior–Black inferior racial ideologies. During the Jim Crow era, the small number of Koreans who worked as staff on the bases or the larger contingent in the seedier camptowns observed the separate and unequal facilities of White and Black members of the military. Since the formal desegregation of the military, the soldiers and camptowns—namely, the restaurants, bars, and brothels within—have remained, in many areas, informally segregated. Black Americans also proliferate along the "front line" of the demilitarized zone and are denied the White GIs' less dangerous assignments in Seoul (Sturdevant and Stoltzfus 1993).

Over the years, South Koreans' encounters with Black troops have been troubled, in part a product of resentment over the injustices they suffer and incur at the hands of the U.S. presence. The woes with Blacks are also owed in part to Korean mimicry of White American racial bias. On the other side of the line, Blacks have either resisted local prejudices or have adopted stereotypes and abused their power over Koreans, potentially signaling the group's own "detour" from White oppression. Needless to say, all parties have exacerbated the tensions and prejudices necessarily spawned by the occupation. Even prior to the end of World War II, colonial Japan had deployed propaganda about Americans' penchant for violence, murder, hypocrisy, and rape (Dower 1986:24), behaviors that White soldiers in Japan would later racialize as Black (Russell 1991:20). In 1970s South Korea, White soldiers admitted that they heard Koreans repeat soldiers' anti-Black epithets without full comprehension of their meaning or the level of animus (Moon 1997:72). In 1971, even the U.S. Army itself reported its culpability in *kijich'on* (military camptown) racial tensions:

> [It is] undoubtedly true in many instances [that] club owners and the hostesses [prostitutes] are discriminatory towards one group or the other [Whites or Blacks] . . . However, it must be recognized that *we* have created this condition through patronage habits and individual or group behavior . . . In many instances, vociferous groups have forced Korean clubs to cater to only a certain group and exclude all others . . . Korean business establishments willingly try to

correct those undesirable practices over which they have control but are in a dilemma when they try to correct a situation which is created and controlled by the patrons. (Eighth U.S. Army "Civil-Military Affairs Newsletter 7–71" 1971:1)

In other words, many of the local Koreans claimed that their discriminatory actions were in fact defensive, necessitated by the White-Black divide imposed by *U.S. military personnel*. As stated in the newsletter, Korean owners of bars/clubs feared that working with Black patrons would alienate the more numerous and allegedly better-paying White customers (Moon 1997:71). Furthermore, sex workers were well aware that they could incur punishment from their White or Black patrons for crossing the racial divide. The divide explains why most of the military base villages were and are racially segregated, with more numerous and better-resourced White establishments and typically fewer and lower-quality Black establishments (Moon 1997:71). In addition, shortly after the first big wave of Korean immigration to the United States in 1970, Black nationalism intensified among soldiers, fueling even more conflict. During this period, the tensions reached a feverishly racialized pitch, as fights between Black and White soldiers and between Blacks and Korean residents were common. According to one incident published by Serious Incident Reports (SIRs) of the Eighth U.S. Army (EUSA) and official U.S.-ROK joint investigations, the violence began when fifty Black soldiers simultaneously entered five camptown clubs, ordered people to leave, and demolished the establishments as an act of protest against Korean clubs' bias (which Korean clubs said they were pressured to follow; Moon 1997:74). The Black soldiers were met by a mob of over 1,000 Koreans who chased them with sickles, threw rocks in retaliation, and physically attacked them (Moon 1997:74). It took U.S. military and South Korean police as well as a decree forbidding U.S. personnel in the camptown to quell the violence. Thousands of Korean nationals protested near the gates against Black violence and the decree (Moon 1997:74). In so doing, they were not simply or solely being prejudiced, but were protesting Blacks' state power over the local population. Of course, racial tensions during this time were not just limited to South Korea. The U.S. Congressional Record noted that "provost marshals in Germany, Korea, Vietnam, and other major military areas reported a 'sharp' to 'alarming' increase in incidents of racial unrest" in the early 1970s (Moon 1997:73). Where South Korea has been unique is in the frequency of conflict between the bases and the surrounding camptowns (Moon 1997:73).

In a context in which dark skin and Blacks were already seen in a less favorable light, such incidents spurred the idea that Black soldiers, more so than Whites, cause trouble. Moreover, although Koreans had become familiar with Whites in multiple favorable roles and statuses much before the first Blacks arrived—benevolent missionaries, U.S. diplomats and presidents, General MacArthur, Audrey Hepburn—their exposure to Blacks was largely limited to soldiers and unsavory mass media stereotypes. Because Koreans generally perceive all American military personnel to be low class, uneducated, and unrefined—part of anti-U.S. resistance—there is little to disrupt the Black image. New immigrant Ms. Yoon (age 48), for instance, had this to say about her prearrival conceptions of Black Americans.

Y: The things I've heard was, like the Blacks in the American military in Korea . . . all I heard about them were negative things.

N: What did you hear?

Y: Like for example, I heard things like this one Black man hit this Korean man . . . Though there are good things about them, too, I've heard that they are physically abusive. Actually, I read that in a newspaper article. If you go to *It'aewŏn* [Seoul camptown] there are many Blacks out there, but I think that since they're career military personnel they don't really care about how they act.

She does not malign Whites for the many similar military abuses they have perpetrated. This could reflect Koreans' weaker tolerance for discrimination from Blacks than from Whites (*Chosun Ilbo*, May 20, 2003), reminiscent of the tendency to "submit to the strong." Furthermore, although she had never interacted with Blacks in the home country, as a professor's daughter she had had fleeting encounters with White American professors. Given these kinds of contacts with high-status Whites, it is not surprising that she had thought all Whites were "high-classed people" prior to leaving Seoul.

Mr. Ha (age 27, 8 months in United States), a recent seminary student, was another respondent who characterized Blacks, not Whites, as the problematic soldiers. Yet he was more critical of the sources of such characterization.

H: I'm sorry to say this, but Korean society has a norm that the Africans [African Americans] are, have, inferior to (seems uncomfortable) . . .

N: Inferior to whom?

H: Us. Yeah.

N: Why do you think they think that?

H: Maybe that's from America. They learned America's racist kind of thinking. That kind of idea just flows through their movies, their cultures. Basically those African Americans coming to Korea do not have high standards
of living or education or social status . . . Maybe on the White side [it] is
usually a businessman, more highly-educated, so that's more sociable.
And I (pause) admit that, I've also been brought up in that norm . . . I'm
sharing their norms although I'm trying not to; but it's just built [up in]
myself.

He reveals that even Koreans like him who try to disabuse themselves of stereotypes have trouble decoupling "Black man" and "low-class soldier." In the process, he elides the fact that most White men in South Korea are also soldiers
from working-class backgrounds. In his reckoning, Mr. Ha also invokes the
Confucianist ethos of South Korean class hierarchies when he reasons that
White men are higher class, hence they should be respected; Black men are
the lower class to be disrespected. He shows that even a strong economy and
technological sophistication do not eclipse a society's problematic racial
ideologies—the United States is a case in point.

Challenging Anti-Black Ideologies

It is important to note that Koreans did not always follow the route of "submission to the strong, mistreatment of the weak" or of racializing Black Americans as "low-class" soldiers and violent occupiers. Although there is a need for
more historical documentation of Blacks' relations with Koreans (and others)
in Asia during World War II and the Korean War, there is some sparse evidence
of Koreans (and Japanese) having treated Black American soldiers well. In
George Lipsitz's (1995:63) analysis of Ivory Perry, a prominent Black American
activist from St. Louis, he finds that Perry attributed the birth of his activism
to his service at Camp Gifu, Japan, and during the Korean War. Lipsitz (1995:63)
writes,

For Perry, meeting Japanese and Korean citizens who seemed to him refresh-
ingly nonracist compared to the white Americans he had known helped him see
that white supremacy was a primarily historical national phenomenon and not
human nature . . . As he remembers thinking on his return to the United States
from the war, "I shouldn't have been in Korea in the first place because those
Korean people they haven't ever did anything to Ivory Perry. I'm over there try-

ing to kill them for something that I don't know what I'm shooting for. I said my fight is here in America."

When Perry met the Koreans abroad, perhaps they were not just grateful to him for helping their country but, as those who had just been liberated from Japan, may have identified with a fellow underdog. Some of my respondents roughly half a century later noted their identification with Blacks as fellow non-Whites. In this way, they were not bent on maintaining a position over Blacks to compensate for their internalized inferiority vis-à-vis others. In brief, they were less conformist and chose to censure White racial dominance. Sixty-six-year-old Mr. Roh, a recent émigré, clearly aligned with Blacks while in South Korea. As a government inspector in the 1950s he had witnessed the Jim Crow segregation of the U.S. military and interpreted it through his own indignation over the occupation.

> When I was in Korea, I felt that Whites were really cold to Koreans. I also felt that way because, after the Korean War, I went to a U.S. army base . . . Well, when a White person and a Black person got in a car, the Black person *always* drove the car and the White person never drove. And they used separate restrooms: there was a restroom for Whites and a restroom for Blacks at the base. So, ever since the Korean War, I realized that White Americans tended to discriminate against races a lot and that they were cold-hearted.

Although he could have focused on Jim Crow segregation as coterminous with Blacks' "naturally" subordinate positioning, Mr. Roh rather went on to describe how Blacks and South Koreans felt more similar to each other than either did to White Americans.

> R: There were these soccer games between the soldiers and the people near the base. The U.S. army did this to try to have a better relationship with the Korean people who lived near the base. When I saw this, I noticed that Whites made their own separate team of only Whites. But the Blacks cheered for the Korean people and didn't cheer for Whites.
>
> N: Why was that?
>
> R: Because we are the weak nation . . . because they knew that they suffered like us, they identified with Koreans and cheered for us, not for Whites.
>
> N: I see. Then, did you speak with Blacks and with Whites?
>
> R: Yes, I did. I did . . . I went to the U.S. embassy to get an American visa . . . There were Black consulates and White consulates. It was the White

consulates, White *female* consulates, who *never* issued any visas to Korean people . . . Black consulates easily gave out visas, but White consulates would scrutinize everything . . . to see if you would benefit their country . . . What also shows their coldness is that most of the consulates in the U.S. embassy in Korea know how to speak Korean . . . but they *never* asked things in Korean. They would either ask in English or use a translator.

N: Do the Blacks speak in Korean?

R: Blacks ask directly in Korean.

Amidst the respondents Mr. Roh was atypical in that he had witnessed more than fleeting interactions between U.S. soldiers and South Koreans. Drawing on his experience, he did not conjure up the happy, nice, carefree White person from America. Rather, he condemned Whites as cold racists, also showing ire for his emasculation at the hands of White American *female* consulates. By extension, he believed that White Americans treated Blacks and Koreans similarly, as Blacks' support for the local Korean soccer team over the fellow American White team attests. He adds that Koreans and Blacks "fully accept each other here [in the United States], too," seeming to forget or dismiss the ways in which both have been conditioned to derogate the other. Regardless of his unique vantage, it is clear that he likens U.S. subjugation of South Korea to White America's racism toward Blacks.

As U.S. mass media texts have highlighted Whites' racist treatment of Blacks under slavery, some Koreans were also dismayed or horrified by movies like *Roots*. Echoing some of the sentiments of Mr. Roh, ten-year immigrant Mr. Oh (age 34) claimed that he had been ignorant of the subjugation of Black Americans until he had watched *Roots* in Seoul:

O: Do you know the movie *Root[s]*?

N: Mhm!

O: I'd never really thought about Black people before I watched that. After I watched that movie, I realized how prejudiced White people were against the Black race . . . I felt it after watching that movie.

Recent immigrant Mr. Kang (age 46) added:

I saw a movie called *Roots* a long time ago and I found out that Blacks were captured from their country and brought to England and started their lives as slaves. Through TV and things like that, I heard that America doesn't really give Blacks a whole lot of opportunity to succeed, but they seem to be doing very well in sports. They're also being discriminated against here . . . and [I] felt sorry for them when I was in Korea.

Although Mr. Oh and Ms. Kang were not as explicit as Mr. Roh above, they alluded to a greater identification with Blacks than with Whites in the realm of racist treatment. In similar fashion, the college student and young professional informants in Seoul, a group who tended to be the most critical of the United States and of White racism, were acutely critical of the oppression of Blacks. Several of them cited Spike Lee's critically acclaimed film *Malcolm X* as disturbingly eye opening. In this way, the younger generations seemed to be grappling, in earnest, with their indoctrination by White racism (especially against Blacks). For instance, although Edward Chang's 1999 survey of South Korean university students revealed that Blacks, particularly African Blacks, were on the bottom of the marital preference hierarchy, my data point to a complex negotiation of prejudices and a nascent awareness of antiracist and social desirability discourses. These baby steps are likely the product of Blacks' recent protests against Japanese blackface/"darky" products; the intensifying cultural interpenetration between the two countries, of which one manifestation is youths' adoration for R&B and hip-hop (though love of culture need not quash prejudice); increased outmarriage with non-Whites; protests against discrimination waged by multiracial children of military couplings; and (politicized) anger over the 1992 LA unrest.[4]

In the focus group interviews with the young students and working professionals, many aspired to rid themselves of the prejudices that they knew themselves to harbor. During one focus group one of the women was visibly disturbed by another female participant's un-self-conscious prejudice toward Blacks. After grimacing and shifting in her seat, she finally looked at her and said, "You know, I think what you're saying is really prejudiced." Even along the lines of intermarriage, South Korean residents sought to disabuse themselves of long-held prejudices. Ms. Lim articulated the principle of "color-blind love":

L: I would like to marry a Korean but if my partner turns out to be a foreigner, then I think that'd be okay.

I: Okay, so a foreigner would be okay; do you care about race, like skin color? . . . how about Black people?

L: If we loved each other I don't think I'll look at skin color; like, it's true that you don't feel connected to Black people but if you love each other it means that you overcame those things.

As an example of the complexity of undoing prejudices, Ms. Lim takes for granted the fact that Koreans "don't feel connected to Black people," a notion partly informed by Korean society's strong exhortations for endogamy (i.e., consanguinity) in the name of the pure blood nation. Yet she challenged such social pressures by being open to the idea of a Black spouse. In another instance, a U.S. immigrant of less than a year, Ms. Um, had interacted (though mostly superficially) with White and Black men at her father's store near Seoul's U.S. military base. She remarked, "Because when my dad had the store, I thought wow, White men looked pretty good, and even the Black men did too (chuckles)!" When she says that "even the Black men" looked good, she shows that she has disabused herself of her society's devaluation of dark skin. In another example, Mr. Park invoked a "universal love" trope to convey his openness to a Black wife.

> P: For marriage, I don't have a set rule that my wife has to be a certain ethnic-
> ity. I don't want to restrict myself, so I don't prefer certain people over oth-
> ers. If I really liked the person, I don't see any problem.
> I: How about a Black person?
> P: Yes, same.

As a cursory way to compare Koreans' words and their practice, I had the good fortune of interviewing Tracy, the Black American exchange student. Although she spent most of her days at the college and consorted mostly with the Kore-ans within, she also encountered everyday service people, like store clerks, and walked the streets of Seoul. She reported, "Koreans are generally nice to me." Of course, she was taken aback by how biologically minded they were, such as when they would say, "All Koreans naturally love kimchi" and "All Koreans are born good singers." In this vein, she remarked, "Koreans do seem to exoticize me, like fetishize me. Like they expect me to be able to sing and dance, that kind of thing; that can get a little interesting (pause). But, at the same time, I think it's much better to be exoticized than, you know, to be racially profiled and shot by cops. When I think of it that way, I don't think it's as bad."

Despite Tracy's belief that Korean stereotyping was relatively minor, her ex-perience of it and my respondents' admissions of struggle point to the diffi-culty of purging prejudices when there are few Black citizens with whom to en-gage. This conundrum was inflected in a discussion of racism that played out at Young People's Church on one Sunday. One of my male team members, an outgoing and fun-loving chap whom I liked, asked me if there was racial discrimination in the United States. Excited by the opportunity to broach the discussion, I replied, "Well, I'm interested in hearing what you would have to say—what do *you* think?" to which he replied, "Yes." I agreed with him. Then he quickly remarked, "You know what? No one at this church is prejudiced, because we're Christians." Because my sociological hat had inured me to the fact that no one escapes the pull of prejudice, at least not without painstaking detoxification, I replied, "That's impressive, but what about intermarriage? Do you think that most people in this church would marry a Black person?"[5] He paused for a second, and in a more quiet voice, said, "No, probably not." Feeling guilty that I had burst his bubble, and to lighten the mood, I said, "I know, it's really tough for any group, not just Koreans or Christians, to get beyond this stuff, you know?" Still in a contemplative mode, he nodded.

Although these attempts at racial rehabilitation suggest the rhizomatic nature of racism, that which entangles Koreans and all peoples, these examples evidence growing condemnation of racism and an awareness of socially desirable responses. These narratives also demonstrate that, unlike many Koreans, these individuals in South Korea did not succumb to inferiority complexes and were not as concerned about having status above others.

American Racism and Mass Media Texts

Koreans who emigrated during the 1970s and early 1980s were not exposed to the same level of antiracist discourse as those who left during the 1990s and into the new millennium. Recent émigrés, in contrast, have been exposed to increasing antiracist discourse and also to the rise in mass media texts that deplore White racism against Blacks. In their assertion that "Korean American racism . . . rides on the coattails of American cultural dominance," Abelmann and Lie (1995:150) pinpoint U.S. mass culture as a central force propagating anti-Black *prejudice* in the home country. In fact, U.S. mass media representations have likely stitched the Black slave, gang banger, drug addict, and one-dimensional entertainer into the South Korean collective consciousness more than any other source. Accordingly, the respondents most frequently invoked cultural representations and, less so, their experiences or factual information when reciting their interpretation of Blacks' racial characteristics. As Joe Feagin (2000:135) argues, the mutually negative attitudes among Asian, Latino, and African American individuals are shaped by U.S. media and "the much larger system of White-managed racism, which these groups had no role in initiating."

Although the immigrant cohorts in this study were exposed to racially ste-reotypical images produced by "White-managed racism," differences existed in the type and amount of images they consumed. Koreans who had emigrated sometime during the 1970s to early 1980s (the "early cohort") tended to restrict their images of Blacks to those of former slaves, servants, and a generally poverty-stricken people. The later cohorts most often invoked the ubiquitous images of Blacks (especially men) as drug addicts and criminals popularized since the 1980s.

Although it was difficult for the early cohorts to remember exactly where they had picked up on Black poverty before emigrating, many of them recalled images of Blacks as slaves or as tribal Africans. This visual mainstay is not sur-prising in light of the 1960s advent of U.S. mass media stereotypes (e.g., *Gone with the Wind* was widely popular) as well as Japan's profound consumerist in-fluence since the late 1960s. When I asked members of the early cohort to rec-ollect what images they had had of Blacks prior to immigration, most sounded like Ms. Go: "Weren't, uh, they like slave people, yeah? I had that kind of feel-ing." Other old-timers like Ms. Pak recounted, "We saw African tribes in the films we watched in school." And Mr. Sohn recalled, "They asserted them-selves; but overall, Blacks were poorer than Caucasians."

As the ROK has long relied on Western news agencies for over 60 percent of its own news content (H. Kang 1991:116–17)—for example, AP, Reuters, AFP, and the BBC—all the cohorts have been exposed to Western-centered news. Unlike their forebears, however, recently arrived immigrants have had expo-sure to more American and other global media, namely through cable. CNN, for instance, has been a staple in middle-class South Korean households in re-cent years. Owing to this increased exposure, immigrants who have come since the late 1980s have been infused with news images of "ghetto Blacks" and crack, the once White "glamour drug" (Reeves and Campbell 1997:63). Jimmie Reeves and Richard Campbell (1997:63) note that raiding footage of crack houses in the mid-to-late 1980s was "incorporated into the 'image bank' available for re-cycling in any network news story about cocaine, [and] . . . became something of a visual cliché." The issue of Black Americans and crack appeared in about one of every four stories in the sample of news videos they studied (1997:63). A more recent study by Travis Dixon and Daniel Linz (2000) found that U.S. eve-ning news broadcasts have *overrepresented* Blacks as criminals and *underrepre-sented* Whites, despite FBI crime statistics to the contrary. It is thus not sur-prising that twenty-six-year-old Mr. Min noticed the frequent depictions of

Black masculinity as low-class, criminal, and depraved (1 year in United States): "Well, Blacks . . . in the movies I'd seen in Korea, they were often portrayed in a negative light. Whites play the good parts; Blacks play drug dealers or gang members." Middle-aged Ms. Paik, also a one-year immigrant, agreed: "They use illegal drugs too much . . . Like in the movies, they show them always doing that kind of thing." Recently arrived Ms. Joo, a longtime Hollywood buff, agreed, despite her awareness of more positive representations of Blacks in recent years, "Well, I don't know about other sources outside of movies [but] they don't really portray Blacks as good people. They always seem to portray Whites as more superior than the Blacks . . . It's gotten a bit better recently, but some time ago, Blacks were always portrayed as a part of a gang, in my opinion. But I don't know what it's really like in real life."

All of the narratives reveal, by implication, that Koreans are not gang members or drug dealers and addicts. Across the cohorts, then, most informants racialized poverty as a Black phenomenon. Such a perception suggests Koreans' sense of themselves as in between. Moreover, Koreans who have generally immigrated to the United States share a proclivity for the American dream mythology, in large part because of its ideological congruence with the Confucian ethos of high education and hard work (I. Kim 1981). Both cultural tropes would point out that only those who do not work hard must be poor—especially, of all places, in "America."

The 1992 LA Unrest as a Watershed

One of the key reasons that recent immigrant cohorts had concentrated on Black criminality more so than on poor, enslaved Blacks is the 1992 LA unrest. The unrest was a watershed moment for the post-1992 cohorts and for South Koreans who watched riveted in shock. On the media coverage of the unrest, Herman Gray (1995:172) writes of it as fixated on "the spectacle of public lawlessness and 'colored' (read in the media coverage as Black) rage" rife with "neoconservative discourses of immorality and irresponsibility." In short, mainstream media coverage largely served as grist for the anti-Black mill. As an example, newspaper reports of Blacks' rage at Koreans for making large profits in Black communities without living in or giving back to the community (*Chosun Ilbo*, May 5, 1992) do not bode well in a Confucianist society that naturalizes social class hierarchies and heralds diligent hard work as the cornerstone of everyone's lives. South Korean media reports about Koreans' extreme suffering in the post-uprising era could also, unwittingly, reinforce prejudices

(*Chosun Ilbo*, May 2, 1992). Consider the following report on post-1992 Los Angeles:

> Many Korean Americans who lost their American dream are committing suicide. Perhaps more disturbing than the suicides are the attacks on Korean Americans by Black gang members. For example, Hyung-Soo Kim who had finally rebuilt his store after losing everything during the L.A. riot last year was beaten to death by Black gang members on February 4th. And in the past three months, three Korean Americans have been killed by Black gang members . . . within a two-day span . . . The *Los Angeles Times* newspaper asserted that these crimes stem from other minorities' anger at Koreans' success in impoverished neighborhoods, which . . . Blacks, Italians, Jews, and Hispanics have failed to achieve. (*Chosun Ilbo*, February 19, 1993:23)

The focus on Blacks here, quintessentialized by many South Korean media outlets' racialization of the 1992 unrest as the "Black riots" (*hŭgin pokdong*), also shifts the floodlight onto Blacks as responsible for the mayhem. The moniker of "Black riots" is also striking insofar as it reveals South Koreans' White-Black construction of the United States. The largest number of arrested protestors and looters in Los Angeles, however, were Latino (E. Park 2002).

Although I will show how some of the informants indicted White racism and Koreans' prejudices as responsible for the unrest, many new immigrants and South Koreans named the "riots" as crystallizing their anger toward and fear of Blacks. As Black Americans setting fires, vandalizing, and attacking innocent bystanders like White male Reginald Denny, flashed across their living rooms and seared into their consciousness, newcomers like Ms. Paik decided with her husband in Seoul that they would not open their future business in a Black-populated area.

> P: Although I only heard it through the news, it was still scary. *That's why* I have some bad feelings about Blacks. Without a doubt, I thought to myself that I shouldn't go near them.
>
> N: Did you have any other reactions to that incident besides your feeling of fear?
>
> P: If we were going to open a business here, we wanted to go some place else where there were no Blacks.

As Ms. Paik was also fearful of Black soldiers in the home country, she seemed to collapse the potential violence and criminality of the soldiers in Seoul and that of the protestors in Los Angeles. In fact, many post-1992 emigrants to the United States collapsed such violence. Residents of Seoul seemed to agree with these new immigrants' recollections. One elderly gentleman, Mr. Shin, demonstrated an acute awareness of Koreans' "middle" position in the color-class-ethnonational hierarchy. Blacks' antagonism toward Korean merchants only seemed to prove the point, what he considers the source of the riots: "When Korean people immigrate to that country, they are above Blacks although they're not above Whites. The reason is that Korean people are quick with information . . . and live better than Blacks do. Therefore, Blacks complained that 'Korean people discriminate against us,' so they rioted."

The Seoul residents who were not driven by the need to stress Blacks' criminal wrongdoing (toward more successful Koreans) followed the other route: identifying with Blacks. Perhaps influenced by the smattering of sympathetic media reports, the Seoul residents interpreted the unrest as catalyzed by White racism and believed that Blacks, like Koreans, were victims of it. Ms. Ha, a student, remarked:

> Before I was sympathetic towards Black people, but then after this incident, I didn't understand why they attacked us Koreans because I think their main targets should have been White people. So it seemed like they were exploited by this group of people [Whites] and were seeking vengeance on another group of people [Koreans]. But when I saw in the news that Koreans often suspected Blacks of being thieves . . . , I felt that Korean Americans' lives were not easy, and also that so many Black people are discriminated against.

These critical narratives reveal the belief among some new immigrants and South Koreans that White oppression justified Blacks' rage. Their critical stance also taught them to challenge media imagery that normalized White superiority and Black inferiority. For instance, Mr. Park, a male student from Seoul, remarked, "We're educated that way by the American mass media. Deep down, we all know it: the media put Blacks in the villain's role and made Whites the idols. Because that's what I was first taught, that's the way I think, even though I try not to think that way."

Certainly, the more positive and normalized images of Blacks in popular culture have had some influence on recent émigrés from South Korea. In fact, this cultural "silver lining" constitutes one major difference between the mass media impact and that of the occupational forces. Although the military largely propagated anti-Black ideologies, mass media representations could portray

Blacks positively and encourage Koreans' identification with the group. For instance, newcomers noted the Black Americans on screen who "looked smart," like Denzel Washington, and who were "living better" and "very strong politically." Their cognizance of more positive images is not surprising given exposure to more racially liberal and multiculturally minded movies and television programs in recent years. As noted, Koreans often cited politically conscious movies like *Roots* and *Malcolm X* as transformative and as fostering a sense of commonality with Blacks as fellow subjects of White rule. Along these lines, Hollywood's recent multicultural ventures have yielded more positive representations of Blackness by containing and rendering them normative rather than inferior (Guerrero 1993). At the same time, Gray (1995) finds that these normative images fundamentally reinscribe racism. That is, Hollywood writers "normalize" Blacks to the extent that they exist merely to service White humanity, with little attention to Black characters' own histories, families, needs, and desires (Gray 1995:169). These contemporary representations of Blackness can be found in the following Hollywood box office hits in South Korea: *Fried Green Tomatoes, Ghost*[6] (among the country's all-time box office hits [*Hollywood Reporter*, January 3, 1995]), *The Shawshank Redemption*, and *Forrest Gump* (which garnered 1.5 million theatrical admissions in Korea [*Hollywood Reporter*, January 3, 1995]). In light of the subordination of Blacks through both "negative" and "positive" stereotypes, it comes as little surprise that Koreans, like the young male student who knew he was being conditioned, struggle to purge them even when they make a conscious effort to do so.

The emulation of Black American hip-hop since the 1990s could also prove one way in which American mass culture has fostered favorable perceptions of Blacks. Yet, as the earlier fieldwork moment with the hip-hop enthusiast and his black doll broached, the appropriation of hip-hop could also move in problematic directions. On the one hand, Koreans rapping and break dancing in a country with few Black citizens and no history of Black movements could reify images of the simpleton entertainer and, given gangster rap, the urban criminal (as well as introducing notions of Black hypersexuality, an ideology that as yet seems unfamiliar there). Similarly, audiences could exploit norms of caricature (Japanese *monomane*) by wearing afros, tanning, and the like, while Korean men might use hip-hop to don the hypermasculinity of Black men (see Maira 2002) without grasping the oppressive context that spawned it. On the other hand, increased engagement with Black American hip-hop could lead to more knowledge of the group's plight in the United States and an understanding of shared oppressions (though in South Korea the rhymes are usually written by Koreans and delivered in Korean). That is, if Koreans use Black American culture as a way to become visible and politically salient vis-à-vis U.S. domination, the two parties might be able to converge as non-Whites fighting White power. To date in South Korea, I have noticed kernels and slices of all of the above, suggesting both hope and concern.

Invisibility in America

In the last chapter, I asserted that Koreans suffer the paradox of being dominated by the United States but being a nation unfamiliar to most Americans. This paradox, coupled with South Korea's subordinate status to the advanced West in the global order, has secured their overall sense of invisibility and partial presence. The paradox further betrays the fact that Koreans are not important to Americans outside of the military-capitalist-cultural dividends the occupation brings. Although the U.S. White-over-Black order has reinforced Koreans' sense of "middle" positioning above Blacks, it has also reinforced to South Koreans that they are not part of the binary at all, hence their invisibility in the United States and, by extension, the globe. In other words, the relationship between the White West and Black peoples has largely muted the existence-cum-salience of other nations such as South Korea. Furthermore, as "Americans," or more precisely, "American" service people, both Whites and Blacks engender and reproduce Koreans' partial presence in their own country.

When focusing on their social position *within* the United States, South Koreans had some idea that White Americans coexisted with Asian Americans. Yet the following narratives make clear that Korean/Asian Americans (or Latinos, for that matter) were not part of the American national identity. Such a perception—that America belongs to Whites, secondarily to Blacks, and to no other group—is shaped by the visibly White-Black "face" of the U.S. military. Similarly, in American mass media, Whiteness is the reference point while Blacks have been the most consistently visible subjects of political discourse about non-Whites in the United States (Entman and Rojecki 2000:xi). Koreans, then, especially in recent decades, have come to the United States with the knowledge that Blacks are "more American" while they themselves lack political visibility and recognition (see Taylor 1994). For those old-timers who left South Korea in the 1970s and early 1980s, America's reference point was White; if there was anyone else, however, there were Black people. Ms. Go recollects her notions of "Americans" prior to her emigration in 1973:

G: like when I was in Korea, actually, I thought everybody who lived here were *White people*, that's what I thought (laughs).

N: Was it because that was all you saw or for other reasons?

G: You didn't see much, *only White and Black*, only two kinds of races living here.

To further demonstrate Koreans' strong awareness of this binary racial terrain, Korean respondents tended to express having little awareness of other U.S. residents of color. In particular, most of the informants expressed surprise at the large Latino population in California given weak knowledge of just how big the population was in the United States. This surprise was especially true among those who immigrated in the 1970s and 1980s, such as Mr. Che: "Yeah, I didn't have any images at all about Mexicans, Latinos before I came. No idea." Another old-timer immigrant, Ms. Pak, agreed.

P: Yes, I couldn't even imagine that there were other races, like Mexicans, here.

N: You didn't have any images, not even in movies?

P: In movies, in American movies, you see mostly Whites. Of course, you see some movies with Blacks in it, and there are movies with both Whites and Blacks in it. That's about it.

Despite some recent émigrés' increased awareness about Latinos, other newcomers claimed little awareness until they had moved to California. Even a Hollywood movie fan like new immigrant Ms. Joo could barely recall seeing any Latinos in the movies.

N: Did you have any impressions of Mexicans or South Americans before you came here?

J: No, not really.

N: Does that mean you didn't really see them portrayed in movies?

J: Rarely.

Similarly, although new immigrant Mr. Roh (age 66, 1 year in United States) knew of Blacks before coming to the United States, he said the following about Mexican Latinos:

N: Before you came here, had you ever met Mexican people?

R: No, never.

N: What image, if any, did you have of Mexicans such as from American movies or news, etc.?

R: I didn't even know that they existed [here in the United States].

Although most new immigrants and South Koreans did not know a great deal about Latinos, they tended to demonstrate much more familiarity than did old-timers. For instance, Latinos' greater visibility in American popular culture in recent decades as well as transnational stories from the United States have made South Koreans more aware of the exoticized media stereotype of Latinos' penchant for festive parties, dancing, and singing. Although there has always been a smattering of Latino entertainers, Latinos in music, such as Ricky Martin, Jennifer Lopez, Marc Anthony, and Christina Aguilera, have certainly abounded in recent years. Newcomer Ms. Paik had taken notice.

N: Before you came here, did you see Spanish, Mexican . . . people in movies?

P: No, not really, but after I came here I saw lots of them.

N: So you didn't see them in movies in Korea, in news, or magazines?

P: Yeah, I saw them like they were energetic and they danced really well. That's all I really knew.

Even those Koreans who had seen images or had heard stories concerning Latinos admitted their inability to identify Latinos until they came to the United States. Many echoed Mr. Pak when she said that it was hard to distinguish Latinos because some had "blond hair and blue eyes." Ms. Kang added, "I saw Americans and Blacks, but other people like Arabs or Latinos, I didn't know much about them. I mean, I'd seen Spanish people in the movies, so I knew that they liked music and singing, things like that, but I couldn't really pick them out or distinguish them. Now that I've been here, I can."

In fact, Koreans' inability to identify Latinos is partly why they continued to perceive the U.S. military in White-Black racial terms. It is not surprising, then, that new immigrants like Mr. Cho (who had lived near a military base) claimed that there were very few Latino soldiers in his home country.

C: [age 68, 1 year in United States] It wasn't anything special for me to see Americans in the U.S., because there are many Americans in Korea.

N: Was it only Americans or were there other people too?

C: In Korea, there are mostly Americans . . .

N: Did you happen to see any Black people or Spanish-speaking people or Asians or any other group in Korea?

C: Yes, there are Black people, maybe some Asian, but there are barely any Spanish people, you don't see them at all. But the biggest number is

American. This is because, first and foremost, the U.S. Army has been stationed in Korea for over forty something years.

When asked about U.S. mass media generally, the vast majority of Koreans invoked White American stars and story lines and were all too familiar with Blacks. Although Asians have been portrayed in Hollywood since the early twentieth century and have become more visible in recent years, Asians / Asian Americans are still less prominent in mass media texts than are Blacks and Latinos. South Koreans could thus rarely recall representations of themselves or of Asians generally in U.S. mass culture. They could not see themselves as part of "America." The interjections of college students and young profession-als in Seoul—those who tend to consume the most American popular culture—are telling. Although they had been garrulous about images of Whites and Blacks in the United States, they fell silent and paused for long periods when they were asked about images of Koreans/Asians in America. Indeed, Mr. Park, a young fan of American popular culture had spoken at length about the im-ages that occurred to him when he thought of Whites (rich) and Blacks (slaves), but when he was asked about Asians, after a long pause, this was his reply: "Well, nothing really comes to my mind."

To be certain, Koreans have begun to notice certain stereotypes. Ms. Jun, a female graduate student in Seoul, disliked the images of "docile Asian women" in Hollywood movies. The South Korean Ministry of Culture and Tourism has also begun to ban films with offensive stereotypes of Korean/Asian characters. Furthermore, coverage of the LA unrest signaled Korean Americans' invisibil-ity, prompting some to criticize the way in which Whites exploited Koreans' political powerlessness by not coming to their aid during the several days of unbridled arson and looting.

The Seoul residents believed that if Korean Americans had not been so politically invisible and palatable—and ostensibly, if the ROK was a superpower—Whites would never have turned a blind eye on Koreans and used them as a buffer between themselves and Blacks. The theme of Koreans' political weakness could also be found in a small number of transnational news stories. Consider a 1988 *Chosun Ilbo* (February 23, 1988) piece on a Mr. Choi: "Mr. Choi sued the [U.S.] government for racial discrimination after he and his Asian co-workers were fired from a police department for no apparent reason. Mr. Choi claims, '*Asians are more vulnerable to racial discrimination than Blacks because of lack of human rights protection programs specific to Asians'* " (emphasis added). Transnational media on the LA unrest, on Black Americans in the political arena, and on experiences like Mr. Choi's, especially in a context of South Korean partial presence, familiarize the people to their political invisibility and weakness in the United States. Simply put, it was not difficult for Koreans to notice that they were not part of the national identity, one of Whites (the citizens) and Blacks (the second-class citizens; P. Collins 2001).

Conceptual Map: Racial Triangles and Hierarchies

Taking together the data from this and the previous chapter, I contend that the racial knowledge and identities of South Koreans, and those who would later emigrate, are deeply influenced by the group's subordinate status to White America and by their various positionings vis-à-vis Black Americans. The dual axes of racial triangulation (C. Kim 1999), slightly modified, are helpful here for conceptually mapping the South Korean context.

Although I borrow the notion of a racial triangle itself and the modified versions of the dual axes that make up that triangle, I should reiterate that, because Koreans are in their home country, their concerns pertain to their place in the United States–led global order as well as the U.S. domestic order. Because South Korean hierarchies and ideologies are integral to Koreans' experiences, the racialization axes in South Korea also differ from those of the triangulation model based in the United States (although they are largely congruent).

With respect to the racial triangle, South Koreans are positioned not along the color line and citizenship line per se, but along a vertical axis I conceptualize as "ethnonational" and a horizontal axis I conceptualize as "political recognition." This horizontal axis of "political recognition" addresses the extent of Korea's visibility/recognition within the United States and the larger global order. The U.S. process of civic ostracism would be imprecise here, then, as South Koreans are in their own country under an independent government (at least formally, and notwithstanding U.S. influence and pressure). Although in this capacity the United States cannot "civically ostracize" South Koreans as inauthentic citizens in their own country, the state-led occupation (and economic, cultural dominance) has relegated Koreans to partial presence within their own borders.

All of the group placements that follow are determined by interrelated social structures, cultural representations, and the everyday interactive realm within South Korea. Overall, the groups' positionings reveal that along the vertical "ethnonational" axis—Koreans' main racialized ranking system—White America occupies the dominant position marked by the top pole: "Light-skinned / Developed / Strong Lineage." In contrast, Black Americans (whom Koreans trace to Africa) occupy the subordinate position marked by the bottom pole: "Dark-skinned / Underdeveloped / Weak Lineage." South Koreans occupy the middle position. In addition to Western-based color and development hierarchies, Koreans' own ethnic nationalism puts them in the middle: below White America but above Blacks and other "originally" third world peoples.

Along the horizontal axis of political recognition (within the U.S., globe), the status of South Koreans is toward the "Not Visible–Disempowered" pole. White Americans occupy the "Visible-Empowered" position and Black Americans come next, though not on equal footing with Whites. These social locations denote that South Koreans are not visible global citizens or American citizens and thus receive little political recognition and resources. In addition, the White-Black demography of the U.S. military as well as Koreans' conflicts with both groups politically empower Whites, then Blacks, above Koreans. To summarize, both the vertical (ethnonational) and horizontal (political recognition) axes capture the multiple ways in which South Koreans are socially positioned along the racial triangle. First, White America is the globe's leader and reference point. Blacks rank on the bottom of the ethnonational hierarchy yet are politically visible given the world's focus on White-Black relations within and without the United States. As such, Blacks are both more "American" and more familiar to the world than are South Koreans. Blacks are also more dominant as armed, English-speaking Americans advantaged by the Status of Forces Agreement at the expense of Koreans in their own country. This racial triangle reveals that while White America is the world and U.S. leader, South Koreans rank both "above" and "below" Black Americans in various hierarchies.

The concept of a racial triangle and of multiple axes is suited to the South Korean context. It accounts for the congruence between Koreans' ethnonational order and the U.S. White-over-Black order, especially ideologies of biology that underpin both (e.g., bloodlines, phenotype). Yet South Korea as a case also departs from the triangulation model insofar as the lack of political visibility (hence, Koreans' insignificance) goes unacknowledged by the theory. Although Asians in the United States can be rendered invisible by processes of civic ostracism (C. Kim 1999), South Koreans tend to be, and feel, more invisible as a byproduct of America's paradigmatic White-over-Black "race" model, an *indirect* process. This sensibility is affirmed by Koreans' partial presence in their own country. It should be noted, however, that those Koreans who left the "homeland" in the wake of the 1992 unrest have had their eyes opened to the *directed* ways in which White America can engineer Koreans' invisibility within White-Black contests. And as we have seen, Koreans have established a tradition of resistance to such injustice.

This chapter, in conjunction with Chapter 3, demonstrates that Korean immigrants are racialized not just within the United States but with respect to Republic of Korea–United States relations. This cross-border relationship largely determines South Korea's overall position in the larger global order—the people's greatest concern (see Espiritu 2003). In other words, U.S. dominance over the ROK and Koreans' responses—understood through cultural logics of color, Confucianism, ethnonationality, nationalism, and so on—have forged an imperialist racial formation. One dimension is White (and Black) America's construction and treatment of South Koreans as third world, inferior, and foreign Others, a plight that Koreans resist and, in so doing, challenge glorified ideals of White America. By extension, Koreans become more "one" in light of the presence of Whites as well as Blacks, whose ethnonational origins themselves are erased by dint of U.S. "race" categories. Among other things, Koreans racially characterize Blacks as "GIs" and "criminals," adopting Whites' racial prejudices as a way to position themselves above. Not only is this a strategy of resistance against Black American state power, it responds to Koreans' subordinate position vis-à-vis the White West and Japan, to their liminality in a White-Black binarized world, and to a fear of regressing back to the "blacker" third world (Russell 1991).[7] This "detour" from oppression (Mulvey 1987:11), however, also exists alongside South Koreans' rejection of White superiority and Black inferiority, hence, their increased identification with Blacks. This pattern, common to most responses to oppression, situates consent and resistance side by side and interrelates them (e.g., resisting Black American state power by drawing on stereotypes of Blacks; Espiritu 2001; Pyke and Dang 2003; Pyke and Johnson 2003). Indeed, even in a U.S. context of multiracial demography and history of antiracist movements rife with liberal "race" discourse, groups of color have reported some of the harshest prejudices toward one another (National Conference of Christians and Jews 1994; Cummings and Lambert 1997; N. Kim 2004; T. Lee 2000; National Conference for Community and Justice 2000, 2005).

Along the dimension of the politics of recognition, Koreans are aware that America's national identity as White-over-Black has rendered their own group less "American" than Blacks and, by extension, less visible and significant in the United States and the world. As I show in the following chapters, Koreans' social position in the home country below Whites and as advantaged and disadvantaged vis-à-vis Black Americans is the map with which they navigate and reshape the new, but not wholly unfamiliar, domestic U.S. racial terrain. As I have stressed, Korean and other immigrants do not come to the United States as a tabula rasa on which American racial ideologies and identities wait to be written. Rather, they arrive already racially triangulated. That is, a constellation of forces tied to U.S. imperialism makes Koreans into racially invisible and not-American subjects, inculcates the group with White-Black ideologies, and prompts them to reckon their social positioning vis-à-vis the two "American" players long before they land on U.S. airport runways. These findings beg further analysis of the global and local inequalities that underpin the racialization of U.S. immigrant actors. I turn now to Korean immigrants' " 'return' to racial America."

5 Navigating the Racial Terrain of Los Angeles and the United States

> *Tell me the story*
> *Of all these things*
> *Beginning wherever you wish, tell even us.*
>
> —Theresa Hak Kyung Cha, *Dictee*

ONCE KOREANS HAD CROSSED THE OCEAN, how did they navigate their insertion into a new racial system? How did the home country context matter in Koreans' *direct* experience of the domestic U.S. racial landscape? Did any of their premigrant understandings change or become complexified? Addressing these questions here, I focus on major transitions concerning "race" that Korean immigrants themselves undergo, such as their move from a nation-based categorization system to one that privileges *racial* (pan-national) identity. Another shift is the move from a cultural system that normalized the open expression of prejudice to a country in which liberal "race" ideology prevails (Bonilla-Silva 2001; Schuman et al. 1997). In light of these changes, I also examine how Koreans—often by way of a cross-border process or comparison—uphold, problematize, and/or reconfigure their understandings of the racialized United States. In so doing, I focus on how Koreans connect the U.S. state in South Korea and that at "home," as well as revisit the mass media imagery and transnational stories by which they had long been conditioned. Moving beyond the racial triangle in South Korea of Whites, Blacks, and their own group, I examine how Koreans become more familiar with, and define themselves vis-à-vis, Jews, Latinos (Mexican and Central Americans), and a panethnic Asian American category in their new California home.

From Ethnonationality to "Race"

Peggy Levitt (2001:11) defines "social remittances" as the "ideas, behaviors, and social capital that flow from receiving to sending countries." In the initial stages of social remittance evolution, migrants are still learning about the receiving context, using the premigrant interpretive frames, grafting old onto new, and creolizing (Levitt 2001:56). Sociologists Won Moo Hurh and Kwang Chung Kim (1984) contend that Koreans follow the "grafting" route, what they call "adhesive adaptation." By this they mean that Korean immigrants graft aspects and relationships of the host society onto traditional Korean cultural forms without any fundamental change to the latter. Although my data show that grafting is not true in all cases, it does seem to be the best account of how Koreans more systematically add an "(East) Asian" identity onto their ethnonational Korean one. Although they still see Koreanness through a lens of blood-based nationalism, they come to fold Asianness into their identity repertoire as a more political and situational identity, as Espiritu (1992) documented historically. Of course, the two identities also inform one another. Depending on context, then, the identities may "creolize," as well.

Almost all of the immigrants, regardless of cohort, conveyed that in South Korea they had rarely thought of *themselves* as "Asian." Although they were fully aware that the world's people could generally be categorized into "White, Black, and Yellow," they did not perceive "Yellow" (or Asian) as their *primary* identity. Rather, in the home country they had fashioned themselves as Korean and were only Asian when they grouped the Eastern region together—the Koreas, China, and Japan—and usually in relation to "the West." In the United States, however, Asianness becomes more salient to the old-timer immigrants. They "become" Asian due in part to White America's effacing of difference among countless Asian ethnics. As an illustration, old-timer Mr. Oh (age 34) pointed to mass media's role in subsuming Koreans under the broader Asian "race," thereby promoting ignorance about his people.

O: Here, there is not a special consideration for Koreans.

N: Oh, by the people living in America?

O: Yes, by American society itself. Other than things like the Korean community center there is nothing that specifies Koreans. Anyway, here it's just "Asian." Also, in the commercials when they're advertising things like cell phones there is a White person, a Black person, an Eskimo, and an Asian person. They don't specify whether that person is Korean or not. You don't know whether that person is Chinese or Korean. It's just Asian, Black, and White. So I thought, "I'm just Asian!" after I came here, when I see things like that.

In addition, I queried Ms. Yi if it seemed that people in the United States could identify her as Korean based simply on her appearance.

Y: Not really, . . . some people ask me if I'm Chinese, others if I'm Japanese.

N: Oh, since they can't tell exactly, do you think when they see us, the first thing they think is "Oriental" or "Asian"?

Y: Of course! That's for sure, they can just tell that by looking at us.

As Ms. Yi shows, many of the Korean respondents were mistaken for the more well-known Asian ethnics: Japanese and Chinese. Owing to Koreans' premigrant fixation on the global order and on U.S. society's greater familiarity with Japan and China, the immigrants grappled with the irony of being lumped into an "Asian" racial category that could be synonymous with the *ethnic* label, "Chinese" or "Japanese." Although they came to accept an Asian identity, they also lamented their lack of visibility in the U.S. Asian ethnic hierarchy. Many respondents attributed Chinese and Japanese Americans' greater visibility and recognition to their longer tenure in the United States, to their more famous cuisine, to China's ancient history and colossal size, and to Japan's global power. Some demographic trends support their greater prominence overall. Chinese Americans, for instance, outnumber Korean Americans in most of Southern California by more than 150,000 (the Los Angeles–Riverside–Orange County Consolidated Metropolitan Statistical Areas [CMSA]; E. Yu and Choe 2003) and by more than 1.6 million nationally (Lai and Arguelles 2003). In addition, Japan's high global status has been affirmed by the low levels of immigration from Japan, hence, Japanese *Americans'* predominantly native-born populace, their highest socioeconomic levels, and highest rates of citizenship and English fluency (Jiobu 1988; see Fong 2002:247). In California, Japanese Americans' percentage of native-born adults is eight times higher than that of Korean Americans (E. Yu and Choe 2003).[1]

It is not surprising, then, that Koreans consistently invoked the connection between Japan's position in the global order and Japanese Americans' position in the United States. They attributed White America's respect for Japan and, by extension, Japanese Americans, to the country's advanced capitalist economy and imperialist history—a dogged location of dominance that had embittered Koreans long before U.S. arrival. When I asked the respondents, then, to rank the various Asian groups in terms of power and resources, *all* of them ranked themselves below their former colonizers. Many of the informants unleashed a sense of inferiority in moments when they traced White Americans' better treatment of Japan to a greater familiarity with, and respect for, the former empire. Upon my asking old-timer Mr. Jung (age 54), for instance, whether Koreans seemed to have "made it" in the United States, he qualified his affirmative response with a case regarding "America's" better treatment of Japan than South Korea in global trade.

> Yeah, the United States exported food . . . They bioengineered the food, the corn . . . I think 80 percent [of Korea's food] is from the United States . . . They found out that they [U.S.] had made a bad change to the food, so they complained to the United States government. The . . . government just answered, "Wait, wait, wait," . . . without acting or anything, but the Japanese had the same problem, ... They complained, so they [U.S.] sent a lot of people to Japan, specialists, to check it over and they did everything right away, they responded! But for Korea, they don't do it (laughs nervously) . . . That's looking down [on Korea], uh? I don't know, I don't understand, you know, why are they doing that? . . . They should be responsible right away. That's bad for the United States to do that.

Mr. Jung's embarrassment by this glaring reminder of the U.S. government's indifference toward South Korea is significant, especially relative to Japan. New immigrant Ms. Kang (age 46) was more openly upset by Koreans' invisibility in the United States.

> Let me tell you about an incident. I went to Las Vegas, but I couldn't speak English well. My younger sister who speaks Japanese well went with me. So when we had to ask something and couldn't say it in English, we tried to see if they knew Korean. But no one spoke Korean there and only when my sister spoke Japanese to the guide, through a Japanese interpreter, were we able to board our plane. I mean, why did they have a *Japanese* interpreter there, but not a *Korean* interpreter? This thought depressed me so much. I get so disappointed when things like this happen!

In short, White Americans' greater familiarity with the Chinese and Japanese, and high estimation of the latter, sensitized Koreans to their "extra-invisibility." Perhaps it is not surprising that some immigrants would pretend that they were Japanese when non-Koreans would inquire after their ethnicity. Newcomer Ms. An expressed her shock and distress by this practice, maintaining, "They shouldn't do that! They should be proud to be Korean!"

Irrespective of the Korean immigrants' disquiet over their weak visibility, it was a watershed experience to move into a racial categorization system in which nationality was not the main marker of difference. Although the immigrants maintained their strong sense of nationalist pride, they also became more cognizant of the shared experiences of Asian ethnics as they spent more time in the United States. Historically, this collective sensibility was one of the catalysts for Asian Americans' struggle to secure a state panethnic category (Espiritu 1992; see Almaguer and Jung 1999). In my study, the clearest indication of Korean immigrants' adoption of the panethnic label was their interchangeable use of the word "Asian" and "Korean" during their narratives. Sometimes when I would explicitly ask the respondents whom they meant by "we" or "us," they would say, "Asians." As I show in the next chapter, Korean immigrants tended to invoke "Asian" when they referred to outgroups' perceptions of them, the U.S. model minority stereotype (not the nationalist version in South Korea), and foreigner-related racial stereotypes and discrimination. In brief, the dialectic between externally imposed categories and internal cultural construction (Nagel 1994), as well as shared political experience, are central to Koreans' incorporation of "(East) Asian" into their identity repertoire.

View of Racialized America from Within

In the United States, Korean immigrants demonstrated that they maintained, expanded on, and/or questioned their views on White Americans that they had developed in South Korea, namely that they were rich, beautiful, liberal, friendly, arrogant, and/or racist. On their premigration understandings, I examine the impact of immigrants' greater contact with Whites and White-dominated institutions in the United States and greater awareness of American "race" history, mainly from a transnational frame.

Politics

The penchant for pro-Americanism among those who immigrate was apparent in narratives about American democracy. Because Korean immigrants' survival in the United States came to depend on this cause célèbre of democracy that had "liberated" them from Japan and assisted them in the Korean War, they were even more grateful for the U.S. government resources that they came to enjoy. In particular, Korean immigrants frequently compared "embarrassing" South Korean politicians with "honest" White American politicians. Although Republic of Korea (ROK) officials' frequent physical altercations at formal meetings have mortified Koreans, U.S. officials have overseen generous social welfare policies "even for immigrants." In a comparative light, some of the first generation respondents expressed shame that the South Korean state, in stark contrast, mistreated its immigrants (see Seol and Skrentny 2004).

Old-timer Mr. Han was a staunch proponent of the American liberal state. Although he lamented South Korean politics while in the home country— "Korean congressmen fight [verbally, physically] really badly at their assembly meetings"—he had admired the United States as "rich" and as boasting "the highest democratic system." After living twenty-four years in the United States, he concluded, "Now I think, though I didn't know about this in Korea, that American people are the greatest citizens . . . *great*, great people."

He maintained this view despite the fact that he could have been embittered by his long fall down the class ladder in the United States, going from movie director to grounds maintenance manager at a condominium complex. Rather than convey the anger and depression common to immigrant men who suffer downward mobility, however, he was grateful for his stable job and government benefits.

In fact, he was so greatly humbled by American democracy that he excluded himself from it. Owing to a South Korean ethos that places importance on men's burial in their authentic nation, he concluded, "*I don't think I deserve a bit of American land, so* . . . since I like fishing, [I'll] have my ashes thrown into the ocean" (emphasis added). He internalized his foreignness, then, by believing that no matter how good a citizen he was—that is, no matter how much he contributed in labor, taxes, and random acts of kindness—he did not deserve to be buried alongside "America's" White men. Another longtime immigrant, elderly Ms. Gim, lauded the U.S. polity, particularly the generosity of Social Security: "Korea and America are completely different . . . how grateful I feel to America because you can live on your own when you reach sixty-five years old. But Korea doesn't have anything like that yet." Not surprisingly, she beamed proudly when she recollected the day that she became a U.S. citizen. Although it would be interesting to know if Social Security's increasingly imperiled state would make rents in her admiration for the United States, it is clear that she sees the ROK state as wanting.

Complaining bitterly about Korean politicians, old-timer Ms. Pak (age 46) drew on her transnational viewpoint to reach the following conclusion: "You know, White Americans are calm, thoughtful, and . . . really talk about their rights. Koreans . . . think only the politicians have power [because] in Korea, the politicians control everything; but here I believe that the government respects, is afraid of the people. Koreans? No, they don't care, they don't care about people" [modified].

U.S. imperialist rule in the home country means that the immigrants have been doubly influenced by "America's" culture of dominance. As a poor, weak nation "in need" and, later, as minority immigrants "in need," Korean Americans engage a continued sense of inferiority to a White American democracy that put the ROK to shame. Indeed, the extent of this internalized inferiority is best summed up by old-timer Mr. Han, the gentleman who did not feel that he *deserved* to be buried in American land. Such rose-colored glasses elide the U.S. state's anti-immigrant practices amid the more liberal ones—as immigrants' recent nationwide protests have borne out—as well as the state's checkered history of failure and corruption.

To be sure, Koreans also begin to problematize glorifications of American democracy after settling in their U.S. home. Given that newcomers especially were all too familiar with the abuses of the U.S. military state in the home country, they already had a cultural schema from which to work. Rather than overwhelmingly laud White America as a benevolent bastion of democracy, some Korean immigrants condemn the history of racial oppression about which they begin to learn. Ms. Li, for instance, came to see a "scary," "awful" side of White Americans, especially with respect to the unequal segregation of indigenous peoples.

> I understand that America took the land that used to belong to Mexicans . . . So since Columbus discovered America, America does not originally belong to the *miguk saram*; they just discovered it . . . And while I was traveling around, I visited a Native American village and I saw that they set it up to make Native Americans gamble; there was a separate village where there was gambling and drinking, selling drugs . . . Seeing that Whites forced them into that area, I felt that America was really awful, scary. America, as a country, is scary. Because even though Americans are making sure the people stay alive, if the U.S. really wanted to protect and love them, they should integrate them into society and revitalize the Native American tribes and help them develop.

Ms. Li reveals her sense of alarm by White Americans' oppression of indigenous peoples. Perhaps her alarm should not be surprising, as she had long been taught to glorify White Americans as humane saviors of South Korea. Furthermore, owing to Koreans' sanctification of land from a nationalist standpoint, the U.S. history with Mexico also raised eyebrows. Indeed, Koreans see the nation's physical characteristics (e.g., land, climate, location) and the people's characteristics as coextensive. For instance, many invoked such tropes as South Korea's four seasons as the reason behind the unrivaled work ethic encoded in Koreans' blood (unlike people in the tropics) and the small size of their land as accounting for the people's narrow-mindedness on issues. Within such a cherished framework of the oneness of land and people, old-timers like Mr. Che and newcomers like Mr. Roh were offended that the United States had "stolen Mexico's land." They also expressed that they finally understood why there were "so many Mexicans" in the United States.

Social Class and Work Ethic

Those who had lived in the United States for a while realized that not all Whites were rich and that the American lifestyle was not necessarily glitz and glamour. For instance, old-timer immigrant Ms. Yi was shocked at the sight of homeless Whites in the United States. Comparing her pre- and postmigration views, she states:

Y: In terms of Whites, I thought that they were cultured, their status was higher than ours, those kinds of things. But I found out that a lot of them were not like that. I found out that there are people who can't read and there are people who don't have much, don't live well.

N: Where did you see them?

Y: On the street. There were homeless people, too.

N: Were you surprised?

Y: Of course! I saw even White people digging through the garbage. I don't know if they were mentally disabled or what. They exist too, I guess.

A newly arrived respondent, Ms. Yoo, was also struck by the fact that people in the United States did not live wealthy and glamorous lives as she had expected. In fact, Ms. Yoo realized that ostentation was a South Korean norm, not an American one as she had expected: "Koreans love to show off and be materialistic and so I wanted to tell them that in the U.S. you don't live that extravagantly. I really wanted to tell people to prepare before coming here, even if they have money."

One of the notions that Koreans tended to maintain after living in the United States was the idea that White Americans did not work as hard as Koreans. To be sure, Koreans often conceded that Whites worked hard, as evidenced by the success of the United States. Yet they believed that Whites did not know how to work themselves weary in the ways Koreans did. Although Ms. Li, a seven-year immigrant, spoke in her interview about how early Koreans got up, how many excess hours they worked, and how "diligent" they were, she noted, in contrast, that "White Americans are the kind of people that are always focused on time; they don't work more than they need to, like overtime, and they don't work less either." Old-timer Mr. Han attributed Whites' less fervent work ethic to an innate national character, hence, returning to the blood trope.

> White Americans also cannot work as hard as us . . . You should know it all stems from *native* character, that is, *native* versus *acquired* character . . . Acquired character is something that can change over a lifetime, but native character can hardly change. I think this difference is very important . . . You know dogs have this curved tail. If you tie this tail down for a hundred years to flatten it, the tail will still curl.

Like many other Koreans, Mr. Han essentializes Koreans' "tails" as curved toward a robotic work ethic, while White Americans' "tails" are not. Koreans' narrative of their exceptional work ethic, a claim of cultural superiority over Whites, acts also as a form of resistance to White American dominance and racism (see Espiritu 2001).

White Ethnicity

Although Koreans still viewed their work ethic as superior to that of White Americans writ large, Jews were the one ethnic group that Koreans deemed above their league. Although old-timers had not known as much about this group prior to emigration, many newcomers had learned of Jews' phenomenal success from heightened discourse about it in South Korea around the late 1980s (www.daum .com 2005). More recent émigrés had also gotten wind of it from their immigrant counterparts, especially in light of Jewish prominence in California. Nevertheless, the Jewish legacy of success became much more palpable to Koreans after settling into their new society. Many old-timers maintained that Jewish people held the most economic power of all minority groups and seemed to have influenced every arena of American life. Consider old-timer Mr. Jung's response to my query about whom he thought had the most power in the United States.

> J: From what I know, economically, the Jewish people are holding it right now, I think they're very strong . . . And also they're mostly, uh, I heard, in the motion picture arena and mostly they're in law, law firms. They're doing that, too; then also trade so that's very powerful. And of course Americans, they're holding strong.

N: Do you think that they're the same as the Jewish, or a little below?

J: If we compare percentages, then the Jewish are more strong. For a small group of people, they're strong. Totally overall, of course, Americans are higher than them but . . . they're strong.

I also queried old-timer Mr. Bae, a businessman, as to whom seemed to have most power in economic, political, or other terms. He replied, "Well, based on my knowledge, the Jewish people have been the most prominent economically. I think that in terms of politics the conservative White people are the most dominant." Another old-timer by the name of Mr. Yoo had mentioned Jews and Koreans as very successful and placed Jews in the following tier of society:

Middle class . . . You know, they're actually discriminated against by the dominant Whites . . . The reason why the Jewish people have achieved success is because, like Koreans, they have put enormous emphasis on the education of their children who eventually work in various fields. Therefore, they can't be ignored even though they're being discriminated against . . . They contribute a lot to American society. They work in every field including politics, economics, society, art, and culture. There's nothing they haven't done.

Like the others, he saw Jewish people as epitomizing the American immigrant success story, while he would lament elsewhere in his interview Koreans' absence in too many fields. In general, Korean immigrants like him seemed to feel somewhat inferior to Jews, whose monumental achievements they were constantly reminded of in California.

White Racism

Most of the old-timers, both men and women, came to learn a great deal about White Americans from the daily interactions they had with them in the workplace. For instance, elderly Mr. Sohn felt that his work experiences in the United States confirmed the sense of superiority that he had expected from Whites before coming: "I thought there could be a sense of superiority, just a little (pause). I thought that, sure. [In the United States, I realized] those people are okay at first but then when we start getting into the upper class, they start competing with us." His notions line up with research in Los Angeles that shows that, in the realm of individual life chances, Whites tend to see Asian Americans as competitive threats (Bobo and Hutchings 1996). Yet, as with Koreans' complicated views on White American wealth, these immigrants also modify their premigrant notions of White Americans as cold and racist.

To be sure, some Koreans had made the distinction between the White American state ("can be scary," "kills people") and individual White Americans before they immigrated to the United States. The general perception, however, was softened by Korean immigrants' belief that Whites were more culturally polite, warm, and friendly than their own group. As noted, this view extends from the historically perceived benevolence of the missionaries and U.S. government but also from the generally more effusive and emotionally expressive norms of interaction among all Americans. During his fifteen years in the United States, for instance, Mr. Bae (age 43) had come to respect what he considered White Americans' more "patient" and "calm" ways than Koreans, a group he considered impatient and anxious (because of "our small country," he said).

> When I see White Americans not being impatient, I try to emulate that, for ex-
> ample, the way they form lines. I don't know if they're like that because their
> minds are more calm and at ease, but something I felt grateful for in the past
> was when I had an accident shortly after I came to America on the freeway . . .
> What I felt grateful for was that the passing cars stopped, made phone calls, and
> helped us. They were all White people. So when I see those kinds of accidents, I
> try to help them . . . Since they've lived here for so long, they are at ease. I'd like
> to be that way. So when I see accidents on my way, I try to help them.

He demonstrates that, upon living in a predominantly White world, Koreans also come to value American norms over Korean ones insofar as smiling at strangers, queuing up, exercising calm in panicky moments, and the like are less common in South Korea. Newer immigrants who had come to the United States with both positive and negative images of Whites had also concluded that the group was, at the least, nice and polite. Newcomer Ms. Joo (age 47) had heard a more complicated pearl of wisdom before she emigrated:

> J: I heard that, in *general*, Whites are polite, but that they smile in front of
>   you and then go ahead and *sue* you for something behind your back. But I
>   heard that if there's no discontent between you and them, then they're
>   generally nice people.
> N: After you came here, did you think what you heard from Korea was true?
> J: I haven't really experienced anything like that yet, so . . . (pause) but I
>   think they're nice.

Ms. Joo's short two-year stay and Korean-only circles had precluded her from interacting with Whites enough to know whether they donned the alleged two faces of nice and litigious. As many of the Korean immigrants reveal, they held multiple and sometimes contradictory perceptions of White Americans based on impressions, representations, experiences, and the "ethnic wisdoms" that circulated amongst their communities and across borders.

White Masculinity and Gender

As noted in the previous chapter, Korean women had engaged ideologies of hegemonic White American masculinity instantiated by the U.S. military, mass media industry, and transnational stories. Despite the hegemonic masculinity of Korean men depicted in the popular culture of *Hanryu* (the Korean Wave) since 1998 and the fanatical desire for these men across Asia (and beyond), the women in South Korea racialized "gender modern" men as White Western and "gender backwards" men as Korean (see Kelsky 2001). In the United States, the women largely uphold these notions as a point of resistance against, and escape from, ongoing Korean Confucian patriarchy in the face of shifting gender arrangements (N. Kim 2006a). More specifically, the women resist Korean men's stronger grip on patriarchy that stems from various forms of emasculation (e.g., women's gains, racism, nativism, declassed status).

Oftentimes, the immigrant women transnationally linked pre- and postmigration masculinity ideologies as they navigated shifting gender relations. For instance, prior to her immigration two years earlier, Miss Moon (age 38) had formed favorable views of White men from hearing her girlfriends in the United States speak positively of their boyfriends and fiancés. Ms. Moon's premigrant imaginings tended to be confirmed by her direct observations in the United States that "proved," in her eyes, what she had thought back in Seoul.

> When I observe the White men here, I notice that they're so simple [easygoing] and they treat my friends really well. I have a friend who's going to get married and, for instance, even if my friend's fiancé is really far from her somewhere, he'll still take her places, then leave, wait until she's done, and then pick her up (laughs); and he also does housework! Because getting Korean men to do that is so hard, you know? They treat them so, so well.

In addition to upholding hegemonic White masculinity, her cross-border lens affirmed her views that Korean men, whether in Seoul or in the United States, tended to shun housework and catering to their female partners. As someone who worked full-time as administrative staff at a Korean-owned dental office, Ms. Moon could no longer easily dismiss the importance of help with housework. Similarly, young skin care esthetician Ms. Suh, a five-year immigrant and single woman, presumed that she would marry a Korean man given her mostly Korean social circles in the United States. Yet she was open to the idea of marrying a White American upon observing her two female cousins in California who "lived well" with their White husbands. To be certain, the women's transnational comparisons did not mean categorical derision of Korean/Asian men as patriarchs. Two young newcomers—both homemakers with Korean husbands—believed that South Korean men were more gender progressive than Korean immigrants, as the immigrants were stuck in the "old" Korea that they had left behind.

The female immigrants also tended to see White men as more open to women's careers and, in fact, justified their own professional desires by pointing to "modern" White American masculinity. To unravel one fitting example, fifty-one-year-old longtime immigrant Ms. Pak was quite content with her career as a registered nurse and insisted that she would never have been more than a bored homemaker in Seoul had she not immigrated to the United States.

> Yes, when I first got here, I just followed my husband here, and I raised my children here. And when I look at what's going on in Korea now, I think I made the right decision by coming here . . . I have a job here . . . Women need to be happy with their own lives, have this sense of achievement . . . in their lives. It's not enough to just eat and spend the money the husband brings home.

Although Ms. Pak still prized forms of Korean culture over American culture, her transnational comparison secured her belief that Korean patriarchy left women bereft of any sense of worth. When I asked her if she would consider marrying a non-Korean, she remarked that if she could "do it all over again," she would marry an "American." In other words, Ms. Pak believed that a White husband would have been more supportive of her career aspirations than her current husband whom, incidentally, she described as more "Americanized" than most Koreans.

Immigrant women who ended up in serious relationships with White men, however, told a more complicated story. Two women, newcomer Ms. Noh and old-timer Ms. Park, believed that they enjoyed more gender reciprocity in these relationships, yet they came to realize that "barriers to communication" on an emotive level and lack of cultural understanding were insoluble issues. Ms. Noh ended up marrying a Korean man and Ms. Park was still looking. The failure of their relationships with White men points to a mismatch between the women's image and their reality.[2] Despite these unmatched ideals, including newcomers' distaste for White soldiers in the home country (especially per their mistreatment of women), the female informants consistently returned to the notion that White masculinity largely explained Americans' more gender egalitarian marriages (see Yuh 2002). The women therefore resisted one form of hegemony, Korean patriarchy, by upholding another, White American masculine dominance over both men and women of color. Such an outcome reveals the complexity of resistance strategies at the intersection of multiple social axes. At the same time, the dynamic does not dissuade women from continuing to date and marry Korean men, as the South Korean women also made clear.

Complicating Blackness and Learning Latinoness

Koreans, especially immigrants of recent vintage, did not just buy into White American dominance but also resisted it before they left Seoul. One point of resistance was the condemnation of White racism against Blacks. The informants built on these early forms of resistance by seeing Blacks in less hierarchical and more humanized ways in the United States. These less-conformist Koreans therefore were not bent on maintaining a position over Blacks to compensate for internalized inferiority vis-à-vis White America. Rather, they came to be interested in Blacks as people and more closely identified with them after experiencing life as racial minorities, as invisible in "someone else's" country. Old-timer immigrant Ms. Jang (age 47) recalled how excited she was by the prospect of "learning about America" and meeting all the different people upon first immigrating. She claims that she did not feel any social distance from the various groups, including Blacks.

> J: As soon as I got here, that was the first time I saw *really* heavy-set people, because you don't normally see a lot of those people in Korea. I was like, "Oh my gosh!" I saw a lot of Black people, oh my gosh, then I saw all kinds of different people and different languages . . . Then um, quickly, I discovered my personality, that I wanna learn everything!
>
> N: So you weren't like, "I feel different from them—I don't really feel comfortable around them?"
>
> J: No, no, actually I felt more attached to them, and it's so different.
>
> N: Like the minority people?

J: Yeah! Minority, it doesn't matter, Caucasian or minority people, it doesn't matter. I felt like, "Oh my God! I want to learn about them!" you know? . . . I really didn't feel the distance. That was the main thing, I didn't *feel* distance.

Unlike some of her immigrant counterparts in the 1970s, Ms. Jang felt no distance from Black Americans and, rather, wanted to learn more about them. According to her, her fervent desire to soak in the new country trumped any negative stereotypes or images.

Recent immigrants also tended to learn early on that the person and the stereotype did not always line up. Ms. An (age 57), a newcomer of eight months whom I recruited from a Korean-run English language school, described her budding friendship with a Black immigrant woman from an African nation despite a fundamental language barrier.

N: What do you think about Blacks now that you've been in the States?

A: Well, yeah, one of them studies next to me . . . She is a Black person, came from Africa, and she's studying here . . . She is very nice and I didn't feel any discrimination.

N: You mean towards you or towards that person?

A: Towards that person. I try to make a conversation with her with body language even if it doesn't make sense. So I realize that people are people— the same (chuckles).

From this exchange, Ms. An reached the conclusion, as did many other newcomers, that people were essentially "the same."

As I noted previously, Koreans who immigrated to the United States in the 1970s and early 1980s knew very little about Latinos in general or about Mexican and Central Americans in Los Angeles in particular. Although some of the immigrants who came more recently were aware of the large presence of Latinos, they knew mostly the popular cultural stereotypes of Ricky Martin and Jennifer Lopez. With time, both old-timers and newcomers had come to understand the more complex situation of the Mexican and Central Americans with whom they interacted in Los Angeles. Several newcomers were struck by their warmth and friendliness. For instance, after living in Los Angeles for a year, Ms. Paik (age 56, 1 year in United States) came to perceive Latinos as much friendlier than fellow Koreans. In fact, she felt more of a personal connection with Mexican Americans (and Whites) than with her own group, a reality that crushed her. Her anguish over this rift was palpable in our interview.

P: It really hurts me inside, in our apartment where 90% of the people are Korean, we don't ever greet each other. You know, because I'm so happy to see them, I want them to say "hello" to me and I want to say it first to them, but because they look so cold and indifferent, I can't even say it . . .

N: Do you think they might also be arrogant because they've been here longer than you?

P: Mhm. Yeah, those who've been here long are cold and disregard us in a condescending way. That's the *biggest* discomfort. At least White people and Mexicans talk to me and smile with ease. That softens things and I feel a heartfelt connection with them.

Others agreed with Ms. Paik's reckoning that Mexican Americans, like Whites, were "nice." For instance, based on her experience working with Mexican Americans in a garment factory, another newcomer named Ms. Joo (age 47, 2 years in United States) considered her co-workers nice and honest.

They're nice at the banks and at the DMV [Department of Motor Vehicles]. If I seem to be at a loss and struggling with my English, they always come up and help me out, even if they might be a little annoyed . . . I used to work at a sewing factory [with Mexican Americans]. The people who work at those places are the ones who have a hard time supporting their families, you know? They were more earnest than I'd thought. Of course, there are selfish people too but, in general, I thought they were really earnest.

Although the immigrants repeated cultural stereotypes, such as presumptions of Mexican Americans not being earnest, the above narratives also revealed Korean newcomers' willingness to criticize their own group (ad nauseam, what some consider a "Korean" trait). The immigrants were very frank about their group's lack of friendliness. Despite South Korean society's more overt and normalized disrespect of subordinates than in the United States, Koreans who frequently interacted with low-income Latinos did not allow class status to dictate all their perceptions or actions. My informal observations also revealed that Koreans who were active in civic and even ethnic organizations—such as community service, church affiliation, or social clubs—interacted in some capacity with Black Americans, Latinos, and other Asian ethnics. At least on the surface, and usually at formal events and fundraisers, they were mutually cordial and respectful and frequently laughed together as the evenings became festive. At one particular Korean high school reunion event, a woman seated at my table said to a Korean male acquaintance that she almost did not recognize him (apparently, he had cut his hair and lost some weight). She told him, "For some reason, you look more Mexican than Korean." I immediately shot a glance his way, wondering how he would respond; he simply smiled and said, "Really?" and then the two launched into, and laughed about, another topic.

Other Koreans, longtime immigrants in particular, seemed to adopt American liberal racial ideology and fold it into their commitment to antiracism. Mr. Che (age 54, 21 years in United States), a longtime immigrant and Chinese medicine doctor, had once run a men's clothing store in a low-income Black Chicago community and had had positive relations with Black patrons. These experiences and his thirst to understand American history seemed to explain his more racially progressive views than the average old-timer (and newcomer). Once he had discovered that much of the American West was formerly Mexico's, he solidified his stance on Mexican immigration to the United States.

> Well, a few years ago I wondered: why is it that these people keep coming to California or New York? I used to think that way. I'd also heard of thefts, Latinos stealing from Koreans, so I didn't like that at all, but when I looked at an American history book I learned that the California land was once Mexico's land, so I don't think there's anything wrong with them coming here and living here since it was their land a long time ago. That's what I think. Another reason is that Manchuria used to be Koreans' land a long time ago . . . Yeah, it's the same thing . . . So it doesn't matter if they are at the border or not! I thought, who cares if they come here when it was once their land?

Through a parallel between Mexican and Korean history and a nationalist lens of authentic ownership of countries, he dismisses the anti-immigration camp's nonsensical exclusion of people from their own land.

Similarly, old-timer Mr. Sohn (age 73, 18 years in United States) had once run a restaurant in New York, one frequented mostly by White patrons but with its share of non-White customers. Owing to his mostly positive interactions with these groups and his own bouts with racism, he had come to abhor anti-Black ideology. He further differentiated himself from the Korean American merchants whom he considered discriminatory toward Blacks in Los Angeles and, in his mind, helped ignite the fires of 1992.

S: Yeah, since they [merchants] interact with those who are poor, generally the problem is if one Black person behaves poorly, we see one as the whole. Of course we can't say that all Blacks are bad.

N: But generally, do you think some Koreans think like that?

S: Yes and those who do are kind of stupid, they don't think at a high level.

N: Where did they learn to think like that?

S: It's just that Koreans naturally racially discriminate against others.

N: Naturally?

S: Yes, they talk about how dark they are; who cares if the color of their skin is dark? I don't think like they do.

Mr. Sohn, like Mr. Che just quoted, seemed sincere about his views.

Parallel to the increasing openness of younger generations in South Korea, some Koreans had also come to accept their children's plausible marriage to Blacks and Latinos or hypothetically consider it for themselves if they were not married. To be sure, the responses could reflect conditioning by social desirability over time, but I present the informants who did not contradict themselves in their interviews and seemed genuine. Nevertheless, such a liberalization of opinion is quite striking in light of formidable taboos against exogamy (blood purity tropes), desire for a Korean family lineage, worries over cultural clashes, as well as South Korean– and United States–based struggles with Black Americans. I asked forty-three-year-old Mr. Bae (15 years in United States), for instance, a soft-spoken and friendly man, "If you weren't married now, do you think that you'd absolutely only marry a Korean?"

B: No, not now.

N: Oh, if you didn't marry a Korean, who do you think it would be?

B: Um, I think someone Asian.

N: Including Southeast Asians?

B: Yes. But since I don't know much about Southeast Asians, I think just Japanese or Chinese.

N: Who would come next?

B: Next, I haven't thought about who'd be next.

N: Well, how about Whites, Latinos, Blacks?

B: Next would be all the same so long as our personalities were compatible.

When I asked him about his preferences for his children, he replied: "As my children grow up and I become influenced by the American culture and live in

America, I come to think that, in my children's case, if they love each other . . ."
Here Mr. Bae is conscious of the fact that, as a U.S. resident, he is adopting
American liberal racial ideology.

Similarly, Ms. Jang, a 1970s immigrant, responded thus to my question:
"For your kids, do you want them to marry Korean or will you let them marry
whomever they want?"

> J: You know what? I think it's very beneficial that you share the same culture,
>   very much so, because you don't have to explain too much, you know? You
>   don't have to pretend too much . . . It's *very* beneficial, but it's their own deci-
>   sion, whatever they feel comfortable with. It's their life and I'd support them.
>
> N: So you'd be okay if they wanted to marry, you know, Caucasians, Latinos,
>   Blacks? . . .
>
> J: Absolutely, absolutely. I'd support them.

Other longtime immigrants, however, proved more contradictory in their
views and perhaps verged on mimicry of socially desirable answers. For instance,
seven-year resident Ms. Li (age 42), who related that she had almost no interaction
with Blacks and Latinos, had at one point in her interview repeated stereotypes of
Blacks. Yet, elsewhere, she deplores racism as Christianity had taught her to do.

> L: If I think in terms of religion, we're all the same people. If we discriminate
>   against people based on their race or things like that, I don't think it's
>   proper, in the end.
>
> N: So you mean we should get rid of that kind of habit?
>
> L: Right, we should get rid of it.

Ms. Li's citing of Christianity leads to an interesting point about Korean churches
and racial ideologies. Although most immigrants to the United States were already Christian or became church affiliated upon settlement (Min 1996, 2000),
as my sample reflects, I did not find Christian identification to yield noticeable
differences in racial understanding vis-à-vis non-Christians. As in the case of Ms.
Li above, Christian teachings could foster Koreans' liberal views on "race," such
as the scriptural wisdoms of "love thy neighbor" and the concept that all are
equal under God. In fact, in the wake of the 1992 unrest, LA churches expended
impressive efforts to build coalitions with Black Americans (Min 1996:136).[3] At
the same time, however, churches as institutions have been found to hyperethni-
cize Koreans to the point that group boundaries become difficult to cross, enabling prejudice to ripen (H. Lee 1993:64; Min 2000). These variegated patterns

among the predominantly Christian Korean American community likely explain the paucity of clear difference between those who do and do not attend church.

Like Ms. Li above, Mr. Yoo conveyed the complexities of rehabilitating from long-held prejudices. An old-timer, he bemoaned what he perceived as a weaker work ethic among Blacks and Latinos than among Koreans, yet was bent on stamping out racial conflicts. Referring to the 1992 unrest, Mr. Yoo, a radio broadcaster, waxed poetic on why Korean immigrants had to stop carrying over home country norms of looking down on those of lower class and national standing.

> Y: Even though I don't know how well I behave, at least I say that we shouldn't do that . . . When I do the broadcasting, I say, "Let's not do this. Let's get along well. Let's try to understand each other" and make those efforts. Many people use expressions like "Han-Black" [Korean-Black] or "Han-Mex" [Korean-Mexican]. They sometimes take the pastors or teachers of the Black community to Korea to reduce the conflicts . . . They also take the leaders of the Hispanic people to Korea and pay for the whole thing. That's necessary. Even though we can't completely get rid of the mutual antagonism against each other, at least we have to try something . . .
>
> N: Did the riot worsen your views of the Mexican or the Latino people?
>
> Y: No, I thought that we'd done many bad things to them and that we shouldn't do that any more. I think that many Koreans changed their ideas, too, after the riot.

Though Mr. Yoo did not always meet his own expectations, he, unlike Ms. Li just before, conceded the point ("I don't know how well I behave"). He was, therefore, cognizant of his own contradictions.

Trans-Pacific Social Remittances

In light of many first-generation Korean immigrants' experiences with American "race," some share old and new understandings with South Koreans in the home country. As someone who lived through the 1992 unrest and was extremely concerned about another such uprising, old-timer Mr. Han implored his South Korean friends, especially those considering immigration, to deplore racism in ways akin to advanced Western societies. He conflates, then, development status and racial ideology: "We haven't reached the level of being on the global stage." He thus issues an invective against racial prejudice and the harsh mistreatment of (immigrant) laborers normalized in South Korea (albeit a society with a forceful labor movement).

H: They disregard Mexicans more [than Blacks], they treat them so harshly . . .
      First of all, the money problem. Employers, you know, Koreans don't pay
      enough. The sewing companies don't pay properly, neither do the restau-
      rants, so I think a riot will break out for sure, then it'll be crazy . . .

N: So do you tell Koreans in Korea about these kind of things?

H: I tell them all the time.

N: Do they understand?

H: Yeah.

Although it is not clear whether he is motivated solely by the instrumental reason of avoiding another unrest, he does send a message that exercises considerable foresight about "race" in California and the United States. Perhaps his
friends would come in with a much different sense of what American business
hierarchies and practices should be or recognize that the need to be higher than
another group wasn't worth it in the end. Incidentally, his message also reinforces South Koreans' view of their country and its people (wherever they go)
as located in the "middle," as in the "middleman" merchant.

In addition, friends and kin considering immigration often queried Korean
Americans about issues of racial strife and hypercriminality in the United
States, a perspective that had widely circulated since the 1980s. Although these
South Koreans considered all of "America" to be hypercriminal, especially relative to their largely gun-free society, some did narrow their focus on Black
(male) criminality, as popularized by reports of Black American soldiers' violent acts and by sensationalized images in mass media. Not least of these were
the stroboscopic broadcasts of Blacks "pillaging" Korean stores and attacking
people during the unrest. Newcomer Ms. Paik (age 56) was having difficulty
convincing her fearful daughter to come to the United States, as school shootings were on her daughter's mind.

My daughter is in her early 30's, she wants to come here and wants to send her
child to study abroad since her dad and I are here. She's trying to come here with
an E2 visa, but she's a little bit worried, and scared of Blacks. She worries that
something might happen to her child, like when he goes to school with them.
She's scared of coming here . . . So I reassured her by telling her it's not like that,
so not to worry. But when I actually reassure her, I worry too.

She shares a transnational message that could potentially disabuse her daughter
of the problematic mass media stereotypes that saturate South Korean society.

Yet, as a newcomer of one year herself, she had not been in the United States long enough to know what the reality of "race" and crime was. An old-timer, Mr. Bae, also conveyed having to pacify his mother's fears.

> B: Sometimes they worry—when I go on a trip or something, my mom wor-
> ries about it . . . When she worries like that, I tell her that not all Black
> people are bad, nor are all White people good. I tell her that it's just about
> individual personality.
>
> N: Do you think that they believe it? Do they understand it?
>
> B: If I tell them that they don't have to worry that much, they understand it.

In his case, Mr. Bae shares more progressive notions with his parents and seems to believe that they understand. Mr. Han earlier also believed that his friends understood why they had to treat Latino employees in a more egalitar-ian fashion in the United States. The fact that South Koreans, who have rarely (if ever) interacted with these groups, who have often heard reports of Black GI violence, and who were saturated by racist mass media imagery, could po-tentially understand suggests both a shifting society as well as the potency of immigrants' "real-life" stories from afar. On balance, however, immigrants' messages both reinforced and problematized South Korean and American ide-ologies on the peninsula.

In this chapter, I revealed that the first generation, often by way of transna-tional lenses, problematized some of the racial stereotypes and American ide-ologies that had become quotidian in South Korea. In fact, these ideas are not just quotidian, but coveted, owing in large part to the country's nationalist im-pulse to displace a collective sense of inferiority, to be higher than, and not regress back to, the "dark" third world. Once in the United States, the immi-grants recognized that there were many exceptions to homogenized portraits of Whites and poor or criminal Blacks. In addition, they became much more versed in the historical oppression of people of color, including indigenous peoples and Mexican Americans, and either adopted norms of social desirabil-ity concerning " 'race' talk" or reached an earnest denunciation of racism. With regard to Whiteness, on the one hand, many immigrant women felt that their premigrant belief in gender egalitarian White American masculinity was affirmed by their observations of, and interactions with, White American and Korean men in the United States. Yet, on the other hand, the women also sub-scribed to the masculinity ideal as a point of resistance against heightened

Korean patriarchy. The implication of this view and similar idealizations, such as of the White American state, White ethnics, and Whites' good graces—notwithstanding narratives of resistance—is Koreans' persistent sense of inferiority to the White West, to "America."

Importantly, the U.S. racialized system had changed Korean immigrants' understandings, in part by prompting them to add "Asian" to their identity repertoire and to complexify a nation-based categorization system. At the same time, Koreans were reminded that, under certain circumstances, the home country status matters. That is, not only was their Koreanness erased by a larger Asian category, but they were less visible than those who hailed from the most dominant Asian nation, Japan, and the more popular one, China. Of the Asian nations (and by "Asia" Koreans typically meant *East* Asia), Korea was last. This is one index of Korean ethnics' sense of extra-invisibility in the realm of U.S. social citizenship, one that would haunt them throughout their navigation of "America's" stormy racial waters.

6 Korean Americans Walk the Line of Color and Citizenship

"Asian Americans: A 'Model Minority' "

—*Newsweek,* December 6, 1982

Even though . . . a Japanese schoolgirl uniform is kind of like blackface, I am just in acceptance over it, because . . . an ugly picture is better than a blank space, and it means that one day, we will have another display at the Museum of Asian Invisibility, that groups of children will crowd around in disbelief, because once upon a time, we weren't there.

—Comedian Margaret Cho on singer Gwen Stefani's "Harajuku Girls"

A SKEPTICAL READER MIGHT ALLEGE THAT, as immigrants, the informants in my study *are* foreigners. I argue, however, that foreignness has been *racialized* as Asian, has become synonymous with Asianness in the United States. The Chicago School itself propagated the characterization (H. Yu 2002), marking the socio-historical racial context into which Asian Americans enter today. In contrast, the foreignness of recent European immigrants who are phenotypically White would not be assumed unless their accents or stories betrayed them. Yet, Asian immigrants would be assumed to be foreigners on the basis of phenotype alone. It is also dubious, on a practical level, to label all first-generation Asian Americans as "foreigners" when many of them are citizens and partake in mainstream American culture. There is also empirical evidence of the foreigner racialization. Mia Tuan (1998) deftly shows that today's third- and fourth-generation Chinese and Japanese Americans—middle class and successful, no less—continue to endure nativistic racial prejudice and discrimination in their everyday lives. To look Asian, then, is to be foreign: exotic, third world, yellow peril, outside competitor. Yet sociological works have tended to focus on the social dimensions that oppress *Black Americans* as the bellwether of *Asian Americans'* fate, yielding conclusions of Asian groups' racial assimilation with Whites in a recreated mainstream (Alba and Nee 2003) or in a new "nonblack" category (Gans 1999; J. Lee and Bean 2004; Yancey 2003). Still, the White-over-Black model cannot explain why Asian Americans are simultaneously an assimilable model minority but an unassimilable racial foreigner. As Robert Lee (1999:13) argues, "the Oriental" is a complex racial representation in part because of its contradictions.

Margaret Cho's Internet blog critique of entertainer Gwen Stefani at the outset of this chapter is a window into these very complex dimensions of "race." Cho's commentary parallels the Korean respondents' linkage of their own mainstream invisibility in the United States to their position as racial foreigners. Cho adds another layer by preferring derisive "yellowface" over no face at all, yet implies that one day Asian invisibility will become a relic of yore, the stuff of museums. In this chapter I examine the premuseum era in which the persistent invisibility of Korean/Asian ethnics dovetails with, and *stretches* from, the South Korean context. The invisible dimension of the social citizenship line,[1] the central focus of this chapter, is evident in Korean Americans' racialized positions vis-à-vis Whites, Blacks, and Latinos within socioeconomic, political, and cultural structures. Koreans' responses, namely, the way they perceive groups' placement within these structures[2]—those that compose the larger system of color and citizenship oppression—offer a central vantage into the nature of racial inequality. More specifically, this vantage reveals the dominant operations of transnational U.S. racialization and *multiple* axes of U.S. racial formation (beyond the singular color line). As those who reside on the margins, the vantage of the immigrants also reveals the interplay of pre- and postmigration cultural logics and forms of resistance. A key theme among the immigrants is the deleterious consequence of invisibility—considering the power that flows from recognition—in the racialized orders of the United States and the world. It is in this vein that Koreans continue to voice the imperative of being "in the middle." It persists as a way to "redress" the dogged saddle of invisibility, one that weighs down immigrants even more in the United States owing to a new status as foreignized racial minorities in a country not their own.

Bringing in the Premigrant Cultural Toolkit

Previously, I demonstrated that imperialist racial formation in South Korea yielded a racial triangle. Although Koreans there were intimately aware of their subordinate position to White America along global and local lines, with respect to Black America they deemed themselves a lighter-hued, middle-class populace with origins in a higher-ranked blood nation (above Africa). The triangle also placed Black Americans, as both members of the occupying military and of the U.S. White-Black binary , as more globally visible and more politically powerful, and thus as more "American" than Koreans or other non-Whites in the domestic United States.

These racial and national positions in South Korea both map onto and get reconfigured by the American racialized system. In broad terms, the first generation's field of vision gets moved toward a primarily "race"-based, not nation-centered, system. As well, the immigrants move from a home country in which the primary and nagging concern is the Korean nation's status in the world. Now, Koreans live in "the imperial center" (Lowe 1996), in an immigrant country that *is* a microcosm of the world. This shift, coupled with an American fixation on "race" and Koreans' foreignized status, direct Koreans' attention more forcefully to the *internal* racial hierarchy of the United States, notwithstanding their persistent global perspective. Finally, in contrast to South Korea, the first generation is socially located relative to a fourth major recognized group: Latinos. This multiracial *reality* of the United States belies the binary construction of the country as White and Black, a binarization upon which most inequalities depend, as postmodernist thought has shown (see Glenn 2002, chapter 1).

Although on a theoretical level the racial triangle is suited to the South Korean case, it is not apt for the U.S. racial context. I argue that in the United States the citizenship and color lines are less discrete and thus overlap and work in circular fashion. Moreover, Latinos are a prominent American group. Despite, in my estimation, the model's limitations, the two axes that it posits are *conceptually* and *analytically* useful. I borrow and modify these two axes in my analysis of the dialectic between top-down racialization and bottom-up responses among Korean Americans. Although I reserve a more in-depth discussion for later in the text, I should point out here that I conceptualize the plight of invisibility as interacting with visible foreignness on the citizenship line. Hence, I conceive of the citizenship divide as not strictly "Insider-Foreigner," but as "Insider-Visible"–"Foreigner-Invisible." I further expand on the theory by conceptualizing the color line as interacting with social class inequality; rather than just "Superior-Inferior," then, the poles become "Superior-High Socioeconomic Status (SES)–Inferior-Low SES." I believe this interaction is central to the color line precisely because it is central to the racial ideologies and material experiences of Asian and Black Americans—for Asians, the Asian model minority, suburban neighbor, and (overseas) economic competitor; for Black Americans, the Black ghetto criminal, unwanted neighbor, and welfare queen; and, for both, the limits of middle-class status to eclipse any of these ideologies and experiences.[3] Finally, as I have shown, social class is a central and *conspicuous* form of inequality in South Korea through which the immigrants interpret other forms of inequality—namely, "race" and nation—and do so in both countries.

The Superior-High Socioeconomic Status–Inferior-Low Socioeconomic Status Axis of Racialization

Socioeconomic Stratification in California

Paul Ong and Tania Azores (1994:125) contend that Korean and other Asian Americans' middle-class standing in their sending countries accounts for why a significant number of Asians in Los Angeles (and beyond) has achieved American middle-class status. Census 2000 data reveal that almost 44 percent of Korean Americans in Southern California[4] age twenty-five and over were graduates of four-year colleges, higher than the rate for non-Hispanic Whites (hereafter referred to as Anglos; 33.3 percent). Many had also held professional and white-collar positions in South Korea (E. Yu and Choe 2003). Yet, and not unimportantly, many Koreans have achieved middle-class status in the United States through the lower-status occupation of ethnic entrepreneurship, an otherwise effective way to overcome labor market disadvantages like limited English-language proficiency, nontransferable professional credentials, and nativistic racial discrimination (Min 1996; P. Ong and Azores 1994; Yoon 1997). In brief, entrepreneurship has served as many Korean immigrants' channel (though, often a rough one) into the American middle class. Table 6.1 provides an overview of Korean Americans' socioeconomic characteristics relative to Whites, Blacks, Latinos, and the Asian American population writ large in Southern California.

In comparing small business ownership among the three Southern California groups, Koreans have a much higher self-employment rate than that of Blacks and Latinos: 21 percent versus 4.9 percent and 6.3 percent, respectively (E. Yu and Choe 2003). In the United States writ large, almost 37 percent of Koreans operate small businesses with employees while 11.3 percent of Blacks and 17.7 percent of Latinos do (comparatively, Koreans' average sales/receipts are also higher; E. Yu 2001). Moreover, Mexican workers, most of whom are undocumented, constitute the largest proportion of Koreans' workforce at 48 percent (Min 1996). Other socioeconomic characteristics are similarly suggestive. As Table 6.1 shows, Korean Americans' household incomes are only slightly higher than those of Blacks and somewhat higher than Latinos' in

Table 6.1 Socioeconomic characteristics by "race"/ethnicity, Los Angeles–Riverside–Orange County, California, 2000

Group	Educational attainment (bachelor's or above)	Employment		Household income (U.S. dollars)	Poverty rate
		Private	Small business		
Non-Hispanic White	33.3%	74.8%	11.0%	$55,082	7.6%
African American	17.8%	69.4%	4.9%	$33,526	23.3%
Latino	6.9%	83.8%	6.3%	$36,154	22.6%
Korean American	44.5%	71.5%	21.0%	$37,957	15.1%
Asian American	42.6%	79.1%	9.3%	$50,896	13.1%

SOURCE: Eui-Young Yu and Peter Choe, Social and economic indicators by race and Asian ethnic groups and Korean population density map: Top 5 metropolitan areas, 2000 (paper presented at Conference of Korean American Coalition–Census Information Center, San Francisco, September 12–14, 2003).

Table 6.2 High- and low-skilled professionals by "race"/ethnicity and gender, Los Angeles County, California, 1989

Group	Men		Women	
	High-skilled professional class	Low-skilled professional class	High-skilled professional class	Low-skilled professional class
Non-Hispanic White	36%	11%	34%	21%
African American	16%	22%	22%	27%
Latino	8%	32%	12%	50%
Korean American	26%	22%	23%	33%
Asian American	26%	22%	22%	44%

SOURCE: Paul M. Ong and Tania Azores, Asian immigrants in Los Angeles: Diversity and divisions, in *The new Asian immigration in Los Angeles and global restructuring*, ed. Paul M. Ong, Edna Bonacich, and Lucie Cheng (Philadelphia: Temple University Press, 1994), 100–129.

Southern California, but Blacks (23.3 percent) and Latinos (22.6 percent) have a higher poverty rate than Korean Americans (15.1 percent; E. Yu and Choe 2003).

In addition, Table 6.2 shows that more Korean/Asian American men hold high-skilled professional positions than Black and Latino men do. Interestingly, Korean/Asian American and Black women's representation in the high-skilled professional class is roughly the same.[5]

Finally, owing to many Koreans' immigration for the purpose of their chil-

Table 6.3 National suburban and urban concentration by "race"/ethnicity, 2000

Group	Suburbs	Cities
African American	33%	53%
Latino	45%	47%
Korean American	57%	40%

SOURCE: Eui-Young Yu, Korean population in the United States as reflected in the year 2000 U.S. Census (paper presented at the Population Association of Korea Annual Meeting, Seoul, Korea, December 1, 2001).

dren's educations given a merciless schooling life and college entrance system in South Korea, many are suburban residents. Although 45 percent and 54 percent of Korean Southern Californians would have to move, respectively, into an Asian American and Anglo neighborhood to achieve full integration in each, 65 percent and 78 percent would have to move into a Latino and Black area, respectively, to do so (P. Ong and Azores 1994:123).[6]

Table 6.3 reveals suburbanization on a national level: 57 percent of Korean Americans live in suburbs and 40 percent live in central cities, more suburban-friendly numbers than is the case for Blacks and Latinos.

Referring again to Table 6.1, it is noteworthy that Korean/Asian Americans have higher educational attainment than Anglos, yet lower median household incomes despite, on average, more earners in their households. Tables 6.1 and 6.2 both show that they also have lower rates of professional/managerial work and have almost double Anglos' poverty rate. In summary, these socioeconomic data point to Korean/Asian Americans' place roughly "in the middle" of the socioeconomic order of Southern California, though notable exceptions exist.

Korean Immigrants Interpret the "Model Minority"

When I asked Koreans directly about racial hierarchies, such as which racial/ethnic group was most powerful in the United States, they reacted as if I was asking the obvious. In addition to saying, "Americans, of course!," many Koreans named Jewish people as even more economically powerful than Anglos. They attributed this feat to the Jewish community's small size, hence, larger proportion of successful people. In fact, for many Korean Americans, Jewish people's "merchant-to-upper-class legacy" in the United States inspired them to follow their forerunners. As longtime transmigrant Ms. Yi said: "If we could get to Jewish people's level, then we'd have made it," implying that Korean Americans had yet to do so.

Although Korean immigrants squarely positioned themselves below Anglos and Jews, they carried over their sense of "middle" positioning above Blacks from South Korea. In this way, their perception of themselves in the middle, and their attendant pride, did not originate in the American model minority ideology per se—at least, not consciously so. Definitions of the ideology—sometimes called the model minority myth—converge around the notion of a "homogenous" Asian group with a "distinctive" cultural penchant for hard work, delayed gratification, academic excellence, and political passivity, a group that can be traced to some Orientalist ancestor (see C. Kim 1999; Osajima 1988; Prashad 2000; Suzuki 1989). Importantly, the ideology emerged as a hegemonic political tool to discredit and "discipline" 1960s Black and other social movements, to represent the opportunity structure and the American dream as color-blind, and to make Asian Americans a buffer between Whites and Blacks (Louie 2004; Prashad 2000). Virtually no Korean immigrant (including old-timers) had heard of the term "the model minority" or knew what it meant. Mr. Che, an old-timer, saw it in a Korean newspaper and actually did not agree with it (in his view, these newspapers "exaggerate[d] things" like Korean success). Everyone else's lack of engagement with the "model minority" likely has to do with the term's prominence in mainly mainstream U.S. discourse and academic circles, an important testament to the salience of premigration notions as opposed to strictly American ones. Indeed, an analysis of the home country context reveals that education was the cornerstone of existence there, hence, high performance in school is not *simply* a form of adaptation to the United States as assimilationist frameworks would stress. In fact, U.S. dominance in South Korea likely hampers Koreans' ability to *anticipate* White Americans' "celebration" of them as model minorities in the United States. Moreover, I did not come across any evidence of the U.S. occupational forces systematically using model minority ideologies in South Korea.

That said, upon explaining to the informants that mainstream Americans have described Asians as more hard working and, thus, more socioeconomically successful than other racial minorities, few were surprised by the sentiment. It was, after all, the way Koreans had long thought of themselves. Armed with their preexisting preference for pale skin, sense of their nation as "middle class," ethnocentric pride in their blood, and stereotypes of Blacks as low-class soldiers or criminals (especially among later cohorts), Koreans naturalize the socioeconomic conditions in Southern California. For instance, immigrants spend much time in Koreatown (Hanin Town) and become quickly aware that predominantly White Beverly Hills is on one side and the predominantly poor ghettoes of Black and Latino South Los Angeles are on the other. In Hanin Town they also observe Mexican and Central Americans, sometimes darker-hued people from poorer nations, working under Koreans (see Min 1996). Yet, irrespective of how much time they spent in "K-town," the first-generation's mostly coethnic circles typically precluded them from knowing the middle-class Black and Latino communities (or pockets of) a bit farther afield.

Against this backdrop, Ms. Yi (age 76, 21 transnational years) echoed the sentiments of many when she associated Koreans' socioeconomic strength in the United States to their high educational attainment in South Korea, an oft-used proxy for intelligence. She draws on the home country's state-administered, severely competitive college entrance system in which the smart people "naturally" get the best educations and thus "naturally" attain the highest social posts. By contrast, her exposure to low-income Mexican immigrants meant that this group did not hail from such a background.

Y: Most of the Koreans that immigrated to the U.S. have scholarships and are educated people so rather than the Mexicans who come here and do all that difficult manual labor, Koreans' level/status is higher . . . Mexicans do all the hard work: pushing carts, they carry all the heavy stuff in restaurants, they help move people's belongings, those are the things that Mexicans do . . . Koreans don't really do that type of manual labor; either [they] do well in a business enterprise and live well off or educate their kids well and those kids get good jobs; this is a common occurrence among Koreans. When I see this, I think that Koreans are smart . . .

N: You mean smarter than other nationalities?

Y: Yes (chuckles, slightly embarrassed).

N: Do you think they're smarter than White Americans too?

Y: Well, Whites are smart too, but Koreans are smart enough to succeed and move up here . . . not anyone can do that, right?

Ms. Yi dichotomizes Koreans as those who do not do manual labor and Mexican Americans as those who do. Yet, not only had I seen many Korean Americans do manual labor in my lifetime, many of my respondents had also started out doing manual labor or were still in such jobs (e.g., janitor, shipper/mover, storage). Although she is aware that Whites are dominant, she sees Koreans as exceptional for being able to "leapfrog" past the class of manual laborers. Koreans' success despite being in a brand new country, not speaking the language fluently, and experiencing racial bias is confirmed by the group's place in the socioeconomic order around her.

Although those who had spent less time in the United States tended to express more one-dimensional views of the work ethic of Latinos (and Blacks), those who had lived in the United States for a longer period tended to have more variegated and nuanced views (see J. Lee 2000). Still, however, this group demonstrated an inconsistent engagement of social desirability norms and antiracist ideologies. For instance, Koreans who either employed, worked with, or served Mexicans in Korean businesses had both positive and negative notions of them (see K. Park 1991). On the one hand, old-timer Mr. Oh remarked, "I'm close with Mexicans [co-workers]." Yet in another statement, he still understood them with respect to a rigid South Korean class hierarchy in which acute deference must be paid to superiors, "They can't think bad about Koreans ... [because] all the Mexicans that know Koreans are all working under Koreans." In addition to such statements, Koreans would recycle the refrain of their group's status as the most diligent in the world (*puchirŏnhae*). Proclaiming their harder work ethic than that of even White Americans, they would repeat, "They sleep eight hours, we sleep four."

Ms. Yi and Mr. Oh are also lucid examples of how Koreans' general need to boast about, and maintain, their status above Latinos and Blacks is traceable to their more heightened insecurity (and, I will show, invisibility) in the United States than in South Korea. Although they were the "ex-nominated" majority back in the home country (i.e., the reference group with the power to label, albeit in an occupied country; Bhattacharjee 1992), they became first-time racial minorities (Espiritu 1989) for someone else's labeling in the United States; everything mainstream around them reminded them of their difference. With respect to everyday living, Ms. Yi was feeling uncertain about her future life in California as an immigrant woman living without her husband (he had recently passed away), and Mr. Oh's musical ambitions had yet to take off in the United States, leaving him bereft of financial security still ten years after his arrival. Both had also experienced interpersonal racial discrimination in the United States, an unfamiliar experience in Seoul. The insecurity of hailing from a subordinate and invisible home country carries over to their need to underscore their "middle" status in the United States. There is little reason otherwise for many Koreans to feel compelled to boast constantly about how smart and diligent they are and to proclaim proudly that they are higher than other groups. Koreans' statements are defensive in another way wherein complacency about their middle status can *displace* the possibility of failure, the possibility that all their immigrant struggles would come to naught. Their need to believe in the deliverance of the American dream yields the Janus-faced ethos that poor people (of color) simply have not capitalized on tremendous opportunity.

American media texts themselves, even the most well-intentioned, mark Blacks' (and others') subordinate position as emblematic of a failed Protestant ethic. Despite the commendable work of media texts like *Roots* (1981) in exposing the horrors of Black enslavement by White America, the dramatic miniseries ultimately reinforced the "anyone can make it" ethic. About the miniseries, Herman Gray (1995:78) aptly writes:

> With *Roots* the popular media discourse about slavery moved from one of almost complete invisibility (never mind structured racial subordination, human degradation, and economic exploitation) to one of ethnicity, immigration, and human triumph. This powerful television epic effectively constructed the story of American slavery from the stage of emotional identifications and attachments to individual characters, family struggles, and the realization of the American dream.

The noted Protestant ethic motif in *Roots* and countless other media texts, its congruence with Confucianist exhortations about work ethic, and the naturalization of unequal systems by both, explain newcomer Ms. Kang's (age 46) hegemonic view of Black poverty despite her "horror" upon watching *Roots* in the home country.

K: But when I came here and saw for myself how they [Blacks] were living here and how they were acting, I kind of thought that they brought it upon themselves. They do things that make other people look down on them.

N: What do you mean?

K: They don't work. I personally think that even if you're not well off in the States, the system is, uh, good.

Her subscription to the American dream ideal naturalized in many media texts and by the state itself precludes Ms. Kang (and any American, really) from comprehending institutionalized racism and thus tracing current Black American poverty to it. As *Roots* itself promoted, Blacks need only take advantage of "America's" endless bounty of opportunities to achieve success; those Blacks who do not have only themselves and their unused bootstraps to blame (see K. Park 1995). The timing of entry, that is, sociohistorical context, is also crucial here, as most Korean immigrants did not arrive until *after* the 1960s social revolutions and the gauntlet the 1960s threw down to meritocracy ideals. In addition, those Koreans who came *after* 1992 had witnessed Blacks targeting Koreans for being the entrepreneurs in the middle and for being successful. Such antagonism serves only to retrench the Protestant/Confucian notion of Blacks not taking advantage of the richest system in the world, a mantra that Koreans have heard and will hear over and over again in the United States. In addition, those old-timers who identify with the Republican Party (owing largely to Christianity) would be further indoctrinated by this "logic," although irrespective of religion the respondents echoed Ms. Kang's sentiments (she herself, a Buddhist). In light of these factors, it should not be surprising that Koreans, as is true of most Americans, are unaware of the structural causes of Black poverty.

Certainly, there are Koreans who depart from the article of faith that their group works harder than any other. Some subscribed to the view that Asians, Whites, Blacks, and Latinos alike had to give it their all for every penny. In addition to problematizing views of their group as *exceptionally* diligent, some Koreans, old-timers in particular, actually criticized their group for working *too* hard and not fulfilling other important responsibilities. In response to my question of why Mr. Han thought Korean/Asian immigrants had achieved a modicum of success in the United States, he replied:

> Because they're diligent, they're diligent people (*puchirŏnhae*). They work day and night! They concentrate on money [but] because of that . . . they don't do a good job of teaching and training their children . . . Though it's good to be diligent, what's the motive for their diligence?: it's not for others, it's not for society, but it's only for "myself," only for making big money, so they ruin their children.

His narrative shows that such hard work undercuts other dimensions of both Confucian and model minority ideology, namely, devotion to family and adherence to collectivism. Another old-timer, Mr. Jung, problematized the notion that Koreans were the best example.

N: So do you think it's true that we're working harder than these other groups and that they should follow us, or do you think that's not really accurate?

J: Yeah, but Koreans are working too much, actually . . . Same in Korea. In Korea, actually, you know a lot of them work harder.

N: Here, do you mean like the immigrants wak[ing] up very early and . . . ?

J: Yeah, they wake up early, work 16 hour days sometimes. That's what *I* did so that's why, that's why I feel this way (laughs)!

Koreans like Mr. Han and Mr. Jung thought that Koreans worked too hard to become solidly middle class or to make "big money," often at the expense of family time. By "big money," many Korean immigrants also referred to the need for coethnics to prove their success (read: claim a sense of worth) by showing off material markers of wealth as is normative in South Korea among the higher classes. Another old-timer, Ms. Jang, did not agree with most Koreans that they were socioeconomically higher than Blacks and Latinos. She based this sentiment on Koreans' weaker agendas in the world of business relations.

J: We're all mixed up.

N: Really, then could we be below them?

J: I think I rate it about the same because it's okay to be proud of the Korean people and [say] they work so hard . . . but guess what? If you go in another community, there is a sub-portion of people just like us. They have a lot of leadership . . . I didn't have an opportunity to *know* other communities all the way until the last ten years, but I had an opportunity to work with the Latino community . . . And I was so surprised, they're very successful in what they do. Sometimes I wish that our Korean community people could see their [Latinos'] strengths, too . . . Even in small business, they're *so* kind to their clients and they really want to make sure they're doing business for the *future* clients, not just the current clients. I think we're a little bit weak . . . The Black and Latino communities focus on *tomorrow*.

Despite some of the informants' sense that Koreans were in a similar socioeconomic strata as Black and Latinos, more often than not Koreans relied upon a transnational frame of ethnic nationalism to explain social class stratification in Southern California. Such a frame meant that they were "somebody." In the following section, the Korean immigrants demonstrate their transnational lens on social citizenship and the limits of model minority valorizations.

The Insider-Visible–Foreigner-Invisible Axis of Racialization

As Claire Kim (1999; see Ancheta 1998; Hondagneu-Sotelo 1997; T. Lee 2005; Okihiro 1994) has shown, the United States is not structured by just one racial division. Beyond the color line is the racial divide of citizenship, one that need not hinge on skin tone but on other heritable traits. About the citizenship line, Jeffrey Alexander (1992:290) aptly writes, "There is no civil discourse that does not conceptualize the world into those who deserve inclusion and those who do not." Here I focus on Korean Americans' experience of the *invisible* dimensions of being on the excluded or, better yet, differentially included (Espiritu 2003), side of "America." I depart, then, from studies that conceptualize the Asian American foreigner status as *solely* a status of the visible pollutant who needs to be purged or contained by federal exclusion laws, by Supreme Court proscriptions of citizenship, and Executive Orders to mass incarcerate—what Claire Kim (1999) aptly calls "civic ostracism." Moreover, Asian Americans are not just *visible* examples of how non-White foreigners evince the meritocracy that is "America." What I *add* to these groundbreaking insights is Asian groups' status as unknown, ignored, hence, "un-citizen"—another dimension of foreignness, one that is especially damning given that identities do not exist outside of recognition of them (see Gutmann 1994). An unrecognized identity, then, is tantamount to not existing. Moreover, an identity recognized (usually by the nation-state) accretes onto itself resources and privileges (e.g., see Espiritu 1992).

As they were in the home country, Koreans were viscerally distraught over their invisible "citizenship" within the United States. Recall the emotional distress of Ms. Kang when the airline had Japanese interpreters but not Korean ones. As I have shown elsewhere, Koreans trace this invisibility to the long history of external subjugation that denied them the recognition that was rightfully theirs. Had their history been different, Koreans imply, their nation could have been on top of the world, or at least higher than it was now. Among the immigrants in my study, Americans' weak knowledge of, or complete ignorance about, Koreans was always linked to a reminder of the home country's low status in the global order. Newcomer Ms. An (age 57) invokes this reminder in her account of Americans' (particularly Whites') inability to distinguish amongst Asian ethnics.

> N: When people couldn't tell what country you were from, did that make you feel more like an Asian as opposed to a Korean, or no?

A: Yes, certainly. If our country was bigger and richer and was more well-known, then when I'd tell them my country it would be more well-known.

Similarly, three-year immigrant Ms. Baek (age 46) was greatly disturbed by Americans' ignorance about Korea (and greater familiarity with China).

You know, when I first got here, I went to a different state, Texas . . . There, I felt it right away, because when you go to some market or walk down the streets when people ask about my nationality they would ask me if I was Chinese. They didn't know Korea at all! I'd say that I am from Korea, "I AM KOREAN" (enunciated slowly in English), but they still didn't understand! They're not familiar with us. Of course not everybody was like that, but since we're such a small minority here, people know about the Chinese but a lot of people don't even know about Koreans!

The narratives reveal multiple dynamics underpinning Koreans' sense of their own foreignness. First, she is reminded that Korea is less familiar than China in Americans' eyes.

Second, not only do dominant White Americans erase Koreans' ethnicity, but, at times, they demonstrate complete ignorance about the Koreas. In this way, Korean immigrants continue to live the paradox of insignificance that many of them had endured before coming to the United States: "America" being in Korea but Korea not really being in "America."

Invisible Vis-à-Vis Black Americans

In part because of U.S. society's ignorance about South Korea, Korean Americans have been placed *outside* of the social citizenry, hence, made to be nearly invisible in the national culture. As I have noted throughout, Korean/Asian Americans' invisibility is also a *byproduct* of the U.S. racial binary in which peoples who are neither White nor Black are erased and muted. Given the occupation, Koreans were well aware of their invisibility in the binarized national identity before coming to the United States. Owing especially to the 1990s cohorts' increased exposure to Black America through mass media texts, hip-hop culture, the 1992 unrest, ongoing conflicts with Black soldiers, porous borders, and so on, Korean/Asian Americans have become more aware than ever before of the *nature* of their invisibility in the White-Black order: weak political power and weak visibility in the nation's culture. To make matters worse, the model minority myth contributes to such invisibility by implying that Asian Americans do not suffer from racial barriers, in effect, pushing the group even further into the shadows of the nation during "conversations" about "race" and rights. I turn to a brief discussion of the weak political power that has kept Korean/Asian Americans in the shadows of the nation.

Political and Cultural Hierarchies in California and Beyond

The political representation of Korean/Asian Americans in Los Angeles and nationwide is generally low and, in some parts of the nation, nonexistent. Despite the fact that California boasts the highest Asian Pacific American (APA)[7] population in the country and despite the increasing efforts of the predominantly foreign-born Asian populace, APAs' political representation and power pale in comparison to those of Blacks and Latinos.

Even with the sanguine prospect that APAs' political clout will increase as their population rapidly grows, Maria Kong and Peggy Saika (2003) warn that that influence may be largely hampered by internal differences. They add that APAs are hurt by the large number of nonnaturalized and not-yet-eighteen Asian ethnics as well as their small population sizes in most states (under 5 percent in all but five; Kong and Saika 2003). Across these factions, Paul Ong and David Lee (2001) contend that Asian Americans suffer from greater political apathy, conservatism, and inconsistent party line voting, largely traceable to their predominantly foreign-born/immigrant status. Despite a history in the United States that dates back to Filipinos' advent as sixteenth-century Manila galleon traders, APAs to this day have constituted twenty-seven of all possible members of Congress.

As detailed in Table 6.4, the group has had a total of five senators, four from the majority Asian state of Hawaii and one from California, home to the largest Asian American population. In addition, there have been fifteen representatives to the House, most of whom hail from California and Hawaii, as well as seven nonvoting delegates from American Samoa, Guam, and the like. Although Blacks have had an equal number of U.S. senators (five) and Latinos have had one more (six), both groups have had a significantly larger number of representatives of the House, respectively, one hundred sixteen and at least eighty-one (including resident commissioners). Although in 2001 Blacks had roughly 9,101 elected officials nationwide (Bositis 2003), in 2005 Asian Americans had 1,228; of this figure only 162 were Korean American (UCLA Asian American Studies Center and Asian Pacific American Institute for Congressional Studies 2005–2006).

Table 6.4 Members of U.S. Senate and House of Representatives by "race"/ethnicity through 2007

Group	U.S. Senators	U.S. Representatives (House)
African Americans	5	116
Latinos	6	81*
Asian Americans	5	22
Korean Americans	0	1

SOURCES: Congressional Black Caucus Foundation, Inc., http://www.cbcfinc.org.index.html; United States Senate, http://www.senate.gov; National Association of Latino Elected and Appointed Officials, *The 2006 Directory of Latino Elected Officials* (Washington, DC: NALEO Education Fund, 2006); UCLA Asian American Studies Center and Asian Pacific American Institute for Congressional Studies, *National Asian Pacific American Political Almanac, 2005–2006,* 12th ed. (Los Angeles: Asian American Studies Center and Asian Pacific American Institute for Congressional Studies, 2006); http://en.wikipedia.org/wiki/African_Americans_in_the_United_States _Congress; http://www.loc.gov/rr/hispanic/congress/chron.html#1900; http://en.wikipedia.org/wiki/List_of _Asian_Pacific_Americans_in_the_United_States_Congress.
* This number is likely a slight underestimate.

Furthermore, Black Americans have run for the U.S. presidency, some of whom have garnered considerable support for their campaigns. Since the interviews and observations, Senator Barack Obama has emerged as a front-runner for the 2008 Democratic nomination, and by extension, the presidency.

To be sure, California boasts the highest number of Asian politicians, but only recently so. Edward J. W. Park (2002:204) writes that the urban political leadership in Los Angeles was almost exclusively Anglo until the 1960s despite the massive influx of Black, Mexican, and Asian Americans as well as Jews into the city forty years prior. Despite Anglo dominance, in 1973 African American councilman Tom Bradley defeated a White American candidate for mayor by bringing together Black and Jewish voters in a city less than 20 percent Black. Bradley proved to be an institution—he was handily reelected in 1977, 1981, 1985, and 1989. To be sure, even in such cases, Blacks' overall political power may be limited (Waters 1999:41). Although Los Angeles, Washington, D.C., Baltimore, New York, Chicago, and Detroit are all majority minority cities (owing to White flight) and have had Black mayors, they are profoundly shaped by the economic decisions of outside Whites and a distant national government (Waters 1999:41).

Nonetheless, as Blacks have been the most politically visible and influential non-White group, Asian Americans and Latinos have been following their lead. Korean and other Asian ethnics continue to lag behind, however. Nearly three-quarters of the random Korean sample in the 1993–1994 Los Angeles Survey of Urban Inequality declared "no [party] preference" (N. Kim 2004). To be sure, Korean Americans expanded their political activity in the wake of the LA uprising (E. Park 2001; Sonenshein 1996) when they, especially small business owners, recognized their lack of political power as partly responsible for the razing of their stores and ethnic town (K. Park 1997:155). Furthermore, the Korean community expended significant efforts to build political alliances with Black community members (Min 1996). Such efforts notwithstanding, Asian Americans have yet to establish the kinds of political institutions that Blacks and Latinos have built in California despite Asians' concentration and history in Los Angeles. Asian Americans simply have too little political representation on all levels to make such empowerment a reality (P. Ong and Azores 1994:125–26).

To add insult to injury, even when Asian Americans are active in politics, the American mainstream typically ignores them. For instance, the Asian American Legal Defense and Educational Fund (AALDEF) found that Asian Americans overwhelmingly voted for John Kerry over George Bush (74 percent versus 24 percent) in the 2004 presidential election.[8] *New York Times* exit polls[9] also revealed that Asian Americans were the only group (among Whites, Blacks, and Latinos) to have *not* increased its support for George W. Bush in 2004 from 2000.[10] Exit poll surveys of Korean Americans found that in Los Angeles 58 percent voted for Kerry while 40 percent voted for Bush. AALDEF also found that Asian Americans voted overwhelmingly Democratic in the 2006 midterm Congressional elections. Despite these unique and influential voting trends, they were rarely mentioned in journalistic media; any focus on the voting behavior of groups of color referred only to Blacks and Latinos.

Unlike Korean Americans' experience as "outsiders" vis-à-vis the White-Black binary, Blacks' membership in this dyad, whether in political or other realms, marked their stronger insider status, notwithstanding their subordination along the color line. The Korean respondents pinned this understanding on five interrelated comparisons between themselves and Blacks: (1) Blacks' greater power and recognition (from Whites) in the realms of politics and national culture; (2) their longer history in the United States; (3) their larger population; (4) their better English facility; and (5) Whites' greater familiarity with Blacks, especially given the aforementioned characteristics. I turn now to the criteria that Koreans invoked to demonstrate Blacks' more "insider" status relative to Asian Americans.

Politics and National Culture

Strikingly, Koreans were most consistent and coherent as a group when discussing their invisibility relative to Blacks. After all, Koreans hailed from a home country in which Black soldiers exercised the political power that flowed from being American. Even Ms. Yoo (age 48), who had recently settled in the United States, had noticed the difference: "It is really hard to see Asian people involved in politics. Occasionally, I see one or two people involved but that's it. Politically, I feel that Blacks are a little above us Asians." She recounts a story to prove her point:

> I've felt the disadvantages of being a minority here . . . Like the doctors, lawyers: even though some Koreans make it into the high class society, compared to White lawyers Koreans wouldn't have much power—like that time when three Korean grandmothers were crossing the street and got killed by a car. They didn't receive any compensation! I believe that it happened because we Koreans don't have much power. I get really upset when these kinds of incidents happen.

She implies that if Korean Americans had had more political power, the grandmothers would never have been dismissed as unimportant. In so doing, she notes that Koreans who climb the professional ladder to become doctors or lawyers, a platitude among Koreans on their children's "many" career options, are still not as powerful as Whites in the same positions. "Race," in this case, eclipses social class. Another informant, longtime Mr. Yoo (age 49), lamented Koreans' low participation in U.S. politics despite a high number of naturalized Koreans.

> They're not interested. Why? Because they became American citizens only to get welfare or things like that. That's wrong. They're not doing what they should do as real Americans. They're not real Americans if they only get what they want and don't give back. Isn't that true? They should vote. Only when we have a higher percentage of the vote, the White House or Washington D.C. will recognize that Korean Americans are active in politics too. *Blacks have that, but we don't!* We're not recognized in that way. (emphasis added)

Here Mr. Yoo makes Koreans culpable for being less active in politics, though he may be overestimating the first generation's lack of interest and underestimating the barriers to participation. Nevertheless, he believes that Korean Americans have a lot of catch-up work to do if they are to gain the attention that Black Americans have from Washington, D.C. Had he been interviewed in 2008, he would likely use Senator Barack Obama's well-received campaign for the U.S. presidency as a case in point. Similarly, another old-timer, Mr. Oh (age 34), claimed he could not place Blacks in just one level of the U.S. hierarchy.

O: Black people participate more in politics than us. They have better participation in politics than us.

N: More than us? Than Koreans?

O: Yeah, of course. There are more politicians. I recognize that.

Elsewhere in the interview, he had used a pan-ethnic lens to exhort that
"Asians," not just Koreans, "had to get more involved!" In recognizing the
much larger number of Black politicians, people like Mr. Oh were also conced-
ing that fewer Koreans than Blacks had assumed a social post considered one
of the most prestigious in South Korea. They also implied that the first generation's reentry into the middle class by way of entrepreneurship did not necessarily integrate them into the political mainstream, toward more authentic
Americanness.

Importantly, the respondents knew that Korean / Asian Americans lacked
not only elected representation but symbolic representation in the political
sphere. Their fixation on this invisibility seemed to extend from their long-
standing concern with their "homeland's" invisibility in a world that referenced the United States / West. They were not visible in American history (the
Korean War = "Forgotten War") nor were they visible as political leaders or
icons, all central dimensions of the national culture. Although the Korean respondents themselves were intimately familiar with iconic Abraham Lincoln,
John F. Kennedy, and Black American figures like Martin Luther King Jr. and
Jesse Jackson, citing some of the foregoing as their heroes, they had no Korean
political leaders or icons whom all Americans would know; neither did the
other Asian groups. In fact, Charles Moskos and John Sibley Butler (1997) contend that Black Americans have contributed so much to the nation that they
deem American culture to be "Afro-Anglo culture." Over the last few centuries,
they argue, African and African American culture has influenced Euro-
Americans in such a way that both groups have created the core national culture that is today's "America." In contrast, they note that other groups like
Korean and Cuban Americans have not been in the United States long enough
to have significantly influenced American culture.[11] The Korean American respondents in my study agree. Many cited Martin Luther King Jr. as an ad-
mirable political and religious leader, a view certainly validated by American
history books (and, more recently, by the mass advertising campaign of Apple
Computers). In contrast, old-timer Mr. Sohn (age 73) said the following about
Korean / Korean American iconic figures.

S: We're really a minority, even among the minority races!

N: Have you ever personally felt that here?

S: Yes, I have, sure. There aren't many of our people or things that are well known here, like our politicians, ministers. None of our Oriental medicine doctors are known. I feel that we really are a minority race.

Mr. Sohn makes a direct link between invisibility and a status as racial minorities within a White majority.

Koreans expressed similar viewpoints about the nation's popular culture. Although they could rattle off many Black American artists and entertainers of household-name stature, such as Whitney Houston and Denzel Washington, old-timer Mr. Yoo lamented Koreans' invisibility in popular culture, much akin to the way comedian Margaret Cho does in the opening epigraph. I asked him, "What should Koreans do to improve their status?" He replied:

Y: We should work in more various fields. Koreans have improved their economic status quite a lot and have achieved the average income of the White American family, but what we still lack are Koreans who work in every field of society: everyone's concentrated in just a few. There are tons of lawyers, tons of medical doctors, but there are few Koreans in fields like the entertainment business. Do you know why?

N: No, why?

Y: The parents prohibit it. "You should be a lawyer, you should be a doctor," they say to their children. That leads the children to do something they don't really want to do . . . There should be people in politics and business, we should have great musicians, artists, and novelists. By that time, when we've settled down in various fields of the American society, we will also be treated fairly.

Consistent with the argument of this chapter, even a status as a doctor or lawyer did not spare Koreans the stigma of foreignness. It is entering into various realms of U.S. society—politics, corporations, arts/entertainment—that will beget recognition and less racial bias. Yet, in advising thus, he does not conform to a multiculturalist celebration of differences, as if groups were on a "level" playing field à la the salad bowl motif. Rather, he acknowledges a hierarchy of difference, one in which Koreans would need to be among the *dominant* White strata to realize the kind of recognition that could eclipse unjust treatment. His conviction that Korean faces in all the mainstream jobs and cultural spaces would invite greater acceptance is reminiscent of past cultural efforts to overcome denied legal and social citizenship. Novels like Younghill Kang's *East Goes West*, Carlos Bulosan's *America Is in the Heart*, or John Okada's *No-No Boy* demonstrate that Asian Americans have used culture to contest their civic exclusion as "Orientals" and to reconfigure what it means to be "American" (R. Lee 1999:13).

American History

Per the emphasis on ethnonationality, Korean immigrants associate one's history in the nation with authentic belonging in that nation. As a predominantly immigrant populace in the United States, they did not feel that they shared Blacks' membership in the nation. Ms. Jun (age 49, 30 years in United States) traced it to African Americans' longer history in the United States.

> N: So you think that, um, Blacks have more political power than Koreans and Asians do?
>
> J: Right now, yeah, yeah, of course! Because they came first.

Another respondent, Mr. Che (age 56, 20 years in United States), had owned a small business in a low-income Black part of Chicago when he first immigrated, yet perceived Blacks to be quite powerful.

> C: Economically and politically, in every way, Anglo-Saxons are definitely at the top since they founded this country, politics, economy, all that. Then the Jewish came and influenced . . . that's how I see it in America.
>
> N: Then who's next?
>
> C: Next, the Black people have an established history in America, therefore I'm sure they have influence.

His placement of Blacks just below Jewish people in the economic and political power structure despite his years of interaction with low-income Blacks attests to the value he places on shared history. He invokes it again in a statement on Whites' better treatment of Blacks than Asian immigrants in the Chicago neighborhood.

> N: Did you ever feel that you experienced racism, such as in certain places or . . . ?
>
> C: Yes I did, but it was the invisible kind. As an example, we Asians and Blacks had many problems but whenever that happened the White police came and took the Blacks' side . . . and never took the Asians' side, that

happened several times . . . They are better to them than to us Oriental people.

N: Why do you think that is, in your view?

C: I think the Blacks have a longer history of living here and White people are just more used to seeing Blacks than Asians, that's why.

Mr. Che's is an interesting, counterintuitive claim given scores of cases of White-on-Black police brutality as well as model minority notions that imply Whites' proclivity toward Asian groups. It is still plausible, however, that the White police were more familiar with Blacks (e.g., had ties to the community), perceived Asians as foreigners, had difficulty understanding them, sought to pacify charges of racial profiling against Blacks, and so on. Nevertheless, Mr. Che believes that the White police subordinated an Asian like himself because he was less familiar. He may have also been connecting the Chicago police to the LA police department's neglect of a burning Koreatown at the hands of mostly Black and Latino protestors in 1992.

Group Size

Population size was also extremely important to Korean respondents. They went from seeing mostly their own faces to being largely invisible in mainstream America. Therefore, they were attuned to being a much smaller group than Black Americans. Newcomer Mr. Gil, for instance, followed up his view of Asians' general lack of power in the United States with this statistic: "As far as I know, in terms of population, Asian people account for less than 10 percent." In addition, some had an erroneous sense of just how populous Blacks were in the United States. Consider old-timer Mr. Oh's (age 34) confusion over my reference to Blacks as "minorities." With a quizzical expression, he asked,

O: Aren't there a lot of African Americans here in America? There are a lot of African Americans here!

N: Oh, right, right. I just used the word "minorities" because that's how they're officially classified.

O: That's how they classify?

N: Yeah, to the best of my knowledge.

O: Oh, my God. You should have told me!

Another respondent, a newcomer named Ms. Min (age 26), made the same assumption as Mr. Oh. Owing to her categorization of Koreans and other

non-Black groups of color as *numerical* minorities, Ms. Min classified Blacks
as members of the majority.

> N: Well, whom do you think are right below Whites, then [in terms of
>   power]?
> M: You mean based on ethnic groups, just whatever I think?
> N: Yes, just what you think in general.
> M: Blacks, and then minorities.

The last two narratives reveal an overblown sense of how large the Black population is in the United States, especially in light of the fact that Latinos have
slightly edged out Blacks in size and, like Asians, are one of the fastest growing
groups. Yet Koreans' thinking might also be the product of a certain teleology.
That is, Blacks' large numbers signified their more "American insider" status
than other non-Whites, although it could have also been precisely Blacks' more
insider status that made their numbers seem larger than life.

English Proficiency

With the advent of the U.S. occupational forces in South Korea, the English
language became a national obsession. Not only do South Koreans frequently
use English rather than *hangŭl* for their store signs, consumer goods, TV commercials, and pop songs, English is mandatory in the school curriculum. Parents with means compete ferociously to get their five-year-olds into the top
schools, which boast the best English language programs. The English language, then, reminded Koreans of their Otherness and inferiority long before
arrival in the United States, something that one could not instantaneously
"get" like Dr. Millard's plastic surgery.

   Although South Koreans learn a great deal about written English, their
training in speech is considerably weaker. The predominantly foreign-born
status of the group in the United States (82 percent in 2000) also accounts for
their relatively low level of English-speaking proficiency (P. Ong and Azores
1994). Census data from 2000 reveal that among adults eighteen years and
older, 29.3 percent of Korean Americans speak English "not well" (UCLA
Asian American Studies Center and Adachi 2004). Lamenting this reality,
twenty-six-year resident Ms. Pak described how even for first-generation immigrants with PhDs, limited English proficiency was a patent barrier to mainstream participation.

I think it's harder because I didn't go to school here . . . I don't have much of a problem with daily conversations but if I wanted to become a leader, the head of an organization, it's hard without a formal U.S. education . . . So first-generation Koreans even with a PhD cannot do things like teaching because they have problems speaking English. They might know a lot but they can't express it well, so it's always limited.

Rather than blame the monolingualism of the United States for devaluing all languages besides English, many respondents focused on their own need to better their proficiency. Newcomer Ms. Kim invoked the difference between Blacks and Korean/Asians when she traced her group's political invisibility to their relatively recent immigration. When I asked whether long-tenure groups like Blacks participated more in politics, she pinpointed language: "Yes, since they have better English language skills." I asked another newcomer, Ms. Joo (age 47), if she felt that U.S. minority groups shared some kind of similarity.

J: Well, Blacks have grown up and lived here so they have their own set of issues that they deal with, but among Asians or Latinos, I think as soon as we get here, our lives get extremely busy and we don't really have the chance to move into a higher class because our major problem is language.

N: So you're saying Blacks don't have that problem?

J: No, Blacks, because they were born here and can speak the language, they're different from us, Asians and Latinos.

Ms. Joo stresses the similarity between Latinos and Korean / Asian Americans in relation to Blacks as English speakers.

Familiarity: "Whites Found Out Who Was Coming to Dinner"

Koreans carry over their sense of partial presence at the hands of Whites from the home country. They arrive painfully aware that White Americans in South Korea were and are complacently ignorant and disrespectful of the nation they occupy. The insignificance of Korea in the American center bore this out. Because Koreans had to wrestle with the persistent paradox of America-in-Korea without the inverse, they fixated on Whites' familiarity with Blacks. Despite their awareness that Whites continued to oppress Blacks, they believed that Blacks' presence in the national identity and culture flowed from Whites' familiarity with and recognition of the group. Much of what Korean Americans have previously stated already supports the point, but it is worth reiterating here. For old-timer Ms. Jun, the first non-White group that came to mind as possibly breaking through the barrier of White U.S. presidents was Blacks. In her narrative, she had started by saying that U.S. society would never really treat any minority person as an equal, but quickly followed with: "Maybe I'm wrong. Like I said, maybe 100 years from now it may be different, you know? You may have the Black president, you never know." In light of Senator Barack Obama's front-runner status in the Democratic presidential primaries at the time of this writing, it will be interesting to see if a Black president will be elected in much fewer than 100 years.

Others denoted Blacks as culturally American or simply called them "American" with no qualification. Old-timer Mr. Han, for instance, con-structed Blacks as "totally American" in thought and practice. As such, he be-lieved he would have more in common with a Latina wife than a Black wife, similar to others' logic that Koreans and Latinos were both outsiders to the White-over-Black paradigm. Another respondent, five-year-immigrant Ms. Noh, agreed and showed a partial awareness of social desirability in the process: "I think there are many smart African-Americans, you know, anyway they're American, they've been living here a long time."

More Invisible Than "Foreigners"

Mexican Americans and Central Americans.   Thus far, an overview of the first generation's understandings of "race" hierarchies in the United States re-veals that along the color line, Whites are positioned at the top ("Superior-High SES") while Blacks and Latinos are generally at the bottom, a pole marked "In-ferior-Low SES." In comparison, the Korean respondents position their group and other Asian Americans in the middle of the axis. On the citizenship line they position their group toward the "Foreigner-Invisible" pole, while Blacks are toward the "Insider-Visible" end (occupied by Whites). Here I discuss Koreans' positioning of themselves vis-à-vis Latinos along this citizenship line.

Parallel to the case of Asian Americans, the general Latino population has been foreignized by way of U.S. conquest and imperialism in Latin America, yielding a similar conflation of Latinos and their home countries. Asian Ameri-cans and Latinos are also similarly racialized as foreign immigrants and economic threats. One difference, however, points to the way in which Asian Americans' foreignness is hegemonically centered on essentialist notions of exoticized differ-ence (à la *Orientalism* [Said 1979]) and on more formal wars and tensions. Latinos' foreignness in the United States—and especially Mexican Americans' status in California—tends to depend hegemonically on *legal* status (Hondagneu-Sotelo 1997) and on the pejorative view of much of Latin America as underdeveloped.

Against this backdrop it is not surprising that Koreans conceived of Mexicans and Central Americans as similar to them: both were predominantly immigrant groups and "neither-White-nor-Black outsiders" (see Cheng and Espiritu 1989; K. Park 1991, 1995). Speaking to the racialized foreignness of Latinos, newcomer Mr. Cho made the comment that, like Asians, "Hispanics aren't really Americans either." Other respondents mentioned shared traits between Asians and Latinos, such as variations in skin tone ("light to dark brown," save the blond-haired, light-eyed Latinos), use of a non-English language, and even cuisine ("both are spicy").

This sense of commonality notwithstanding, Koreans positioned themselves socioeconomically above Latinos. At the same time, they considered Latinos less invisible and foreign along the citizenship line. They recognized Latinos' greater population size and stronger political and cultural influence in Los Angeles and nationwide. With respect to culture, Koreans were struck by the ubiquitous presence of Spanish (the unofficial second language of the United States). Akin to their view of Blacks, Koreans like old-timer Ms. Pak (age 51) acknowledged Latinos' stronger political power, hence, greater visibility.

P: Latinos (pause), overall, I think they're doing better than us . . . because first of all, Hispanics learn the language faster and therefore adjust faster, and they're outspoken, speak out a lot. We never do. Asians never really do. We don't have anyone who speaks on our behalf. When there was the riot, who did we have?—that lawyer . . .

N: Oh, Angela Oh [Korean American lawyer interviewed by nearly all major media outlets for the "Korean voice" on the riots]?

P: Yeah, she appeared all of a sudden, but there's no one that's done a lot in particular.

Another old-timer, Mr. Pak (age 54), also remarked on Latinos' and Blacks' political prowess:

P: But in terms of politics, we Koreans don't have many avenues to participate in it.

N: So we're lower than Latinos and Blacks?

P: Lower.

Since the interviews, the election of LA Mayor Antonio Villaraigosa, a Mexican American whom some have described as having indigenous features, as well as massive immigration protests have likely crystallized Koreans' views.

Given Koreans' view of language as an essence of ethnonational identity and a source of power, many shone a spotlight on U.S. society's adoption of Spanish as an informal second language. Koreans even called Mexicans (and other Latinos) by their language: the "Spanish." Although old-timers had been around Latinos for so long that they tended to take for granted the ubiquitous presence of Mexican culture, newcomers really took notice. Ms. Joo, for instance, felt that "Mexicans learn English faster than us." Another newcomer, Ms. Min, perceived Asians and Latinos to share the same strata with respect to power and resources (behind Whites, then Blacks), yet she qualified:

M: I think Hispanics have more advantages here in California though.

N: When compared to Koreans, Asians?

M: Yes, people speak both English and Spanish wherever you go. But you know that Korean is just optional! . . . English and Spanish are always there. I haven't seen a single place where they don't have these two options, no matter what job it is . . . So, I think it's for sure that the Spanish have more advantages.

On the same issue of the overall U.S. racial hierarchy, newcomer Ms. Du (age 24), who perceived language as the linchpin of power, put "Spanish" people right under Whites.

N: Oh, Spanish people. So you think they're higher than Korean or Asian people?

D: Mm, yeah.

N: Why's that?

D: Because in the U.S. almost 40 percent speak Spanish. Language is so important. If I go out and speak Korean no one really pays attention but if I go out and speak Spanish, then a lot of people pay attention because they know how to speak it. I think being able to communicate through language gives you that kind of power.

Here again is the link between recognition and power ("no one really pays attention").

Another undercurrent in the Koreans' narratives was that all White (and Black) Americans were familiar with Mexico. After all, Mexico and California were separated only by an oft-traversed line, not to mention that California was once Mexico. In no way could Koreans say the same about U.S. society's awareness of the Koreas. Finally, the respondents were aware of the commercial explosion of Latino and Latina entertainers.[12] Latinos have gained so much prominence that television network ABC broadcast in 2006 the ALMA awards (Spanish for "spirit"), created by the National Council of La Raza (NCLR), the largest national Hispanic civil rights and advocacy organization in the United States. The fact that a major network like ABC broadcast a Latino awards ceremony and in *prime time* speaks volumes about Latinos' increasing visibility in the United States. It will be interesting to see when, if ever, an Asian American entertainers' award show will be aired on national prime-time television. Owing to these forms of visibility, Korean immigrants saw themselves as the more invisible foreigners than Latinos, akin to their perception of themselves in relation to Japanese and Chinese Americans.

Overview

Throughout their interviews, the Korean respondents conjured up their weaker visibility compared to Blacks in the United States and in the world as the occupation and U.S. "cultural imperialism" had instilled in them. Once Korean immigrants are in the United States, however, their invisibility vis-à-vis White America (and weak visibility relative to Black America) becomes an everyday, interpersonal reality, not just one that extends from macro forces like the military, mass media, cultural economy, and the like. Partial presence in the home country coupled with invisibility in the United States and the world is therefore heartbreaking for many Korean immigrants, whose overriding ambition has been to gain recognition as "equals" of America / the White West and, secondarily, Japan. It is largely this heartbreak that undergirds some Korean Americans' misguided promotion of themselves in model minority–like fashion above Blacks and Latinos. Lisa Sun-hee Park (2005:6) contends that Asian Americans' claim to social citizenship (here, in the Korean case, on the basis of ranking above Blacks and Latinos) serves as an *adaptation strategy* to prove oneself the "good immigrant." They must do this in light of U.S. society's pressure on immigrants to prove their economic worth as the yardstick for whether they deserve to stay. She finds that even second-generation Asian Americans feel perpetually compelled to have to prove their worth as good, model minority immigrants in order to overcome their denied social citizenship (L. Park 2005). In my sample's case, Koreans' ready subscription to the model minority ideology is further abetted by home country frames of color-class-ethnonationality and, importantly, a Californian socioeconomic structure that seemed only to prove the point.

To be certain, one could conceivably argue that Korean Americans' "success," which "confirms" American dream and meritocracy ideals, could signal Koreans' "Americanization." That is, Koreans "become American" by dint of their emulation of the Protestant ethic and distance from the "bad minorities" who supposedly belie the ideal.[13] Yet, I contend, the Protestant ethic is illusory precisely because model minority valorizations of Asian Americans are based on essentialist notions of the "race" and its culture (C. Kim 1999; Tuan 1998). The Orientalism of model minority ideologies attributes Asian Americans' success to their "exotic" cultural practices. Not only does extolling Asian groups in these ways reify foreignness, but model minorities have been excluded, vilified, and murdered precisely for being "foreigners" who are too good at what they do.

Korean immigrants' vantage from the margins revealed how racial/national oppression in the home country and related cultural logics were central to their reception of their social locations in the United States. On a theoretical level, however, the American-centered frame of both segmented and (neo)institutional assimilation models precludes an identification and analysis of such processes. Global/transnational frames fill this lacuna by shining a light on the process of how imperial powers racialize groups long before their "return to the imperial center" (Lowe 1996:16). A global/transnational perspective also affords an understanding of how immigrants themselves navigate racialization across borders. By starting at the point of U.S. foreign relations, then, the home country moves toward the center, away from the periphery, of scholarly analysis. Thus conceived, scholars are able to displace assumptions that often unintentionally extend from American-centered and, at times, ahistorical frameworks. Such a framework could also displace models that employ White-Black inequality as the yardstick for how much "race" matters for Asian Americans and the predictions of "whitening" and racial assimilation that emerge from them. A global/transnational rendering can move scholars toward richer understanding of the different *and* related processes by which groups are racialized, as Claire Kim (1999) brilliantly shows in her theory.

In this transnational and multiracial vein, Koreans, like other Asian Americans, are responding to being unknown-cum-insignificant, but they are also reacting to the civic ostracism (C. Kim 1999)—the repression within so-called liberty (Alexander 1992:300)—that they endure. It is to this form of discrimination as visible foreigners, culminating in Korean immigrants' differential inclusion in the watershed LA unrest, that I turn.

7 Visibly Foreign (and Invisible) Subjects
Battling Prejudice and Racism

I really realized that Korean immigrants were left out from this society and we were nothing . . . Is it because we are Korean? Is it because we have no politicians? . . . Where do I find justice? They [Blacks] have a lot of respect, as I do, for Dr. Martin King . . . he was the model of nonviolence . . . They like to have his spirit. What about last year? . . . I was swallowing the bitterness.

—Mrs. Young-Soon Han, whose liquor store was
destroyed in the 1992 unrest[1]

IF SEGMENTED ASSIMILATION THEORY (Portes and Zhou 1993) were to integrate social citizenship into its formulation—in this case, the conspicuous foreignness of Asian Americans—then its selective assimilation path would likely not conceive of immigrants' retention of ethnicity as solely enabling upward mobility. It would see the retention of ethnicity as also fanning the flames of anti-Asian racial stereotyping and discrimination. Although Korean immigrants rely on ethnic networks to gain socioeconomic security and mobility (e.g., Min 1996; K. Park 1997; Yoon 1997), the benefits of ethnicity are complicated when "race" and citizenship are more forcefully considered. For instance, most assimilation/whitening theories do not consider the fact that Asian Americans' movement up the socioeconomic ladder incites backlash against the "foreigner competition," thus *stunting* assimilation into the national citizenry. Such backlash betrays the relationality of the "model minority" and "forever foreigner" ideologies. As Gary Okihiro (1994:142) has aptly shown, the model minority and the yellow peril are not opposite poles, but "form a circular relationship that moves in either direction." That is, the moments when Asian Americans have been considered "too model a minority"—in other words, too much competition (see Olzak 1992)—are the same moments in which they have been ostracized most virulently as "foreigners" (see Newman 1993). This nativistic racial discrimination underpinned the nineteenth- and twentieth-century anti-Asian exclusion acts spearheaded by European immigrant labor, the acute

Japan bashing during World War II and the 1970s and 1980s, the efforts by elite universities to stem the tide of Asian American admissions in the 1980s (Takagi 1993), racism against Judge Lance Ito of the 1995 O. J. Simpson trial, the racial profiling of Asian American Democrats after the 1996 John Huang–Bill Clinton campaign scandal, the wrongful 1999 imprisonment of nuclear scientist Wen Ho Lee for ostensibly being "a Chinese spy," and many more. Simultaneously, the model minority image can assuage fears of Asian Americans as the masculinized yellow peril and thereby allow both representations to exist side by side (Okihiro 1994).

In more recent years, the 1992 LA unrest is a prime example of the way in which Korean/Asian Americans are simultaneously subordinated by both racial positions, what I call "foreign model minorityhood." The U.S. state's neglect of, and indifference toward, Koreans during and after the unrest shares a disturbing parallel with U.S. constructions of South Korea and its people: unfamiliar and unimportant ("we weren't taught about Korea"), weak, subordinate, and foreign ("gooks," "coolies"). This form of transnational racialization accounts for the similar racial ideologies in both countries (notwithstanding differences) and why these themes emerged in Koreans' descriptions of their bouts with prejudice and discrimination.

Many of the Korean immigrants who experienced the LA unrest and whose voices I share in this chapter spoke with as much passionate melancholy nine years after the event as did Mrs. Young-Soon Han in the chapter epigraph, even if they had not lost a business. Although this chapter focuses on the prejudice and discrimination that Korean immigrants suffer for being a *visible* outsider and a *visibly* successful non-White, it also addresses both dimensions of "foreign minorityhood," wherein the 1992 LA unrest was tragic evidence of Koreans' simultaneous invisibility. In their own retelling, the Korean respondents trace the discrimination and racism they suffer to U.S. perceptions of Korea, to being seen as racial foreigners, and to being too model a minority in the United States. They also saw the factors they highlighted previously as enabling: weak recognition and power in politics and the national culture, Whites' weaker familiarity with Koreans/Asians in comparison to Blacks, uneven English proficiency, a relatively small population, and their absence in the United States at its inception. In the process, they also invoke home country constructions of nation and comparisons between their pre- and postmigration status.

Last but not least, the potency of Korean Americans' resistance is impressive. In light of U.S. dominance over South Korea, immigrants' penchant for pro-Americanism, and their naturalized beliefs about "owners" of nations, they could have *excused* White prejudice and discrimination and resigned themselves to it. Yet, because Koreans suffer as they spend more time in the United States and thereby hone their antiracist lenses (see Chapter 5), they do not take the indignities of "race" lying down. Indeed, their long-standing struggle with external powers like "America" and attendant inferiority issues have in many ways readied them to defend their honor, a fight that some of them expected to wage. For those who do not expect it, however, the contradiction of American democracy and American racism inflames resistance.

Antiforeigner Discrimination on the Job

The incidents in the accounts that follow are examples of Americans' or U.S. institutions' mistreatment of Koreans for "intruding" on the United States. Many of the informants shared their experiences of nativistic racial prejudice and discrimination that occurred in sites in which they frequently interacted with White Americans. For instance, old-timer Ms. Park (age 46) shares a fascinating story about how her sister dealt with a White female customer's antiforeigner prejudice at her small business.

> OK, once, my older sister had an ice cream store and one old lady came, she said (in old lady voice), "Go back to your country!" that's what she said, and my sister who can speak very well, she said, "*You* go back to your country, this is *my* country, I'm a native Indian!" . . . So she said "No! I was born here." . . . [My sister] said, "You get, go back to your country, you came from England!" . . . The woman said, "I pay taxes," so my sister said, "*I* pay taxes, there is no reason, you know, for you to treat me like this . . . If *you* make any [more] noise, please, you'll have to step out because you're not the only customer I have."

Owing to the fact that some Koreans think their group resembles Native Americans in appearance, Ms. Park's sister subverted the White woman's prejudice by taking on an indigenous identity, that is, claiming to be more authentic than a potential descendent of British colonists. From the sister's vantage point, what better way to respond than to claim herself a "Native Indian"?

Other Korean Americans shared incidents that occurred in predominantly White American workplace settings. Many felt that Koreans and other Asian groups faced distinct disadvantages here that denied them a fair shake. These experiences reflect Angelo Ancheta's (1998:66) assertion that one dimension of the foreigner status is that of an outside "competitor," one who incites "economic antagonisms." I present snapshots of four accounts of such struggles, starting with Mr. Koh (age 54, 20 years in United States).

K: After I came here, I felt like I became "yellow."

N: Yellow? You mean, you felt like a yellow minority?

K: Yeah. We are "yellow." We have an accent. At work, it's faster to climb up for Whites, but it's slower for us because I'm an Oriental; immigrants are discriminated against in the company . . . I went to personnel in human resources to report it and to quit . . . There was this White guy [whom I fought with] . . . The manager sided with [him] over me even though I was right, [so] I reported it and went to the personnel department and fought hard to try to get rid of that manager.

The next two respondents traced nativistic racial prejudice to competition over resources too precious for "foreigner" Asians/Koreans but to which Whites felt entitled. In the first passage, Ms. Park (age 46) details White Americans' discrimination against her during her stint as an animator for Walt Disney Company. Because she and many other animators were offered contract renewals if they performed well during an initial probationary period, her success incited jealousy and competition from her White co-workers. In anger, Ms. Park recollected:

P: I thought they were friends, but their attitude changed and they also [started to] report whatever I did, you know, they reported it to my supervisor . . . So I told my supervisor, "Look, I cannot stand any of this," because one of the [co-worker] guys [said], "Oh! I can smell the garlic. I don't like it." [I said,] "What do you mean?" [He said,] "You ate *kimchi* [spicy Korean dish], right?" I hadn't eaten *kimchi* at that time, so eventually I told him, "Oh! I don't like cheese, the smell of cheese!" you know? They said, "Oh! I don't like you." They found out I had a master's degree. They didn't like it. Caucasians don't like it, you know . . . Eventually I couldn't stand it, because at that time finances were stable enough for me, so I said, "Without you guys and this job, I can do whatever I want." That's why I quit the job.

N: Oh, you quit?

P: Yeah, which I regret to this day because the salary was so good (laughs). Yeah, but also people had said that Caucasians had discriminated, you know, against any Asian or Black, whatever. I didn't want to believe it, you know? But it really happened that directly. You know, to point out, criticize the way I talk, . . . the smell I have, those kinds of things, it was really cheap. [modified]

Mr. Bae, another old-timer (age 43, 15 years in United States), understood Whites' antipathy as fostered by their own unwillingness to match Koreans' diligent work ethic and related fear of losing out to Koreans and other Asian ethnics. As in Ms. Park's example, backlash against the "foreign" competitor inspired the discrimination.

B: When they look at how hard we Koreans and Asians work, they think that they'll lose their jobs because of us. There'd be no problem if they just worked harder . . . I also experienced that in a previous job, for example, with the manager. Because I had more personal experience, the owner preferred me in terms of my quality of work and everything, so as someone higher-up than me, the manager was very jealous of me.

N: How do you respond when you experience such attitudes?

B: I'm kind of patient. I tend to tolerate a lot and overcome the situation that way. For example, that manager said racially discriminatory things to me, but I just couldn't stand it after a while. Because of that, I once had a big fight with the manager. I can stand everything else, but that kind of racial discrimination, I can't.

When I asked another old-timer, Mr. Sohn (age 73), if he had ever experienced any racial discrimination, he recounted a vignette from the early 1980s involving a White male co-worker at a meat-packing plant. His story thus differed from the others insofar as U.S. dominance over less-developed Korea, not necessarily competition, was the apparent subtext of the slur, a mimicry of U.S. state ideologies abroad. With verve, he recollected:

I had an argument with a co-worker . . . I had a lunchbox with me, but I dropped it when someone bumped into me. Then this White guy came up to me, pointing at my lunch box saying, "That's made in Korea, isn't it?" So I yelled, "NO! Look at this, this is 'Made in USA.' " I told him to *look* because back then the products that were made in Korea, like now the stuff made in China, were considered really cheap. But now people respect the Korean products that say "Made in Korea." I was so very angry then. I put it right in his face and said, "Look it! 'Made in USA!' "

In addition to Mr. Sohn's subjection to derogatory American perceptions of Korea, Ms. Park herself ("Disney") was belittled by her White co-workers for eating the Korean food kimchi and smelling like garlic (a staple of Korean cuisine), that is, for polluting the erstwhile White and modern American office with her smells of the lower country. In both cases, the two were made painfully aware of Whites' pejorative views of Korea and of their embodiment of the country, despite their status as Americans.

The narratives reveal other thematic similarities, notwithstanding important differences. Both longtime blue-collar worker Mr. Koh ("yellow") and Ms. Park underscored being "Asian" and having poor English skills as the source of Whites' discrimination against them. As is typical among the U.S. informants, they, along with Mr. Bae ("manager"), showed their pan-ethnic sensibilities by characterizing the discrimination as anti-*Asian*. Ms. Park and Mr. Bae also specified that this prejudice rested on Whites' view of them as Asian/"yellow" economic competitors, again, as too good at what they do. Mr. Koh and Ms. Park both characterized the moment as not just an individual-level event, but as part of an institutional problem—Mr. Koh: "Because I'm an Oriental; immigrants are discriminated against in the company" and although Ms. Park quit Disney, she felt she had to, as: "people had said that Caucasians had discriminated, you know, against any Asian or Black, whatever." Taken together, these experiences seemed to yield a more textured understanding of the U.S. opportunity structure than that which they first brought with them. Although all four members revealed their faith in hard work to propel them upward and that "race" could be tempered by social class, they also perceived "race" to be insurmountable in light of glass ceilings, White Americans' fear of immigrant and Asian competition, and derogatory views of Korea.

"Race" could also seem insurmountable because U.S. antidiscrimination laws have yet to expand to include considerations of subordination along citizenship lines. Asian Americans thus suffer from weak protection in the workplace, particularly in comparison to antidiscrimination laws designed for Black Americans (Ancheta 1998:80). Importantly, the lack of consideration for nativistic racism, immigration, and Asian–U.S. relations by the state could only exacerbate Asian Americans' sense of alienation in the White American labor market. Mr. Koh, for instance, felt that there was no one at his workplace to represent his grievances toward his White American supervisors. Ms. Park did not get the backing she desired from her supervisor. And, as small business owners like Ms. Park's sister, Koreans generally have little institutional recourse with customers who come in and act on their racial prejudices. At the same time, all four respondents did not passively allow the barriers of "race" to go unchallenged. For Mr. Sohn, a newly arrived immigrant, to shove a lunchbox in a White male's face when likely surrounded by lots of other "Americans" arguably took guts. He resisted his co-worker's slur by defending his own Korean identity and home country. Also striking was how Mr. Koh ("yellow") and Ms. Park ("Disney") quit their jobs as a strategy of resistance. Despite the fact that they really needed those jobs, or later realized that they did, they chose not to face constant racial assaults at work and to contribute to a company that did not support them. Even mild-mannered Mr. Bae ("manager") who normally tried to avoid exploding over racism could no longer stand the slights of his White manager and fought back. Their forms of resistance reveal that they considered the antiforeigner treatment—that is, being treated as beneath White workers, outsider immigrants who took resources, bad English speakers, and "backward" third world people[2]—to be unconscionable. They believed that Asian immigrants like themselves had a right to be in the United States and to all the resources and privileges of White Americans.

Another old-timer, Mr. Han, shared a story about discrimination from his time working at his grounds maintenance job. It was unique from the four above in that he was not sure what caused the trangression. This uncertainty reveals that the burdens of "race" do not simply involve clear, explicit forms of bias and discrimination, but the very fact of having to wonder whether "race" was the basis of such treatment (see Feagin and Sikes 1994). After I asked him, "Have you ever experienced racial discrimination in the U.S.?" he replied:

H: Of course, several times . . . I had many bad experiences with African-Americans, and White people are racist.

N: Oh, you mean in general?

H: Yes, naturally. But the problem is its extent, whether it's harsh or just a little, but for example, when I was cleaning once in Ventura, I went from building to building with a bucket . . . That was twenty years ago. A couple of young White people came close to me with their truck, then they threw out *all* the water in my bucket. I don't know if that's because I'm Korean or not.

What is immediately striking is that this is the same gentleman who deemed Whites "nice" and the world's "greatest citizens," suggesting that contradictory perceptions ("White people are racist") can coexist. It is also interesting that this twenty-year-old incident stuck out in his mind amidst his many noted struggles with racial prejudice (perhaps being at the mercy of White youth was most humiliating). He had shared elsewhere in his interview how he was once beaten and held at gunpoint by Black Americans because "they thought all Koreans had money." Like him, many other Korean Americans had claimed that Blacks and Latinos seemed to discriminate against them just as much as Whites did, if not more. Whether or not such a perception is accurate, it is safe to say that the hegemony of "race" and racism leaves no one immune from racial ideologies, as the accusations traded between Blacks and Koreans have laid bare.

In fact, the respondents identified the key government offices to which all immigrants had to report, like the then-Immigration and Naturalization Service (INS) and the Department of Motor Vehicles (DMV), as the loci of their worst experiences with Blacks and Latinos. Because 25.7 percent of Blacks, and increasingly Latinos, proliferate in federal and state government jobs in Southern California (E. Yu and Choe 2003) and the Golden State writ large (Jiobu 1988), Koreans' legal rights and privileges often seemed to be sanctioned or proscribed by Blacks and Latinos. In this context, Korean immigrants tended to express anxious vulnerability. For instance, recent émigré Mr. Hune (age 26) shared what he considered to be a Black DMV tester's bias against him.

> I have not gotten my driver's license yet. I got 100 percent correct when I took the written exam. When I was out for the road test, a Black guy rode with me. I have driven for 8 years . . . I'm a good driver, but when I took the exam, . . . he asked me to make a right turn. I answered, "Yes" because I wanted to give the impression that I was polite; I wanted to let him know that I could understand English and communicate. He said, "Hey, hey, hey, ssshh!" And when he first came out, I'd said, "Nice to meet you. I'm [Ron]," but he said, "Hey, sshh, let's go." That made me angry, so I think he fundamentally does not like Koreans . . . [So] after that, he told me, "Park over there," then he said, "Too far!," but he said it really harshly, not nicely. It made me really angry, so after that I drove really roughly, even crazily (makes noise), *Voom voom wee!*, so that's why I failed. I let him off at the DMV, so I still carry an international driver's license to this day.

Mr. Hune's driving test for his license put him in a subordinate position to a Black American DMV examiner, one who would determine whether Mr. Hune would be able to drive in California, a state in which one is practically immobile without a car. Moreover, it was in the moments that he tried to demonstrate that he could understand English (indicating his anticipation of the examiner's foreigner stereotypes) that the examiner responded rudely in Mr. Hune's eyes, ultimately angering him. In his narrative, when he wonders whether the gentleman did not like Koreans, he elaborated later that perhaps the LA unrest had fueled such animus. Koreans were thus cognizant that beyond Korea's low or competitive status and its dirty smells, American events such as the "riots" fueled prejudice. As we have seen, many Koreans attributed their fear of, and anger toward, Blacks to the "riots" they watched in South Korea. In another instance, young newcomer, Ms. Suh, spoke to these interminority tensions when she said: "Blacks and Latinos get more picky with us, they discriminate more, while Whites are nicer." Yet she along with others would name their struggles with discrimination at the hands of Whites elsewhere in their interviews. Perhaps Korean Americans simply remembered Blacks' and Latinos' bias against them more readily because they expected Whites to be the biased ones and because it stung to be mistreated by another minority. Perhaps those who were most affronted were driven by what they perceived to be Blacks' and Latinos' disrespect for Koreans' socioeconomic position above them.

The Language of "Race"

In the following narratives, anti-Korean and anti-Asian subordination hinges on language discrimination. Nearly all of the respondents had some tale about mistreatment on the basis of their accented or barely there English. Koreans' ire over such mistreatment extends in part from their longstanding sensitivity to the language "handicap," a key variable holding up their sense of inferiority. As an example, soft-spoken seminarian student Mr. Ha (age 27, 8 months in United States) stayed on the theme of Blacks' and Latinos' discrimination against Korean immigrants in government offices.

H: They have a tendency of looking down upon people who do not speak English that well, or don't know the procedure; like if you go to the DMV, you don't know what to do or if you go to the bank, the system is really different. And even [if] you're really good at English, you don't know the vocabulary at all, so then they just kind of look down upon those people.

N: Did you ever feel like someone looked down upon you because they thought your English wasn't perfect?

H: Uh huh, in the bank or DMV, especially African Americans or Latin Americans . . At the DMV I was almost fighting with the Black guy, yeah. [modified]

Although John seemed to be soft-spoken and even-keeled, he chose to actively resist what he considered discrimination. Old-timer Mr. Yoo relayed a story about Whites' denigration of Asian English.

Y: If your pronunciation is strange, some Americans pretend that they don't
understand you, I've heard about that happening a lot . . . [T]hey pretend
not to understand and ask, "What? What?" repeatedly.

N: Have you ever felt that way?

Y: Of course, of course! . . . I remember soon after I'd come here, when I was
buying something in a supermarket, this happened. Though I thought to
myself that it was possible that they truly hadn't understood me, at that
moment, I was suspicious and wondered, "Is it because I'm Asian?" No
matter what, it's very possible that that would be why.

His narrative links Whites' sense of language superiority over Asian Americans
to their sense of racial superiority. Simply put, language is racialized. Some respondents, especially newcomers like Mr. Pai (age 26), stated that they had yet
to experience any racial discrimination, in part because they were always
around Koreans. When I asked Mr. Pai about mistreatment based on language,
however, an anecdote immediately came to mind.[3]

A while ago, I went fishing; we of course brought our permits. We brought
everything we'd possibly need but those officials came over and asked, how long
were we there, they asked that kind of thing . . . I couldn't communicate in English; we'd say something, then they'd say, "No, no, no!" As we were leaving, I
heard them say something like, "Oh I really don't want to meet those kinds of
people again" . . . I thought, "You little twit, you try coming over to Korea!" and
I was so upset that day anyway because I hadn't caught a single fish! (mutual
laughter)

Despite this obviously unpleasant experience with law enforcement, Mr. Pai had
initially not considered the officers discriminatory, mentioning that it seemed
natural given South Koreans' own discrimination against non-Korean-speaking
foreign workers in the "homeland." Yet, owing to the link between language and
nativistic racial subordination, it is not surprising that Mr. Pai said afterward, "I
guess that's a form of racism, huh?" He is an example of how newcomers start
to learn that imperfect English is associated with an Asian racial phenotype.

Being Invisible

The above instances of discrimination demonstrate Koreans' visibly foreign
status in a country in which White Americans are the normative citizens and,
by dint of the binary, Blacks are the secondary Americans. Yet, aside from

being a visible outsider, Koreans also related their invisibility, a plight that had long troubled the group, because it reified a sense of not existing or of existing as an insignificant people. Although it is more difficult to track such forms of discrimination, some of the Korean respondents spoke of being made to feel only partially present and insignificant. Ms. Song, who had emigrated a little over three years ago for graduate study (and who spoke near-fluent English), described her early days in Texas: "When you go to a very good shop, expensive shop, they don't talk to you, right? Unless you dress very, you know, you're dressed up or whatever. They don't talk to you, they totally ignore you. And I think it has something to do with my being Asian. Well, in Texas, there are not many Asians at all."

Although Ms. Song intimates that dressing as if one is wealthy attracts sales associates' attention, she also states explicitly that her Asian phenotype is what makes her not worth the time, that is, it makes her invisible to the workers there. Her linkage of invisibility to the small population of Asians in Texas can be embedded within Korean Americans' larger discussion of being unfamiliar to (White) Americans, hence, easily ignored.

Another respondent, Mr. Oh (age 34), felt most like "a minority," when he recounted being ignored at a restaurant where there were no Asians but, in his words, mostly "White and Black people," the two groups whom he considered to be "American" throughout his interview. After I asked Mr. Oh, an old-timer, whether he had experienced discrimination, he replied:

> O: In some situations . . . like yesterday. They don't look at me, they don't look at me like this (gesticulating eye contact). I think the fact that they don't look at me makes me feel like I'm being ignored.
>
> N: Oh, that they don't look even once?
>
> O: Yeah, not looking at me at all. They think of me as a puppy or a statue, or something like this . . . I went to Utah once by bus. Over there, they look at you like this (imitates a shocked face) because there aren't many Asians, they look at you really weird. In California, there are a lot of [Asian] people . . . and supposedly they are very kind, kind to minority people, yeah, I don't know (chuckles nervously), personally, I never felt that they [were] nice to me because I'm Asian, but I think that they will [some day]. [modified]

In his narrative, he weaves between being invisible (being ignored in the restaurant) and visibly foreign (being gawked at in Utah), revealing that the lived experience of Korean/Asian Americans often involves both dimensions. Most striking about his narrative is the way he compares invisibility to being inhuman: a "puppy" (e.g., an animal, a sidekick) or a "statue" (e.g., inanimate). Much like the protagonist of Ralph Ellison's *Invisible Man* (1952), he felt defined rather than able to define himself.

The 1992 LA Unrest: A Case of Invisibility and Differential Inclusion

No historical moment better captures the racial visibility as well as the invisibility of Korean immigrants than the 1992 LA unrest. Furthermore, nothing elucidates better the U.S. state's grip over South Korea, a power that affords it the liberty to do what it wills with Korean Americans domestically. In many ways, the federal and state government's neglect of Korean communities and livelihoods also presupposed Korea's and the immigrants' lack of power (hence, lack of consequential reprisals). What would the ROK state do? Punish the United States and risk losing the military troops that safeguard them from North Korea/the world and the U.S. investors that keep their economy alive? What would Korean Americans do, a group with relatively weak political power? Even when South Korean officials ventured to Los Angeles and walked amidst the rubble, they left without doing much of anything (Abelmann and Lie 1995:28–29). In short, the U.S. government's decision not to assist Korean Americans is a sobering reminder of the U.S.–Asian relations and the global racial inequalities at the heart of anti-Asian subordination (K. Chan and Hune 1995; Espiritu 2003). Under this formulation, then, the U.S. state's high regard for and intimate ties to Japan could have yielded a more favorable response. To be sure, such responses are largely determined by diplomatic relations at the time, as made painfully clear by the World War II mass incarceration (and the early 1990s was tense between Japan and the United States), yet the global and local connection remains.

Although the U.S. state's neglect points to Korean Americans' invisibility, mass media discourse brought the group into view by writing about and televising them as victims and victimizers. Mass media coverage was thus a key architect in representing Korean Americans as at once hard-working model minority victims (Cho 1993; Palumbo-Liu 1994) and foreigner ghetto merchants (E. Kim 1993; J. Park 1999). The former construction, the immigrant model minority victim, was invoked during the unrest to delegitimate, as it had historically, Blacks' claims of institutionalized White racism. On this pattern, Sumi Cho (1993:203) found that conservative journalists painted Korean shopkeepers as hard-working, law-abiding members who became "a surrogate army acting out the white suburban male's American dream—bearing arms against Black men." They singled out Korean Americans as "legitimate victims" worthy of "praise and sympathy" (Cho 1993:203; see Palumbo-Liu 1994). By so doing, conservative opinion makers exercised the process of differential inclusion—in other words, integrating the group into the nation with little power to represent itself to serve the ends of those with such power. That is, elites legitimated the ideology that the White American system was not the problem, Blacks were.

Yet, Korean Americans were not just constructed as hard-working model minorities wronged by Black and Latino gangbangers. Mass media and public discourse also represented Korean merchants as foreigners, as not-Americans. For instance, images abounded of Korean immigrants wailing unintelligibly in the Korean language as their entire livelihoods turned to ash and dust around them. Another endlessly recycled clip was of Korean American men as handkerchief-clad, gun-toting vigilantes, shooting indiscriminately and hotheadedly at unknown targets (although many of them had been shot at first [E. Kim 1993]). The profound impact of foreigner constructions like these was manifest in the heaps of hate mail sent to University of California, Berkeley, professor Elaine Kim by self-identified White Americans who were incensed by her personal essay in *Newsweek* magazine. In it, Dr. Kim had accused the news media of "using Korean Americans and tensions between African and Korean Americans to divert attention away from the roots of racial violence in the United States," implicating the corporations and the state in the unrest and in Black and Korean Americans' general lack of understanding of each other (E. Kim 1993:222). Her many detractors responded thus:

> How many Americans migrate to Korea? If you are so disenchanted, Korea is still there. Why did you ever leave it? Sayonara.

> [Her] whining about the supposedly racist US society is just a mask for her own acute inferiority complex. If she is so dissatisfied with the United States why doesn't she vote with her feet and leave? She can get the hell out and return to her beloved Korea—her tribal afinity [*sic*] where her true loyalty and consciousness lies [*sic*].

The denigration of Dr. Elaine Kim as a forever foreigner—a "model minority" University of California, Berkeley, professor, no less—is at the heart of the foregoing prejudiced rants. For one, she made clear in her essay that she was born in the

United States, where her parents had been for six decades. The angry letter writers also seemed to forget that six decades was longer than the tenures of many Euro-Americans. Moreover, that the letter writers showed so little sensitivity toward the plight of Korean Americans a mere three weeks after the unrest is also telling.

Adding insult to the injury sustained by the "surrogate white" and forever foreign Korean American community (Palumbo-Liu 1994), media discourse also pegged Korean Americans as *the ultimate* anti-Black racists. Recognizing the perennial red herring, one all too common to processes of differential inclusion, Cho (1993:203) argued that such finger-pointing served to deflect attention away from institutionalized White racism: "Already anguished by the not-guilty verdicts of the four white police officers, liberal journalists sought to redeem themselves . . . From this angle, Korean Americans, not white Americans, became the primary instigators of racism against African Americans." Indeed, "Korean racism" against Blacks became a virtual article of faith owing to the endless, stroboscopic broadcast of a Korean female merchant shooting a Black female teenager in the back of the neck. The incident occurred in South Central Los Angeles in March 1991 (around the time of the Rodney King beating) when Soon Ja Du fatally shot LaTasha Harlins after a dispute and a physical altercation between the two. Notwithstanding the LA Korean community's claim that Ms. Du was mentally unbalanced (Cho 1993:204), the sentence she received was essentially a slap on the wrist: a $500 fine, probation, and 400 hours of community service. Judge Joyce Karlin, a White American woman, meted such a sentence on the grounds that Du was not a menace to society (see K. Park 1996). Irrespective of the speculation over Karlin's designs on political office, the sentence, coupled with the ubiquitous image of Du shooting Harlins and White police officers abusing Rodney King, solidified Black community protest against Korean Americans. In the end, Black and Korean Americans suffered from the mutual prejudices that were fueled and refueled by the mass media and elites (Abelmann and Lie 1995; Cho 1993; E. Kim 1993).

The Invisible Victims (and Victimizers) of 1992

Notwithstanding the brutal murder of Harlins and the reproof of her killer, Du, the invisibility of Korean Americans reared its head when the numerous homicides of shopkeepers in Black and Latino communities were met with indifference, with few killers brought to justice. In the wake of three murders of Korean American merchants in one day, a Korean American social service worker asked in a manner reminiscent of Mrs. Young-Soon Han in the epigraph: "Yes, her [Harlins's] life was important, but what about the dozens of Korean merchants? What about their lives? Don't they matter?" (Abelmann and Lie 1995:152). Eui-Young Yu (1992) found that within a two- to three-year span beginning in 1990, at least twenty-five Korean American merchants had been killed by non-Korean gunmen.

As noted, the model minority myth has partially reproduced Korean / Asian Americans' invisibility by celebrating the group as politically passive. In light of these depictions of apathy, the mainstream mass media frequently mute Asian Americans' voices on political issues even when those issues bear on them directly, such as the 1992 unrest (E. Kim 1993). If any Asian groups garner attention at all, they are usually Japanese and Chinese Americans, also true of the coverage of the unrest (E. Kim 1993). This sleight of hand made Elaine Kim and other Korean Americans "sensitive to an invisibility that seems particular to us. To many Americans, Korea is but the gateway to or the bridge between China and Japan." Such liminality also revisits the possibility of a more favorable U.S. response had the entrepreneurs and town been ethnically Japanese, notwithstanding other potential responses.

The most salient way in which Korean Americans were rendered invisible, however, was the noted nonresponse of the police and fire departments in Korean Americans' time of greatest need. There is no starker contrast to this inaction than the government's deployment of thousands of National Guardsmen and military personnel to preempt attacks against the richer, predominantly White neighborhoods of Beverly Hills and Westwood. Although Koreatown is nestled between these posh communities on one side and South Central Los Angeles on the other (with whom its lines are blurred), the troops ran past the thick smoke billowing from Koreatown and "South Central" toward the choice real estate and designer boutiques of predominantly White Los Angeles (see E. Kim 1993). Hurting the cause, the mass media granted little airtime to the nonresponse, saying little about the frantic 911 calls from Koreatown and South Los Angeles during the first two days of the unrest, April 29 and April 30, and about the few police or fire trucks that came. The coverage thus failed to underscore U.S. government / police negligence as the reason why Korean American men could not rely on the police and had to take up arms themselves. Had the media discourse done so, the sensationalistic clips showcasing Korean vigilantes' "alien" behavior (i.e., shooting "senselessly" from store rooftops) would have been cast in a whole new light.

Many of the informants, particularly old-timers who had endured the unrest and who had generally a more sophisticated understanding of U.S. "race"
relations than did newcomers, focused on White America's erasure of, and indifference toward, Korean Americans and Koreatown (see K. Park 1995). Despite the respondents' identification of Black Americans as ultimately responsible for the physical destruction, old-timer immigrants consistently traced the
source of the unrest to Whites' oppression of Blacks. In fact, Koreans' exposure
to this "American Dilemma" in the home country in news stories and conversations, Hollywood movies, and, for some, personal experiences seemed to cement their deep awareness of this cancer and of its spread to Koreans as a third
party in the United States. After all, the 1992 unrest had erupted in response to
the acquittal of four *White* police officers who had severely beaten *Black* motorist Rodney King.[4] Moreover, the acquittal was meted out by a mostly White
jury in predominantly White and conservative Simi Valley, a home to many
police officers over forty miles north of "South Central." At the same time, Koreans' belief that Blacks were the majority of the "rioters" when Latinos were in
fact the largest number arrested (E. Park 2002) testifies to the ongoing potency,
from Seoul to Los Angeles, of the White-Black lens through which they make
sense of "race" in the United States.

In the respondents' retelling of the fate of Black and Korean Americans
could be heard the vocabulary of "institutionalized racism," though indirectly,
given the use of the term mostly among scholars/activists. Focusing on such
racism against Blacks, old-timer Ms. Go responded thus to my query about her
knowledge of the unrest: "*In my view, it's a White and Black conflict.* Koreans
were the victims who lost in this, you know what I mean? We were just innocently subjected to that. Fundamentally, it's a Black-White conflict, how the
court ruled wrongly against Rodney King so Blacks rioted, but it was us who
became the victims" (emphasis added).

Unlike Ms. Go, however, most of the respondents also traced the unrest,
its ability to persist for so long and wreak such havoc, to the U.S. state's remiss indifference. They pointedly blamed White America for ignoring Korean Americans' cries for help, turning them into unnecessary victims of institutionalized discrimination. In recollecting Koreans' torched livelihoods
and charred ethnic hub, many respondents' indignation rose with their
voices. As a broadcaster at Los Angeles's main Korean ethnic radio station,
Radio Korea, old-timer Mr. Yoo's ire revealed how close he was to the scene
and to the facts of the case.

Y: All the police blocked them when they were heading towards Beverly Hills from the South area, but there were absolutely no police at all around the Koreatown area. They just let them do it. That's a very important fact, actually! . . . They wouldn't have treated it like that if, for example, it had happened in a purely White-concentrated area! They would've defended it even with some military troops, so why didn't they? It's because it's a place where minorities live, that's why.

N: Do you mean, then, that it was racial discrimination when the White police didn't help Koreatown?

Y: Yes, I even thought that right at that time. I even said it in my broadcasting. I said that it was "discrimination." What I told you now is actually what I said in my broadcasting at the time.

Mr. Yoo's broadcasted interpretation was likely quite influential, as during the unrest Korean merchants and militia groups depended on Radio Korea's reports for their respective responses to the bedlam. Another old-timer, Mr. Che (age 56), who had said that it was *sa-i-gu* (4-2-9, or 4/29, the first day of the unrest) to which all his feelings of being "a minority" in the United States were harnessed, felt similarly cheated.

If this were Korea the police probably would have prevented the thefts, but these police officers were just standing there watching . . . even though they saw it they let them steal. On the street when some Koreans tried to put out a fire, the police stopped them from doing it . . . It's these things that I don't understand! I don't know if they [police] were out of their minds, or what, but think about it, the riot started out in the Black area, then spread to Koreatown, then to Beverly Hills—it was only then that the police started to be more active. I realized then that they [Whites] only protect themselves.

Mr. Che believed that if the unrest had happened in South Korea, the leaders would have identified with the "victims" by virtue of shared ethnic/national identity. In the United States, the gulf between Whites and Korean Americans excluded his group from consideration as fellow "Americans." Even old-timer Ms. Jung, someone who adored the United States and the American lifestyle and had most consistently chalked up racism to "human nature," was critical of the nonresponse.

J: The Caucasian people, they are very logical people, okay? If they're going
      to plus and minus and [they know they're] not going to get anything out
      of it, they won't do anything.
N: So they're going to turn their back on you?
J: Uh huh, if they think it is a worse situation for them. [modified]

Unlike the old-timers, the newcomers stressed Blacks' destruction of Korean businesses. Understanding little about the racial context, they impugned
Blacks' behavior during the unrest.[5] In so doing, they depicted Blacks as more
authentically American than themselves. Said Ms. An (age 57, 8 months in
United States):

> Yes, I was a little mad at them. Whether they were treated badly or nicely, it is
> someone else's life. They ruined everything and made some people have no
> place to go. So I don't like them, but on the other hand, I thought that if they
> had been treated better, [like] if I were in those Koreans' positions, I would've
> treated them better, like my brothers and sisters . . . [But] killing people and
> setting fires make me mad, sure. Isn't it sort of discrimination since *they've lived
> here longer, because this is their country?* (emphasis added)

Ms. Noh stated similarly, "You know, though I didn't see the situation, Koreans
just thought of Blacks as 'Oh, those people are scary since they have guns' . . . of
course Blacks came and stole and robbed, but *since we're living in their country,* I
think [Koreans] should have been ready for that kind of trouble and they should
have been nicer to Blacks" (emphasis added; age 31, 4 years in United States).

Like other newcomers, Ms. An and Ms. Noh conform to John Ogbu's (1991)
conceptual distinction between Blacks as "domestic minorities" and Koreans
as an "immigrant minority," one I consider oversimplistic.[6] Notwithstanding
these various points of entry among the first generation, most Korean Americans' belief that the unrest was not simply senseless Black criminality pointed
to their understanding of the accretion of the histories, injustices, and self-
perpetuated ills that were the American story. They identified White-over-
Black racism, the foreignizing of Korea and Koreans, their status as an immigrant group (newer, less familiar, worse English), mutual prejudices between
Black Americans and their group, and their weak visibility in U.S. politics and
the national culture (largely self-perpetuated).

The profound impact of this differential inclusion, of being part of the nation
as visible foreigners and invisible subjects, came to life in my interviews and in

the field. Without fail, I was treated to the incantations from the first generation (and some from the second generation) that I use my research to familiarize the United States / world to Korea and its people. Although most were emphatic that I show the "impressive" and the "goodness / brotherly love" that was Korea, others, somewhat to my surprise, saw me as a vehicle to wake Koreans to their severe problems and limitations (read: "fighting with each other," "obsession with class status," patriarchy, and, what I turn to next, the Korea-in-America problem). Some also considered me a valuable political vehicle that could alert the U.S. government to Koreans' especial struggles and needs ("we need someone who can let them know"). Although I reserve the burdens of that understandable pressure for my methods discussion (Appendix), the salient point I gleaned from their exhortations was the depth of their felt invisibility. They needed me—any outlet, for that matter—to bring them out of the shadows and to unmute their voices. There were also harsher edges of Korean/Asian invisibility, those that became apparent at the organizational gatherings in Los Angeles. Time and again, Korean Americans were acutely self-conscious about how White and other non-Korean guests at their functions would perceive their imperfect English or overuse of Korean, programmatic glitches, food quality, the "class" of the venue, and the like. In addition, I felt their seemingly visceral longing for an authentic national home in the tears that streamed down their faces as they joined hands and sang the Korean folk anthem, *Arirang*, or songs by the 1980s duo Haeparagi (Sunflower) at the close of their school reunion and hometown association events. Some of the second-generation children in attendance would shed tears beside their parents, realizing an emotional space that left no one untouched.

Self-Foreignizing: The Politics of Similarity and Difference

It would be remiss to argue that the Korean informants blamed in toto the White government, Whites, and Blacks for the discrimination they suffered during the unrest and in everyday American life. Korean Americans also understood *themselves* as responsible for reinforcing their own foreignness and invisibility. Interpreted thus, many Koreans challenged their peers who had resigned themselves to their group's foreignness, a product of the Whiteness of America as well as Koreans' essentialist view of national belonging ("our roots are Korea anyway"). Many bemoaned "foreign" ethnic networks like Koreatown and ethnic entrepreneurship as patent roadblocks. Their concerns were often animated by the belief that they belonged in "America" just as much as any one else, yet even in so thinking, they would presuppose their own foreignness.

Over-Ethnicizing

Koreatown and Ethnic Networks.   Koreatown (Hanin Town) is much more than an immigrant way station or a dizzying plethora of stores catering to Korean needs. It also acts as an "anchor of identity" to which all Koreans can refer amidst the multicultural terrain of Los Angeles (Tangherlini 1999). The word *multicultural* is apt here, because Koreatown is populated mostly by Latinos. Korean ethnics make up less than 15 percent of the population (Asian Americans comprise 33.9 percent), in part because of the criminal activity there at night and the residents who fled after the 1992 unrest. In fact, an open-ended survey of Koreatown residents found that their greatest concern was crime (40 percent).[7] Despite the town's hermetic and seedy character, its lower-cost housing and other resources are in demand by the mostly newly arrived, low-income, and elderly Koreans who call it home (E. Yu 1990). In part because White Los Angelenos deem it a "foreign" enclave, Koreans often brand it "not-America," reproducing the notion that Korean/Asian ethnics and Latinos are not Americans.

As an example, old-timer Ms. Jang (age 47) prided herself on her independence from Koreatown as an early immigrant:

> I didn't know when I was here the first three years [that] the Korean community had expanded this far and this much. Once I saw it, I was like, "Oh, my God!," they stick so [much] to the Korean community, you know? So my hope is, since you're in the USA, people need to make spare time to learn about this culture, that's the only way you can [live in] this country, you can occupy [a] better job, you could get into the mainstream more. [modified]

True to many interviewees' reports of Koreans as acutely self-critical, several bemoaned Koreans' ethnic self-segregation. Old-timer Mr. Pak (age 54, 26 years in United States), for instance, explicitly advocated a strategy of contact with Whites:

> Even though they're in America, they live in the exact same way as they do in Korea . . . They should get rid of it as soon as possible . . . They work hard to survive, but I think that Koreans should change their attitude some. They have to learn English more and need to, well, like Koreans usually eat Korean food, go to Korean churches, read Korean newspapers, and watch Korean TV. It's a completely Korean lifestyle even though we live in America . . . Because we live in America, you should make American friends, and because my wife and I can

speak English on some level, we have American friends and have opportunities to talk to them, but most other Koreans don't.

He prescribes not only that Koreans speak and live the lifestyle of White America but, perhaps most importantly, befriend and be familiar to "Americans." This motivation also became clear when he followed up with another solution: "We need to make our *kimchi* (Korean pickled cabbage) less spicy so that Americans will like it." To know Koreans, then, was to know their food.

Others more explicitly implicated Koreatown in their battle with foreignness. Unconscious of the bounty of premigration human capital (PhD, high social class) that afforded his leap over this ethnic way station, herbal doctor Mr. Bahng (age 46, 7 years in United States) described Koreatown thus:

> It's like Korea in the early 1960s if you look at it from an economic point of view, like the houses . . . There are poor people there and many who work hard so they can live better lives. What I would like to see is for them to live in America . . . When I came to the States I didn't start working in Koreatown, I started to work in America. In Koreatown, there are way too many Chinese medicine clinics and I thought, "Why don't they go into America and get out of Koreatown?"

That he set up his practice in predominantly White and affluent Beverly Hills should serve as testament to how paramount going to "America" was. As an intermittent patient, I had occasion to observe him at his practice, noticing that he self-consciously treated the White (and some Black) patients with the utmost respect and never ever missed an opportunity to explain Korean culture and Korean Buddhist philosophies to "America."

Inferior and Foreigner Jobs.   On the one hand, "K-town" (Koreatown) was a blessing, housing such valued ethnic resources as rotating credit associations and business networks, churches, and the coveted after-school tutoring programs widespread in South Korea (Zhou and Kim 2006). Yet, among Koreans, it was also a curse. Many lamented Hanin Town, insular networks, and especially ethnic entrepreneurship for reinforcing their foreignness and precluding their *occupational* assimilation into the White mainstream.

In general, Asian entrepreneurs in California tend to be concentrated more heavily in less desirable and highly competitive niches than Anglo entrepreneurs, such as in wholesale and retailing. Small business work is also plagued by self-immolating long hours, lack of family and leisure time, a substantial rate of failure (L. Park 2005), as well as acute intra-Korean competition and interracial conflicts (Yoon 1997). As Paul M. Ong and Tania Azores (1994:114) write, "Self-employment may be a better option than the limited opportunities in the labor market, but it is not a guarantee of economic success on a par with Anglos."

Issues of low occupational prestige, however, are overlooked by those who celebrate Asian American class mobility (Barringer, Takeuchi, and Xenos 1990; Hirschman and Wong 1981), such as sociologists who predict whitening or like forms of racial assimilation. Low occupational prestige, however, has in no way eluded the first-generation Korean immigrants with whom I spoke. Although it is true that they recognized growing numbers of Korean professionals (e.g., lawyers, doctors), they also knew that mostly the young generations coming of age occupied these jobs, those who had yet to establish a "Korean American mainstream" and seemed a long way off from doing so. Koreans' concern has been shaped, as well, by U.S. ideologies that measure immigrants' right to be in the country by their economic contributions (see L. Park 2005). The psychic burdens of knowing that one does not contribute to white-collar America and of coming from a home country that derides small business work fuels Koreans' anxiety about their Laundromats and liquor stores.

Also significant to the equation was the small businesses' representation of Korean downward socioeconomic mobility in the United States. This downward movement was a product not just of language and cultural barriers, credentialing differences, or ethnic niches but also of nativistic racial discrimination in the mainstream labor market (see Min 1996). In my sample, roughly two-thirds of the immigrants had college degrees (or higher) and most of the men had held professional and managerial jobs. In the United States, however, most became small business proprietors or low-skilled professionals (sales, service, textile/apparel workers, technicians). The male informants were especially critical of what they considered their inferior and foreigner jobs, hence, the overrepresentation of their voices below. Although women also commented on "Korean jobs," the men demonstrated the most anxiety about their emasculating move from "mental" to "physical" labor, in part because they had been the sole earners in South Korea.[8] Their pre- and postmigrant lens made their fall down the class ranks seem longer and the landing more painful.

In response to my query about the U.S. racial hierarchy, Ms. Joo (age 47, 2 years in United States) made explicit that White Americans shunned the "3-D" ("dangerous, dirty, difficult") immigrant jobs that many Koreans, especially

those starting out like her, had to take (e.g., urban small business, janitorial/
service, manufacturing).

> White people don't do those jobs but they make the people who are new to this
> country do those kinds of jobs . . . Some Korean person said something as a
> joke that people in those jobs should stop working all at once so that White
> people would realize that what we were doing was really important . . . They
> just think they are in the highest ranks.

Note her acute awareness that it was only Whites' *designation* of immigrants' "3-
D" jobs as undesirable that made them so. However, many more respondents bemoaned their ethnic economies as fettering their chance to move up and mainstream. As one example, Mr. Chun (age 51, 10.5 years in United States) attributed Koreans' "below-middle" social position in the United States to their less
than prestigious occupations. He underscored the typically unsafe character of
small business work, alluding to the danger of Koreatown and other urban areas
where he and his peers set up shop.[9]

> C: I think Koreans stand somewhere below the middle tier [of U.S. society].
> N: Why a little below? . . .
> C: Because I believe the real middle-tier groups have to have safe occupa-
>   tions and I believe Koreans are not strong enough to have reached that
>   point. Koreans usually own grocery stores or markets and these stores are
>   not safe places to work. If they did some other kind of job, I would cate-
>   gorize them a little above the middle tier but most of them own liquor
>   stores, groceries, or doughnut shops.

Mr. Gil (age 37, 7 months in United States) similarly indicted Koreans for their
ethnically segregated business practices that left "Americans" and Mexican
Americans out of the fray.

> If you want to sell alcohol, don't do business the Korean way, do it the Ameri-
> can way. Start your business in such a way that everyone can come to your esta-
> blishment, including Koreans, Americans, and Mexicans, but they always cater
> to Korean customers. That's the problem.

As a poignant account of how lack of occupational prestige foregrounds
Koreans' minority and foreign status vis-à-vis White Americans, Mr. Sohn
(age 73, 18 years in United States) recounted:

In Manhattan, if you go to those buildings next to Central Park—isn't that where Jacqueline Onassis lives?—anyway, inside those buildings they're like palaces, so I heard through my friend who does work delivering fresh vegetables that when he went to those rich houses, he found a different world there; he felt belittled doing this business of bringing vegetables to these rich people. The customers place orders over the phone for vegetables and then he brings them right to their house in a bucket. One time when he left some rich people's house, they left money in a jar for him, a 100 dollar bill for tip, which actually made him feel alienated . . . and he thought, no wonder us minorities feel belittled whenever we come into contact with these Whites. At that point, he felt, "There's no way minorities can do better than Americans" . . . And I personally felt the same way when I went to Long Beach and I'd see all these incredibly *huge and nice* houses there, then you realize how well Americans are living. So that's when we feel like the "minority."

Mr. Sohn's narrative supports Hurh and Kim's (1984:141) finding from their classic study that longtime immigrants' main comparison group was Whites more than South Koreans or other Korean immigrants. Even if the vegetable delivery business paid the bills, it was ethnically Korean; it was beneath the White America emblematized by Park Avenue and Long Beach mansions. In the end, it was "alienating" and belittling to be the non-White service worker reaching for his tip.

Taken together, the narratives stand in partial contrast to recent findings on the value of ethnic resources (Portes and Zhou 1993; Waters 1999; Zhou and Bankston 1998; see Portes and Rumbaut 1996). That is, these immigrants ultimately hope that they will *not* have to use Korean-only socioeconomic networks and pathways to become mainstream citizens. As valuable as these ethnic resources are, Koreans see their concentration in ethnic jobs and circles as racially/ethnically typecasting them. That is, they identify a tautology whereby Korean proliferation in ethnic small businesses reinforces the foreignness of precisely the Korean/Asian people who run them. By being critical of their ethnic jobs and lifestyle, they considered the very vehicle that paved most of their way into the American middle class—small business proprietorship—to be a major roadblock to their becoming mainstream. Indeed, they believed they were targets of White American racist indifference during the LA unrest in part because it was "just" Korean-owned businesses and Koreatown. Such a sentiment is not insignificant, as Korean Americans, like most Asian ethnics, are a predominantly first-generation group. So long as they keep entering the country and continue proliferating in community leadership, Korean and other Asian ethnics will be hard pressed to deplete, or one day expunge, their ethnic towns and networks.[10]

It should be noted that Koreans' commitment to this "politics of similarity" with mainstream America crystallized in response to the 1992 unrest (J. Park 1999). The watershed awoke their political consciousness about the need to claim "America" as their own, lest they be crippled by another unrest (J. Park 1999).[11] Ever since those fateful April days, Korean Americans have more actively mobilized and have engaged the mainstream political process (E. Park 2002). Jung Sun Park's (1999) study of Korean Chicagoans' response to the LA unrest found that they countered their racialization as foreigners by proclaiming themselves "Korean *Americans*," no longer mere "Koreans." This move runs counter to Claire Kim's (2000) argument that, in response to conflicts with Black American residents, Korean Americans were mainly interested in protecting their "middle" status in the racial order and, thereby, the racial order itself. Rather, Park's (1999) research and my study demonstrate that Koreans' move toward a politics of similarity with White and Black Americans also signifies their desire to *disrupt* their foreigner position, hence their desire to *alter* the racial order. The unrest taught them the dangers of liminally existing between Whites and Blacks (E. Park 2002).

I take Park's argument a step further by showing how Korean Americans exhort a politics of similarity as a means to enter the American mainstream and move closer to authentic social citizenship. Guided by multiculturalism's tenet that groups should be accorded the social right of recognition for their differences (see Taylor 1994), Korean immigrants forge a *politics of similarity* as social citizens while maintaining a *politics of difference* ethnically (see Rudrappa 2004). In this way, they do not aspire for the ex-nominated status (Bhattacharjee 1992) that they enjoyed in South Korea, as they seek to *maintain* their difference rather than become the group whose power lies in being the *unmarked* reference point for all other groups. Drawing on their premigrant lenses, they aspire to be marked as visible Korean minority members of the American mainstream. In this way, mainstreaming would be the one stone that killed two birds—elevating Korean Americans and Korea—and simultaneously a third—their ability to overturn their global and local invisibility-cum-insignificance. Although they aspired to forge a "mainstream Korean America," they did not fall prey to the pretense that they could *be* mainstream America.

"Forever Foreigner"?

In light of many Koreans' belief in the American dream opportunity structure and democratic system, I queried about the link between Koreans' hypothetical parity with White Americans along all dimensions and social acceptance of Koreans. Of the forty-seven Korean Americans sampled, only two felt that it was possible for Whites to see Koreans as equals in the event that they gained parity along *all* dimensions. Although they believed that all of the trappings of "Americanness" would help them fit in, the trappings could not afford them the respect of a real "American" short of being born a White person. To convey Koreans' conviction about the strictures of "race" for them as well as their culturally "American" children, I focus on the narratives from the old-timers only, most of whom had been "Americans" for decades. Worth noting, however, is that most of the recent émigrés aligned with their veteran counterparts. This stands to reason if one considers their recent exposure to White American abuse of power, their new experience of first-time minorityhood in the United States, and thus initial bouts with uncertainty and instability, what Hurh and Kim (1984:141) call the "exigency stage."

All of the passages below are responses to my question (hereafter, the "parity question"): "Do you think White Americans would treat us as equals once we have reached all of the exact same levels as they have in U.S. society?" Although the premise that Whites would always distinguish racially between themselves and others was the most common response, some Koreans highlighted Whites' anti-immigrant sentiment against those who came to "their" country. Consider Ms. Gim's (age 69) perspective:

G: Well, I think that there will still be some difference anyway.

N: Why?

G: I just think that way.

N: Can you guess why?

G: I don't know, but I just think that there'll still be some discrimination. Although this is the United States and a country mixed with immigrants, the owners of the country are the White people, you know? We're just people who followed them here and live here, therefore, I guess there'll be some discrimination.

Consistent with his earlier-quoted experience with the racist manager whom he finally challenged, Mr. Bae (age 43) highlights the absurdity of Whites' racial prejudice by way of an argument reminiscent of Gunnar Myrdal's (1964) "American Dilemma" thesis.

> I don't think so. When I heard in Korea that Americans discriminated against people, I thought, How could they discriminate against people while they were saying that they were the most superior citizens? How could they be the most superior citizens with that kind of foolish idea? After I came here, I saw that they took really good care of *animals*, and sometimes they took better care of animals than they did human beings. Therefore, I think that that's their duality. Of course, not everybody is like that; it's less visible in places like California. [But] from what I've heard, White people think that Asians, because we have a different color, are snatching or taking away their places.

His notion of Whites' unwillingness to share the country's bounty with non-Whites undergirds what he thinks all immigrants feel: "I think that it's the feeling of living in another's house. Because it's not my own country, it's less comfortable even if you've lived here long. It feels like you're living in someone else's home."

In a related vein, most other respondents cited "color" or racialized phenotype alone as sufficient grounds for Whites' construction of Korean / Asian Americans as persistent foreigners. That is, as long as Koreans did not look White, they would always be seen as less than White. In a narrative akin to Mr. Bae's discomfort in a predominantly White "house," Ms. Pak admits candidly that Koreans would always be a people apart. Bear in mind that she is a strong English speaker, a twenty-six-year resident, a U.S. citizen, and a self-described "Korean American."

> P: No matter how much I deny it, in the eyes of the people here, even if you're third- or fourth-generation Korean American, you know how they don't say you're "American" because of your appearance . . . Even if we get U.S. citizenship later on, we cannot become owners of this country if you look at our status or appearance. It's like renting a room at a house that belongs to someone else . . . If there are as many Asians as there are Americans, the concept that "I'm Asian," "I'm American" will disappear, but I think it's still a very long way before that happens . . .
>
> N: Even if you're a minority with the same economic and political status?
>
> P: Looks. Because Asians look different to begin with, when they see us they see Asians. No matter how hard you try to fix your appearance . . . Even if

you get plastic surgery to change the shape of your eyes, even if you color your hair yellow, you're still Asian. I think Asians can't become American because of our appearances.

Here Ms. Pak takes a subtle jab at the many Asians and Asian Americans who alter the very thing that makes them foreign, their racial phenotype. To the parity question, longtime immigrant Ms. Jun (age 49) replied with the same small dose of faith in the passage of time as did Ms. Pak, but with the same conviction that it would take much to reverse present reality.

J: Nope, I don't think so. (with certainty)
N: And why is that?
J: Um, because we're not Caucasian! (scoffs as if a stupid question)

Similarly, another old-timer, Ms. Park, pinpointed "race" as a barrier to her becoming a U.S. citizen, all despite a twenty-year life in the United States and her love of the American democratic system.

P: I have a green card. I never applied for that [citizenship] because I don't feel like I can really become, uh, I don't feel like I'm ready to be American.
N: Oh, do you think you'll ever feel ready?
P: No, I don't think so . . . Because you know, I don't think anybody really, no American will really think I'm American because of the way I look.

She would therefore remain a South Korean citizen. Finally, wealthy Mr. Bahng (age 53) recaps the common theme that a "middle" (model minority) positioning is not enough to overtake their status as foreigners. To the parity question, he replied:

No, they would think that a Korean immigrant has succeeded. It doesn't matter. You pay all the taxes, live in a nice house, ride in a nice car, have American citizenship, so it doesn't appear that there should be a problem, right? If you have an American citizenship you're American in that sense because this is a multi-ethnic / -racial nation, but in actuality, you're still Korean.

These sentiments among the respondents reveal their belief in the immutability of "race." They believe that the U.S. opportunity structure would prevent them from realizing a *complete* politics of similarity. Simply put, they would be mainstream Korean Americans who could *approximate* Americanness but never be *the* Americans. Such a status claim was the province of Whites. Although the respondents did not always state explicitly that U.S. dominance over South Korea accounted for their views, it stands to reason that ranking beneath a racially distinct imperial power could shore up a sense of the insurmountability of "race."

In addition, U.S. society's denial of social citizenship to Asian Americans is precisely what motivates the group to become mainstream Korean Americans. In this way, their premigrant ethnonational identity is strengthened by dint of the racial discrimination they endure in the United States, a finding that lines up with other transnational studies (Foner 2000; Glick Schiller 1999; Kasinitz 1992). Given the perception of the immutability of "race" and the purity of the Korean bloodline (*tanil minjok*), on the one hand, they maintained their transnational lens on South Korea as the ancestral and symbolic ethnic "home." On the other, they believed that they should mainstream by declaring to "America" and the world that they were making the United States their home as well, their mainstream home. Although they did not want to use Korean-only mobility channels, they sought to make visible to a wide-eyed American and global audience the impressive culture and exceptionally talented people that were Korea. With such recognition would come movement up the domestic and global ladder.

This strategy also evidences the belief that they *could move into the mainstream* precisely because of their impressive national intelligence and diligence. In a similar vein, Sharmila Rudrappa (2004:188) finds that first-generation Indian Americans perceive their culture thus: "The elements that make up the various ethnic rituals may be exceptional, but the morals that structure their daily immigrant lives are portrayed as being identical to American values." Korean immigrants subscribe to the same belief in their simultaneous difference and similarity vis-à-vis White America as a way to join the nation's mainstream. They believe that their culture (Confucianism, Oriental medicine, kimchi) is distinctive and often superior ("our bloodline explains our great culture") but not so distinctive that their value systems are unlike those of mainstream White America (hard work, sacrifice). In fact, the similar tune of Confucian and Protestant ethic mobility values is part of "America's" appeal.

Owing to Koreans' cognizance that their phenotype precluded authentic social citizenship, they passed on the lesson of occupational mainstreaming onto their children and others' children (Confucian age hierarchies allow elders to impart wisdom onto *all* Korean youth). They made this effort to ensure that when the next generation became white-collar professionals in the core economy, they would do so *as Koreans*, not as mere Asians or, worse, as "wanna-be Whites" with altered eyelids and bleached blond hair (see Kibria 2002a; Min and Kim 1999).

In this chapter, I found that Korean Americans encounter and resist racial discrimination against their group as visible foreigners, typically as "foreign model minorities." Again, the depth and consistency of their resistance speaks volumes about their willingness to scrutinize their pro-Americanism and face contradictions ("How could they discriminate . . . while . . . saying that they were the most superior citizens?"). They must wrestle with the seeming "contradiction" between the model minority and persistent foreigner, one that, below the surface, betrays a circular relationship. This circularity explains why Asian American groups' "success" has not lifted them out of their foreigner status and into the ranks of American authenticity. A key limitation of the racial triangulation model, then, is its lack of a theoretical emphasis on the overlap between, and the intersection of, the color line and the citizenship line (notwithstanding Claire Kim's [1999] acknowledgment of it in her *explanation* of the model).

Dominant society's elevation of Asian Americans to model minority heights is debilitating for *all* groups of color insofar as the maneuver is used to "prove" the color blindness of U.S. opportunity structures. The model minority myth thereby effectively reproduces the racial status quo in which Asian Americans are subordinated, most consistently along citizenship lines. Again, the deliberate use of the model minority myth to counter the aims of civil rights and liberation struggles (that on many fronts have helped Asian Americans) and to eradicate affirmative action policies (that in many areas have helped Asian Americans [P. Ong 2000]) should remind us of the hegemonic interests behind the existence of racial ideologies. That is, Asian Americans are "model minorities" so long as they "stay in their place" (L. Park 2005). As I have shown, the 1992 LA unrest emblematized Korean Americans' status as differentially included insofar as elites included the group in mainstream discourse, and they were *able* to do so, precisely because the Korean Americans were subordinate and partially present (see Espiritu 2003:47). Coverage of the unrest used Korean immigrants to legitimate the U.S. opportunity structure, deflect from White racism, sensationalize intraminority "racisms," and uphold Asian foreignness and Black depravity. Stretching its work in South Korea to its own backyard, the White American state capitalized on the group's partial presence and intensified it, by treating "Korean ethnics" as nonexistent and unimportant.

Also stretching their cultural glasses from the home country to Los Angeles, Koreans drew on their dogged invisibility, sense of inferiority, and the belief that one must *be* its nation to conclude that Koreans were reifying their own foreignness. They bemoaned Koreans' inability to publicize its greatness from the echelon of a "mainstream Korean America." In criticizing thus, many respondents did not seem cognizant that they presupposed their essential foreignness whenever they exhorted that Koreans stop being so Korean (e.g., there was no parallel demand for White Americans to learn about Korea, especially considering that the United States had long been there). Moreover, Koreans' attempts to showcase their "good immigrant" status, such as their need to covet their "middle" positioning in the color-class order, presupposes that, at heart, they are immigrants rather than the Americans they have been since 1903 (see L. Park 2005:97). They did, however, recognize the fiction of their foreignness in the moments that they resisted Whites' authenticity ("You . . . go back to your country, you came from England!").

In view of the noted complex struggles, Korean immigrants had much hope for the next generation, all despite the sobering reality of "race." As I show in the next chapter, however, the second generation's struggles with foreignness and invisibility reflected the racial histories and structures that profoundly vexed the first.

8 Second-Generation "Foreign Model Minorities"

Battling Prejudice and Racism

"Go back to your country!" As if I ever left?
—I Was Born with Two Tongues, Asian American spoken word troupe

AS DO THE YOUNG ADULT ASIAN ETHNICS of "I Was Born with Two Tongues," the second-generation Koreans in my study must perpetually defend their presence in "America." In this way, struggles with antiforeigner discrimination and the desire to be "mainstream Korean Americans" are not simply first-generation phenomena. In this chapter, I examine the second generation's bouts with nativistic racial prejudice and discrimination despite, and *because of*, their "model minority" achievements, a plight I call "foreign model minorityhood." In making these arguments, however, I do not suggest that only the second-plus generations will ultimately determine the "fate" of the group, a claim generally espoused by the field of mainstream immigration sociology (Fouron and Glick Schiller 2002). Such a conceptualization assumes that the first generation will cease immigrating or will become insignificant actors, both in numbers and influence (see Massey 1995). It also universalizes Europeans' especial opportunities for generational mobility that were, in actuality, denied to groups of color (Blauner 1972), such as legally excluded Asian Americans (see Massey 1995). Claims that diminish the import of the first generation are also premised on mainstream U.S. norms, not on Confucian age hierarchies and duties that instruct younger generations to respect, listen to, and follow the older generations.

Although this book is concerned principally with first-generation Korean Americans' navigation of U.S. racialization across unequal borders, it is crucial that the "foreignness" of the second generation, both *despite* and *because of* "model minority" achievements, is empirically examined. It is even more crucial in light of predictions of Asian American racial assimilation, especially by works that do not empirically interview or observe Asian Americans' experiences with "race" (e.g., Alba and Nee 2003; Bonilla-Silva 2002; Gans 1999; J. Lee and Bean 2004; Warren and Twine 1997; Yancey 2003). The relationship between Asian Americans and "race" continues to be oversimplified or erased despite the battery of studies that systematically speak to and ethnographically observe later-generation Asian Americans' struggles with racism (e.g., Chen 1999; Espiritu 2003; Kibria 2002a; Maira 2002; Purkayastha 2005; Pyke and Dang 2003; Pyke and Johnson 2003; Tuan 1998, 1999; Wu 2002; Zhou and Bankston 1998).

Method

For this supplementary data sample I conducted in-depth, open-ended interviews with twenty second-generation Korean Americans. So as not to tap a social network, only two were the children of members in my primary sample. By "second-generation" I refer to those who are United States–born ($n=7$) or who had immigrated by age eleven ($n=13$, median age at arrival=7). I recruited the sample from churches and schools; from social, community service, and political groups; and by processes of snowball sampling. The sample consists of nine women and eleven men who range from age 17 to 42 (average age = 26.6). Aligned with demographic trends, the vast majority of the respondents come from families who fall somewhere in the small business to white-collar middle class. Three respondents' parents are part of the blue-collar middle class. All are college graduates except for one finishing college and two college-bound high school seniors. Those with careers had also attained middle-class status. Occupations included attorney, physician, teacher, practitioner in education, nonprofit administrator, journalist, designer, and corporate businessperson.

The First Generation and the Ethnic Mainstream

Corroborating the first generation's claims, most of the second-generation Korean Americans reported that parents or elders had fostered pride in their Koreanness and had encouraged or pressured them to pursue only the most prestigious occupations, especially physician and lawyer. Because the parents often immigrated for their children's educational opportunities, the second generation felt that they had to live up to their parents' tremendous sacrifices. Seventeen-year-old Hagen sums up well the link between ethnic pride and ethnic pressures. When I asked her if she thought Korean cultural traditions were important, she replied in the affirmative, and explained,

"Like you should know where you're from, because you don't look like that beautiful Italian girl sitting next to you[1] . . . Because you should feel proud of who you are, that's how I feel." Hagen believed that pride in Koreanness was necessary to overcome inferiority complexes vis-à-vis Whites, such as the European beauty standard that haunts Koreans in both countries. Indeed, many second-generation Korean/Asian Americans have bankrolled cosmetic surgery in the United States to look more like "that beautiful Italian girl" (see Kaw 1993). At the same time, Hagen considered the parental pressure on the children for the sake of the ethnic group to be excessive. In her own case, her mother supported her aspiration to be a singer and actress, in part because of Koreans' invisibility in popular culture, but her father had opposed it until recently. On the first generation broadly, she remarked: "They wouldn't let their children go out and do what they really wanted to do, they usually tell them, 'You have to go to college, you have to become a doctor or a lawyer.' You know, like put pressure on them a lot, like, 'Go to Harvard, go to Yale.' "

To be sure, not all first-generation parents pressured their children into narrow job and college options. As I showed, some, like Hagen's mother, were concerned with the lack of Korean representation in popular culture. Yet, it is striking that most of the respondents' parents fixated on their children's entrance into mainstream white-collar America. Jenny, currently a law student, had originally pursued the "other" option, medicine, because of the frequent incantations for her to do so.

J: Part of it was, because like I've always heard being a doctor is really good.

N: From your parents or other Koreans?

J: Yeah, like from other Koreans, so I just naturally, you just have it ingrained in your head for so long that you just do that. And I did discover that it was those things that I was actually good at.

Jacquelyn, a seminary student, had defied her parents' orders concerning her college major:

My parents wanted me to go into either Med or Pre-Law . . . So I took biology and a math class and I totally hated it. My first year I was just exploring and trying out everything and when I took an African-American history class I absolutely loved it. It was so interesting and so fascinating and something that I really wanted to study more; the more I took it, the more I loved it. And so I finally said this is what I wanted to do and they just thought it was the most bizarre thing. They'd always ask, "Why don't you study Asian Americans?"

Another respondent, Ron, had conformed to his parents' wishes and became a medical student. He spoke of how his parents told him and his brother to "Americanize" by becoming the perennial "mainstream Korean Americans." Ron begins his narrative by describing how his father would teach them life lessons every day as he drove them to school.

> He would be like, "Family is like a car, and the car has four wheels, and in our family we have four wheels, so every wheel has its job and when one wheel falls off then the car can't go, so all of the wheels have to work together." This was like his very subtle way of being like, "You guys have to do your jobs" . . . The good thing was that my parents never said, "Oh, you have to get straight As" . . . It's funny, which brings up another point: my dad would say to me, "I just want you guys to be all Americanized," but he never explained to us what that meant, so we had to find out. And for me, when I heard him say that, I think that the very essence of being American is having this amount of diversity being from an immigrant background and making something of that.

Ron therefore interpreted his father's message of Americanization not as a green light to "whiten" but to promote one's diversity as an immigrant and make "something of that," that is, to do well for one's *ethnic* group.[2]

Visibly Foreign, Not-American

Korean Americans' struggles with nativistic racial discrimination were not restricted to the first generation. Despite some of the second generation's adoption of the model minority ideology and great faith in the U.S. opportunity structure (see Stacey Lee 1996), they narrated the discrimination they faced as visible foreigners, that is, as those who were conspicuously out of place and thus not-American. They also maintained that their invisibility hampered their social citizenship in their own country.

In addition to their bouts with nativistic racism, the second generation claimed to have learned much from their own parents' struggles with it. They were well aware of how far their parents had to come, from leaving Korea and having to be first-time racial, linguistic, and cultural minorities in a White-dominated country. For instance, Carol, a graduate student and part-time teacher, recollected her shock when a police officer assumed that middle-aged Asian Americans could not speak English.

> I remember once when we were driving and my mother got pulled over and, you know, my parents speak English, they can read, everything; and he looks at me and he tells me, "Could you please tell your mom in your language that I pulled her over because . . . ," right? And then she's like, "Excuse me, I speak English!" and he was like, "Oh, I'm sorry" and he was really surprised. And I totally remember that and I remember it was so awful. I was like, "Oh my gosh," he just assumed that she didn't. And my mom was really upset about that . . . I talked to my friends about it and they said it happens all the time.

Carol was deeply upset that her mother was treated as a foreigner and that such treatment was commonplace. Her narrative reveals that Carol herself was marked as foreign by the officer's assumption that she could speak an Asian language and thus somehow embodied Asian culture ("tell your mom in *your language*"). In another example, Tim's parents ran a dry cleaning store. In light of his parents' struggles as small business proprietors, he responded in the following way to my question: "Do you think Korean Americans face institutional discrimination in the United States?"

> T: I think it's complex. When you're talking about the first generation, you know I think a big factor [of] why they go into small business is because opportunities in the mainstream are not available to them.
>
> N: You mean, because they're discriminated against?
>
> T: Yes.

Central to their understanding of the first generation's struggles with disempowerment and political invisibility was the 1992 LA unrest. Narratives from male respondents were especially forceful owing to their identification with their fathers' suffering and protection of the family store during the life-threatening unrest. As Taehan (age 23), a magazine editor, relived his family's loss of its Koreatown business through his retelling, his feelings in 1992 of alarm, sadness, fear, and anger came to the fore. He begins his narrative by describing his father's response to the unrest.

> T: He watched TV until the night and it was like images of buildings burning and fucking people just acting like totally nuts, you know? . . . I remember, there was like this total tension . . . And like my father (pause),

I mean he's screwed in his own way but inside he's a really gentle person. He's not the kind of person that's going to be like erupting and wheeling a gun and like popping off. Although after his businesses got burned, and one of my uncle's businesses hadn't been touched yet, they all kind of went to his business to protect it. And I remember like, he was leaving the house and he was really devastated about what was going to happen, (pause) he was telling me that it could be really dangerous and like that he might not even come home if things got really bad. Yeah, I was like in total shock.

N: Do you think, even if for a short time, you got angry at African Americans or Latinos?

T: Not for a short time but for a long time, I think I was angry at the world around me, you know?

Unlike Taehan's family, Todd's family in Claremont did not lose their liquor stores despite the eruption of riots in that area as well, some thirty miles east of downtown Los Angeles. Yet, Todd (age 26), an attorney, was just as upset as Taehan when he recounted the unrest. Unlike his counterpart, however, he more explicitly assigned fault to the U.S. mass media and government.

My dad slept in the store for like three days. You know, every night that the riots were going on he slept in the store. I wanted to, but my dad wouldn't let me, which says a lot about him . . . So yeah, we worried about the store getting burnt down and my dad getting killed. It was a really big deal. A lot of my parents' friends, they lost their businesses . . . Especially for Koreans of my generation, that was the defining cultural experience of this country and the greatest single disillusioning thing that has ever happened. Until the riots I truly believed in the American Dream. I believed in egalitarianism, I believed in meritocracy, and after the riots I didn't believe in any of it . . . Here I am reading in the L.A. Times how, you know, it probably is the Koreans' fault 'cause they went into these neighborhoods and they didn't give the Blacks enough jobs . . . Nobody's on the Korean side . . . That's why like it's ludicrous to me when Americans talk about getting Nazis [for] war crimes or they want to go and punish the Japanese for their comfort women, well they don't admit to any wrong they did nine years ago! That's one thing about America that makes me angry. Korea has a lot of problems, but it doesn't pretend to be like the bastion of ideology [of] greatness and liberalism and fairness, that's why I think America is much more hypocritical.

For both Taehan and Todd, watching their fathers potentially meet death and realizing dominant Whites' complete disregard for Korean ethnics had taught them that "America" was unjust. In Todd's mind, the United States discriminated against Asian immigrants in the same stroke that it glorified itself as the "bastion of . . . greatness and . . . fairness." Todd resists U.S. institutionalized racism by comparing the United States and South Korea in a way that favors his ancestral "homeland," a common form of resistance (Foner 2000; Glick Schiller 1999; Kasinitz 1992; Kibria 2002b; N. Kim forthcoming).

Although these second-generation members became conscious of anti-Asian bias in light of their parents' lack of belonging in the United States, as borne out by the 1992 unrest, they also became conscious of it through their own struggles with their status as foreigners and "foreign model minorities." Being foreign, whether along visible or invisible lines, was a current running through all the second-generation informants' experiences of racial prejudice and institutionalized racism.

Many of the second-generation informants recounted their experiences of being treated as foreigners ("chinks") by the majority White population in the neighborhoods and schools in which they grew up. A "kids will be kids" explanation would be much too simplistic and capricious here, as the racial taunts often served as the most traumatic memories for some and were the building blocks of their adult identities and political consciousness. Forty-two-year-old Joe, a non-profit administrator, struggled with an inferiority complex from grade school to college. He begins his narrative by recollecting his first day of kindergarten at a predominantly White American school after having emigrated from Seoul.

J: Because I didn't speak English very well, I was speaking still in Korean so it was difficult for me to communicate. I liked to eat Korean food and the kids would make fun . . . I was one of the few Asians in the whole elementary school, so they would call me names. They made fun of my name, so very early, early on, you know, it was clear to me that I was *different* . . . As the years progressed and kids continued to make fun of me, they would call me "flat face" a lot. I remember looking in the mirror thinking, "Do I really have a flat face?," things like that.

Yet Joe's struggles with a sense of racial inferiority, struggles that sent him scrutinizing himself in front of the mirror (again, prompted by the European aesthetic standard), did not end in elementary school. He came to reject his Korean/Asian identity in favor of Whiteness.

J: It made me conscientious of it in a negative way. So I, uh, you know, up until high school, pretty much early college, I rejected my Korean identity . . .

N: When you say rejected, what does that mean?

J: Um, it means not wanting to date any Korean girls or being associated with other kids that were Korean; you know, the food that you ate and I didn't want to speak Korean . . . So, you know, I was pretty much negating everything about your culture and wanting to fit in, wanting to be White.

In an interesting parallel, the second generation's sense of inferiority flowed from being Korean in "America" while that of the first generation was initiated by an "America" (and Japan) in Korea. The reaction of Jacquelyn (age 27), a seminary student, to the racial taunts at school stood in contrast to Joe's.

I got so much of that, or even walking down the street, they would start saying things to you like, "Oh, look at that chink" and so that made me more like, "I'm going to hold on to my Koreanness" and prove to them that I could be all Korean and still interact with you at your level or whatever. Whereas I think some people would go the other way and say, "Forget being Korean. I really want to hide that identity so I could be better accepted." I went the other way.

Indeed, it seemed that one of the major reasons Jacquelyn still identified proudly as a "Korean American" had to do with her cumulative struggles with racial prejudice since childhood. Although Joe (above) had initially rejected his Korean identity, he later came to embrace it in a process of politicization first sparked by the "racial wrongs" he and others faced as youths. He eventually became a nonprofit worker for all people of color and was instrumental in bringing Blacks and Koreans together during times of strife, such as after the LA unrest.

Many of the respondents also shared their bouts with racialized bias and discrimination as adults. Taehan, whom we met as a victim of the 1992 unrest, recounted one not-so-enchanted evening in San Francisco with much angst:

A good example of it was like the whole millennium New Year's bash, right? I was dating this girl and we went up to my friend's place . . . We got really drunk, and we were counting down the new year and it's just like, it couldn't have been a better moment: this beautiful girl I'm with, having a great time with my friends. And this guy walks up to me, he was this bald White guy and he's totally wasted and he's got this cigarette with the wrong end in his mouth and he's about to light the butt . . . I'm like, "Hey, buddy, buddy! You gonna light the butt end!" And he's like "Oh!" and I don't know what seized him, but he turns around and he starts making like Chinaman noise like "*CHING CHONG!*" whatever and he starts saying this shit to me and I couldn't believe that this was happening. It was this really great moment completely spoiled by this asshole.

Taehan spoke with an air of tragedy about how he went from being *a person* enjoying a time-honored celebration (with a "beautiful girl") to being a "*Chinaman*" foreigner who needed to be taunted by the "real Americans." This theme of happy moments utterly spoilt by "race" prejudice played out during my time in the field as well. In one instance, some Korean American organizations had decided to take part in a progressive political rally downtown. Energized by the large number of progressive people coming together for justice, we were in high spirits until a woman registering people to vote (who looked non-White) approached the Asian American woman walking next to me, June. After querying about her registration status, June paused to think. Abruptly, the woman said, "Oh, you're not from here anyway," and walked away. We both looked at each other in tragic disappointment. At a progressive rally, this was the last thing we hoped to hear. In his own spoiled moment, Taehan was torn about how to respond to the drunk White male, a common struggle among groups of color.

> He looked like he didn't even know what he was doing and I'm with this girl, so I let it go, right? . . . But to this day I feel like I should have smashed that guy's face in and every time I don't smash some guy's face in, I feel like I should have . . . Part of me says I did the right thing not to hurt that guy, but you know there are a lot of things that happen where there's some kind of weird similar racist thing that occurs and I let it go, 'cause usually the person who does it is like some weird asshole, you know, who isn't worth a food stamp.

Taehan's ire reveals his conviction that racism is wrong and that the perpetrators should know it. What he neglects to mention, however, is that his desire to "smash [the] guy's face in" likely had to do, as well, with the White male's emasculation of him (and in front of his "beautiful girl"), a common problem for Asian American men who are subordinated by ideals of hegemonic White manhood and masculinity (Chen 1999; Eng 2001; Espiritu 1997; N. Kim 2006a). Beyond mere racism, then, Taehan may have wanted to "smash" faces in to discredit the gendered racism that depicts Asian men as passive and effeminate.

Other male informants shared stories of their simultaneous "race"-gender marginalization, such as in the realm of sports. For instance, Lance (age 24), a financial analyst, spoke of the epithets typically hurled at him for being an Asian American basketball player, two statuses that are often not conjoined in mainstream representations of athletic masculinity. At about 5'5", Lance would also be labeled the stereotypically short Asian man.

> L: I also played high school sports and I was the only Korean that played in my, only Asian guy, basically, on my team and stuff. And I'm also like the smallest guy on the team and most of the Asians are smaller than everyone else, so you really get the stereotype that, you know, Asian people suck at sports, which might be justified because we haven't really represented in any of the sports . . . So you hear it a lot and they say how much you suck at it, "You're no good!" and stuff, and you just have to like block it out, I guess.
>
> N: Would you say something kind of spiteful back?
>
> L: I mean I would curse at them, but that's about it.

Though he seemed an easygoing person, Lance, like Taehan, conceded that he was bothered by the constant emasculation he faced as an Asian American in the hypermasculine realm of basketball ("I would curse at them"). Similar to Taehan, he seemed conflicted over how to fight back. Although Yao Ming would make his debut as Houston Rockets center (and tallest NBA player at 7'6") about a year after the interview, studies show that Asian American men continue to be seen as more nerdy and studious than athletic, more weak than strong (see Chen 1999; Espiritu 1997). Neither Yao Ming nor the many Asian and Asian American basketball leagues (see King 2002) seem to be enough for U.S. society to think of men like Lance when they conjure up "basketball player." As for gendered racial ideologies of Korean/Asian women, Jacquelyn remarked: "I've heard, especially for women, that they're quiet and submissive and ah, like docile, like, I guess. Something like those things are attached to me and I didn't really like it. I was pretty clear about making that known." Because Jacquelyn attended a seminary school in which other students had stereotyped Asian woman as those who do not speak up in class or disobey men, she engineered her behaviors to explode the images in their heads.

Being a "Foreign Model Minority"

Many of the respondents had endured the trials of "foreign model minority-hood." By that I mean that these second-generation Korean Americans were foreignized and discriminated against in settings that showcased their high socioeconomic status. In this regard, they faced racial bias or the glass ceiling both *despite* their embodiment of the model minority ideology and *because* of it. Grace (age 38) is an example of the first, of being mistreated despite her high status. As a successful attorney Grace often faced the perennial burden of "race" suffered by middle-class non-Whites: having to constantly decipher whether or not her "race" shaped the way she was treated in predominantly White settings (see Feagin and Sikes 1994). She said, "I sometimes feel like when I get rude treatment, treated rudely by a clerk or something at the courthouse, you know, the thought does cross my mind: 'Is it because I'm Asian? Is it because I'm female?' Those thoughts do cross my mind."

Tom (age 29), a physician, prefaced his narrative by describing how horrible the racial taunting he suffered as a child had made him feel. He then remarked:

T: Even like one of the hospitals that I rotate through now, it's like a VA hospital and they may say, "Hey, Bruce Lee!" or something . . . Some of the patients, like these, uh, African American patients—well, it's just because I think most of the patients are African American at the VA—they'll say "ching chong" or whatever, some derogatory term . . . And I can tell you, my colleagues have had bad experiences, like there's a fellow resident of mine who's Japanese and he's also a radiologist. I think he went in to interview a patient and then the attending went in after and the attending was Austrian and the patient was also Austrian and uh, I guess the patient told him, "You know, it's good to be seen by another countryman and, you know, not a . . ." (long pause)

N: Chink?

T: Well, it was a derogatory term; it was in German so it ["race" prejudice] is still around, I guess, but people won't say it to our face.

Despite the fact that Tom was a physician, the so-called model minority, he became nothing more than Asian martial arts fighter "Bruce Lee," an oft-exoticized image in American popular culture, and his physician friend became a racial epithet. Their status as racialized foreigners eclipsed their high socioeconomic status on which the model minority ideology has largely been based;

his foreignness outweighed his esteemed and authoritative status as a doctor. Also striking about Tom's narrative is his shift from talking only about his Japanese friend to including himself as a victim of prejudice ("people won't say it to *our* face"). Owing to the American public's practice of lumping together all groups who appear (East) Asian (Espiritu 1992), such as the universal "chink" label or a variant thereof, Tom understands that what happened to his Japanese friend could have just as easily happened to him. Perhaps this explained why he was rather uncomfortable relating the Black veterans' and Austrian's prejudice (more "uhs" and pauses in these moments).

Audrey, an attorney at a high-powered law firm, noted how she had faced *blatant* racism only when she moved to her upscale, predominantly White, West LA neighborhood. Previously, she had been surrounded by Asians / Asian Americans in the Bay Area where she had grown up and at her alma mater, the University of California, Berkeley.

> My next door neighbor right here (pointing), she's Caucasian. I just don't really like her and when we moved, she gave us such a hard time about where to park our car . . . I mean, just name it, she's done it. She had a Christmas party and our neighbor down the hall was invited but we weren't invited. I never felt that [blatant racism] until now, now that I'm here in Brentwood . . . Just the fact that we were excluded didn't make me feel good. I really don't like this area; most of them are Caucasian . . . Now that I'm thinking, the [previous] owners here were Caucasians but they rented it out to UCLA students who were all Asians, and I guess the guys had parties, broke condo association rules and maybe they thought we were going to be the same way, I don't know. When I first came, she even asked, "So does your dog bark and does your baby cry?" I felt like she was discriminat[ing] against us because we were Asian, I don't know, I didn't appreciate that at all.

As Audrey recounted this story, she was clearly distressed and concerned about how long she could live under such conditions. She, like everyone else, wanted to feel at home in her domicile and not have to constantly prove her differences from "bad Asians" (i.e., the UCLA students). Rather than be able to relax in her posh condominium that she and her husband had bought through their hard-earned "model minority" salaries, she lived under the pressure of White American neighbors seeing and treating her as "those bothersome Asians" with loud babies who were unworthy of an invite to their potentially loud parties.

Although the above respondents struggled with foreignness *despite* their high socioeconomic standing, other Korean Americans noted that White Americans singling them out as model minorities also made them feel like foreigners. I asked Todd, an attorney at a predominantly White law firm, the following: "Do you think stereotypes attached to Asians have ever been something put on you?"

T: Oh, I mean the model minority stuff, like "You work hard and you're smart," everybody always attaches that stuff.

N: What's the reaction that you have?

T: I mean I'm not that good at math so . . .

N: Do you tell people that?

T: Yeah, I mean I've had to deal with situations where—and these are very well meaning White people who literally come up to you—they're like, "You know, I like to hang out with Asians because they're like me. They like to work hard, they're smart, and they're disciplined just like me." You know, that's really offensive. They don't even realize it's offensive. They think it's a compliment like, "You're so achievement oriented! Good for you!" . . . No, it's very offensive.

I asked the same question of Sora, someone who had made clear throughout her interview that she believed that opportunities were bountiful in the United States and that hard work did pay off. Many others shared this sentiment. Sora had a doctorate in pharmacy and a high-paying, coveted job as a marketing manager for a top pharmaceutical company, yet she somehow felt irked by the model minority ideology.

S: Actually my current boss, I really think that he just feels that Koreans are, you know, modest, extremely hard working, and bright individuals . . .

N: How do you often react?

S: You know (pause), I'm pretty like a mild personality person and so it probably doesn't bother me a whole lot, but regardless of if it's a positive or negative stereotype, *they're still stereotypes*, you know? If you think about it that way, it does get a little irritating, you know? (emphasis added)

The reason Todd and Sora found the "positive" model minority stereotype so "offensive" and "irritating" was because it was a constant reminder that their White American bosses and co-workers saw Todd and Sora as an Asian image, not as individuals. In addition, White Americans' marking of Asian Americans as "just like us" also betrays the belief that non-Whites are pejoratively "different" until proven otherwise. Lastly, being patted on the head for being "a good 'race' " is belittling, especially when the head pats stop once Asian Americans show signs of potentially disrupting, rather than accessorizing, the U.S. racial order. For instance, elite universities' altered weighting of standardized test scores to stem the tide of Asian American admissions in the 1980s (Takagi 1993) and Americans' fears of Japan's global ascent (and potential superiority [Jung 2006]) are prime examples of how a "good minority" can instantly become a yellow peril. In brief, Todd and Sora were not Todd and Sora; they were foreign model minorities.

Invisible and Foreign

Some skeptics might allege that invisibility is merely a South Korean and a first-generation experience. My data, however, find it to be a central dimension of the second generation's struggles with "race." The debilitating racial ideology of the Asian foreigner necessarily rests on the partial presence, or erasure, of the group. To illustrate, Sung, a high-achieving, college-bound high school senior, related just how invisible he was to Whites from Kentucky and Idaho. He shared his frustration despite the fact that he had spent most of his interview wanting to portray himself as undeterred by all the racial ignorance he had faced in his life. Despite putting on his best "cool pose" (see Rose 1994)—perhaps as a way to subvert ideologies of unmasculine Asian American men—Sung's narrative reveals that some incidents really tested his cool.

S: White people can't tell the difference between Koreans, Chinese people and Japanese people; and some White people don't even know what an Asian person is . . .

N: What do they think Asians are?

S: Well, like I went to a basketball tournament and there was a team from Kentucky there and like they didn't know I was classified as an Asian . . . I don't think there's many Asians in Kentucky . . . Something sort of similar happened to me too once in the South. We were actually kind of scared because they had never seen Asians before. Well, like my friend's relatives [are] from Idaho, they're scared of Asians; so like, I scare them (wry smile).

N: So you purposely scare them?

S: Yeah.

N: Like what do you do to scare them?

S: I just run up to their car and say (loudly) "Hi, how you doing?!" and yeah, they get scared.

N: So it kind of annoys you, then?

S: Yeah. It does.

Sung's need to be cool is evident in his response. Rather than educate the White Idahoans about who Korean/Asian Americans are, he used his Otherness to subvert their dominance and exploit their fears. He was clearly bothered by the fact that his existence could be unknown and erased and that, when it did become known, he was gawked at and feared.

In the institutional realm, the second generation had little problem citing the invisibility of Korean/Asian Americans. Indeed, numerous studies point to the lower returns Asian Americans receive for their education, some estimating that their college degrees receive seven times less protection from poverty than do Whites' degrees (see Lai and Arguelles 2003). Asian Americans are also greatly underrepresented as managers in several occupational sectors: government, private employment, and higher educational institutions (both public and private; Xie and Goyette 2004).

Audrey, a University of California, Berkeley, graduate and successful attorney who hailed from an upper-middle-class family, was unequivocal about Asian Americans' invisibility in the top socioeconomic echelons of U.S. society. She made this claim in response to my question of whom she considered the most dominant and influential group in the United States.

Oh my gosh, Caucasian would be very dominant, I mean, even in the legal profession, you rarely see an Asian partner in a firm. I know for a fact there are so many Asian lawyers but why aren't they becoming partners, you know? Most are White males that are partners. If you go to any medical school, college, you see White males as achievers. I rarely see an Asian guy as the chief of the medical staff . . . And I actually can't wait until we have an Asian or a Black President in the U.S., but it will never happen.

Here she alludes to institutionalized racism and its effects on both Asian and Black Americans, such as exclusion from the U.S. presidency. Even Black Americans, whom she described elsewhere to be the most powerful non-White group in U.S. politics, would, in her mind, never be able to rule the United States. As with the first generation, it would be interesting to ask her now what she thought of Senator Barack Obama's strong chances at the U.S. presidency.

Sora wanted to be more optimistic than Audrey about the glass ceilings in pharmaceutical corporations. Like Audrey, however, she recognized the thickness of the glass.

> S: I just even look at my own work environment. There are hardly any Asians like in upper management levels.
>
> N: Is that the history of most big [pharmaceutical] corporations?
>
> S: Oh yeah! I think so; at this other company I was at a few years ago, it was worse because at least here [in] Southern California, there are a few Asians here and there, but out East, hardly . . . I think still corporate America has a hard time envisioning other people in those types of positions.
>
> N: Do you see it as kind of being discriminatory or not?
>
> S: Yeah, I do! Because I think a lot of it is just, I don't know, they're actively keeping people out; at least where I am now, they are trying.

Although Sora seemed wishful about racial progress, she recognized that White Americans are not used to having Asian American CEOs and vice presidents running big drug companies.

As with the first generation, the second generation seemed to be most keenly attuned to Asian Americans' invisibility in the realms of mainstream culture and politics. Like their elders, the second generation believed that they were less powerful than Blacks and Latinos along political and cultural lines. To be certain, a minority of respondents ($n = 4$) recycled the standard color line when I asked them about overall racial hierarchies in the United States: Anglo White and Jewish people are on top, then Asian Americans (meaning *East* Asian), then Latinos (meaning Mexican/Central Americans), then Blacks. Yet, some of these same people would then qualify how there were "well-off Blacks" who were "above well-off Asian Americans" and how there were "poor Asian Americans" ranked "lower than every group." Given multiple axes of inequality—such as color, social class, and social citizenship—most of the respondents, like the first generation, found themselves unable to proffer the single hierarchy of the color line offered up by many social scientists (i.e., Asian Americans just below or alongside Whites). The second generation often claimed, rather, "I'm not sure that there's one answer."

To illustrate Korean Americans' understanding of their position along multiple hierarchies, I provide a narrative by Tim, a patient rights advocate.

I don't think you can really order that in a straight hierarchy; let's take the issue of Korean American versus African Americans. If you're talking about African Americans in the inner city and Koreans who own a liquor store in them, then you have an economic arrangement [in] which the Korean Americans are in power over the African Americans, where[as] if you talked about different sectors of society, African Americans are definitely more represented in academia in terms of professorships and government, mainstream media. And so I think, of course Korean Americans don't have that power. They're trying to, but they don't.

This was a point he stressed often in his interview. Earlier he had responded to my question of discrimination against Korean/Asian Americans by noting the group's cultural invisibility: "In terms of culture, uh, in terms of cultural worth, we're underrepresented. *For the most part we don't exist,* you know, aside from Ted Koppel's *Nightline* thing on Korean Americans and the riots" (emphasis added). Again, cultural representation is a form of political power. Many other respondents agreed that Blacks were way ahead politically, citing greater group cohesiveness and central figures like Jesse Jackson and Al Sharpton.

Heesu, a graduate student, also cited Black Americans' power in academia and their bigger clout in politics and mainstream culture. Our exchange starts with my comment on her belief that there was no single vertical hierarchy of "races."

N: You can actually do different ones where you say economically, for example [this] or politically [that]. You can use any criteria you want.

H: I think in terms of political power and cultural power, African-American and Latinos do a lot better than Asians.

N: And when you say cultural power . . .

H: Not just media like popular media, but like even in academia or I think a lot of that has to do with, just that African-Americans were the first minority in size, and language facility.

Heesu is careful to note that Asian Americans are not simply invisible in mass media but that they lacked representation in academe. Moreover, she, like the first generation, invoked Black Americans' "first" minority status, their larger size, and their English facility.

Some respondents, however, interpreted Asian Americans' lack of visibility in mainstream society as signaling Blacks' overall higher status than Asian Americans. These respondents focused more on the axis of social citizenship

than on the axis of socioeconomics/color to understand Asian Americans' overall social location in the United States. For instance, Lance believed that Black
Americans' longer history and greater cultural power gave them a slight edge
over Asian Americans. After citing Whites as the most dominant, he stated:

> L: It's hard to say, I would like to say Black people [next] because they've been
> around probably the second longest, but I mean, they're really up there or
> they're really down, most of them are really in the bad areas of society . . .
> [But] like all of the movies, music, athletics,[3] it's almost all like Black
> people . . . I don't know, you want Asians?
>
> N: Sure.
>
> L: Asians next, below, you know, Black people.

As he perceived Blacks to be bifurcated into either wealthy or poor classes, he
seemed to want to place Asian Americans below the wealthy subgroup, including the highly visible Black entertainers and athletes in the nation's culture. Yet,
Blacks' "second longest" tenure in the United States and proliferation in the
national culture ultimately prompted him to place Asian Americans below
Black Americans in aggregate terms.

An aspiring actress-singer, Hagen (age 17) cited Asian Americans as the
least powerful group in the United States owing to political and cultural invisibility. She maintains this perspective despite the fact that she hails from an
upper-class family: her father is a tae kwon do grand master and CEO of
schools, and her mother is a co-CEO and a businesswoman. Her narrative begins with my question: "Who do you think has the least amount of power and
resources and control [in the States]?"

> H: Um, well I think the Asians, they really haven't come up and because the
> Asians, we don't really cry about it [racism] but the Blacks have been
> through [a lot] and they start crying about it. For us, I guess it's not really
> like that . . . Koreans—not the Koreans but the Asians—we work hard just
> for our own life, not for the whole group of Asians.
>
> N: So that's kind of why we're on the bottom?
>
> H: Yeah, I think so.
>
> N: So [then] who's sort of after Whites . . . ?
>
> H: Blacks.

Here, it sounds as though she is buying into hegemonic notions of Blacks
complaining by way of the "race" card, but it appears that she sees *not* "crying"

about racism as precisely why Asian Americans lack power and are at the bottom of the social order. Later, Hagen recognizes the difficulty of Asian Americans participating in U.S. politics in light of their "other countries," while most Blacks were descendants of the enslaved. "That's why in the government, there's Whites and Blacks and the Latinos; the Asians it's harder because we have our own world. We have China and Korea and like our own countries, so that's a lot different because America is their country; for Blacks, America is their country. They don't even know if they're from Africa, you know?"

Although it is not clear whether Hagen is mistakenly presuming the lack of immigrants among Blacks, what is clear is that she recognizes Asian Americans' origins in Asia as precluding their singular devotion to "America." In identifying the transnational ties among Asian groups, she, as a member of the second generation, references her own identification with the ancestral "homeland" ("our own countries"). Although Hagen does not make explicit that Asian Americans are themselves "Americans," she, like the first generation, sees a solution in the culture industry (Horkheimer and Adorno 1972). In fact, she was one of the few respondents who actively sought to be that actress-singer on television and movie screens and in concert venues who would become the household name, more specifically, the Asian-sounding name.

H: Right now, I don't feel like a minority in my daily life, but I do in my business . . . There's no Asian people, you know? It's really, really sad and I'm trying to break that, you know?

N: Do you think that if we were more exposed in the entertainment industry, that that would also elevate our standard?

H: Yes!

Tom (age 29, physician), another respondent who did not believe that Asian Americans had enough power to be in the middle of the racial order, echoed another common sentiment that Latinos, not just Blacks, were also culturally mainstream: "First of all, there are a lot more Latinos than Asians, I feel like, and they're pretty much accepted in the mainstream like in terms of acting, in the media and entertainment industry, in sports. You don't see as many Asians in the movie industry or like the Grammys. I can't think of too many Koreans off-hand or Asians off-hand, not like Jennifer Lopez."

Carol is an example of someone who highlighted Korean/Asian Americans' own culpability in the group's invisibility and disempowerment. She, like

Lance and Hagen above, disagreed with the popular and scholarly construction of Asian Americans as in between Whites and Blacks.

N: What you hear a lot is that Whites are on top, African-Americans or Latinos are on bottom and Asians are in the middle. Do you think there is any accuracy to that or we can't really say that?

C: Hmm (pause), I don't think it's that accurate . . . I think people, that's just what they were either taught or just what they've come to believe, because everybody else does.

Carol justifies her answer by underscoring Asian Americans' lack of political power. After blaming the group's insatiable appetite for economic success ("they always want more"), she sees the first generation's lack of political participation as partially culpable for the group's invisibility.

C: Even like Koreatown, like my best friend, she used to work for KAC, Korean American Coalition, and so they would try to get all Koreans to register to vote and kind of make them aware of issues in the community and things that could affect them. She was saying it's so difficult to get them involved. Even when you go to their house and you're like, "Just sign here and you're registered to vote," they *don't want to worry* about that. You know, [just] go to work, go to school and whatever happens in America will just take care of itself.

N: Do you think there's anything else they should be doing besides politics or . . . ?

C: There's a lot, you know like Black history month, things like that, like making other people aware of their history, accomplishments . . . I know things because my parents told me or because I went to Korean school; but if you don't have that then you're not going to know.

Rather than cite the need for more Korean/Asian Americans in mass media culture, Carol also believed in cultural dissemination in the civic arena, such as a Korean/Asian American history month.[4] However, in her view, the younger generations themselves would first need to be schooled on Korean history and culture. In many ways, she echoes the internal criticisms registered by the first generation: excess focus on economic survival (or achieving wealth), insufficient participation in mainstream politics, weak (multi)cultural politics, and the like.

Poppy (age 27), a public school teacher, summed up nicely what many second-generation members prescribed that Korean/Asian Americans do to gain national recognition, hence, greater membership in the country:

> I think that we need to really pursue our creativity and do things that we want to do, yeah, because we're so underrepresented in different areas, and I think that the best recognition could come out from pursuing what you're good at, pursuing what you want, what's in your heart . . . I would like to see more Koreans in different areas whether it be the arts, in theater, theater arts, music arts, you know, visual arts, in education, yeah, and other areas.

In effect, Poppy was appealing to young Korean Americans to move beyond the white-collar world and into the world of arts and education. Like much of the first generation, she did not believe that prestigious occupations would afford full-scale membership in the nation's social citizenry. Compared to the first generation, however, Korean Americans, as those raised in the United States, were not as bent on doing so by promoting ethnic rituals and nationalistic pride or by raising South Korea's status in the global order, though many saw value in it. As the narratives demonstrated, they were much less compelled to hold onto their "model minority" status above Black Americans and Latinos, as growing up amidst racial/ethnic heterogeneity and antiracist discourse further militated against it. Many respondents also identified with Latinos and Black Americans, whether in choosing to defy parental pressures to major in African American studies or working in nonprofit and activist circles to serve all communities of color. In their own way, the second generation chose to reproduce sameness by emphasizing both Koreanness and Asian Americanness simultaneously. Panethnicity, then, was a much more salient part of their lives, identities, and political consciousness than was true of the first generation (see Tuan 1998).

We Can't Erase Our "Race"

More like the first generation, however, the second generation did not believe that being mainstream Korean Americans, or even achieving parity with White Americans on *all* societal levels, would ever translate into Whites treating them like fellow Whites. Although parity, mainstream visibility, and a racial model that acknowledged Asians rather than just Whites and Blacks might afford them greater social citizenship, their phenotype could only bring them to the reaches of "approximate Americanness." The responses I present below are a snapshot of the overwhelmingly negative responses[5] to the "parity" question that I also asked of the first generation: "Do you think White Americans would treat us as equals once we have reached all of the exact same levels as they have in U.S. society?"

TODD: [*age 26, attorney*] No . . . What does it mean to make it in a country? I mean, like a piece of trailer park trash sitting in Arkansas thinks he's better than me and I make four times what he does. Because he's White he can walk into any restaurant: a nobody, nobody, [but] he's a White guy! . . . I mean you look at his people, it shows spotted ancestors, so if money's making it, I guess we've made it, but you know, it's a lot more than that!

Not only did Todd reply in the negative, but his disillusionment with White America led him to problematize the currency of social class in a racist society altogether. What follows is a battery of like responses:

JOE: No.

N: Why do you not think that?

JOE: Um, 'cause Whites think Asians are foreigners.

N: Even if we were just like them in all levels of society?

JOE: No.

N: So you think appearance would still make a big difference then?

JOE: Mhm! (age 42, nonprofit administrator)

DAVID: [*age 26, graduate student*] No.

N: And why no?

DAVID: 'Cause the human animal is a very visual animal.

JENNY: [*age 28, graduate student*] No.

N: You don't think so?

JENNY: Yeah. I think that because we're always going to be different.

N: You mean, in the way we look?

JENNY: Yeah! The way we look. I think with other immigrants, Caucasian immigrants from Europe or whatever, it's easier for them to blend in and you can't really tell [but then they say]: "Oh my parents are actually from Italy" or whatever . . . But with Asians or Koreans I think it's very obvious . . . [Plus] we haven't been here as long. I think it's always a sense like, "Oh, they're the outsiders."

JOHN: [*age 18, college student*] No, I think everyone sees everyone as their own specific race.

N: So you don't think anyone would see us as White, ever?

JOHN: No.

N: Like if we lived in a very posh neighborhood?

JOHN: No, I don't think so.

Unlike the others, Heesu, a graduate student, replied that she did not believe that Koreans could ever reach complete parity with Whites in the first place. Another respondent, Ron, concurred with the others that Whites would always distinguish non-Whites as different, yet he refused to jettison his Koreanness to "whiten" even if doing so would bring huge social dividends. To him, as he stated at the outset of this chapter, multiculturalism in a context of equality was the desired goal.

R: I wouldn't want them to [see me as White]!

N: Why?

R: Because I'm, I'm not them!

N: Are you proud of that?

R: Yeah, I'm damn proud of that!

As the foregoing narratives demonstrate, many of the respondents agreed with Ron that mainstreaming as Korean/Asian Americans would afford them greater membership in "America" but never its fullest form. Authenticity was the province of Whites and Whiteness, a fact to which they were resigned. In effect, second-generation members like Ron, and much of the first generation, did not want it any other way.

Like the first generation, the second generation understood the way in which the straitjacket of "race" proscribed their full inclusion and authenticity as "Americans." No amount of money, flashy materialism, Ivy League diplomas, and white-collar promotions could erase their "race," its signification of foreignness, and its alibi of the "foreign model minority." They therefore strove to make the most of abridged possibilities by one day becoming mainstream Korean ethnics, that is, "approximate Americans." Central to their understandings and that of all Korean Americans was the 1992 LA unrest. This induction into American "race" relations seared into their political consciousness and threw into relief their differential inclusion in the U.S. nation.

The second generation resented the dominant group's exploitation of Asian American invisibility, namely, ignoring Korean Americans in their greatest time of need because they could.

In order to present the U.S. opportunity structure as meritocratic and to validate "blame the victim" notions, Whites have celebrated Asian Americans as model minorities on the path to "whitening," passing Blacks along the way. These notions of "whitening" are inaccurate insofar as they assume that Asian Americans are not fundamentally hurt by "race," specifically, by racialization and subordination tied to immigration, citizenship, and larger global inequalities. As the testimonies from successful Asian Americans lay bare, whitening theses overlook the fact that Asian Americans have been *pitted* against Blacks and other non-Whites in the service of White American dominance. This hegemonic project has relied on gestures toward whitening, such as "model minority" celebrations, but not with the intent of delivering a White status. Nor do the first or the second generation desire in any way to jettison or submerge their Korean/Asian identity to take on a White one as portended by Euro-Americans' own identity assimilation around the mid-twentieth century (Warren and Twine 1997; Yancey 2003). As my study and other works show (Espiritu 2003; Kibria 2002a; P. Ong and Azores 1994; Rudrappa 2004; see Massey 1995), Asian American groups do not desire to jettison or dilute their ethnic identity to become part of the White category or to assimilate into a more homogenized grouping in which their difference is erased. Their life experiences in the United States—and, for the first generation, in the home country—made abundantly clear that they would never be accepted as White Americans in the first place.

Transnational Feedback

Racial Lessons from Korean America

"America Is in the Heart"

—Carlos Bulosan

TRANSNATIONAL MESSAGES, as channeled through mass media and personal exchanges, proved a potent influence on immigrants' premigration racial knowledge about the United States. This chapter explores what social remittances (Levitt 2001) the first-generation immigrants, along with the second generation, sent back to South Korean kin and friends. Although it is much beyond the scope of this study to ascertain how these Korean Americans' messages bear directly on the home country's understandings of "race" and racism in the United States, it is important to chart what stories and ideas immigrants *are* sharing in this cultural loop. I pay attention to what Korean Americans convey about their social locations in the U.S. racial system, how they craft their messages in light of group rifts across borders, and the implications of such information for South Korean society. Questions I pursue include, Did Korean Americans speak at length about their lack of political and cultural power relative to Blacks and Latinos, thereby affirming South Korea's sense of their invisibility in "America" and the world? And/or did immigrants convey their continued sense of themselves as below Whites but above Blacks (and Latinos), perpetuating nationalism and the society's problematic responses to their internalized oppression? As well, did South Koreans highlight their proliferation in inferior and foreigner jobs, in part, as a way to coach the next wave of émigrés onto a different path? Because stories concerning the Korean diaspora often circulate and become part of the cultural landscape of South Korea (Abelmann and Lie 1995), these stories, especially those sent from "America," tend to have a ripple effect. The 1992 LA unrest / "Black riots" (*hŭgin pokdong*) is a prime example of the reverberations that racial conflict in the United States can have in immigrant "homelands" across the globe. These cultural reverberations continually feed and reconfigure South

Koreans' experience of racialization forged by the political, economic, and cultural realms of U.S. imperialism.

These conversations were especially relevant for those South Koreans who were considering immigration to the United States. The respondents in my study noted, however, that the prospective migrants' focus on logistics—how to get sponsored, how much money to save and bring—often dampened in-depth conversations about racial hierarchies and relations with out-groups. The Korean Americans even claimed that they did not share much about their own struggles with racial discrimination, particularly if their kin and friends were reluctant to immigrate because of worries over racism. They did, however, share their new realizations about the nature of " 'race' in America," often in subtle and implicit ways.

As noted, South Koreans who immigrate tend to articulate more pro-American sentiments. They immigrate in large part because they take as an article of faith the openness and largesse of the U.S. opportunity structure. Many also come to escape political and personal troubles, to seek new American adventures, and live out imagined ideals. These are the reasons they make the long, costly, arduous, and emotional journey away from the comforts of family, white-collar jobs, and ex-nominated status. In contrast, those Koreans who stayed behind (especially since the 1980s) have tended toward greater anti-Americanism and have maligned the immigrants as Korean Benedict Arnolds and as those who are ashamed of their own national family. These unflattering perceptions have guided Korean immigrants' choices about what to share with certain South Koreans.

The Korean Benedict Arnold and Horatio Alger

Extending from South Koreans' duality regarding the United States, many Seoul residents reported having envied those who had gone to thrive in the land of milk and honey, even as anti-American sentiments rolled off their tongue. Although images of immigrants robbing the nation of its "material and human assets" preceded the 1980s (Abelmann and Lie 1995:80), these became de rigueur in the anti-American decade of the 1980s and ever since. A common trope about United States–bound Koreans was that of the traitor who left the "homeland" in the rubble left by centuries of national suffering: China's conquests, Russia's attempts at domination, Japanese colonization, poverty/underdevelopment, the Korean War, the U.S. military occupation, the divide with the North. Rather than devote themselves to making the nation a better country, if not the best, these Koreans left precisely for the country that had already become the best; they selfishly left for the dream life. The ammunition for these salvos was the belief that emigrants had rejected their own subordinate nation and thereby denied their own family, their own selves (see Balibar 1991). The immigrants' shame in their national family also made rents in what was meant to be a rock-hard nationalist ethos. Critical of Korean immigrants, a 1962 newspaper editorial by a South Korean read: "If you are ashamed of your country's own culture, no matter how wealthy you live in another nation, your life can only be compared to that of a servant. If the parents do not stop living like a servant in the US, there is no way that their children can escape living like servants, no matter how fluent they are in English" (*Chosun Ilbo*, May 7, 1962).

Within this context, it is not surprising that one pejorative for immigrants in the United States is "*ttong-po,*" a play on the word *tongpo,* meaning "fellow countrypeople." "*Ttong,*" however, means excrement. Although South Koreans do not blame the children as much as they do the immigrant parents, such sentiments manifest in open disapproval of Korean Americans who speak English or poor Korean while in the ancestral "homeland" (Kibria 2002b; N. Kim forthcoming). When my younger brother, whose level of Korean is limited mostly to food words, had been with me in the country, older men—from taxi drivers to subway passengers—have liberally used their Confucian parental privileges to criticize him for speaking English. Interrupting our conversations, they would gripe: "Your parents are from Korea, you have a Korean face, why can't you speak Korean? How can you know who you are if you don't know anything about your *ppuri* (roots)?!" Next to my bewildered brother, I would explain in Korean, "*Ajŏsshi,*[1] he was born there, he's grown up in a mostly White country, he tries but it's hard—you can try to understand a little, yes?" They would usually respond with an insistent "But still . . ." In their diatribes, they often implied the notion of United States / Western contamination of Korea and its blood, the longstanding ideological formation against external powers that I have noted. In more recent years, to be sure, South Koreans appear to have become more accepting, or perhaps they have just resigned themselves to the fact. Yet the sentiment continues to rumble below the surface.

South Koreans were able to feel vindicated when their economy gained even more rapid-fire strength in the 1980s through the early 1990s, marked by their hosting of the 1988 Olympics. In fact, Abelmann and Lie (1995:78) found that the Korean immigrant community, especially after the unrest, began to voice their regret over having left. Few could come close to the profligate lifestyle of those in Seoul who had amassed wealth from land speculation in particular and who were wont to flaunt it. Although the rate of Korean return migration has generally not been high, a *New York Times* survey found that during the 1985–1995 economic boom period, return migration had increased seven- to eightfold (*Chosun Ilbo*, August 23, 1995:39). Immigrants also returned during this time after finding the racial and linguistic isolation and exclusion in the United States insufferable, especially after the 1992 unrest (*Chosun Ilbo*, August 23, 1995). In 1995, for instance, the rate of immigration to the United States decreased and that of return migration increased. Since the 1997 International Monetary Fund (IMF) crisis, however, the trends have reversed (*Chosun Ilbo*, August 23, 1995).

Partly owing to these uneven trends, South Koreans bifurcate U.S. immigrants into those who live a misery of low-class jobs and racism or as those who succeed and live the good life. The most widely read South Korean newspaper, *Chosun Ilbo*, has presented both views. As early as 1947, a South Korean Ambassador to the United States was quoted as saying, "All Korean Americans seemed to be doing well, and their lives are very abundant" (*Chosun Ilbo*, October 12, 1947). In more recent years, the newspaper has highlighted immigrants' impressive capacity to earn and send their children to good schools, all in the face of racial discrimination (*Chosun Ilbo*, May 20, 2002). These accounts offer up successful Korean Americans like Michelle Wie and Chan-ho Park to prove the point (*Chosun Ilbo*, May 20, 2002). At the same time, articles since the 1970s have published stories of graduates of Seoul University, the Harvard of South Korea, and immigrants with U.S. doctorates living bereft of the good life given massive corporate layoffs and meager opportunities (e.g., dishwasher, janitor, security guard; *Chosun Ilbo*, December 29, 1971). Later, the 1992 LA unrest would thrust these dismal perceptions into the spotlight. Whether South Koreans explained the "riots" by blaming Blacks or blaming Korean immigrants, they began to construct immigrant life "over there" as overworked misery plagued by "race" wars. In fact, the "riots" were only fodder for South Koreans who most fiercely critiqued their overseas coethnics as self-interested national traitors (Abelmann and Lie 1995:28), what I call "Korean Benedict Arnolds."

Koreans in the United States are mindful of these contentious and dualist sentiments whenever they share accounts of their lives with those across the ocean. They are acutely aware of the home society's disapproval of immigrants and utter disgust when some immigrants visit thinking themselves to be better after living in the dream country. Even when the Korean immigrants insisted they did not put on airs, they claimed to suffer rejection from their overseas brethren. Old-timer Mr. Yoo, for instance, had lived for three years in South Korea after the LA unrest in order to reacquaint himself with his "homeland" and to better report about it in his Radio Korea segments. His sojourn taught him how different and distant he was from his counterparts in South Korea.

> Y: When I went there, I couldn't easily fit myself in because I lived in America so long. There were some things that [we] *couldn't understand* about each other . . . That means that I've been much more Americanized without even being aware of it. I wasn't aware!
>
> N: Oh, what kind of difference did you feel, for example?
>
> Y: Difference in thinking. I became much more *liberal* living here without even knowing it. I came to have a broader understanding of people.

He went on to say that one of the aspersions South Koreans cast his way was that of national traitor: "People in Korea blame us as those who had deserted their own country even though they themselves desire to come here, right?" In 2000, these antipathies still held sway. In my interviews there, older South Korean respondents would often say, "Those immigrants who disconnect themselves from their roots/nation (*ppuri*) are bad people." A Mr. Yoo, in his fifties, maintained: "Although what they say seems to make them look good, actually they're taking Korean possessions to foreign countries. If they made money abroad, they should support their families in Korea . . . If they were born with a Korean bloodline, why do they look down on Korea and take money out of Korea where there's not a lot of money? That's bad!"

Although U.S. immigrant Mr. Yoo, the gentleman who had lived in his home country for three years, would likely deem such a rant duplicitous, his dual experience of being a South Korean traitor and racially "foreignized" in the United States engendered his belief that Korean immigrants had to accept their status as partial members of both countries. Simply put, they fully belonged nowhere. At the same time, he knew that the first generation would need to claim "America" more publicly as their home in order to become mainstream Korean Americans, the noted strategy of choice.

We're Superhuman Workers

Although old-timers sometimes had to be careful not to appear boastful about their American lives or judgmental of the home country, both newcomers and old-timers alike would speak freely with their close kith and kin. They often reinforced nationalist tropes in their tales of how diligent (*puchirŏnhae*) and adept Korean immigrants had to be in order to survive. Newcomer Ms. Kong (age 28), for instance, noted that despite her and her husband's willingness to work hard, they both realized that they could not have the flexible schedules they had in Seoul. She shared her observations with her South Korean friends who were curious about U.S. life.

> I tell them how diligently Koreans work here. I explained the situation by re- minding my friends that over there we all watched movies at least once or twice a month and went out and ate foreign food like at a nice cafe, and every year at summertime, we matched our vacations and visited each other; but I told them that kind of life is not possible here. They said, "Really?" I told them that even if we do a small business here, we couldn't just shut it down to go travel and leave it unattended.

Although the ethos of Koreans' exceptional work ethic was taken as a priori, Koreans in the United States seemed to surpass that ethic even to the surprise of South Koreans.

In Seoul, a female graduate student named Ms. Lee had heard from her own transnational contact, a friend of a friend who studied abroad in the United States, that Korean Americans were indeed very hard working. She related: "He said that the people in the States seemed more diligent and hardworking than the people here, probably because they are minorities and they think they should try harder to survive." Another South Korean, a gentleman in his sixties named Mr. Shin, had no contact with any immigrants in the United States, but he had heard similarly glowing accounts of immigrants' exceptional work ethic and successes.

> People have said that Koreans become successful in the U.S. because of their strength for living and their diligence and knowledge, there are many excellent people among them who do extremely well in universities or become lawyers or mayors. Our Koreans who were born in this small country went to that big country and thrived in many competitions, even to become mayors which re- quired getting a lot of votes; because of [that] they have been treated well and they've settled down well. This is very honorable. In a word, I'm proud. I be- lieve that any Korean, as long as they are not crippled by anything, can live well when they go to any country without being underneath anyone.

Although he seemed to know little about the many hardships of Korean immigrants in the United States—such as the scant number of mayors—his nationalist pride seemed to want to override any potential negative aspect of immigrant life.

As I introduced in Chapter 5, Korean immigrants at times reinforced such ethnonationalist pride and affirmed their middle status by repeating stereotypes of Black and Mexican Americans to South Koreans. In so doing, they normalized South Koreans' frames of color-class-ethnonationality and reified the nationalism that many Koreans tended to use for their problematic "detour" through oppression. However, some immigrants dispelled stereotypes of Blacks not working hard, demystified the trope of Koreans' exceptional work ethic, and thereby destabilized South Korean's pride of being in the middle. Immigrant newcomers like Ms. Kim were especially struck by how hard Americans worked despite her premigrant impression of a more leisurely life of plenty. She told those abroad: "*Everybody* here lives in a sincere way and works hard." She derived this conclusion from working with Latino immigrants at a Korean-owned clothing store. Mr. Bahng, a Chinese medicine doctor, frequently remarked during his interview how impressed he was by the "very strong work ethic in America." He shared his observations with those abroad: "I tell them that because it's a multicultural society, I meet a variety of people, so I know that people in America work hard regardless of race." He went on to say, "Nothing's for free in America. Here beggars wash your car windows and demand money for their services." In other words, no racial group could afford to slip up in "America." These sentiments are quite a radical departure from Korean society's naturalization of class status and veneration of Koreans as the hardest workers the world over. Immigrants told them, rather, that everyone in "America," from the CEO to the beggar, had to earn every penny.

These messages could also reinforce the moves in South Korea toward socially desirable norms on "race" talk and the antiracism that has begun germinating among young adults in particular. Despite formidable societal taboos against exogamy, pressures for blood purity, worries over culture clashes, and resistance to Blacks' state power (as part of anti-Americanism), some of the South Koreans conveyed an openness to intermarriage with Blacks/Africans (and with Latinos and Southeast Asians). During my six months of fieldwork and multiple personal trips over the years, two Korean-Black couples/pairings jolted me out of the taken-for-granted scenery of everyday life. I glimpsed a twenty-something Korean female holding hands with her Black male partner (of similar age) as they walked out of a megachurch in Sunday dress. It was not clear to me if the second pair I saw was a couple, but in this second case, the young Korean female and Black male seemed intimate in the way they were with each other. They were dressed in civilian clothes (jeans and nice shirts) and stood on a subway station escalator several steps ahead of me.[2] In both cases, I panned my eyes across the surrounding people. Although some innocently stared as I did, I did not witness anyone frothing at the mouth or whispering unflattering disapproval in each other's ears, common behaviors especially among the middle-aged and elderly populace (to be sure, church typically pressures people into niceties, and I was only afforded a quick glance at both pairings). Yet, most Korean (female)-Black (male) matches are made in the military camptowns. Both because most GIs do not venture farther than the camptowns or nearby environs and because of mainstream society's visceral animus toward relationships between Korean women and U.S. soldiers, interracial couples have usually stayed within those bounds. When I saw the two couples on different occasions in late 2000, I therefore witnessed something I did not anticipate seeing within the mainstream public, let alone more than once. Although I knew from the rest of my trips there and my native-born contacts that such sightings were not routine, Seoul has become more cosmopolitan and people visit from all over the world.

Also potentially signaling a watershed in the offing are the segments of Korean society that genuinely respect and appreciate hip-hop, inspiring the frenzy of MC, break dancing, and pop and lock training on the peninsula. Moreover, hip-hop / R & B / pop sensation Rain, ranked first in *Time* magazine's 2006 online poll of the "100 Most Influential People Who Shape Our World" (ahead of Stephen Colbert), seems to have a genuine respect for hip-hop and has met with interested Black American stars like Diddy and Omarion.

However, no one has brought "race" and racism to the fore more publicly than the Pittsburgh Steelers' Hines Ward (Super Bowl XL Most Valuable Player). Since my interviews, Ward, the child of a Korean mother and Black American father, traveled to his birthplace in 2006 and established the Hines Ward Helping Hands Foundation to assist multiracial children overcome discrimination, the first of its kind. South Korea celebrated and welcomed him as "a Korean" hero, involving a meeting with the ROK president at his Blue House and a constant media blitz. While there, Ward actively spread antiracist ideology, namely the liberal humanism of "love knows no color," and he publicly cried when he recounted his struggles with racism in the United States. His visit and charity work have spurred South Korean legislators to introduce laws barring discrimination against all multiracial children. Many Koreans, however, including Ward's Korean mother, express skepticism that the country is simply capitalizing on Ward's celebrity to bring honor unto itself. They may be right, but the reception still marks a landmark change from a mere twenty years ago, one that is forcing the Korean nation to learn more about what racism is, the overall American "race" history, and to confront moral questions about its own inequalities and discriminatory practices. Change could also be realized by Black American soldiers recognizing the oppressive nature of the U.S. occupation as well as their own prejudices against Korea/Koreans. In summary, the fact that South Koreans are increasingly marrying various out-group members and are not living as sequestered lives reveals that even in a blood-nationalistic society collectively embattled over its oppression, change is possible. That is, not all Koreans are animated solely by a nationalistic need to submerge an oppressed history, offset internalized inferiority, and resist all Black American soldiers.

The Model Minority and Its Foreign Partner in Crime

In addition to demystifying notions of their group's exceptional diligence and work ethic, immigrants also informed those considering migration about the inferior and foreigner status of Korean small business work—its low occupational prestige, its hyperethnic character, and its locales in many racial minority areas. Certainly, the coverage of the 1992 LA unrest popularized these notions. Transnational exchanges with immigrants or return migrants could also affirm the picture of an unfavorable work life in the United States. Old-timer Mr. Pak, for instance, had tried to convince his siblings to immigrate. They had come close to doing so until tales from jaded return migrants led to a change of heart.

> P: At that time [1980s/1990s] the Korean economic situation was quite good, so they didn't want to come because they knew that they had to live a hard life once they got here.
>
> N: How did they know that?
>
> P: When the Korean economic situation was good, those people who had immigrated and went back to Korea told them . . . They told them that they had to lead a hard life, that they couldn't communicate successfully, that they had to do manual labor if they came to America.
>
> N: Did you agree with that view?

P: Yes, so I couldn't force them . . . I told them to make their own choice, and they didn't come.

The first-generation immigrants in my study who visited the "homeland" but not as "prodigal sons or daughters" expressed having difficulty interacting with their old South Korean friends. Mr. Koh, a middle-aged old-timer aptly summed up this difficulty: "Whenever I go back, the difference I feel is that my friends there are still in the professional class while I became low-collar-class in the U.S. That's the difference that I feel." These kinds of transnational exchanges coupled with widespread knowledge of the LA unrest had informed South Koreans that their immigrant counterparts were ultimately the outsiders, the racialized foreigners who worked "3-D" jobs in "America:" the dirty, difficult, and dangerous. Irrespective of their knowledge that many immigrants climbed back into the middle class after performing these jobs, the perception was unflattering.

When immigrants talked about their group's foreignness, they recapitulated the theme of ethnic insularity and ethnic jobs as complicit in their own foreignness and marginality. Old-timer Mr. Sohn (age 73), a South Korean corporate businessman turned immigrant meat packer and restaurant owner in the United States, related this message in his perception of immigrant life.

I told them "Do not come here if you haven't studied English first. Just live in Korea if you haven't studied English because then you'll have to live in Koreatown and if you live in Koreatown, then you're not living in the USA. Why do you have to come all the way here if that's the case? Are you coming to make money? Then just live there a little less financially secure."

Mr. Sohn reifies Korean Americans' foreigner status by claiming that Koreatown is "not living in the USA." That is, Koreans would have to live amongst Whites, not a mini Korea, to be part of an authentic U.S.A. In practical terms, he believes that making money is not sufficient reason to be an immigrant minority confined to not-America, thus reinforcing to South Koreans one of their negative conceptions of immigrant life.

At the same time, given their construction of nation, South Koreans likely received the immigrants' persistent foreignness in "America" as unremarkable. That is, the immigrants' authentic nation (roots, *ppuri*) was Korea while "America" was "owned" by Whites. Notwithstanding these constructions, the Koreans in the United States also believed that bias against them as fundamentally foreign was unjust and that the group need build a "mainstream Korean America." In fact, immigrants' disquiet over Koreans' current position in the United States belied the "naturalness" of the racial foreigner position, constituting a disruption of the South Korean conceptualization of nation and belonging. As an example, by advising would-be immigrants to come and work if they had learned English, the first generation implied that Koreans in the United States were not stuck, that they could partake in the occupational, cultural, and political mainstream ("live in the USA"). By extension, Koreans could gain recognition for the home country and its people, though within the limits of the one thing that they knew could never be erased: their looks.

Social Remittances on "Race" and Racism

When I asked the immigrants whether they shared with South Koreans accounts of their racial experiences or relations, most of them claimed that they had not. They found that explaining these issues was, in effect, futile. Old-timer Mr. Yoo summed it up well when he said, "They could never understand without having lived here." In fact, it would be surprising if South Koreans were able to grasp the everyday reality of being a racial minority in White-over-Black America. Although those in the home society could understand the immigrants' invisibility given their own battles with it, they could not grasp the *experiential* dimensions of everyday "race" experiences, such as language/identity problems and severely proscribed social citizenship.

To be sure, the first-generation immigrants were also culpable, as they seemed to avoid in-depth exegeses on the racial discrimination they faced, in part to stave off South Koreans' negative images of American life and the vindicating "I told you so." Korean immigrants likely felt compelled to convince South Koreans (and themselves) that their trials across the ocean were, in the end, worth it. Old-timer Mr. Bahng, the successful Chinese medicine doctor in Beverly Hills, however, summed up why immigrants' rosy portraits of "America" were problematic and dangerous: "The reason why Koreans are misinformed is because the Korean immigrants who came to visit Korea didn't tell us about their struggles. They should tell us, and maybe some people do, but more than five out of ten won't talk about their struggles."

Not surprisingly, it was the second generation who felt more at ease delving into racial inequality when talking with South Koreans. Certainly, they shared with the first generation a desire to correct Euro-American ideologies and blatant prejudices in South Korea. Yet, regarding the strictures of "race" and racism in the United States, it was the second generation who felt compelled to explain the indignities, even when those abroad did not seem to or want to understand. Todd, an attorney, had conveyed to me in his interview how jaded he had become by racial discrimination (especially at his mostly White law firm) and how he had come to "love Korea" as a result (see Foner 2000; Glick Schiller 1999; Kasinitz 1992; Kibria 2002b; N. Kim forthcoming). He especially felt compelled to indoctrinate his cousins who seemed to fall on the pro-American side of the ideological duality.

> T: They're often very naïve. I've noticed they're very surprised that I had these sort of, you know, anti-American feelings . . . [I said] "In Korea you have the advantage, race is not a filter through which you have to view life," and that is incredibly, a stress-reducing thing to have, and so they're very fortunate in that way. But they don't really relate to that; you can't really explain to them that, "you don't have to think about race, that's good," because they don't think about it. And then they're like, "There's racism against Koreans?"
>
> N: Do you talk about what your interactions are like with White Americans?
>
> T: Um, I do try to explain that . . . I don't think they're really surprised, but then I think that it's disappointing to them that America is like that; I try to be very honest with them because a lot of them are always like, "If only I could go to America." I tell them, "Listen, you got it pretty good here!," especially my cousins who are upper middle class . . . I'm like, "No, stay here, you will not have a better life than this in America."

Todd's explanations of "race" as a "filter through which [Korean Americans] have to view life" seem to make some sense to his cousins despite their lack of full comprehension. Although his cousins glorified the United States, at least as a place to live, they had yet to immigrate.

Joe—a nonprofit administrator, in part for coalition-building projects involving Koreans, Blacks, and Latinos—sometimes received calls from the ROK government inquiring about the plight of Korean Americans in the United States. This is what he told them.

> J: Well, I try to describe to them what racism is really like and how minorities have to struggle against a lot of racism and, you know, the acculturation challenges for younger Korean Americans as opposed to immigrants.

N: And why are there more challenges for younger people, do you think?

J: Well, because they have to grow up in this society. It's different than coming here as an adult [when] your identity is basically formed, you're basically trying to survive . . . whereas younger people have to try to figure out how to fit.

N: When you tell them about racism here and about "race" as a big deal, do they get surprised?

J: I don't think they understand racism in a very deep way but I think that they get it that there would be this natural tension between people who look different . . . Plus, you know, CNN and the news is global and they can see the tension like the riots and all that stuff . . . But one conversation, it would be very hard to change them.

Joe believes that South Koreans have some sense of the centrality of " 'race' in America" based on a naturalized explanation of racial tensions (". . . between people who look different"), but could not understand "in a very deep way."

In a similar vein, I asked Hagen (age 17) if and what South Koreans seemed to think about Korean Americans' experiences as minorities in the United States. In her response, she provided a vignette about upper-class Koreans who immigrated without deep awareness that racism could handcuff them in ways they could not anticipate.

H: Everyone is the same [there] so like when they come here they think they're like, you know, the top of the game [upper class], but they're really not . . . And they don't realize that they're a minority, but if you were born out here, it's like we realize it. You know, we know it because we face it, and we've faced it since we were born.

N: Do they understand that when you try to explain that to them?

H: No, because it's like when you're raised with something for so long, you don't listen; it's like you listen, but it doesn't click.

Of note is the indirect message that Korean Americans who spoke of racial discrimination against them were sending to those abroad: the invisibility and foreignness of South Korea in the larger world order. That is, if South Korea were a more dominant, respected, and stable country, White Americans would regard its ethnics much more highly. To be sure, if South Korea had been a more dominant nation-state to begin with, "America" would not have been able to wield such power over it and so many Koreans would not have subsequently left to struggle and toil "in someone else's house."

Understanding Racial Orders in Seoul

Although most Korean Americans did not believe that South Koreans could fully comprehend the everyday experiences of American "race" and racism beyond the level of, say, the occupation, it is worth exploring how their overseas brethren understood group rankings in U.S. racial/ethnic hierarchies. My focus here on such rankings differs from my previous focus on South Korean residents' interpretations of the 1992 unrest, general U.S. mass media representations, and American military might. Of course, the South Koreans' views of U.S. racial hierarchies also flowed from these sources, because most did not have close, sustained ties with immigrants. Ms. Kim was an exception, however. Her close friend in the United States who frequently visited had remarked on Korean Americans' hyperinvisibility. She recounted, "For example, when we were watching Park, Chan-ho on TV [then-star Los Angeles Dodgers pitcher] he was saying how in Korea he is treated as a hero and we go crazy about him, while no one really knows about him in the States." Although in no way was the Korean immigrant populace in the United States disinterested, Ms. Kim's friend noted the stark contrast between the fanaticism of South Koreans and the indifference of the average American. That is, even prominent Koreans, like Major League Baseball pitchers, were relatively invisible in the United States.

The rest of the Seoul residents had no regular and intimate correspondence with immigrants and, perhaps not surprisingly, had some difficulty identifying racial/ethnic orders in U.S. society. In addition, their use of "nation" as a main unit of categorization made *racial* ordering difficult, as was true for some of the first-generation immigrants. Yet, they drew on globalized mass media (e.g., TV, Internet) and texts about the LA unrest, stories they had heard among the people, information they learned in school, and so on, to craft their perceptions. Several, for instance, seemed to focus on Black Americans' (and other people of color's) greater visibility and political power relative to Korean Americans. Although this is not surprising in light of Black Americans' role in the occupational forces and prominence in popular culture, what is striking is how much lower they seemed to position Koreans. Although a few focus group members stated simply that all non-Whites in the United States were below Whites and thus "similar to one another," others proffered Korean Americans' weaker position.

Ms. CHE: They [Koreans] are ranked 4th if there are 5 ranks.

I: Do you think you could briefly pick 5 ranks?

Ms. CHE: Well, using 5 ranks seems unnatural. Instead, when I look at it simply or abstractly, our position is not on the bottom, but it's not in the middle yet either.

MR. YOO: I agree.

In another focus group, members provided groups in rank order based on how much combined economic and political power the groups wielded, but could not really point to other reasons why they ranked as they did.

MR. HAN: Mmm, [in order] Anglo Saxons, Jewish people, Japanese, South Americans, African Americans, etc. . . . .

MR. PARK: Jewish people first, then Caucasians, then Blacks, then South Americans. A little below, but in about the same position would be Japan, then China. And us? We would be in the et ceteras.

These men placed Blacks and South Americans above Koreans (though one placed Japanese Americans near Whites), relegating their brethren close to the bottom of the U.S. racialized hierarchy or within the bottom-dwelling "et ceteras." It is apparent that these young adults put great stock in political power and visibility and did not harness all power to social class. The perception of Japan across the focus groups reveals the common emphasis on nation and development status. Such a view, however, precludes awareness of historical and persistent racial discrimination against Japanese Americans along social citizenship lines (see Tuan 1998).

As noted, other South Koreans hinted toward the racially triangulated positions among White, Black, and Korean Americans by acknowledging *multiple* racial hierarchies, not a singular one. They identified Korean Americans' socioeconomic position above Blacks, but they also identified their smaller population and weaker political and cultural power than Blacks. The focus group format also allowed group members to inform and develop one another's ideas. Mr. Bang began one exchange by reckoning that Whites and Blacks were in roughly the same strata.

MR. BANG: Isn't it about the same there?

I: What do you mean by that?

MR. BANG: Black athletes in sports do better and so do Black singers and Black actors/actresses.

Ms. Lee: However, politically and economically Whites are more (pause)—has there been a Black president yet?

A similar theme emerged in another exchange.

Ms. Park: [After Whites and Jewish people] I think Blacks and South Americans would be powerful because there are a lot of them. I guess the minorities would pretty much all be the same, then?

I: So Koreans belong to the smaller-size minority groups below Whites, Jewish people, Blacks, and Latin Americans?

Mr. Yoo: [But] wouldn't we be close to Blacks?

Ms. Lim: Yeah, wouldn't we? But then, although we might be . . .

Mr. Yoo: — richer than Blacks—

Ms. Lim: Yeah, richer, there are so many more Black people so wouldn't they have stronger power overall?

In an individual interview, Mr. Dong also addressed the multiple positionings of Blacks and Koreans and invoked the "Spanish" as the lower class.

I: The Spanish are the lower class. Then, what about Korean people?

D: They might not experience as much contempt as the Spanish because they have some economic power, although they don't look much better than them in the U.S.

I: What about Blacks?

D: It's kind of hard for me to say without having been in the U.S. . . . . What I think is that many Blacks have done well economically compared to before and there are also many Blacks in high social positions. Although Blacks might suffer from racial discrimination, I think they are better off than the Spanish. I think right now the Spanish are the most exploited class.

I: What about Asians? You can include Koreans or not, up to you.

D: The East Asian nations—Korea, China, and Japan—should have some economic power. Japan and China should especially because of their long history of immigration in the U.S., at least from my outsider's view.

Note that he excises Korea after his initial mention of its economic power, as Koreans did not have the "long history of immigration in the U.S." of Japanese and Chinese ethnics, a key concern among the first generation as well. Moreover, he believes that Koreans "don't look much better than" the Spanish, the lowest and most exploited group, in his view. Although he acknowledges Koreans' economic power, he does not describe his group as occupying "high social positions," a characteristic he reserves for Black Americans. Had he and many of his Seoul counterparts been interviewed in 2008, it stands to reason that their view of Black Americans as sociopolitically empowered would be affirmed by Senator Barack Obama's status as one of the likely Democratic nominees for U.S. president.

Taken together, the narratives are striking insofar as the Seoul residents could have chosen to rate their group high à la ethnic nationalism as well as skin color and social class orders. They could have sought to downplay their status beneath the White West and Japan. Rather, many placed Korean Americans below Blacks and Latino groups or situated each group in positions of both advantage and disadvantage relative to one another. That is, although Koreans/Asians may have had more overall economic power, Blacks had more political/collective and cultural power. After all, South Korea has had its own complex relationship to White and Black America. In their reckonings, then, most of these young adults at the start of the new millennium did not share the compulsion of the older generations of South Koreans and earlier immigrant cohorts to highlight and covet only their "middle" status. They were more candid about the weakness of South Korea and its people. However, they also had the benefit of drawing on the 1992 unrest, an instructive historical moment that the earlier immigrants did not have the privilege of knowing. Owing in large part to the young adults' engagement of the event, albeit ranging from cursory to intimate knowledge, they recognized that Korean immigrants' status as storeowners in low-income Black and Latino communities was unstable, signaled only partial power, and could not eclipse other forms of subordination. Even from a cursory glance of the media coverage, one would be hard pressed not to notice Korean immigrants' lack of power and recognition.

It is plausible that more meaningful exchanges with Korean Americans, among myriad other sources, could foster South Koreans' deeper understanding of the American history and reality of racism and antiracism concerning all groups. Perhaps if fewer South Koreans impetuously branded immigrants as Benedict Arnolds living the good life or suffering the miserable life, Korean Americans could speak more candidly about "race" and its many indignities. And in speaking about it, Koreans in the United States would necessarily stop shrouding in secrecy the unrosy parts of their lives. To initiate the process at all, in fact, they would have to believe that baptism by fire was *not* the only way that South Koreans could develop greater understanding. Indeed, if both parties could change their biases to foster more candid and informative channels of transnational communication, an understanding of the connection between U.S. racialized imperialism and the U.S. domestic racial system could be in the offing. Thus made, the connection would afford an understanding not only of the institutionalized racism behind the treatment of Korean immigrants but also behind "America's" decision to migrate to Korea in the first place. It would elucidate why Black Americans proliferated in the U.S. military that migrated to the Korean nation and shed light on the parallels between both groups' treatment at the hands of hegemonic White America (see Lipsitz 1997).

To be sure, young adult South Koreans are demonstrating a more diverse and complex understanding of the American racial landscape, one that immigrants of the 1970s and 1980s could not have had. By the dint of more variegated exposure and contacts as well as shifting norms, South Korean society is beginning to understand that Black Americans are not just "uneducated GIs" who come to their country and are more than just "the criminals" on the television and movie screens. They are also respected actors, athletes, community leaders, and politicians. And the multiracial children among them who did not choose to be the offspring of the United States–ROK relationship could grow up to fight for greater tolerance, like Hines Ward. In addition, some respondents, though few, are more aware of the social plight of the "Spanish." By virtue of being more familiar with these groups' multifarious social positions, the young adults problematized such ideologies as the reductive anti-Black racism carried into South Korea by "America."

With respect to Korean Americans, the Seoul residents recognized the limits of social class in the absence of cultural and political power, acumen that is impressive for a group of respondents living in an overtly class-stratified and class-fixated society. Aside from the 1992 unrest they may have been influenced by South Korean newspaper coverage of the problem in recent years. In 2002, for instance, *Chosun Ilbo* reported that Korean Americans were not "blending in" with mainstream American society, had "not gotten involved much in American politics," and lagged behind even Chinese and Japanese American politicians in high office (*Chosun Ilbo*, May 20, 2002:3). By taking note of these struggles, the young South Korean generation problematized their coethnics' categorical middle status in the United States and did not parlay this status to make themselves look and feel better, as did other (generally older) South Koreans. On balance, their views, and those of Koreans in the United States themselves, stand in contrast to the sanguine projections of whitening and racial assimilation among some U.S. pundits and scholars. Engaging directly with these Asian groups, whether through interviews or field observations, reveals more complex and variegated issues of power than such projections seem to allow.

10 Postlude

THIS STUDY CASTS A DIFFERENT LIGHT onto my mother's stories about "America" with which I began the book. Like the accounts of Koreans in Seoul and the United States, hers are not simply colorful vignettes about times gone by. Rather, they are life experiences profoundly shaped by U.S. power over South Korea, a nation indelibly racialized by an imperialist United States. It is no surprise, then, that my mother came of age in the 1940s and 1950s with a profound sense of gratitude to a *miguk* ("the Beautiful Country"), represented by White American General MacArthur, and with little to countervail the glorified image and icon. Gratitude to MacArthur and visions of Katharine Hepburn and Elizabeth Taylor also gave rise to unsavory outcomes. Much like the Korean War victims who visited Dr. Millard in an effort to look like him, the U.S. presence stirred my mother's sense of shame in her own eyes, sending her in front of a mirror every night to draw lines with her finger that she prayed would remain. The U.S. presence also prompted unflattering whispers about Korean women who had relationships with American soldiers. In her hometown of Pusan, my mother also noticed that the Black American soldiers seemed to be set apart from those who were White, a pattern she would also notice in her new home of New York City. Indeed, the U.S. military and cultural presence was what drew her, as it did scores of other Koreans, to the United States. Once one of her friends had left after catching "American Fever" and after she herself tired of her parents' matchmaking, my mother made up her mind to pack up her life and spend the rest of it in the "Beautiful Country," all the while telling her parents that she was taking a "short trip." That short trip has lasted thirty-six years.

These are only some of the outcomes, both direct and indirect, of U.S. imperial dominance over South Korea. Much beyond my mother's story, South Korea as a society has long negotiated "America's" White reference point, racialized biases and injustice at the hands of the U.S. military, anti-Black ideologies, and other toxic realities of racial/national oppression. Once South Koreans become Korean Americans in the United States, they find themselves situated at the nexus of United States–ROK relations and the domestic American racial order (see K. Chan and Hune 1995; Espiritu 2003; Lowe 1996). This form of transnational racialization as negotiated by Koreans lies at the heart of my analysis. The process reveals that U.S. imperial rule has already racialized the eventual Korean immigrants as lesser (dependent), foreigner ("gook"), and invisible (not worth knowing), and it has done so partly by way of the U.S. White-over-Black model. Because this binary model has sent the message that no other group belongs to the American fabric, it, coupled with foreigner ideologies, have already deprived Koreans of social citizenship in "America" (i.e., the privilege of being authentic members of the nation). In U.S. society, no other event in American history would more viscerally demonstrate the lack of regard for South Korea and the denial of social citizenship than the 1992 LA unrest. Koreans are not passive in this process, however (see Glick Schiller 2005). As immigrants, for instance, they respond to dominant transnational racialization by forging racial understandings, identities, and resistance strategies in a cross-border framework. They do so largely within the logic of (South) Korean cultural categories (Sahlins 1981), categories that themselves often correspond with, or complement, those of American society. Despite the importance of this transnational perspective, however, it has been missing in U.S. racialization and immigrant incorporation theories.

A transnational perspective reveals, however, that U.S. imperial rule has socially located Koreans vis-à-vis not only White Americans but also Black Americans. This tripartite/triangle positioning composes imperialist racial formation in South Korea—in other words, the dynamics of "race"/nation forged by the hegemonic relationship between the state and social movements. On Koreans' negotiations of U.S. dominance, I find that the group, primed by parallel sensibilities about Japan, generally internalized their inferiority vis-à-vis White America, notwithstanding resistance (the two often interrelate). With regard to Blacks, they, on the one hand, saw themselves as higher along color-class-ethnonational lines. On the other hand, they recognized their weaker visibility in the realm of United States/global recognition as well as their subordinate status to Black

Americans along nation-state lines. Indeed, South Korean resistance to the U.S. occupation, hence to Blacks as well, fostered and exacerbated prejudice. These prejudices were especially common among those who emigrated after the 1992 LA unrest and who collapsed Black political violence in the home country and Blacks' politicized attacks against Koreans in Los Angeles. Formed not only in their resistance to Black political power in both countries, Koreans' prejudice also stemmed from a *need* to be above Blacks (i.e., in the middle), in order to compensate for their collective inferiority to the White West and Japan. Upon the nation's development in the 1970s, they, like Japan, sought to distance themselves from the "third world" and the "Dark Continent" they once resembled (see Russell 1991). Some Korean immigrants continue to follow this "detour" from oppression (Mulvey 1987:11) as a way to deal with racial subordination in the United States. In addition to the U.S. socioeconomic order, their middle or in-between status is naturalized by the U.S. model minority ideology. To be sure, Koreans in the home country have begun identifying with Blacks as part of their resistance to White America. Despite the dearth of interaction with Blacks and history of antiracist movements in the country, they, along with the younger South Korean generations in particular, are repudiating the "detour" and beginning to make new history.

Concerning U.S. immigrant life more generally, Korean immigrants came to modify their triangle lens from the home country to accommodate the domestic racial order. The immigrants adapted to the U.S. hierarchy's principal focus on "race" (pan-nationality) rather than ethnonationality. In addition, they engaged a fourth major group, Latinos (namely California's Mexican and Central American populace), a group that is overlooked by Claire Kim's (1999) racial triangulation model. Inserted into this new racialized system, the first generation draws on a *premigrant* lens of subordination and invisibility to understand their "foreigner" status in the White-Black order and their "extra-foreignness" vis-à-vis Japanese and Chinese ethnics and Latinos. In brief, the following factors—the conflation of "American" and "White" in U.S. ideology, the construct of "owners" of nations, the group's related invisibility and foreignness, and the limits of "model minority" status—shore up the first generation's belief that they would never be treated like Whites. As a watershed, the 1992 unrest drove the point home. In light of their own struggles with "foreign model minorityhood," second-generation Korean Americans concur with the first. Yet, Korean Americans writ large are not placated by fatalism and, hence, inert. Rather, the immigrants' problematize their pro-American tendencies and begin to deem prejudice and racism unjust. In so doing, they increasingly identify with Blacks and Latinos as fellow racial minorities who suffer under a White system. Old-timer Korean Americans' placement of blame on White America for the unrest, rather than on the Blacks and Latinos who burned their ethnic town, elucidates the point.

Koreans' *resistance* to their own foreignness and invisibility also problematizes Claire Kim's claim that, especially in times of racial strife, Korean Americans work to "[protect] their collective position within the racial order and thereby the order itself" (2000:158). As I have shown, Korean immigrants also seek to *disrupt* their foreigner position and, by extension, the racial order that subordinates them thus. In other words, although my study concurs with Kim's (2000) claim that Korean immigrants benefit from, and therefore protect, their middle (entrepreneurial) positioning along the traditional color line, I find that they also seek to insert themselves into mainstream U.S. politics and culture in order to disrupt their foreignness and invisibility as citizens. In actuality, they seek to approximate Black Americans' prominence in U.S. politics and in the nation's culture. They show that they would be thrilled to have as many influential household names in the nation's history, arts and entertainment, and electoral politics, from Martin Luther King to Oprah Winfrey to Barack Obama.

More specifically, they aspire to be "approximately American" by way of a "mainstream Korean America." As such, neither they nor the second generation *desire* a "White" or unhyphenated American identity. Rather, both generations respond to their cross-border racialization by aspiring to *mainstream* their ethnic difference. At the same time, their awareness that White Americans would always hold the lead position points to their cognizance of the limits and exclusions within the mainstream itself. To some extent internalizing and reinforcing their own foreignness, the first generation subsequently advised their children as well as peers considering emigration to move away from ethnic niches and networks toward mainstream white-collar jobs, electoral politics, and acclaim in American popular culture. Such warnings against "foreignness" teach an (indirect) racial lesson to South Koreans about immigrants' social position in the United States. The reluctance among immigrants to discuss racism, however, precludes enriched consciousness-raising, thereby shielding the U.S. state in both countries from greater challenges. Further regarding the nation-state, the desire for a "mainstream Korean America" points to the first generation's simultaneous identification with the ROK *and* the United

States. Although both nation-states' power could be reified by immigrants maintaining their gaze on the ROK and looking more to the United States than before, the immigrants' cognizance of the exclusions inherent to both has also challenged state power.

At the analytical level, these findings on Korean Americans in the United States push our thinking on the racial ideology of the "forever foreigner," of the American who is confounded with Asia rather than with the country she lives in, sometimes the only country she knows (Tuan 1998; see Ancheta 1998; C. Kim 1999). The specificity of this oppression is marked by the racialization of Asian groups not exclusively along the color line (as praiseworthy "model minorities") but also along the citizenship line (see Moraga 1981). In contrast to the premise of racial triangulation theory (C. Kim 1999), the color line and the citizenship line are mutually constitutive, what I call "foreign model minorityhood." To be sure, citizenship is not a primary social axis for Asian Americans only. It is also a key axis along which Latinos/as are racialized. Like the case of Asian Americans, the social location of Latino groups largely hinges on U.S. perceptions of, and relations with, the Latin American home countries. In the contemporary United States, however, *legal* citizenship is more specific to the hegemonic treatment of many Latino groups than of Asian ethnics (see Hondagneu-Sotelo 1997). The racialization processes, therefore, should not be conflated. I also do not suggest that Black Americans enjoy the full rights of legal and social citizenship that White Americans do. In the past Black Americans were disenfranchised despite legal citizenship; indeed, they remain second-class citizens (see P. Collins 2001; Du Bois 1969). Yet, at the level of relational racialization, the fact that Black Americans have not faced similar federal exclusion laws, have not been mass incarcerated as enemies during wartime, and are not as frequently asked where their real country is or whether they can speak English suggests that they are, at least, considered "Americans," even if second-class Americans (see Tuan 1998:8). In contrast, the Americanness of Asian groups in and of itself remains problematic. Again, the struggles of the groups are different, though related.

Expanding conceptually and analytically on received notions of racialized foreignness in the scholarly literature, I have argued that Asian Americans are not just *visibly* foreign; that is, they are not simply conspicuous outsiders ("Exclude the yellow peril!") or visible when hegemonic ends call them to be ("The system works: look at those model minorities!"). Rather, I add that the subordination of Asian Americans has hinged on the *invisibility* of this group, not simply in the United States ("No one helped us during the LA riot!") but also in the United States–dominated "homeland" ("They never told us military officials anything about Korea"). Although it is apparent that the dimensions of visible foreignness and invisible subjectivity overlap and can be mutually constitutive, this book underscores that the "foreigner" status goes beyond being *visibly* Asian within a nation-state that upholds itself as White and secondarily Black.

The study's overall findings also bear implications for extant sociological theory. For instance, one way in which Korean Americans sought to disrupt their foreignness was to minimize their reliance on, and containment within, ethnic networks. Such a process both lines up with and departs from segmented assimilation theory (Portes and Zhou 1993). The selective path whereby immigrants move up socioeconomically by deliberately maintaining ethnic ties holds insofar as Korean Americans heavily rely on ethnic resources as a way to move into the middle class. They will most likely follow this path for many years to come. They even seek to maintain their ethnic identity and culture upon integrating into the mainstream. Yet, counter to the selective assimilation path, Korean Americans do not see their reliance on ethnic resources and networks as always and everywhere beneficial, particularly in regards to *social citizenship*. They consider these forms of their ethnicity to reinforce their foreigner and invisible status in "America." Because invisibility in the United States and the globe had been their concern long before arrival, Korean Americans recognized their need to *reconfigure* their ethnicity such that it overlapped with *mainstream White American* channels. In turn, American social citizenship, the theory goes, would be within closer reach. Such a formulation shows that the group's hopes for a mainstream Korean America involved forging at once a *politics of similarity* and an ethnic *politics of difference*. The first generation in particular desired a mainstream soapbox for their ethnonationality in order to familiarize American society, and the world, to Koreans' exceptional culture (see Rudrappa 2004). Such a process cannot be captured by segmented assimilation theory alone given a focus on the *benefits* of ethnic resources and on the socioeconomic dimensions of U.S. inequality at the expense of social citizenship concerns.

In general, the findings of this study seek to move beyond theoretical accounts that conceive of immigrant racial minorities' encounters with American "race" hierarchies as playing out only in the United States. Notwithstanding important differences, the theories used to explain U.S. immigrants and "race"—versions of racial triangulation (P. Collins 2001; C. Kim 1999) and assimilationist accounts (Alba and Nee 2003; Gordon 1964; Portes and Zhou 1993)—tend to underappreciate the global and transnational scope of U.S. racial dominance and immigrants' use of cross-border lenses to negotiate it. Although Kim's (1999) racial triangulation account gives primacy to the racialization of Asian Americans along citizenship lines and as part of a multi-ordered system of racial inequality, the remaining theories do not. The present study sought to show, however, that the experience of Korean Americans—and many U.S. immigrant groups, for that matter—cannot be fully captured without considering U.S. global and transnational relations of power and their connection to specific forms of racialization. These racializing processes include foreignizing future Asian immigrants or disseminating across the globe ideologies of White superiority and Black inferiority.

Along methodological lines, this study revealed that going to the sending context affords a richer and more accurate understanding of the nature and scope of U.S. power abroad, especially its migrating institutions and ideologies. More specifically, studying both the home country and the U.S. site enables scholarly acumen into the ways U.S. racial/national dominance generates ideologies of U.S. groups of color and shapes immigrants' own cultural toolkits. I therefore contend that it is not possible to grasp fully the U.S. immigrants' experiences of "race"/ethnicity—and to avoid reproducing American-centrism in the process—without analyzing the home country and its ties to the United States in our theories, methods, and analyses. An intellectual lens and research design of this type requires, then, an openness to transnationalism as "a valuable *conceptual* tool," in the words of Yen Espiritu (2003:4), "one that disrupts the narrow emphasis on 'modes of incorporation' characteristic of much of the published work in the field of U.S. immigration studies" (emphasis in original). Furthermore, a global and transnational framework compels scholars to analyze the impact of American empire, particularly its reliance on racial inequality globally and locally. With slight modifications, this study corroborates Abelmann and Lie's assertion that "the primary source of Korean American racism [prejudice] toward African Americans is the American racial ideology" (1995:150). Although Korea's indigenous *color-class* hierarchies that lend themselves to anti-Black racism are salient, it cannot explain why Koreans attributed the American *racial* characteristics of inferiority, urban poverty, (gun) violence, criminality, and hyperathleticism to Blacks (see Russell 1991). In addition, Japan's racialization of the globe as White West / Asian middle / African bottom, which Korean society has adopted, was originally borrowed from Euro-American conceptualizations

(Russell 1991). Moreover, this racialization of the global order did not crystallize in Japan or South Korea until after the United States had occupied both countries (and, subsequently, the East Asian Tigers were born). Even Japan's anti-Black commodity racism was not in full swing until *after* the U.S. occupational forces arrived and propagated such ideologies on Japan's own turf (Russell 1991). To be sure, Korean and Japanese color-class hierarchies had to line up for the U.S. White-over-Black order to make sense, and Koreans, even as an oppressed nation and people, have exercised agency in determining what purpose these racial ideologies will serve. These dynamics, however, do not change the fact that American *racial* ideologies of Blacks were a primary source of *racial* prejudice on the peninsula. Before "America's" arrival, the Koreans (and Japanese) used (and continue to use) racialized nationality, not pan-national "race," as their *main* unit of categorization. Had the White-led U.S. military not been such a potent force in South Korean history, then, Korea would have likely maintained its focus on color and ethnonationality only ("African primitivism" and underdevelopment versus an urban, criminal, entertaining "race"). And more likely than not, had the United States (and Japan) not exercised imperial domination, Koreans would not have engaged in such protracted and complex battles with internalized inferiority in the first place. While it is true that all countries would be expected to feel inferior should they rank below a world superpower, direct imperialist domination by a higher "race" is what makes the battle so protracted and complex among the subordinated.

Finally, a scholarly focus on the impact of American empire compels us to reenvision U.S. history as not merely one of immigrants going to "America," but one of "America" first going to the future immigrants (Espiritu 2003:24). Simply put, if the United States has been transnational in its state projects of power, it is remiss to ignore immigrants' transnational experience of the United States. In analyzing the impact of these processes on Korean immigrants, for instance, one finds that the group folded into their cultural toolkits in the United States the derision and Othering of the Koreas and Koreans by the occupational forces, the White-Black segregation in the U.S. military, the mass media representations of Whiteness and Blackness, the transnational Korean media and interpersonal exchanges sparked by U.S. imperialism, and so on. It is extremely difficult to capture these processes linked to U.S. power without witnessing them as real-life processes in the home country and, further, from the immigrants' vantage point. I would maintain this view even if the U.S. state should choose to whittle down the military concentration in South Korea and

Japan, as some currently speculate will occur. It would be surprising if a reduction in U.S. bases and troops, even to the smallest denominator, would mean a drastic decline in U.S. influence and pressure on these two countries, especially South Korea. Contemporary imperialism relies not only on global armament but on restructured capital, in the Pacific region in particular. Moreover, given the underdevelopment of their own military forces, the ROK and Japan will continue to look to the United States for assistance if greater threats or armed conflicts should arise (say, with North Korea), thereby perpetuating unequal relations with the superpower.

Although this study focused on a group who hailed from a country directly dominated by the United States, I do not believe that the framework or even some of the findings apply only to immigrants who match Koreans' circumstances. For instance, because this study was situated within the larger context of U.S. imperialism in Asia, immigrants from other Asian countries that have been subordinated in similar fashion—such as Japan/Okinawa, the Philippines, Vietnam, Laos, and Cambodia, to name a few—would be influenced by racial ideologies instantiated by U.S. military and mass cultural dominance (see Espiritu 2003; Lowe 1996; Palumbo-Liu 1999; Russell 1991). In addition, Latin American and Pacific Island countries that continue to be subordinated by direct U.S. (military) rule would likely yield similar patterns. Of course, Latin Americans' experiences and understandings would be distinct in light of the White and Black ancestry shared among most of the populations. Yet both Asian and Latino groups would suffer the consequences of U.S. racial/national domination and would simultaneously learn about, and respond to, the conspicuous binary "race" model of the United States.

In a broader vein, it is safe to say that no immigrant-sending country has escaped the cultural influence of the United States, especially in this era of contemporary global capitalism. In fact, cultural influences are central to glorifications of "America" that spur mass migrations in the first place (Abelmann and Lie 1995; Espiritu 2003). Beyond constructing the United States as desirable, however, U.S. mass media also disseminate American racist ideologies to a world audience (Feagin 2000). This profound influence accounts for the centrality of U.S. mass media in the present study. It is the hope of this study that future research will also consider the force of American global culture in home countries in their analyses of U.S. immigrants.

With regard to many disciplines' current scholarly frenzy over the fate of the American racial landscape, this book problematizes the increasingly accepted sociological account that Asian Americans (and Latinos) are racially assimilating (Bonilla-Silva 2002; Gans 1999; J. Lee and Bean 2004; Warren and Twine 1997; Yancey 2003). These prognostications, although intellectually stimulating, do not consider the dimensions along which Asian Americans' (and Latinos') racial status depends, namely global inequalities (e.g., United States–Asian relations) and hierarchies of citizenship; nor do these works cite the qualitative and quantitative studies that incorporate such dimensions. Moreover, predications of Asian American and Latino whitening take as a priori and use as a paragon Southern and Eastern European immigrants' whitening trajectory. Yet, historians at present are debating heatedly over the veracity of such a shift in the first place—that is, Southern and Eastern European immigrants may have always been White (e.g., Arnesen 2001; Guglielmo 2003). The path of "whitening" that Asian Americans and Latinos are ostensibly undergoing, then, may have no historical precedent.

To be certain, the accounts of Bonilla-Silva (2002) and Gans (1999) acknowledge that the White racial system largely elevates Asian groups for its own hegemonic reproduction. The larger and more pressing point that they and others make is that White American dominance has been secured by exercising racial power over *all* non-Whites (see also Almaguer 1994; Feagin 2000; C. Kim 1999, 2000). Unless scholars and activists investigate how such dominance has hinged on racializing all non-Whites in *different* and *related* ways (C. Kim 1999, 2000; see Almaguer 1994; Ancheta 1998; T. Lee 2005; Omi and Winant 1994), a fundamentally unequal system will remain in large part because all non-Whites will lose in an internecine war over whose oppression matters more. In the absence of frameworks of different and related racialization, social scientists will inadvertently reproduce the racial ideologies of our sociological forefathers (H. Yu 2002) that, as we saw, continue to haunt today. Erasing "race" altogether, then, necessitates both a new and retrospective examination of the sources of racism against Asian Americans and all groups of color. Let us begin, then, with "America's" migration to Asia.

Reference Matter

Appendix: Research Methods—Working in the Transnational Field

QUALITATIVE RESEARCH IS CENTRALLY CONCERNED with meaning-making, not with the "measurement principle" of quantitative research. Qualitative researchers therefore seek to make sense of, or to interpret, phenomena in terms of the meanings people bring to them within natural settings (Denzin and Lincoln 1994:2). Owing to these natural rather than contrived settings, qualitative research is at once a contextualized and an in-depth understanding. To this end of a contextualized and in-depth analysis, I sought to address the lacuna of the immigrant home country context. That is, I found that the originating society was rarely analyzed in studies of immigrants' navigation of racial/ethnic ideologies, identities, and politicized responses. I found this oversight curious given U.S. dominance over many of the countries, whether historically or presently, from whence the immigrants came. I brought this question and lens to my research design and fieldwork. My project thus serves as one of myriad examples of how global/transnational research can be done, even with all the logistical difficulties and the complexities of multiple social worlds.

Interviews

Los Angeles County

In 2001 I conducted the primary fieldwork of in-depth, open-ended interviews with forty-seven first-generation Korean Americans who reside in greater Los Angeles, California. Collectively, the Los Angeles–based interviews allowed for respondents to share their own stories on their own terms. Moreover, I conducted the interviews in a personal, conversational manner and in the Korean language (unless they desired to speak in English) to facilitate informants' comfort with, and openness to, discussing sensitive and uncomfortable topics such as racial/national inequalities and prejudice. In addition, interviews are particularly important for uncovering the experiences and perspectives of minority groups whose voices traditionally have been muted (K. Anderson and Jack 1991; Frankenberg 1993).

I recruited first-generation Korean Americans from various ethnic, civic, and social organizations, from churches and schools, and from processes of snowball sampling. To avoid networks of respondents I recruited from as many separate sources as was possible. Only those who met the following criteria were selected: residence in South Korea prior to coming to the United States, emigration as adults, and U.S. settlement (and among recent émigrés, intent to settle). This sample was roughly evenly divided into two subsamples of "newcomers" and "old-timers" designated as less than five years and more than five years, respectively. Interviewing recent émigrés was necessary to (1) make note of their "homeland" racialized ideologies before too much time elapsed and memory reconstructions abounded, (2) compare their views with Seoul residents for reliability purposes, (3) capture initial reactions to becoming a minority and to learning the U.S. landscape, and (4) assess comparative differences with "old-timers," who tend to be more aware of social desirability norms and antiracism, more secure and stable in the United States, more conflicted about their ties to the home country, and so on.

Regarding sample characteristics, the socioeconomic status of the Korean American sample in Los Angeles was largely middle class, a status I assessed based on informants' and their parents' education levels, occupations, and incomes and by self-description. Although sociologist In-Jin Yoon (1997) asserts that more working-class Koreans have emigrated in recent years, the Koreans in my sample mostly hailed from middle-class backgrounds and worked back, or were working back, into some semblance of it in the United States (see P. Ong and Azores 1994). Between the few working-class respondents and their middle-class counterparts, I did not find differences in nationalist leanings or in racial perceptions (notwithstanding other differences). Most of this subsample were married (all presented themselves as heterosexual).

It was relatively easy to find old-timer Korean Americans in Los Angeles to meet with me, in part because of their desire for greater visibility in the United States. Only a few informants were put off by what I told them would be longer than an hour interview, especially given their extremely busy work lives. In contrast, it proved much more difficult to find and gain the consent of recent émigrés given their lack of time and the cultural norm of "saving face," especially during times of low socioeconomic security. I drummed up the idea of going to Koreatown adult language schools where many recently arrived Koreans studied English. To do so, I first had to ask permission of the owners and administrators of these schools, most of whom then provided me access to teachers whose class time I would interrupt with my announcements.

Seoul

In general, interviewing in Seoul was not an easy task. In fact, many professors in the United States and in South Korea had advised me against conducting interviews with the middle-aged population in Seoul. They cautioned that interviews outside of university institutions were not culturally common, even if presented as a research practice, and that my status as "a Korean from America" (a youngish female one, at that) set me further apart. This served as one of the first examples of my lack of "insiderness" in my ancestral homeland despite my similar phenotype, Korean language facility, and my parental origins in the country. My experience thus complicates the "insider/outsider" binary as fashioned by Merton (1972; see Võ 2000). In part to circumvent the rarity of individual interviewing, I settled on focus groups as one of my primary methods. Focus groups are of great utility in situations in which linguistic and cultural differences exist between researchers and participants (Morgan 1993). In addition, focus groups can effectively capture the participants' shared and collective meanings (Frey and Fontana 1991), even more vital in a collectivist cultural system like South Korea.

The difficulty of accessing respondents was not a major setback, however, as I had planned all along to emulate the background characteristics of those who tended to immigrate to the United States: middle class and well educated like the focus group members. Moreover, the students and young professionals hailed from various cities on the peninsula, like many Seoul residents in general, and thus represented more than the city's native-born populace. Students in general have also been at the (often bloody) helm of social change in South Korea and were a good barometer of where the society was and where it was headed. My research assistant, Heejin, conducted the focus group and the individual interviews, given the potential bias my presence as an American might introduce. I was in attendance, however, at all four focus group interviews as a "quiet helper" and "note taker" for Heejin, the interim "principal investigator."[1] Prior to the interviews she and I had worked together on the protocol and tested it with our network of personal contacts outside of the focus groups. After further training, she conducted two individual in-depth interviews. Still determined not to limit my sample to young adults, however, I defied the advice I was given and would eventually gain the perspectives of thirteen older-generation South Koreans with the help of my research assistant and other native-born residents. We recruited these informants from our networks, those of other residents, and from public sites where older South Koreans congregated.

In Los Angeles, the informants were asked questions under the broad themes of immigration; race relations, in-groups and out-groups, ideologies, prejudice, discrimination; interrelated identities and experiences of "race," class, gender, ethnicity/nation, culture; and the home country and transnational dynamics. In Seoul, all interview respondents, both younger and older, were asked items germane to racialized perceptions of who "Americans" were (or who "lived in America"), evaluations of them vis-à-vis their own identities as a people, the sources of these ideas (e.g., occupation); Korean Americans and immigration; transnationalism; global/international and U.S. hierarchies (East Asia); various forms of culture; and politics and movements.

Ethnography

Seoul

In both sites, Seoul in particular, I conducted supplementary (participant) observation in conjunction with the interviews. In general, ethnography exposes the frequent differential between what people *report* and what they *do* in their everyday lives. Mindful of this methodological advantage, I stayed alert as to whether or not South Koreans' interjections about racial ideologies and other American influences aligned with, contradicted, or were more simplified than their actual engagement of them. Yet, because ethnography cannot tap certain parts of a person's history or cognitions, the act of interviewing is a central component of participant observation. The fact that I began observing before I delved into the interviews further allowed me to see the kinds of racialized conceptions and engagements of "Americanness" in which I was interested. Hence, these observations were instrumental for modification of the focus group schedules.

My informal participant observation involved regularly taking part in Seoul's Young People's Church.[2] It was located at a university campus and was a vibrant, growing place of worship (and socializing) that catered to young adults and young families. The male minister frequently delivered the message of the church's mission: to make youth the central architects of the future. I spent every Sunday from morning until late afternoon or night at this church, sometimes going there one to three times more during a given month to take part in church activities. My role there was as a member of the larger congregation and of a small group (fifteen to twenty people) who met after worship service to study and relate Christian philosophies to everyday life. We as small group "Team #53" also socialized over meals and enjoyed leisure activities together.

As someone who believed in God but had not always attended church, my participant observation at Young People's Church served both a research as well as a personal function for me. In light of this, I did not have to "deceive" my informants, as other ethnographers sometimes have to do in various field settings. To my satisfaction, the small group ("Team #53") interactions yielded very fruitful observations. For instance, despite the fact that most Koreans have come to construct Christianity as a *Korean* cultural marker (S. Chan 1990), I identified (White) American influences in their acts of Christianity from the Korean-translated American/European Christian songs they sang to the popular culture they engaged in this often skit- and performance-heavy setting. I came to learn that scores of Korean youth were familiar with White American Christian figures and singers and, on occasion, were able to discuss issues of "race" and racism with me, someone they could trust as a friend.

Second to Young People's Church, my overnight visits to my aunt's house every weekend served as a great source of informal ethnography, because I could witness directly a middle-aged couple and their thirty-something sons watch reports about the United States or American programming itself (and televised Hollywood movies), their reactions to these texts, and the ways they engaged one another while they watched (see Lembo 2000). I did not consider myself to be a thoroughly biasing actor in their presence, because they had had little occasion to learn my political opinions prior to my arrival in Seoul for intensive fieldwork. Furthermore, because I was low on the age and gender hierarchy in South Korea, my views mattered very little in the household (although, at times, my residence in the United States conferred status and privileges onto me). Our lack of intimate knowledge of one another's political opinions and my low status in certain situations enabled me to observe the ways they perceived and evaluated me as an "American." I could also observe the racialized dimensions of their understanding of who "Americans" were and what they were like.

Finally, I observed every second that I was in public, taking note of everyday people and their actions, the "glitter" of popular culture, the dizzying consumerism of global capitalism, and people's humorous reactions to me when I would tell them I was "a Korean from America." The data—sights, sounds, smells, conversations—enveloped me everywhere and proved to be some of the most stimulating and memorable moments of my research.

Los Angeles County

Although my observations in Los Angeles County and its Korean communities are based in part on my upbringing in these communities, throughout the course of 2001 I made a point to observe Korean ethnic organizations—namely community service, church, and school or hometown reunion clubs—in which people I knew or interviewees were involved. There I could witness and hear about how Korean Americans conceived of their positioning in the United States, the issues that most concerned them, and sometimes how they interacted with other racialized/ethnic groups. Here, issues of nationalistic pride and struggles with racial discrimination and "foreignness" came to the fore.

Newspaper Research

Research assistants and I also drew on archived newspaper texts (1920–2000) from the top-circulating South Korean newspaper, *Chosun Ilbo*, as well as more recent print journalism in both countries between 2001 and 2007. The South Korean newspapers were useful for providing information on how media outlets—and how regular citizens in editorials—interpreted the United States, its racial dynamics, Korean immigrants, and the palpable presence of the U.S. military, popular culture, and "America" generally in the peninsula.

In short, my use of multiple methods—various forms of interviewing, formal and informal participant observation, and past and present newspaper data—constitute a triangulation of sources that can enhance the validity of the study's findings (Denzin 1978). The combination of these methods allowed for depth and breadth of analysis concerning immigrants' racialization as well as their ideological formation in Seoul and Los Angeles. Despite my multiple sources of data and carefully thought-out design, I did not intend for this research to generalize to all South Koreans or Korean Americans. Rather, in line with the extended case method (Burawoy 1998), I honed my inquiry on how macro-level structures/discourses and everyday people are mutually constituting and how we can fine-tune our theories to account for such a dialectical relationship. My research shows, then, how studying everyday people and their meaning systems is a statement on the way the world works.

Logistics and Analysis

While I was in the LA site I frequently took notes after the interviews, usually in my car after each one was completed or late at night if I had conducted two or three in one day. In Seoul I usually took shorthand notes during the various interviews. In both sites, I typed up field notes whenever I was at home. Transcription, translation, and coding of interviews from both settings proved to be more daunting than I had expected; this stage cost me more money, demanded more time, and sapped more energy than I ever could have imagined. Research assistants here were indispensable.

I began informal analyses during the data collection process by note taking and memo writing in a journal I carried around with me. As with the (global) extended case method, however, I also brought theoretical lenses to both field sites, such as racialization (triangulation), racial formation, cultural globalization, transnationalism—and constantly pondered their applicability, lack thereof, or refinement as I engaged with the world (Burawoy 1998). Both processes allowed me to build questions or probes into my interview schedules as well as cut or rewrite items that were premised on improper assumptions.

The process of analysis involved coding the Seoul and the LA data (interviews and field notes) separately but through similar and different code categories for each site. In light of certain shared questions that I asked across both, I later analyzed these data together to capture thematic divergences and convergences. Using ATLAS.ti qualitative analysis software, I found that many of the quotations (or variations of them) belonged to more than one code category (which made for daunting, yet rich, data analysis). I then grouped codes into metacategories, or what the program called "code families." Through such a coding process, I noted themes such as the nature of local/global racialized ideologies and identities; the processes of immigrants' pre- and postarrival racialization (involving volition and ascription); and issues of assimilation, transnationalism, and variants thereof.

Issues in the Field

Subjectivity

As John Aguilar (1981:16) has remarked about the insider/outsider debate within the social sciences, "Epistemological concerns have been raised that insiders are 'too close to home' and will miss the obvious, whereas outsiders curious about their new environment will make 'valuable discoveries.' " But is this formulation accurate? Indeed, was I an insider because I was ethnically Korean in South Korea? Perhaps yes, certainly when compared to the less "insiderness" of a White, Black, or Vietnamese American visitor, but to what extent did my differences with native South Koreans and with the first generation in the United States—along lines of nation, culture, age/generation, gender, class/education—still position me as an "insider?" Linda Võ (2000:28) aptly problematizes the insider/outsider dichotomy as falling prey to the very essentialism of racialized/ethnic categories that social scientists so painstakingly critique and eschew.

To start with my experience in Seoul, I was simultaneously insider and outsider on multiple levels. My presence in South Korea and its disruption of taken-for-granted definitions of Koreanness was made most apparent when I chose to interview elderly South Korean men at Tapgol Park, where they infamously gather to play Korean board games. It was in this instance that I felt my outsider status most viscerally. Although it is true that ethnic communities have been and continue to be suspicious and distrustful of researchers not from their own ethnic group (Blauner and Wellman 1977), it is also true that ethnic researchers do not automatically gain the trust of coethnic communities or organizations (Loo 1980), especially when they hail from a distant (and more powerful) nation-state.

At Tapgol Park I was immediately conspicuous given my female gender, younger age, and schoolish backpack. Upon explaining that I was a Korean American exchange student conducting a project, many were eager to talk to me and persistently interrupted me during one of my interviews to get my attention (it seemed that in their old and sometimes lonely age they enjoyed talking about themselves to an inquiring party). However, my "outsiderness" as an American student became extremely problematic when during my interview with an elderly gentleman, one of the middle-aged men lambasted me in front of the large crowd, shouting that I was going to repeat all the negative things that Koreans said about "America" or about Black people and that I was a traitor who had no right to be there.[3] All of a sudden the gentleman whom I had been interviewing—an apparently impressionable chap—refused to continue speaking with me. Simply overwhelmed by such instantaneous public humiliation, by the assailant's seemingly unwarranted, vein-popping fury at me, and by persistent reminders of my lack of belonging in Korea—not to mention exhaustion from living abroad and conducting intensive fieldwork—I could do nothing to prevent my tears from spilling forth. I was swiftly escorted away by sympathetic middle-aged men who grumbled under their breaths about male senility. One had done graduate research before and thus empathized with my predicament; the other was a Christian minister who granted me an interview to brighten my spirits. In this way, gender also factored into my humiliation in that I was playing the emotionally unstable "girl" who needed older men to "help" her, all within an overtly patriarchal society (unlike what I believed to be a more covert but, in many ways, equally pernicious gender-stratified U.S. society). I kept trying to explain to them that my emotional outburst was aberrant, but they focused instead on admonishing me not to return to the park.

One reason for my outburst that I did not share with the two concerned gentlemen was my own personal bias that I had brought to the field. Indeed, to an extent I had romanticized how much of an insider I actually would be in South Korea. I was initially intrigued and excited by life as a racially/ethnically majority member, to live in a society where the majority looked like me. I quickly learned that I had underestimated how much of an outsider I was in reality. Yet, this romanticism and my subsequent rude awakening can inform our scholarly ruminations about methodology. For instance, as a third-generation Japanese American studying in Japan, Dorinne Kondo (1990:303) expressed that "temptations of romanticism or apologism are great, but our different positionings could at the very least create the possibility for accounts written from perspectives different from dominant perspectives in mainstream social science." That is, my common ethnic background could mitigate Orientalist interpretations of South Koreans and their lives. In addition, the instability of my existence enabled me to conceptualize the very dilemmas that simple insider-outsider binaries missed, such as the upside of being at once within and without the circle. In other words, it was my vigilance in understanding "them" from the outside that demanded that I be open, that I engage all of what I thought to be the "undesirables" of the South Korean context.

In fact, this openness and my focus on the South Korean actors (rather than the other way around) could often lead to cultural dissonance. For instance, at Young People's Church the women would comment on my dress (one chided me for revealing more skin than most others, which I later observed to be true);[4] in other instances, it was my style of dance (very "unique," "natural/free") and my vocal annoyance at Korean elders who I thought were mistreating us youth (particularly middle-aged men who reprimanded females).

Similarly, at my aunt's home my not-so-Korean comportment (loud laugh; in-dividualistic ways; "strange" requests) jarred her and my relatives out of their taken-for-granted sense of Korean identity. For instance, despite knowing bet-ter, I would sometimes slip and overuse the Korean words for *I* or *you* until my aunt made a point to tell me that that I should use them less (given a collectivist language system of *we, us*). As Kondo (1990:11) put it, I could be a "living oxy-moron" and an even more puzzling one given an "eminently biological" defini-tion of Koreanness. Yet, in moments that I presented high Korean cultural lit-eracy or went along with the gender norm of catering to the every need of my male cousins and uncles, South Koreans saw me as "naturally" Korean and placed me in culturally meaningful roles, such as daughter/niece. I came to be-long in the church and in my aunt's home at the same time that they saw me as somewhat incomplete or "in progress."

Akin to my experience in Seoul I was simultaneously outsider and insider in the LA site, albeit in a more familiar context. Gender became salient when I found that many Korean immigrant couples assumed that I should talk to the man, not the woman, within their heterosexual coupling. Because I was ini-tially concerned that this inequity would yield a predominantly male immi-grant sample, I made efforts to recruit the wives as well. In fact, some of the women secretly whispered that they would grant me an interview in private; in the end, I interviewed a larger number of female than male respondents.

With regard to the ways that the first-generation Korean immigrants per-ceived me, a "second gen," they typically employed the Korean Confucian lens of collectivist parenting whereby I was "one of their children" in need of their wise counsel. Specifically, they enjoined me to learn the ins and outs of Korean history (often assuming that I knew little), to give primacy to my Korean cul-tural heritage and identity, and to use my research to better the community's status in the United States. Yet, in somewhat of an ironic twist, my upbringing and high educational attainment in the United States also gave me privileges they did not have, insofar as my capacity to become a "professor"—typically a higher occupational social status than theirs—and my English fluency enabled me to represent and promote the Korean community in ways they could not. In addition, I felt my "Americanized" cultural and educational status most when I sought to recruit from the adult language schools: here I was a PhD stu-dent asking very recent émigrés with the most insecure status of all Korean im-migrants to help me with *my* research. I was concerned about the "power ef-fects" of reflexive research, such as domination of "scientist" over "the studied"

(Burawoy 1998). To account for my specific "privileges," I made sure to respect Korean age and gender hierarchies in communicating with them and ultimately found myself with more interested people than I could interview.

The Theories of Methodology

When I entered the field, I focused primarily on theory building that pertained to my primary data collection method, various methods of interviewing, and that could be applied to my secondary data collection, participant observation and archival analysis. I was thus guided primarily by the grounded theory approach (Glaser and Strauss 1967). Although ethnography served as secondary data, I also drew on aspects of the extended case method (Burawoy 1998). Unfortunately, *Global Ethnography* (Burawoy et al. 2000), a book treatment of the globalized extended case method, was published as I wrapped up fieldwork. I was happy, however, to find that I had followed some of the conceptual paths and employed some of the practices that make global ethnography enriching and effective.

Grounded theory draws from the discovery of relevant social and psychosocial aspects of human processes. In contrast to the deductive empiricism of quantitative research and the theoretical starting point of the extended case method, a grounded approach represents an inductive process of generating theory anew. This method was suitable insofar as little theory had been generated on transnational racialization processes, especially in the context of imperialism. In addition, the theory was helpful in allowing me to be a tabula rasa in South Korea, one on which the people, thoughts, everyday practices, and representations would be etched. From there I could generate theoretical ideas. I was also guided by the theory's search for similarities across differences, because I was comparing two different societies to ascertain the similar impact of U.S. imperial rule (while also pursuing the differences between immigrant and South Korean life).

At the same time, grounded theory's positivism seeks to generalize from moments that are too insulated from larger related forces; this is where the tenets of extended case method proved helpful. Rather than solely "discover" theory from the ground, then, I brought the model of racial triangulation (C. Kim 1999) to the field, both as a way to ascertain its applicability and to explore its limitations, such as its focus only on the United States. I did not seek, then, to generalize to an entire population but to reconstruct theory by absorbing "anomalies" (Burawoy 1998:16). Starting with theory enabled me to meet another key premise of the method, to extend out from micro processes to macro forces. That is, rather than conceive of the micro as an expression of the macro, a one-way relationship, I followed the theory's conceptualization of the macro-micro link as a two-way process largely driven by external forces that are themselves dynamic (Burawoy et al. 2000). Applied to my study, I understood immigrants' ideologies and identities on the one hand, and the U.S. armed forces, U.S. cultural economy, and transnational influences on the other, to be mutually constitutive and driven by the "external force" of U.S. imperialism.

Employing both grounded theory and the extended case method in a global context moves the field of vision beyond the idea of an atomized nation that has little relationship to global processes, what Wimmer and Glick Schiller (2003) call "methodological nationalism." Grounded theory allowed me to generate new ideas and connections by my movements beyond the United States and into another country deeply connected to the United States. Also moving beyond bounded territories, Burawoy et al. (2000:29–32) render the globe "an object of theorization in its own right." Burawoy et al. encourage us to conceive of global forces as produced by contingent social processes—in other words, global connections between sites (the transnational of which are the "most directly global experience")—as well as by actors' imaginations, which themselves can reconfigure globalization. I followed this theoretical lens by examining how immigrants negotiate the *connections* between racial ideologies in their home country dominated by the United States and in the "imperial center" itself (Lowe 1996:16). In so doing, I revised United States–based theories by capturing immigrants' negotiation of racialization in both societal contexts.[5]

After conducting my study, I find background information on the home country, especially one that has had a relationship to the United States, to be an insufficient way to analyze immigrant processes. With the support of my study, I contend that immigrant groups' cultural experience of, and lenses on, U.S. dominance in the home country must be central to the framework of understanding their ideologies, identities, and behaviors in the United States. This framework requires, then, that immigration scholars who have resisted the conceptual lens of the global and the transnational to shift dramatically their paradigms toward cross-border analyses of U.S. political projects, mass media forms, social ties, and imaginings/symbolism. I argue that such processes are germane not only to the first generation but to later ones. Indeed, there appears to be little sign of slowed emigration from the major sending regions, a phenomenon that indelibly shapes the U.S. racial/ethnic landscape as well as the immigrants' progeny. This mutual influence between the generations is especially true among the Asian American population in which cultural age hierarchies as well as elder leadership typically guide the ideologies and practices of the overall group. In addition, second-generation groups, especially those of color, have been looking toward the ethnic "homeland" or the culture as a way to resist racial marginalization in the United States (Foner 2000; Glick Schiller 1999; Kasinitz 1992; Kibria 2002b; N. Kim forthcoming; Maira 2002; Purkayastha 2005).

In addition to a global lens, I brought to the research the effort to better the world I was studying, an idealism that indeed carried me through this labor of love. From the start of my project, I have believed that examining the impact of U.S. imperialism on immigrants' racially structured lives could do something to benefit Koreans in both countries. I have also been motivated by dangerous silences that needed interrupting. That is, I sought to investigate whether Korean/Asian Americans were indeed struggling less and less with "race" and racism as the theories predicted, an investigation that the overall field of sociology has rarely done at Asian Americans' and everyone's peril. To be sure, I knew all along the limitations of qualitative research in the realm of direct policymaking, and, since my completion of the project, I am more sobered by what seems a yawning gap between academic research and movements for social change. At the same time, qualitative research exposes the contradictions and complexities that challenge hegemonic power, such as the "natural" ideologies that justify inequality (Burawoy 1998; Glick Schiller 2005). Through talking and living with the people, we expose how they are affected by power in ways that are not monolithic and omnipotent, and how people push back against power. These contradictions and anomalies are the moments that invite everyday resistance, the pathway to most collective movements. The scholarly job of documenting the contradictions also means resisting the impulse to paint a singularly rosy picture of a marginalized community simply to expose the depths of its oppression or, more simply, to "save face" in a social context that has derided them because of their racialized faces. Although I am sensitive to inequalities and oppression, such a representation also verges on victimizing the population, as if the oppressed cannot make mistakes and should always be able to triumph over structural power. Although some of the things that the informants said, quite literally, broke my heart, I have taken pains not to allow my status as an ethnic/racial insider to bias me into manipulating the image of "my" communities. Rather, putting a spotlight on the uglier sides of power, the messy contradictions, can point to social change. My attention, then, to Korean immigrants' adoption of Euro-American racial ideologies (from which no group can escape) has served the dual purpose of showing that the piece of the oppressor lies in all of us (Lorde 1984) and that the trajectory of that path can be traced, no matter how complex. Unraveling this process also encourages Koreans and other groups of color to be cognizant of such processes endemic to oppression, that is, if they have yet to face them. In short, despite the inequalities mired in the methods we use to study social inequalities, I hope I have done the people who spent their time with me justice. At the least, I hope I have given all of us cause for reflection.

LA respondents: First generation

Name	Sex	Age	Time in United States	Occupation at time of interview
Mrs. An	F	57	8 mos.	homemaker
Mr. Bae	M	43	15 yrs.	dental technician; small trade business
Mrs. Baek	F	46	3 yrs.	homemaker
Mr. Bahng	M	53	8.2 yrs.	Chinese medicine doctor
Mr. Byun	M	37	23 yrs.	minister (Korean church)
Mr. Che	M	54	21 yrs.	Chinese medicine doctor (ran clothing school)
Mr. Cho	M	68	1 yr.	retired (business)
Mr. Chun	M	51	11 yrs.	textile manufacturing business
Mrs. Du	F	24	5 mos.	homemaker and dental hygiene student
Mr. Gil	M	37	7 mos.	manufacturing small business
Mrs. Gim	F	69	10 yrs.	retired homemaker (co-ran photo business)
Mrs. Go	F	51	25 yrs.	textile designer
Mr. Han	M	64	24 yrs.	maintenance/janitor
Mrs. Jang	F	47	21 yrs.	data processing client relationship director
Mr. Jin	M	27	9 mos.	Web design student
John Ha*	M	27	8 mos.	seminary student
Ron Hune*	M	26	2 yrs.	graduate student
Mrs. Joo	F	47	2 yrs.	disabled education assistant (Korean services)
Mrs. Jun	F	49	30 yrs.	custom house broker
Mr. Jung	M	54	24 yrs.	hospital supervisor
Mrs. Kang	F	46	3 yrs.	homemaker
Mrs. Kim	F	54	7 mos.	sales associate (Korean clothing store)
Mr. Koh	M	54	20 yrs.	retired (factory worker)
Mrs. Kong	F	28	1.3 yrs.	homemaker and language student
Mrs. Li	F	42	7 yrs.	singing lessons business
Mr. Min	M	26	1 yr.	engineer
Mrs. Min	F	26	2 yrs.	trade company loan officer
Miss Moon	F	38	2 yrs.	dental hygienist
Mrs. Noh	F	31	4 yrs.	homemaker
Mark Oh*	M	34	10.5 yrs.	auto body shop cashier; church music director
Fred Pai*	M	26	9 mos.	warehouse manager (Korean business)
Mrs. Paik	F	56	1 yr.	homemaker
Mr. Pak	M	54	26 yrs.	picture framing business
Mrs. Pak	F	51	26 yrs.	registered nurse
Miss Park	F	46	20 yrs.	Chinese medicine business (former animator)
Miss Pike	F	44	2 mos.	N/A
Mrs. Ra	F	25	6 mos.	homemaker and language student
Mr. Roh	M	66	1 yr.	retired (government inspector in S. Korea)
Paul Ryu*	M	31	3 yrs.	seminary student
Mrs. Shin	F	29	6 mos.	secretary (Korean services)
Mr. Sohn	M	73	43 yrs.	retired (meat packer; owned Japanese restaurant)
Mrs. Song	F	28	3.5 yrs.	public health graduate student
Miss Suh	F	27	5 yrs.	skin care beautician
Mrs. Um	F	29	1 yr.	homemaker
Mrs. Yi	F	76	21 trans. yrs.	homemaker
Mr. Yoo	M	49	19 yrs.	Korean radio broadcaster
Mrs. Yoon	F	48	2 yrs.	dental hygienist

*Denotes male who has never been married

LA respondents: Second generation

Name	Sex	Age	Occupation	Romantic status
Audrey Kim	F	30	attorney	married
Carol Kim	F	23	part-time student teacher	single
David Chang	M	26	student	single
Grace An	F	38	attorney	single
Hagen Park	F	17	student (sings/acts)	single
Heesu Kim	F	24	student	single/ bisexual
Jacquelyn Lee	F	27	student	single
Jenny Hur	F	28	student	engaged
Joe Song	M	42	nonprofit administrator	married
John Park	M	18	student	single
Lance Kim	M	24	financial analyst	single
Poppy Son	F	27	teacher	single
Ron Jun	M	27	medical student	single
Sam Oh	M	29	manager of a learning center	single
Sora Ryu	F	31	pharmaceutical marketing manager	married
Sung Bae	M	17	student	single
Taehan Ko	M	23	editor	single/ bisexual
Tim Cho	M	26	patients' rights advocate	single
Todd Paik	M	26	attorney	single
Tom Chung	M	29	physician	married

Seoul respondents

Name	Sex	Age	Education
Bokhi Lee	F	51	junior high school graduate
Daehyun Suh	M	61	college graduate
Doo-hwan Chun	M	23	college student
Eunjee Lee	F	23	graduate student
Haengbok Han	M	26	college student
Haewon Jung	F	20	college student
Han Gil Yoo	M	22	college student
Heesun Kim	F	51	junior high school graduate
Hong-gil Dong	M	22	college student
Hosung Jang	M	46	college graduate
Hye-soo Ha	F	24	college student
Hyonah Che	F	28	graduate student
Hyung-jun Park	M	26	college student
Hyungsook An	F	52	some college
Jae-ook Shin	M	65	high school graduate
Jahmi Jun	M	26	MA recipient
Jeongah Paik	F	55	high school graduate
Minhee Jung	F	60	college graduate
Minkyung Chong	F	21	college student
Mino Bang	M	25	college student
Minsun Park	M	79	high school graduate
Pil Baek	M	55	college graduate
Rucy Yoo	M	54	college graduate
Sang Min Park	M	23	college student
Shimi Oh	F	51	college graduate
Shin Kim	M	79	college graduate
Shinha Park	F	23	graduate student
Sohee Kim	F	21	college student
Su-heng Lim	F	26	graduate student
Yong Joo	F	22	graduate student
Yongsoo Kim	M	28	college student
Yun Lee	F	23	college student

Notes

Chapter 1

1. I define "ideology" as a group's set of sociopolitical beliefs. The term often serves a legitimating function, such as in the name of White supremacy or for the purposes of resisting an oppressor. Other examples abound.

2. I employ Kim's (1999) definition of racialization: the creation and characterization of racial categories.

3. Some of the authors support their claims by drawing on interviews they themselves did not conduct and/or on journalistic media (e.g., Bonilla-Silva 2002; Warren and Twine 1997). Within the parameters of empirical data, however, these sources do not seem sufficient to support such heavyweight concerns as the transformation of American racial structures.

4. On this process with respect to anti-Black ideologies, see Abelmann and Lie (1995).

5. I borrow Joan Scott's definition of "discourse" as "a historically, socially, and institutionally specific structure of statements, terms, categories, and beliefs . . . Discourse is thus contained or expressed in organizations and institutions as well as in words" (2003:379–80).

6. Forman (forthcoming) accounts for the differential power of racial or ethnic groups by conceptualizing prejudice as culturally realized in the context of dominant and nondominant ideologies. The prejudices of unequally positioned groups, then, serve different and unequal projects.

7. By "internalized," I refer to the process by which oppressed groups unconsciously legitimate their own oppression by believing in their own inferiority (Baker 1983).

8. However, Japan's war against the United States and Black Americans' symbolic hope in a Japanese victory to dismantle (global) White dominance gave rise to some

unanticipated and generative alliance-building between Black Americans and people of Japanese descent in the United States and in Japan (Lipsitz 1997).

9. One exception is Levitt's study (2001:107) in which she found that anti-Black sentiment in the Dominican Republic shaped migrants' persistent anti-Black prejudice and transnational affirmation of it from the United States.

10. I thank Moon-Kie Jung for pushing me on this point. I also agree with his view that triangulation may be *empirically* appropriate only in particular historical cases or for specific research questions. On another note, although Kim (1999) applies the axis of social citizenship to Asian Americans only, I believe that it can be made specific to the case of Latinos, a group that has been racialized as foreigners largely on the basis of *legal* status (see Hondagneu-Sotelo 1997), but also by way of United States–Latin American relations (see Chapter 6).

11. Although the experience of small business owners in low-income Black and Latino communities is not the focus of my study, my interviews with such merchants, I will show, shine light on their resistance to foreignness and invisibility.

12. By "first-generation immigrants" I mean adult immigrants to the United States ("immigrant" because the vast majority are not transmigrants).

Chapter 2

1. Also from personal communication with John Lie.

2. Throughout, I use "Ms." and "Mr." as prefixes to surnames to conform to the Korean cultural practice of addressing strangers or elders through more formal, honorific language. I choose not to stipulate the marital status of women by using the "Miss" or "Mrs." prefix, as there is no equivalent for men. Whenever I am the interviewer, I write "N" whereas I write "I" to denote my research assistant interviewer.

3. In a more recent example and within the realm of popular culture, Kellner (1992) argued that the privileging of the color white in *Miami Vice* supported the privileging of the White protagonist Crockett over his Black partner, Tubbs.

4. It is interesting that Korean women have not seemed to follow the more recent American beauty aesthetic of "light brown" skin. To be sure, I witnessed and was also informed about a fad whereby Korean women desired a pale face but a tanner body. Perhaps this emulated Americans' association of a tan with fitness and leisure or their tendency toward "colonial appropriation" of Blackness. It is an appropriation because few light-skinned women tan beyond the aesthetically pleasing light brown tone of a Jennifer Lopez. It is highly uncommon to see tanning products or magazine representations of beauty promoting the skin complexion of Black actresses such as Grace Jones. It will be interesting to see if and how this beauty aesthetic changes in the United States and how Korean women will continue to respond (or not), such as in the above "mixed light-tan" manner.

5. In the premodern era, Japan perceived "proper place" to mean the natural

ordering of national or ethnic groups in the global scheme of things, with the Japanese leading Asia, and the rest of the world, in perpetuity.

6. I owe this insight to Kyeyoung Park.

7. From personal communication with Kyeyoung Park.

8. During my fieldwork in 2000, it broadcast "oldies" like *Norma Rae* and *Missing in Action* to more recent movies like *Jurassic Park*. On other stations, all of these movies would be dubbed in Korean.

9. On average, people spend thirty-four minutes each weekday reading newspapers and, on weekend days, thirty-nine minutes. Men spend more time reading newspapers than women (K. Lee 1999).

10. There are other joint ventures as well, such as MTV Asia.

11. Despite the fact that a large number of Latinos have been serving in the U.S. military in recent decades, South Koreans have been so conditioned by racial categories of White and Black that virtually all of the respondents in this study were unable to distinguish Latinos as a separate group until they got to California. In other words, they either lumped Latinos stationed in Korea with Whites or lumped them with Blacks. This is not a testament to ignorance, but rather to the influence of Japanese and U.S. dichotomies of White and Black, especially in a self-perceived homogenous society of "only Koreans." Finally, I found no reports of South Korean conflicts with Latinos as a group. All reports pertained to White and Black soldiers.

12. The information in this paragraph comes from Eui-Young Yu (2003).

Chapter 3

1. Following Frankenberg (1993:1), I define "Whiteness" as a location of structural advantage ("race" and national privilege), the standpoint of Whites, and a set of cultural practices that are usually unmarked and unnamed.

2. I owe this insight to John Lie.

3. I say "transmigrant" because for twenty years she had lived between the United States and South Korea for visa reasons.

4. The information in this paragraph comes from Millard (1955:313, 319, 334).

5. I owe this insight to John Lie.

6. Although the United States continues to occupy the ROK, it "officially" left Japan in 1952 but formally controlled Okinawa until 1972 and Iwo Jima until 1968 (although a large deployment remains today). There are parallels, such as military crimes and anti-U.S. movements. In contrast to the ROK, however, 75 percent of the bases in Japan (and many of the tensions) are in Okinawa (Fujiwara 1987:12, cited in Lie 2001), a more distant island/people that Japan has subordinated as a non-Japanese minority.

7. So as not to reify racial stereotypes or power relations between researcher and informant, I modified English language passages that contained grammatical errors. In these instances the word "modified" appears after the passage.

8. It is interesting to me that the two respondents who mentioned *Breakfast at Tiffany's* did not discuss the racist portrayal of Mr. Yunioshi (Mickey Rooney in yellow-face). Perhaps it reflects how "natural" such portrayals of Asian men are (e.g., as sinister, unattractive, asexual) or how marginal he is to the two main White stars, Hepburn and Peppard. It also reflects Koreans' fixation on Whites, "America's" reference point.

9. I witnessed this when my South Korean friend and I walked by a large group of very sharply dressed women frantically beautifying themselves for what looked like a photo shoot. When I asked my friend what the women were doing and why the nervous excitement, she informed me that they were taking their picture for the Ewha yearbook, which many families referenced to pick out potential wives for their sons.

10. According to Yuh (2002:248n24), the U.S. role has been essentially confirmed by journalist Tim Shorrock (1996a, 1996b) who found corroborating evidence through the Freedom of Information Act.

11. Korean Americans in the United States also participated as part of a diasporic political struggle. Edward Chang (1988) notes that Korean Americans protested the ROK state's suppression of the student dissidents and intervention in U.S. immigrants' lives, as well as the U.S. role in the massacre.

12. As an example of fierce local pressure, once *Fatal Attraction* broke through red tape in 1988, it faced angry mobs linked to Korean firms that previously had enjoyed a movie monopoly (*Financial Times*, October 5, 1989). The mobs blocked the entrances of theaters showing the movie, "released live snakes in theaters that sent terrified movie-goers fleeing into the streets" and used smoke bombs and tear gas (*Financial Times*, October 5, 1989). The result was the "fatal" end of a disastrous seven-week run for *Fatal Attraction*.

13. As a result of these land problems and South Koreans' increasing resentment toward the base, Yongsan Garrison will be relocated southward to Camp Humphreys near the city of Pyongtaek in 2008.

14. After finding a document that confirmed the AP journalists' earlier account of military-issued orders to shoot South Korean civilians, American historian Sahr Conway-Lanz (2005, 2006) concluded that the Pentagon's position was "untenable." The AP journalists have concurred.

Chapter 4

1. I owe this insight and phrase to John Lie.

2. Literally, "older sister," per Confucianist emphasis on respect for those older.

3. As Kyeyoung Park (1994) found, some Black Americans were "freaked . . . out" by Korean shopkeepers' worship of Buddha in their stores; as well, survey research finds notions of Asian exoticism and foreignness to be common among Americans.

4. Since my interviews, Pittsburgh Steelers' Super Bowl XL's Most Valuable Player, Hines Ward, established in 2006 a foundation to help biracial children in South Korea

overcome discrimination (he himself is Korean-Black). Celebrated and welcomed as "a Korean" hero in the home country, he has actively spread antiracist ideologies, namely the liberal humanism of "love knows no color."

5. This question has its problems as well, given the fact that individuals can also be attracted to, and marry, people of color *because* of racial stereotypes.

6. The reason for *Ghost's* success in Korea (roughly one in every ten Koreans seeing the film; *Hollywood Reporter*, January 3, 1995) was Koreans' cultural reading of it based on Buddhist principles. Movie executives found that the audiences were enchanted by Patrick Swayze's character as a spirit protecting his lover, Demi Moore, "because he personified the theme of reincarnation" (*Hollywood Reporter*, January 3, 1995). Hence, America's sign system of eternal love and life was interpreted within the logic of Buddhism. It is also noteworthy that this movie draws heavily on the racial codes of light-skin / white = good and dark-skin / black = bad.

7. I borrow from Russell's (1991) application of this argument to the case of Japan.

Chapter 5

1. To be sure, the foreign-born / native-born divide is somewhat of a false dichotomy, as child immigrants are also foreign born.

2. As a related point, second-generation Korean American women's outmarriage rates with Whites and others are significantly higher than those of Korean immigrant women; to be sure, the second generation is increasingly marrying other Asian Americans more so than Whites (Sharon Lee and Fernandez 1998; Qian and Lichter 2007; Shinagawa and Pang 1996).

3. Korean churches reached out by promoting scholarship programs (for young Black students), cultural exchanges, joint religious services, and clothing and food donations. One of the largest Korean churches in Los Angeles spent around $20,000 for these efforts in 1991 alone (Min 1996:137).

Chapter 6

1. On citizenship see Marshall (1973), Canning and Rose (2001), and Glenn (2002).

2. It is plausible that rank-order questions may lead informants to answer when they have not formulated strong opinions or to simplify their responses from the outset. I do think, however, that these items are suggestive of hegemony insofar as groups in power often force people into ranked categories in egregiously simplified ways, typically for the purpose of legitimating power. Thus, everyday people are conditioned to think in such a manner as well. In addition, despite the potential difficulty of answering rank-order questions, my informants demonstrated a patterned view of themselves as socioeconomically in between, yet as less politically and culturally powerful than Blacks and Latinos. In this way, their answers to rank-order items tended to match the themes or assumptions of their other narratives. Finally, on a logistical level, I made sure to preface

that the informant could specify various kinds of rankings rather than conform to one hierarchy or not answer if they were so inclined. In general, I found that the informants tended to answer the rank-order question pretty readily; those who were uncertain usually said "I don't know" or "That's too hard a question."

3. Although sociological scholarship largely treats "race" and class as separate systems whereby "race" is not an epiphenomenon of class (Omi and Winant 1994; Willie 1978), it acknowledges that Whites' subjugation of Blacks has involved the intersection or interaction of "race" and class (P. Collins 2000; Omi and Winant 1994). Indeed, America's color line pivoted on these intersections to erect Whites as the educated, propertied slave owners counterposed to the uneducated, unpropertied Black slaves. The ideology of White superiority and Black inferiority, then, has been tied to (though not always dependent on) high and low socioeconomic status, respectively. Moreover, White economic dominance and Black impoverishment still today, notwithstanding the advent of the Black middle class (Neckerman, Carter, and Lee 1999), are traceable to slavery and other racist institutions (Massey and Denton 1993; Oliver and Shapiro 1997). The fact that neither the advent of the Black middle class nor Whites' composition of the largest segment of the poor has fundamentally unraveled color line ideologies shows not only the power of "race" over class, but that of monolithic images over complex realities. The model minority myth represents another such paradox.

4. All references to Southern California refer to Los Angeles–Riverside–Orange County CMSA (Consolidated Metropolitan Statistical Areas) unless I state otherwise.

5. Some of these similarities with Black Americans might explain why some Koreans, as I will show, placed Blacks and Koreans in a similar socioeconomic stratum.

6. To be sure, most Korean Americans in the United States rent their domiciles (UCLA Asian American Studies Center and Adachi 2004).

7. Wherever I use "APA" I refer to census data that include Pacific Islanders.

8. The Asian American Legal Defense and Educational Fund (AALDEF) national poll, November 10, 2004, cited in 80-20 initiative.net (2004–2005). AALDEF provided the only 2004 Asian American–specific national exit poll.

9. *New York Times* exit polls, 1992, 1996, 2000, 2004, cited in 80-20 initiative.net (2004–2005).

10. Exit poll data from National Korean American Service and Education Center (NAKASEC), Korean Resource Center (Los Angeles), Korean American Resource and Cultural Center (Chicago), and Young Korean American Service and Education Center (YKASEC)—Empowering the Korean American Community (New York), November 4, 2004, cited in 80-20 initiative.net (2004–2005).

11. However, the book as a whole lacks an analysis of power and structural inequality, both with regard to the army model and to the construction of American culture.

12. Latinos have defined their own genre of music and have impressively established the global Spanish-language television stations, Univision and Telemundo. Latinos have

boasted many more household names in the entertainment scene than have Asian Americans (to name a few, in recent years, Ricky Martin, Jennifer Lopez, Marc Anthony, Christina Aguilera, Andy Garcia, Antonio Banderas, and Penelope Cruz).

13. I thank Alford Young Jr. for this point.

Chapter 7

1. From Anna Deveare Smith's *Twilight: Los Angeles, 1992* (1994). The passage originally included phonetic pronunciation not included here.

2. Incidentally, even today many Americans know little about South Korea, such as about its robust economy in recent years.

3. Newcomers especially would say that they had yet to experience any racial discrimination, but they would often think a little more and recount some kind of brush with it.

4. It could be argued that the "caught in the crossfire" argument also reflects Korean Americans' desire not to admit their culpability. Korean Americans, however, readily concede their racial prejudice as a cause, as I have shown.

5. To be certain, many Black Americans also supported the Korean Americans they had befriended and tried to help protect stores during the mayhem (Abelmann and Lie 1995). In support of resource competition theories, for instance, Jennifer Lee (2000) argues that less tension exists between Korean merchants and middle-class Black clientele. To be sure, middle-class Blacks, like their lower-income counterparts, tend to prefer Black-owned businesses in their communities.

6. Espiritu (2003:47–48) challenges this distinction by rewriting the historical narrative as one of the United States violently bringing in and differentially including *all* people of color whether through slavery, conquest, or labor demands.

7. This information comes from the LA Community Project Survey cited in Cruz and Patraporn with Adachi (2006).

8. Ten of the women in the sample were housewives in search of work (some were learning English); not surprisingly, they were all newcomers. Four other women were working in independent small business ventures (Chinese medicine, music/voice, two in cosmetology). Another had run a photo developing business with her husband, and three were vocational or graduate students. The rest held mostly pink-collar jobs—office workers, dental hygienists, teachers, and textile designers—while three were in higher status positions, such as custom house broker, corporate relationship director, and so on.

9. Incidentally, prior to 2000 most Korean businesses were on the margins of White suburbs (E. Yu 1990); by 2000 they proliferated in suburbs *and* central cities (E. Yu 2001).

10. Finally, these narratives reveal the flaws in universalist claims about immigrants, such as John Ogbu's (1991) notion that "voluntary" migrants can grin and bear racism in the United States. He adds that they are more optimistic about the future because

their new status is better than that in the home country. Korean Americans, however, typically had much higher occupational prestige in South Korea, consider U.S. racism to be unconscionable, and actively resist it.

11. Korean American and other cultural producers have also represented the 1992 unrest through visual arts and literature in order to navigate the persistent social ills of the nation since the 1990s, a process in the name of a better future (Song 2005).

Chapter 8

1. On the second generation's general sense of inferiority to White women, see Pyke and Johnson (2003). On internalized racism, see Pyke and Dang (2003).

2. As Lisa Sun-hee Park (2005:88) found among second-generation Korean and Chinese Americans, Ron conceives of the U.S. immigrant struggle in a manner akin to the film genre of westerns, wherein the immigrant father is a hero figure who teaches his children to be like him in a harsh world. By the children doing so, heroes and happy endings are born and reborn.

3. Although many respondents cite Black entertainers (especially in music) and athletes, they cite less frequently the powerful (male) business moguls behind the artists/athletes, for example: Robert L. Johnson (Black Entertainment Television, Charlotte Bobcats), Russell Simmons (Def Jam, Rush Communications), Antonio "L.A." Reid (Arista Records, The Island Def Jam Music Group, LaFace Records), Damon Dash (entrepreneur, Dame Dash Music Group), and Dallas Austin (Rowdy Records). Of course, there are those who are at once entertainers/athletes and businesspeople: Oprah Winfrey (Harpo Productions; O, The Oprah Magazine; O at Home), Quincy Jones (Qwest Records, music impresario), Babyface (LaFace Records, Edmonds Production Co.), Diddy (Bad Boy Records, Sean John clothing), Jay-Z (Def Jam, Roc-a-Fella Records and Films, Rocawear clothing, New Jersey Nets), Dr. Dre (Death Row Records, Aftermath Entertainment), Jermaine Dupri (Island Records, So So Def Recordings), Nelly (Derrty Ent., Apple Bottom jeans, Charlotte Bobcats), Magic Johnson (Magic Johnson Enterprises), Michael Jordan (Charlotte Bobcats; Jordan Brand clothing), just to provide a short list.

4. Incidentally, Asian Pacific American Heritage Month already existed at the time of the interview (May of every year) but it is not nearly as well-known as Black History Month.

5. Only three of the twenty respondents thought that Whites would have to see Korean/Asian Americans as equals if they matched Whites on every societal level. Even these responses, however, were filled with qualifications of conditions that would need to be met for "equal treatment" to happen.

Chapter 9

1. Friendly form of address for men who are not kin related.

2. Although the woman could have been a tourist, South Korean women, as in her

case, tend to wear the same trends in makeup, hair clips, clothes, shoes, cell phone accessories, and so on. Such conformity was often how some South Koreans, especially at the beginning of my stay, could discern that I was from elsewhere.

Appendix

1. Of course I was concerned that the students would wonder about my "native authenticity" despite the fact that I never opened my mouth. Given that young women in Seoul often culturally "homogenize" their appearances (in line with essentialism, some even said that they could tell a Korean American by her body shape), I often conferred with Heejin about a look and style that approximated the "norm" as closely as possible. It seemed to work, because the focus group participants were just as critical of the United States as they were laudatory of it in my presence.

2. Although all the names of observation sites and the actors involved have been changed, all other details are unfabricated.

3. This also could have reflected many native South Koreans' censure of Korean immigrants who left for the United States as "traitors" (see Chapter 9).

4. In my assessment, Seoul summers are incredibly hot and humid, and I could not bring myself to wear the heavy dress suits of the native women simply to "fit in" better at my research sites. I had my own boundaries of need that I could not cross (I was honestly afraid of heat spells). I did, however, try to find more concealing, lighter fabrics to be respectful of the cultural dress code and so as not to be too conspicuous.

5. One criticism that can be leveled at both grounded theory and the (global) extended case method pertains to conceptions of culture. Focusing on Burawoy (1998), Nina Eliasoph and Paul Lichterman (1999:228) argue that his conceptualization, although it acknowledges that culture and social structure interpenetrate, does not clearly account for the fact "that people apprehend social structure only through culture" and that "culture is itself a structure." To illustrate their point, they discuss that the way in which actors *talk* about social phenomena, such as the topic of globalization, dictates their behaviors. As well, structure is not just constraining but facilitating. That is, cultural processes can *produce* groups. For instance, they argue, "the social contexts that people create for open-ended dialogue *are structures* in their own right, and people create them in culturally patterned ways" (Eliasoph and Lichterman 1999:231). My study incorporates these two critiques by foregrounding the way in which South Koreans and Korean immigrants produce a new cultural structure as they navigate transnational processes spurred by global power (i.e., U.S. imperialism). Yet, I believe that this emphasis on culture in general, as pathbreaking and stimulating as it is, needs to articulate more clearly when cultural structures, as opposed to social structures, account for phenomena—or when both are equally important—and why that is.

Bibliography

Abelmann, Nancy, and John Lie. 1995. *Blue dreams: Korean Americans and the Los Angeles riots.* Cambridge, MA: Harvard University Press.

AFN Korea. 2005. American Forces Network Korea. http://afnkorea.net (retrieved May 1, 2005).

Aguilar, John. 1981. Insider research: An ethnography of a debate. In *Anthropologists at home in North America: Methods and issues in the study of one's own society,* ed. Donald A. Messerschmidt, 15–28. Cambridge, MA: Cambridge University Press.

Alba, Richard, and Victor Nee. 2003. *Rethinking the American mainstream: Assimilation and contemporary immigration.* Cambridge, MA: Harvard University Press.

Alexander, Jeffrey. 1992. Citizen and enemy as symbolic classification: On the polarizing discourse of civil society. In *Cultivating differences: Symbolic boundaries and the making of inequality,* ed. Michele Lamont and Marcel Fournier, 289–308. Chicago: University of Chicago Press.

All Empires History Forum. 2007. Chinese letters in Japan, Korea, and Vietnam: Past, present, and future. http://www.allempires.com/article/index.php?q=chinese_letters (retrieved July 30, 2007).

Allen, Ernest, Jr. 1994. Waiting for Tojo: The pro-Japan vigil of Black Missourians, 1932–1943. *Gateway Heritage* 15(2):16–33.

Almaguer, Tomás. 1994. *Racial fault lines: The historical origins of White supremacy in California.* Berkeley: University of California Press.

Almaguer, Tomás, and Moon-Kie Jung. 1999. The enduring ambiguities of race in the United States. In *Sociology for the twenty-first century: Continuities and cutting edges,* ed. Janet Abu-Lughod, 213–39. Chicago: University of Chicago Press.

Ancheta, Angelo N. 1998. *Race, rights, and the Asian American experience.* New Brunswick, NJ: Rutgers University Press.

Anderson, Benedict. 1983. *Imagined communities: Reflections on the origin and spread of nationalism*. London: Verso.

Anderson, Kathryn, and Dana C. Jack. 1991. Learning to listen: Interview techniques and analyses. In *Women's words: The feminist practice of oral history*, ed. Sherna B. Gluck and Daphne Patai, 11–26. New York: Routledge.

Ang, Ien. 1996. *Living room wars: Rethinking media audiences for a postmodern world*. New York: Routledge.

Appadurai, Arjun. 1990. Disjuncture and difference in the global cultural economy. *Public Culture* 2(2):1–24.

Arnesen, Eric. 2001. Whiteness and the historians' imagination. *International Labor and Working-Class History* 60:3–32.

Axelbank, Albert. 1967. Why the reelection of Park is practically certain. *New Republic*, April 29, 1967, 9–11.

Baker, Donald G. 1983. *Race, ethnicity and power: A comparative study*. Boston: Routledge and Kegan Paul.

Balibar, Etienne. 1991. The nation form: History and ideology. In *Race, nation, and class: Ambiguous identities*, ed. Etienne Balibar and Immanuel Wallerstein, 86–106. New York: Verso.

Barr, Patricia. 1965. *The coming of the barbarians: The opening of Japan to the West, 1853–1870*. London: Penguin.

Barrett, James, and David Roediger. 1997. Inbetween peoples: Race, nationality and the "new immigrant" working class. *Journal of American Ethnic History* 16(Spring):3–44.

Barringer, Herbert R., David T. Takeuchi, and Peter Xenos. 1990. Education, occupational prestige, and income of Asian-Americans. *Sociology of Education* 63:27–43.

Basch, Linda G., Nina G. Schiller, and Cristina Szanton Blanc. 1994. *Nations unbound: Transnational projects, postcolonial predicaments, and deterritorialized nation-states*. Langhorne, PA: Gordon and Breach.

Batur-VanderLippe, Pinar, and Joe Feagin. 1999. Racial and ethnic inequality and struggle from the colonial era to the present: Drawing the global color line. *Research in Politics and Society* 6:3–21.

Bauman, Zygmunt. 1992. *Intimations of postmodernity*. New York: Routledge.

BBC News. 2005. Country Profile: South Korea. http://news.bbc.co.uk/1/hi/world/asia-pacific/country_profiles/1123668.stm (retrieved December 30, 2005).

Bhattacharjee, Ananya. 1992. The habit of ex-nomination: Nation, woman, and the Indian immigrant bourgeoisie. *Public Culture* 5:19–44.

Blauner, Bob. 1972. *Racial oppression in America*. New York: Harper and Row.

Blauner, Bob, and David Wellman. 1977. Toward the decolonization of social research. In *The death of White sociology: Essays on race and culture*, ed. Joyce A. Ladner, 310–32. New York: Random House.

Bobo, Lawrence, and Vincent L. Hutchings. 1996. Perceptions of racial group competition: Extending Blumer's theory of group position to a multiracial social context. *American Sociological Review* 61:951–72.

Bobo, Lawrence, James R. Kluegel, and Ryan A. Smith. 1997. Laissez faire racism: The crystallization of a kinder, gentler, antiblack ideology. In *Racial attitudes in the 1990s: Continuity and change*, ed. Steven A. Tuch and Jack K. Martin, 15–42. Westport, CT: Praeger.

Bodde, Derk. 1953. Harmony and conflict in Chinese philosophy. In *Studies in Chinese thought*, ed. Arthur F. Wright, 19–80. Chicago: University of Chicago Press.

Bonilla-Silva, Eduardo. 1997. Rethinking racism: Toward a structural interpretation. *American Sociological Review* 62(3):465–80.

———. 2000. "This is a White country": The racial ideology of the western nations of the world-system. *Research in Politics and Society* 6:85–101.

———. 2001. *White supremacy and racism in the post–civil rights era*. Boulder, CO: Lynne Rienner Publishers.

———. 2002. "We are all Americans!": The Latin Americanization of racial stratification in the USA. *Race and Society* 5(1):3–16.

Bonilla-Silva, Eduardo, and Tyrone Forman. 2000. "I'm not a racist, but . . .": Mapping White college students' racial ideology in the USA. *Discourse and Society* 11(1):50–85.

Bonilla-Silva, Eduardo, and Amanda Lewis. 1999. The new racism: Racial structure in the United States, 1960s–1990s. In *Race, ethnicity, and nationality in the United States: Toward the twenty-first century*, ed. Paul Wong, 55–101. Boulder, CO: Westview Press.

Bornstein, Robert F. 1989. Exposure and affect. Overview and meta-analysis of research, 1968–1987. *Psychological Bulletin* 106:265–89.

Bositis, David A. 2003. *Black elected officials: A statistical summary, 2001*. Washington, DC: Joint Center for Political and Economic Studies.

Brooker, Paul. 1991. *The faces of fraternalism: Nazi Germany, Fascist Italy, and Imperial Japan*. Oxford, UK: Clarendon Press.

Bulosan, Carlos. 1973. *America in the heart: A personal history*. Seattle: University of Washington Press.

Burawoy, Michael. 1998. The extended case method. *Sociological Theory* 16(1):4–33.

Burawoy, Michael, Joseph A. Blum, Sheba George, Zsuzsa Gille, Teresa Gowan, Lynne Haney, Maren Klawiter, Steve H. Lopez, Seán Ó Riain, and Millie Thayer. 2000. *Global ethnography: Forces, connections, and imaginations in a postmodern world*. Berkeley: University of California Press.

Canning, Kathleen, and Sonya O. Rose. 2001. Gender, citizenship, and subjectivity: Some historical and theoretical considerations. *Gender and Society* 19(3):427–43.

Cha, Theresa Hak Kyung. 2001. *Dictee*. Berkeley: University of California Press.

Chan, Kenyon S., and Shirley Hune. 1995. Racialization and panethnicity: From Asians in America to Asian Americans. In *Toward a common destiny: Improving race and ethnic relations in America*, ed. Willis D. Hawley and Anthony W. Jackson, 205–33. San Francisco: Jossey-Bass.

Chan, Sucheng. 1990. Introduction. In *Quiet odyssey: A pioneer Korean woman in America*, by Mary Paik Lee, xxi–lx. Seattle: University of Washington Press.

Chang, Edward T. 1988. Korean community politics in Los Angeles: The impact of the Kwangju uprising. *Amerasia Journal* 14(1):51–67.

———. 1999. *The racial/ethnic attitudes of Korean college students survey*. Riverside: University of California–Riverside.

Charles, Carolle. 1992. Transnationalism in the construct of Haitian migrants' racial categories of identity in New York City. In *Towards a transnational perspective on migration: Race, class, ethnicity, and nationalism reconsidered*, ed. Nina Glick Schiller and Linda Basch, 101–24. New York: New York Academy of Sciences.

Chen, Anthony S. 1999. Lives at the center of the periphery, lives at the periphery of the center: Chinese American masculinities and bargaining with hegemony. *Gender and Society* 13(5):584–607.

Cheng, Lucie, and Yen L. Espiritu. 1989. Korean businesses in Black and Hispanic neighborhoods: A study of intergroup relations. *Sociological Perspectives* 32:521–34.

Cho, Sumi K. 1993. Korean Americans vs. African Americans: Conflict and construction. In *Reading Rodney King/reading urban uprising*, ed. Robert Gooding-Williams, 196–211. New York: Routledge.

Clark, Donald N., ed. 1988. *The Kwangju Uprising: Shadows over the regime in South Korea*. Boulder, CO: Westview Press.

Collins, Patricia Hill. 2000. *Black feminist thought: Knowledge, consciousness, and the politics of empowerment*. 2nd ed. New York: Routledge.

———. 2001. "Like one of the family": Race, ethnicity, and the paradox of US national identity. *Ethnic and Racial Studies* 24(1):3–28.

Collins, Sharon M. 1997. *Black corporate executives: The making and breaking of a Black middle class*. Philadelphia: Temple University Press.

Committee of 100 Survey. 2001. *American attitudes toward Chinese Americans and Asian Americans*. Washington, DC: Organization of Chinese Americans.

Connell, R. W. 2005. Masculinities and globalization. In *Gender through the prism of difference*, 3rd ed., ed. Maxine Baca Zinn, Pierrette Hondagneu-Sotelo, and Michael A. Messner, 36–48. New York: Oxford University Press.

Conway-Lanz, Sahr. 2005. Beyond No Gun Ri: Refugees and the United States military in the Korean War. *Diplomatic History* 29(1):49–81.

———. 2006. *Collateral damage: Americans, noncombatant immunity, and atrocity after World War II*. New York: Routledge.

Cornell, Stephen E., and Douglas Hartmann. 1998. *Ethnicity and race: Making identities in a changing world*. Thousand Oaks, CA: Pine Forge Press.

Cose, Ellis. 1993. *The rage of a privileged class.* New York: HarperCollins.

Crofts, Alfred. 1960. Our falling ramparts. *The Nation,* June 25, 1960, 544–48.

Cruz, Melany, and R. Varisa Pataporn with Dean Adachi. 2006. *Neighborhood profile: Los Angeles County's Koreatown.* Los Angeles: UCLA Asian American Studies Center.

Cumings, Bruce. 1981. *The origins of the Korean War: Liberation and the emergence of separate regimes, 1945–1947.* Princeton, NJ: Princeton University Press.

Cummings, Scott, and Thomas Lambert. 1997. Anti-Hispanic and anti-Asian sentiments among African Americans. *Social Science Quarterly* 78(2):338–53.

Denzin, Norman K. 1978. *The research act: A theoretical introduction to sociological methods.* New York: McGraw-Hill.

Denzin, Norman K., and Yvonna S. Lincoln. 1994. *Handbook of qualitative research.* Thousand Oaks, CA: Sage.

Dikoetter, Frank. 1994. Racial identities in China: Context and meaning. *China Quarterly* 138:404–12.

Dixon, Travis L., and Daniel Linz. 2000. Overrepresentation and underrepresentation of African Americans and Latinos as lawbreakers on television news. *Journal of Communication* 50(2):131–54.

Dower, John W. 1986. *War without mercy: Race and power in the Pacific war.* New York: Pantheon Books.

Du Bois, W. E. B. 1969. *The souls of Black folk.* New York: Signet Classics.

Ehrenreich, Barbara. 1995. The silenced majority: Why the average working person has disappeared from American media and culture. In *Gender, race and class in media: A text reader,* ed. Gail Dines and Jean M. Humez, 40–51. Thousand Oaks, CA: Sage.

———. 2002. "Maid to order." In *Global woman: Nannies, maids, and sex workers in the new economy,* ed. Barbara Ehrenreich and Arlie R. Hochschild, 85–103. New York: Henry Holt and Company.

Eighth United States Army (EUSA) Office of the Assistant Chief of Staff, Headquarters. 1971. Civil-Military Affairs Newsletter 7-71:1.

80-20initiative.net. 2004–2005. Evidence of the second consecutive APA bloc vote. http://www.80-20initiative.net (retrieved June 5, 2006).

Eliasoph, Nina, and Paul Lichterman. 1999. "We begin with our favorite theory . . .": Reconstructing the extended case method. *Sociological Theory* 17(2):228–34.

Ellison, Ralph. 1952. *Invisible man.* New York: Random House.

Elms, A. C., and Stanley Milgram. 1966. Personality characteristics associated with obedience and defiance toward authority command. *Journal of Experimental Research in Personality* 1:282–89.

Eng, David. 2001. *Racial castration: Managing masculinity in Asian America.* Durham, NC: Duke University Press.

Entman, Robert M., and Andrew Rojecki. 2000. *The Black image in the White mind: Media and race in America.* Chicago: University of Chicago Press.

Espiritu, Yen L. 1989. Beyond the "boat people": Ethnicization of American life. *Amerasia Journal* 15(2):49–67.

———. 1992. *Asian American panethnicity: Bridging institutions and identities.* Philadelphia: Temple University Press.

———. 1997. *Asian American women and men: Labor, laws and love.* Walnut Creek, CA: Alta Mira Press.

———. 2001. "We don't sleep around like White girls do": Family, culture, and gender in Filipina American lives. *Signs* 26(2):415–40.

———. 2003. *Homebound: Filipino American lives across cultures, communities, and countries.* Berkeley: University of California Press.

Essed, Philomena. 1991. *Understanding everyday racism: An interdisciplinary theory.* Thousand Oaks, CA: Sage.

Fanon, Frantz. 1963. *The wretched of the earth.* New York: Grove Press.

Feagin, Joe R. 2000. *Racist America: Roots, current realities, and future reparations.* New York: Routledge.

Feagin, Joe R., and Melvin Sikes. 1994. *Living with racism: The Black middle-class experience.* Boston: Beacon Press.

Featherstone, Mike, ed. 1990. *Global culture: Nationalism, globalization and modernity.* London: Sage.

Foner, Nancy. 2000. *From Ellis Island to JFK: New York's two great waves of immigration.* New Haven and New York: Yale University Press and Russell Sage Foundation.

Fong, Timothy P. 2002. *The contemporary Asian American experience: Beyond the model minority.* 2nd ed. Upper Saddle River, NJ: Prentice Hall.

Forman, Tyrone. Forthcoming. Conceptual and methodological challenges to studying racism and prejudice in the post-civil rights era. In *Racism and methodology,* ed. Eduardo Bonilla-Silva and Tukufu Zuberi. Lanham, MD: Rowman & Littlefield.

Fouron, Georges, and Nina Glick Schiller. 2002. The generation of identity: Redefining the second generation within a transnational social field. In *The changing face of home,* ed. Peggy Levitt and Mary Waters, 168–210. New York: Russell Sage.

Frankenberg, Ruth. 1993. *White women, race matters: The social construction of Whiteness.* Minneapolis: University of Minnesota Press.

Frey, James H., and Andrea Fontana. 1991. The group interview in social science research. *Social Science Journal* 28(2):175–87.

Fujiwara, Akira. 1987. Tennō to Okinawasen [The emperor and the Okinawa War]. In *Okinawasen to tennōsei [The Okinawa War under the emperor's control],* ed. Akira Fujiwara, 9–45. Tokyo: Rippū Shobō.

Gans, Herbert. 1999. The possibility of a new racial hierarchy in the twenty-first century

United States. In *The cultural territories of race: Black and White boundaries*, ed. Michèle Lamont, 371–90. Chicago: University of Chicago Press and Russell Sage Foundation.

Gayn, Mark. 1981. *Japan diary*. Rutland, VT: Charles E. Tuttle Company. (Orig. pub. 1948, New York: William Sloane Associates.)

Gibson, Margaret. 1988. *Accommodation without assimilation: Sikh immigrants in an American high school*. Ithaca, NY: Cornell University Press.

Gilroy, Paul. 1987. *"There ain't no black in the Union Jack": The cultural politics of race and nation*. Chicago: University of Chicago.

Glaser, Barney G., and Anselm L. Strauss. 1967. *The discovery of grounded theory: Strategies for qualitative research*. New York: Aldine Publishing Company.

Glenn, Evelyn N. 2002. *Unequal freedom: How race and gender shaped American citizenship and labor*. Cambridge, MA: Harvard University Press.

Glick Schiller, Nina. 1999. Transmigrants and nation-states: Something old and something new in the U.S. immigrant experience. In *The handbook of international migration: The American experience*, ed. Charles Hirschman, Philip Kasinitz, and Josh DeWind, 94–119. New York: Russell Sage Foundation.

———. 2005. Transnational social fields and imperialism: Bringing a theory of power to transnational studies. *Anthropological Theory* 5(4): 439–61.

Goldberg, David Theo. 2002. *The racial state*. Oxford, UK: Blackwell Publishers.

Gordon, Milton M. 1964. *Assimilation in American life: The role of race, religion, and national origins*. New York: Oxford University Press.

Gray, Herman. 1995. *Watching race: Television and the struggle for "Blackness."* Minneapolis: University of Minnesota.

Groves, Don. 1998. Asian flu batters healthy o'seas B.O. *Variety*. http://o-www.lexisnexis .com.linus.lmu.edu/us/lnacademic/results/docview/docview.do?risb=21_T2750832946 &format=GNBFI&sort=RELEVANCE&startDocNo=1&resultsUrlKey=29 _T2750832949&cisb=22_T2750832948&treeMax=true&treeWidth=0&csi=139224& docNo=1 (retrieved December 21, 2007).

Guerrero, Ed. 1993. *Framing Blackness: The African American image in film*. Philadelphia: Temple University Press.

Guglielmo, Thomas A. 2003. *White on arrival: Italians, race, color, and power in Chicago, 1890–1945*. New York: Oxford University Press.

Gutmann, Amy. 1994. Introduction. In *Multiculturalism: Examining the politics of recognition*, ed. Amy Gutmann, 3–24. Princeton, NJ: Princeton University Press.

Habermas, Jürgen. 1989. *The structural transformation of the public sphere: An inquiry into a category of bourgeois society*. Cambridge, MA: MIT Press.

Hall, Stuart. 1980. Race, articulation, and societies structured in dominance. In *Sociological theories: Race and colonialism*, ed. UNESCO, 304–45. Paris: United Nations Educational, Scientific and Cultural Organization.

———. 1991. The local and the global: Globalization and ethnicity. In *Culture, global-ization, and the world-system: Contemporary conditions for the representation of identity*, ed. Anthony King, 19–39. Binghamton: Department of Art, State University of New York.

———. 2003. The whites of their eyes: Racist ideologies and the media. In *Gender, race and class in media: A text reader*, ed. Gail Dines and Jean M. Humez, 18–22. Thousand Oaks, CA: Sage.

Hanley, Charles J., Martha Mendoza, and Sang-hun Choe. 2002. *The bridge at No Gun Ri: A hidden nightmare from the Korean War*. New York: Owl Books/Henry Holt and Co.

Hardt, Michael, and Antonio Negri. 2000. *Empire*. Cambridge, MA: Harvard University Press.

Harvey, David. 2003. *The new imperialism*. New York: Oxford University Press.

Heine, William. 1990. *With Perry to Japan: A memoir by William Heine*. Honolulu: University of Hawaii Press. (Orig. pub. 1856.)

Henderson, Gregory. 1968. *Korea: The politics of the vortex*. Cambridge, MA: Harvard University Press.

Hill, Robert A., ed. 1983. *The Marcus Garvey and UNIA Papers*. Berkeley: University of California Press.

Hirsch, Jennifer S. 2003. *A courtship after marriage: Sexuality and love in Mexican transnational families*. Berkeley: University of California Press.

Hirschman, Charles, and Morrison Wong. 1981. Trends in socioeconomic achievement among immigrant and native-born Asian Americans. *Sociological Quarterly* 22:495–513.

Hondagneu-Sotelo, Pierrette. 1997. Working 'without papers' in the United States: Toward the integration of legal status in frameworks of race, class, and gender. In *Women and work: Exploring race, ethnicity, and class*, ed. Elizabeth Higginbotham and Mary Romero, 101–26. Thousand Oaks, CA: Sage.

Horkheimer, Max, and Theodor W. Adorno. 1972. *Dialectic of enlightenment*. New York: Crossroads/Continuum.

Hunt, Darnell M. 1997. *Screening the Los Angeles "riots": Race, seeing, and resistance*. Cambridge: Cambridge University Press.

Hurh, Won Moo, and Kwang Chung Kim. 1984. *Korean immigrants in America: A structural analysis of ethnic confinement and adhesive adaptation*. Rutherford, NJ: Fairleigh Dickinson University Press.

International Action Center. 2001. Statistics on crimes committed by U.S. troops in South Korea. International Action Center (reprinted from http://peacekorea.org, June 23, 2001). http://www.iacenter.org/Koreafiles/ktc-civilnetwork.htm (retrieved May 1, 2006).

Jiobu, Robert M. 1988. *Ethnicity and assimilation: Blacks, Chinese, Filipinos, Japanese, Koreans, Mexicans, Vietnamese, and Whites*. Albany: State University of New York Press.

Jo, Moon H. 1992. Korean merchants in the Black community: Prejudice among the victims of prejudice. *Ethnic and Racial Studies* 15(3):395–411.

Jung, Moon-Kie. 2006. *Reworking race: The making of Hawaii's interracial labor movement.* New York: Columbia University Press.

Kang, Hyon-du. 1991. *Media culture in Korea.* Seoul: Seoul National University Press.

Kang, Jong Geun, and Michael Morgan. 1988. Culture clash: Impact of U.S. television in Korea. *Journalism and Mass Communication Quarterly* 65:431–38.

Kasinitz, Philip. 1992. *Caribbean New York: Black immigrants and the politics of race.* Ithaca, NY: Cornell University Press.

Kassarjian, Harold H. 1969. The Negro and American advertising, 1946–1965. *Journal of Marketing Research* 6(1):29–39.

Kaw, Eugenia. 1993. Medicalization of racial features: Asian American women and cosmetic surgery. *Medical Anthropology Quarterly* 7(1):74–89.

Kearney, Michael. 1995. The local and global: The anthropology of globalization and transnationalism. *Annual Review of Anthropology* 24:547–65.

Keller, Nora Okja. 2002. *Fox girl.* New York: Penguin Books.

Kellner, Douglas. 1992. Popular culture and the construction of postmodern identities. In *Modernity and identity,* ed. Scott Lash and Jonathan Friedman, 141–77. Cambridge: Basil Blackwell.

Kelsky, Karen. 2001. *Women on the verge: Japanese women, Western dreams.* Durham, NC: Duke University Press.

Kibria, Nazli. 2002a. *Becoming Asian American: Second-generation Chinese and Korean American identities.* Baltimore: Johns Hopkins University Press.

———. 2002b. Of blood, belonging, and homeland trips: Transnationalism and identity among second-generation Chinese and Korean Americans. In *The changing face of home: The transnational lives of the second generation,* ed. Peggy Levitt and Mary C. Waters, 295–311. New York: Russell Sage Foundation.

Kim, Claire J. 1999. The racial triangulation of Asian Americans. *Politics and Society* 27(1):105–38.

———. 2000. *Bitter fruit: The politics of Black-Korean conflict in New York City.* New Haven, CT: Yale University Press.

Kim, Elaine H. 1993. Home is where the han is: A Korean-American perspective on the Los Angeles upheavals. In *Reading Rodney King/reading urban uprising,* ed. Robert Gooding-Williams, 215–35. New York: Routledge.

Kim, Illsoo. 1981. *New urban immigrants: The Korean community in New York.* Princeton, NJ: Princeton University Press.

Kim, Lili M. 2001. The pursuit of imperfect justice: The predicament of Koreans and Korean Americans on the homefront during World War II. PhD dissertation, University of Rochester, Rochester, New York.

Kim, Nadia. 2003. Guests in someone else's house? Korean immigrants in Los Angeles negotiate American "race," nationhood, and identity. PhD dissertation, University of Michigan–Ann Arbor, Ann Arbor.

————. 2004. A view from below: An analysis of Korean Americans' racial attitudes. *Amerasia Journal* 30(1):1-24.

————. 2006a. "Patriarchy is so third world": Korean immigrant women and migrating White Western masculinity. *Social Problems* 53(4):519–36.

————. 2006b. "Seoul-America" on America's "soul": South Koreans and Korean immigrants navigate global White racial ideology." *Critical Sociology* 32(2–3):381–402.

————. Forthcoming. Finding roots: Korean American youth visit their "homelands." In *Diasporic homecomings: Ethnic return migrants in comparative perspective*, ed. Takeyuki Tsuda.

King, Rebecca Chiyoko. 2002. Eligible to be Japanese American: Counting on multiraciality in Japanese American basketball leagues and beauty pageants. In *Contemporary Asian American communities: Intersections and divergences*, ed. Linda Trinh Võ and Rick Bonus, 120–33. Philadelphia: Temple University Press.

Kondo, Dorinne K. 1990. *Crafting selves: Power, gender, and discourses of identity in a Japanese workplace*. Chicago: University of Chicago Press.

Kong, Maria, and Peggy Saika. 2003. Disparities in giving to APA communities. In *The new face of Asian Pacific America: Numbers, diversity and change in the 21st century*, ed. Eric Lai and Dennis Arguelles, 217–18. San Francisco and Los Angeles: Asian Week and University of California, Los Angeles, Asian American Studies Center Press.

Lai, Eric, and Dennis Arguelles, eds. 2003. *The new face of Asian Pacific America: Numbers, diversity and change in the 21st century*. San Francisco and Los Angeles: Asian-Week and University of California, Los Angeles, Asian American Studies Center Press.

Lauterbach, Richard. 1947. *Danger from the East*. New York: Harper and Brothers.

Lee, Heon Cheol. 1993. Black-Korean conflict in New York City: A sociological analysis. PhD dissertation, Columbia University, New York.

Lee, Jennifer. 2000. Striving for the American dream: Struggle, success, and intergroup conflict among Korean immigrant entrepreneurs. In *Contemporary Asian America: A multidisciplinary reader*, ed. Min Zhou and James V. Gatewood, 278–94. New York: New York University Press.

————. 2002. *Civility in the city: Blacks, Jews, and Koreans in urban America*. Cambridge, MA: Harvard University Press.

Lee, Jennifer, and Frank D. Bean. 2004. America's changing color lines: Race/ethnicity, immigration, and multiracial identification. *Annual Review of Sociology* 30:221–42.

Lee, Kyung-Ja. 1999. Country experiences: Korea. *Contemporary Women's Issues* 83. http://linus.lmu.edu/search?/tcontemporary+women%27s+issues/tcontemporary +womens+issues/1,1,1,B/l856~b1333293&FF=tcontemporary+womens+issues&1,1,,1,0/

startreferer//search/tcontemporary+women%27s+issues/tcontemporary+womens
+issues/1,1,1,B/frameset&FF=tcontemporary+womens+issues&1,1,/endreferer/ (retrieved December 21, 2007).

Lee, Margaret J. 1999. Seoul's celluloid soul: Korea's local film quota has Hollywood
hopping. *The Nation* 269(18):30–31.

Lee, Mary P. 1990. *Quiet odyssey: A pioneer Korean woman in America.* Seattle: University of Washington Press.

Lee, Robert G. 1999. *Orientals: Asian Americans in popular culture.* Philadelphia: Temple
University Press.

Lee, Sharon, and Marilyn Fernandez. 1998. Trends in Asian American racial/ethnic
intermarriage. *Sociological Perspectives* 41(2):323–42.

Lee, Stacey J. 1996. *Unraveling the "model minority" stereotype: Listening to Asian American youth.* New York: Teachers College Press.

Lee, Taeku. 2000. Racial attitudes and the color lines at the close of the twentieth century. In *The state of Asian Pacific America: Transforming race relations, a public policy
report,* ed. Paul Ong, 103–58. Los Angeles: Asian Pacific American Public Policy Institute, Leadership Education for Asian Pacifics (LEAP), and University of California, Los Angeles, Asian American Studies Center.

———. 2005. Bringing class, ethnicity, and nation back to race: The color lines in 2015.
Perspectives on Politics 3(3):557–61.

Lee, Yoo-Lim. 1994. South Korean star search: After new law, advertisers race to sign
foreign celebrities. *Advertising Age International* 65:l14.

Lembo, Ron. 2000. *Thinking through television.* Cambridge, MA: Cambridge University
Press.

Levitt, Peggy. 2001. *The transnational villagers.* Berkeley: University of California
Press.

Lewis, Amanda E. 2004. What group? Studying Whites and Whiteness in the era of col-
orblindness. *Sociological Theory* 22(4):623–46.

Lie, John. 1998. *Han unbound: The political economy of South Korea.* Stanford, CA: Stanford University Press.

———. 2001. *Multiethnic Japan.* Cambridge, MA: Harvard University Press.

———. 2004. *Modern peoplehood.* Cambridge, MA: Harvard University Press.

Lim, Hy-sop. 1978. A study of Korean-American cultural relations with emphasis on
Koreas' perception of American culture. *Korea Journal* (June):4–14.

Lipsitz, George. 1995. *A life in the struggle: Ivory Perry and the culture of opposition.*
Philadelphia: Temple University Press.

———. 1997. "Frantic to join . . . the Japanese army": The Asia Pacific war in the lives
of African American soldiers and civilians. In *The politics of culture in the shadow
of capital,* ed. Lisa Lowe and David Lloyd, 324–53. Durham, NC: Duke University
Press.

———. 1998. *The possessive investment in Whiteness: How White people profit from identity politics.* Philadelphia: Temple University Press.

Loewen, James W. 1971. *The Mississippi Chinese: Between Black and White.* Cambridge, MA: Harvard University Press.

Loo, C. 1980. Community research among Asian Americans: Problematic issues and resolutions. In *Issues in community research: Asian American perspectives* (occasional paper #5), ed. Alice K. Murata and Juanita Salvador-Burris, 15–22. Chicago: Pacific/Asian American Mental Health Research Center.

Lorde, Audrey. 1984. *Sister outsider.* Trumansburg, NY: Crossing Press.

Louie, Vivian S. 2004. *Compelled to excel: Immigration, education, and opportunity among Chinese Americans.* Stanford, CA: Stanford University Press.

Lowe, Lisa. 1996. *Immigrant acts: On Asian American cultural politics.* Durham, NC: Duke University Press.

Lyman, Princeton N. 1968. Korea's involvement in Viet Nam. *Orbis* 12:563–81.

Maira, Sunaina Marr. 2002. *Desis in the house: Indian American youth culture in New York City.* Philadelphia: Temple University Press.

Marshall, T. H. 1973. *Class, citizenship, and social development.* Westport, CT: Greenwood Press.

Massey, Douglas S. 1995. The new immigration and ethnicity in the United States. *Population and Development Review* 21(3):631–52.

Massey, Douglas S., and Nancy A. Denton. 1993. *American apartheid: Segregation and the making of the underclass.* Cambridge, MA: Harvard University Press.

McClintock, Anne. 1995. *Imperial leather: Race, gender and sexuality in the colonial contest.* New York: Routledge.

———. 1997. "No longer in future heaven": Gender, race, and nationalism. In *Dangerous liaisons: Gender, nation, and postcolonial perspectives,* ed. Anne McClintock, Aamir Mufti, and Ella Shohat, 89–112. Minneapolis: University of Minnesota Press.

Meade, E. Grant. 1951. *American military government in Korea.* New York: King's Crown Press.

Merton, Robert K., ed. 1972. Insiders and outsiders: A chapter in the sociology of knowledge. In *Varieties of political expression in sociology,* 9–47. Chicago: University of Chicago Press.

Millard, D. Ralph, Jr. 1955. Oriental peregrinations. *Plastic and Reconstructive Surgery* 16:319–36.

Min, Pyong Gap. 1996. *Caught in the middle: Korean communities in New York and Los Angeles.* Berkeley: University of California Press.

———. 1998. *Changes and conflicts: Korean immigrant families in New York.* Boston: Allyn and Bacon.

———. 2000. The structure and social functions of Korean immigrant churches in the

United States. In *Contemporary Asian America: A multidisciplinary reader*, ed. Min Zhou and James V. Gatewood, 372–91. New York: New York University Press.

_____, ed. 2006. *Asian Americans: Contemporary trends and issues.* 2nd ed. Thousand Oaks, CA: Pine Forge Press.

Min, Pyong Gap, and Rose Kim, eds. 1999. *Struggle for ethnic identity: Narratives by Asian American professionals.* Walnut Creek, CA: Alta Mira Press.

Mirikitani, Janice. 1995. "Looking for America." In *We, the dangerous: New and selected poems.* Berkeley: Celestial Arts.

Mitchell, C. Clyde. 1951. *Korea: Second failure in Asia.* Washington, DC: Public Affairs Institute.

Mittelberg, David, and Mary C. Waters. 1992. The process of ethnogenesis among Haitian and Israeli immigrants in the United States. *Ethnic and Racial Studies* 15(3):412–35.

Miyamoto, Masao. 1979. *As we saw them: The first Japanese embassy to the United States.* Berkeley: University of California Press.

Moon, Katharine H. S. 1997. *Sex among allies: Military prostitution in U.S.-Korea relations.* New York: Columbia University Press.

Moraga, Cherríe. 1981. La guera. In *This bridge called my back: Writings by radical women of color*, ed. Cherríe Moraga and Gloria Anzaldua, 27–34. New York: Kitchen Table Press.

Morgan, David L. 1993. *Successful focus groups: Advancing the state of the art.* Thousand Oaks, CA: Sage.

Moskos, Charles C., and John Sibley Butler. 1997. *All that we can be: Black leadership and racial integration the army way.* New York: Basic Books.

Moya, Paula. 1996. Postmodernism, "realism," and the politics of identity: Cherríe Moraga and Chicana feminism. In *Feminist genealogies, colonial legacies, democratic futures*, ed. Chandra T. Mohanty and M. Jacqui Alexander, 125–50. New York: Routledge.

Mulvey, Laura. 1987. Changes: Thoughts on myth, narrative, and historical experience. *History Workshop* 23(Spring):3–19.

Museum of Public Relations. 2006. The African-American image abroad: Golly, it's good! http://www.prmuseum.com/kendrix/abroad.html (retrieved June 3, 2007).

Myrdal, Gunnar. 1964. *An American dilemma: The Negro problem and modern democracy.* New York: McGraw-Hill.

Nagel, Joane. 1994. Constructing ethnicity: Creating and recreating ethnic identity and culture. *Social Problems* 41:152–76.

National Asian Pacific American Legal Consortium. 1994–2002. *Audit of violence against Asian Pacific Americans.* Washington, DC: National Asian Pacific American Legal Consortium.

National Association of Latino Elected and Appointed Officials. 2006. *The 2006 Directory of Latino Elected Officials*. Washington, DC: NALEO Education Fund.

National Conference for Community and Justice. 2000, 2005. *Taking America's pulse*. New York: National Conference for Community and Justice.

National Conference of Christians and Jews. 1994. *Taking America's pulse*. New York: National Conference of Christians and Jews.

Neckerman, Kathryn M., Prudence Carter, and Jennifer Lee. 1999. Segmented assimilation and minority cultures of mobility. *Ethnic and Racial Studies* 22(6):945–65.

Neelankavil, James P., Venkat Mummalaneni, and David Sessions. 1995. Use of foreign language and models in print advertisements in East Asian countries: A logit modeling approach. *European Journal of Marketing* 29(4):24–38.

Newman, Katherine. 1993. *Declining fortunes: The withering of the American dream*. New York: Basic Books.

Ogbu, John U. 1991. Immigrant and involuntary minorities in comparative perspective. In *Minority status and schooling: A comparative study of immigrant and involuntary minorities*, ed. Margaret A. Gibson and John U. Ogbu, 3–33. New York: Garland.

Okihiro, Gary Y. 1994. *Margins and mainstreams: Asians in American history and culture*. Seattle: University of Washington Press.

Oliver, Melvin L., and Thomas M. Shapiro. 1997. *Black wealth, White wealth: A new perspective on racial inequality*. New York: Routledge.

Olzak, Susan. 1992. *The dynamics of ethnic competition and conflict*. Stanford, CA: Stanford University Press.

Omi, Michael, and Howard Winant. 1994. *Racial formation in the United States: From the 1960s to the 1990s*. New York: Routledge.

Ong, Aihwa. 1996. Cultural citizenship as subject-making: Immigrants negotiate racial and cultural boundaries in the United States. *Current Anthropology* 37(5):737–51.

———. 1999. *Flexible citizenship: The cultural logics of transnationality*. Durham, NC: Duke University Press.

Ong, Paul M. 2000. The affirmative action divide. In *The state of Asian Pacific America: Transforming race relations, a public policy report*, ed. Paul M. Ong, 313–61. Los Angeles: Leadership Education for Asian Pacifics (LEAP), Asian Pacific American Public Policy Institute and University of California, Los Angeles, Asian American Studies Center.

Ong, Paul M., and Tania Azores. 1994. Asian immigrants in Los Angeles: Diversity and divisions. In *The new Asian immigration in Los Angeles and global restructuring*, ed. Paul M. Ong, Edna Bonacich, and Lucie Cheng, 100–129. Philadelphia: Temple University Press.

Ong, Paul M., and David Lee. 2001. Changing of the guard? The emerging immigrant majority in Asian American politics. In *Asian Americans and politics: Perspectives, experiences, prospects*, ed. Gordon H. Chang, 153–72. Stanford, CA: Stanford University Press.

Osajima, Keith. 1988. Asian Americans as the model minority: An analysis of the popular press image in the 1960s and 1980s. In *Reflections on shattered windows: Promises and prospects for Asian American studies,* ed. Gary Okihiro, Shirley Hune, Art Hansen, and John M. Liu, 81–91. Pullman: Washington State University Press.

Palais, James B. 1995. A search for Korean uniqueness. *Harvard Journal of Asiatic Studies* 55(2):409–25.

Palumbo-Liu, David. 1994. Los Angeles, Asians, and perverse ventriloquisms: On the functions of Asian Americans in the recent American imaginary. *Public Culture* 6:365–81.

———. 1999. *Asian/American: Historical crossings of a racial frontier.* Stanford, CA: Stanford University Press.

Park, Edward J. W. 2001. The impact of mainstream political mobilization on Asian American communities: The case of Korean Americans in Los Angeles, 1992–1998. In *Asian Americans and politics: Perspectives, experiences, prospects,* ed. Gordon H. Chang, 285–310. Stanford, CA: Stanford University Press.

———. 2002. Asian Pacific Americans and urban politics. In *Contemporary Asian American communities,* ed. Lisa Trinh Võ and Rick Bonus, 202–15. Philadelphia: Temple University Press.

Park, Jung Sun. 1999. Identity politics: Chicago Korean-Americans and the Los Angeles "riots." In *Koreans in the hood: Conflict with African Americans,* ed. Kwang Chung Kim, 202–31. Baltimore: Johns Hopkins University Press.

Park, Kyeyoung. 1991. Conception of ethnicities by Koreans: Workplace encounters. In *Asian Americans: Comparative and global perspectives,* ed. Shirley Hune, Hyung-Chan Kim, Steven S. Fugita, and Amy Ling, 179–90. Pullman, WA: Washington State University.

———. 1994. The question of culture in the Black/Korean American conflict. In *Black-Korean encounter: Toward understanding and alliance,* ed. Eui-Young Yu, 40–51. Los Angeles: Regina Books.

———. 1995. The reinvention of affirmative action: Korean immigrants' changing conceptions of African Americans and Latin Americans. *Urban Anthropology* 24:59–92.

———. 1996. Use and abuse of race and culture: Black-Korean tensions in America. *American Anthropologist* 98(3):492–99.

———. 1997. *The Korean American dream: Immigrants and small business in New York City.* Ithaca, NY: Cornell University Press.

Park, Lisa Sun-hee. 2005. *Consuming citizenship: Children of Asian immigrant entrepreneurs.* Stanford, CA: Stanford University Press.

Parreñas, Rhacel Salazar. 2001. *Servants of globalization: Women, migration, and domestic work.* Stanford, CA: Stanford University Press.

Peterson, Mark A. 2000. Korean slavery. Discussion Paper. Provo, UT: David M. Kennedy Center for International Studies, Brigham Young University.

Portes, Alejandro, and Rubén G. Rumbaut. 1996. *Immigrant America: A portrait.* 2nd ed. Berkeley: University of California Press.

Portes, Alejandro, and Min Zhou. 1993. The new second generation: Segmented assimilation and its variants. *The Annals of the American Academy of Political and Social Science* 530:74–96.

Prashad, Vijay. 2000. *The karma of brown folk.* Minneapolis: University of Minnesota Press.

Purkayastha, Bandana. 2005. *Negotiating ethnicity: Second-generation South Asian Americans traverse a transnational world.* New Brunswick, NJ: Rutgers University Press.

Pyke, Karen, and Tran Dang. 2003. "FOB" and "whitewashed": Identity and internalized racism among second generation Asian Americans. *Qualitative Sociology* 26(2):147–72.

Pyke, Karen, and Denise L. Johnson. 2003. Asian American women and racialized femininities: Doing gender across cultural worlds. *Gender and Society* 17(1):33–53.

Qian, Zhenchao, and Daniel T. Lichter. 2007. Social boundaries and marital assimilation: Interpreting trends in racial and ethnic intermarriage. *American Sociological Review* 72: 68–94.

Rainbow Center. 1994. Rainbow News Letter #3, Rainbow Center, Flushing, N.Y. January 1994, 8.

Reeves, Jimmie L., and Richard Campbell. 1997. Coloring the crack crisis. In *The media in black and white,* ed. Everette Dennis and Edward C. Pease, 61–70. New Brunswick: Transaction Publishers.

Robinson, Michael Edson. 1988. *Cultural nationalism in colonial Korea, 1920–1925.* Seattle: University of Washington Press.

Rose, Tricia. 1994. *Black noise: Rap music and Black culture in contemporary America.* Middletown, CT: Wesleyan University Press.

Rudrappa, Sharmila. 2004. *Ethnic routes to becoming American: Indian immigrants and the cultures of citizenship.* New Brunswick, NJ: Rutgers University Press.

Russell, John. 1991. Race and reflexivity: The Black Other in contemporary Japanese mass culture. *Cultural Anthropology* 6(1):3–25.

Sahlins, Marshall D. 1981. *Historical metaphors and mythical realities: Structure in the early history of the Sandwich Islands Kingdom.* Ann Arbor: University of Michigan Press.

Said, Edward W. 1978, 1979. *Orientalism.* New York: Vintage.

———. 1993. *Culture and imperialism.* New York: Alfred A. Knopf.

Schmid, Andre. 2002. *Korea between empires, 1859–1919.* New York: Columbia University Press.

Schuman, Howard, Charlotte Steeh, Lawrence Bobo, and Maria Krysan. 1997. *Racial attitudes in America: Trends and interpretations.* Rev. ed. Cambridge, MA: Harvard University Press.

Scott, Joan W. 2003. Deconstructing equality-versus-difference: Or, the uses of post-structuralist theory for feminism. In *Feminist theory reader: Local and global perspectives*, ed. Carole R. McCann and Seung-Kyung Kim, 378–90. New York: Routledge.

Seol, Dong-Hoon, and John D. Skrentny. 2004. South Korea: Importing undocumented workers. In *Controlling immigration: A global perspective*, 2nd ed., ed. Wayne A. Cornelius, Takeyuki Tsuda, Philip L. Martin, and James F. Hollifield, 475–513. Stanford, CA: Stanford University Press.

Shin, Gi-wook. 1998. Nation, history, and politics. In *Nationalism and the construction of Korean identity*, ed. Hyung-il Pai and Timothy Tangherlini, 148–65. Berkeley: Institute of East Asian Studies, University of California, Berkeley.

Shinagawa, Larry, and Gin Yong Pang. 1996. Asian American panethnicity and intermarriage. *Amerasia Journal* 22(2):127–52.

Shorrock, Tim. 1996a. Ex-leaders go on trial in Seoul. *Journal of Commerce*, February 27, 1996, A1.

————. 1996b. Debacle in Kwangju. *The Nation*, December 9, 1996, 19–22.

Smedley, Audrey. 1993. *Race in North America: Origin and evolution of a worldview*. Boulder, CO: Westview Press.

Smith, Anna Deveare. 1994. *Twilight: Los Angeles, 1992*. New York: Anchor Books/Doubleday.

Sonenshein, Raphael J. 1996. The battle over liquor stores in south central Los Angeles: The management of an interminority conflict. *Urban Affairs Review* 31:710–37.

Song, Min Hyoung. 2005. *Strange future*. Durham, NC: Duke University Press.

Stoler, Ann L. 1995. *Race and the education of desire: Foucault's "History of sexuality" and the colonial order of things*. Durham, NC: Duke University Press.

Sturdevant, Saundra P., and Brenda Stoltzfus. 1993. *Let the good times roll: Prostitution and the U.S. military in Asia*. New York: New Press.

Suzuki, Bob. 1989. Asian Americans as the model minority. *Change* 21:13–19.

Takagi, Dana Y. 1993. *The retreat from race: Asian-American admissions and racial politics*. New Brunswick, NJ: Rutgers University Press.

Takaki, Ronald T. 1998. *Strangers from a different shore: A history of Asian Americans*. New York: Penguin Books. (Orig. pub. 1989.)

Tanaka, Stefan. 1993. *Japan's Orient: Rendering pasts into history*. Berkeley: University of California Press.

Tangherlini, Timothy R. 1999. Remapping Koreatown: Folklore, narrative and the Los Angeles riots. *Western Folklore* 58(2):149–73.

Taylor, Charles. 1994. The politics of recognition. In *Multiculturalism*, ed. Amy Gutmann, 25–73. Princeton, NJ: Princeton University Press.

Tomlinson, John. 1999. *Globalization and culture*. Chicago: University of Chicago Press.

Tuan, Mia. 1998. *Forever foreigners or honorary Whites? The Asian ethnic experience today*. New Brunswick, NJ: Rutgers University Press.

————. 1999. Neither *real* Americans nor *real* Asians? Multigeneration Asian ethnics navigating the terrain of authenticity. *Qualitative Sociology* 22(2):105–25.

UCLA Asian American Studies Center and Asian Pacific American Institute for Congressional Studies. 2005–2006. *National Asian Pacific American Political Almanac, 2005–2006.* 12th ed. Los Angeles: University of California, Los Angeles, Asian American Studies Center and Asian Pacific American Institute for Congressional Studies.

UCLA Asian American Studies Center and Dean Adachi. 2004. Socioeconomic status of Koreans in Los Angeles County, California, and the United States. Los Angeles: University of California, Los Angeles, Asian American Studies Center.

Vickerman, Milton. 1999. *Crosscurrents: West Indian immigrants and race.* New York: Oxford University Press.

Vō, Linda T. 2000. Performing ethnography in Asian American communities: Beyond the insider-versus-outsider perspective. In *Cultural compass: Ethnographic explorations of Asian America,* ed. Martin F. Manalansan IV, 17–37. Philadelphia: Temple University Press.

Wagatsuma, Hiroshi, and Yoneyama Toshinao. 1980. *Henken no Kōzō* [The structure of prejudice]. Tokyo: NHK Books.

Wallerstein, Immanuel. 1974. *The modern world system,* vol. 1. New York: Academic Press.

Warren, Jonathan W., and France W. Twine. 1997. White Americans, the new minority? Non-Blacks and the ever-expanding boundaries of Whiteness. *Journal of Black Studies* 28(2):200–218.

Waters, Mary C. 1999. *Black identities: West Indian immigrant dreams and American realities.* Cambridge, MA: Harvard University Press.

Williams, Patricia J. 1991. *The alchemy of race and rights: A diary of a law professor.* Cambridge, MA: Harvard University Press.

Willie, Charles V. (1978). The inclining significance of race. *Society* 15:12–15.

Wimmer, Andreas, and Nina Glick Schiller. 2003. Methodological nationalism, the social sciences, and the study of migration: An essay in historical epistemology. *International Migration Review* 37(3):576–610.

Winant, Howard. 2001. *The world is a ghetto: Race and democracy since World War II.* New York: Basic Books.

Wu, Frank H. 2002. *Yellow: Race in America beyond Black and White.* New York: Basic Books.

X, Malcolm, and Alex Haley. 1965. *The autobiography of Malcolm X.* New York: Ballantine Books.

Xie, Yu, and Kimberly Goyette. 2004. *A demographic portrait of Asian Americans.* New York: Russell Sage Foundation and Population Reference Bureau.

Yancey, George. 2003. *Who is White? Latinos, Asians, and the new Black/Nonblack divide.* Boulder, CO: Lynne Rienner Publishers.

Yoon, In-Jin. 1997. *On my own: Korean businesses and race relations in America*. Chicago: University of Chicago Press.

Yu, Eui-Young. 1990. *Korean community profile: Life and consumer patterns*. Los Angeles: Regina Books.

———. 1992. "We saw our dreams burn for no reason," *San Francisco Examiner*, May 24, 1992, editorial page.

———. 2001. Korean population in the United States as reflected in the year 2000 U.S. Census. Paper presented at the Population Association of Korea Annual Meeting, Seoul, Korea, December 1, 2001.

———. 2003. Entrepreneurs par excellence. In *The new face of Asian Pacific America: Numbers, diversity and change in the 21st century*, ed. Eric Lai and Dennis Arguelles, 57–62. San Francisco and Los Angeles: Asian Week and University of California, Los Angeles, Asian American Studies Center Press.

Yu, Eui-Young, and Peter Choe. 2003. Social and economic indicators by race and Asian ethnic groups and Korean population density map: Top 5 metropolitan areas, 2000. Paper presented at Conference of Korean American Coalition–Census Information Center, San Francisco, September 12–14, 2003.

Yu, Henry. 2002. *Thinking Orientals: Migration, contact, and exoticism in modern America*. New York: Oxford University Press.

Yuh, Ji-Yeon. 2002. *Beyond the shadow of camptown: Korean military brides in America*. New York: New York University Press.

Zhou, Min, and Carl L. Bankston III. 1998. *Growing up American: How Vietnamese children adapt to life in the United States*. New York: Russell Sage Foundation.

Zhou, Min, and Susan S. Kim. 2006. Community forces, social capital, and educational achievement: The case of supplementary education in the Chinese and Korean immigrant communities. *Harvard Educational Review* 76(1):1-29.

English-Language Newspapers/Periodicals

09/21/82. "Comments on interracial marriages." *Korean Central Daily News*.

11/15/86. "South Korea's American signal." *Washington Post*.

10/05/89. "Snakes alive in Korea's cinemas." *Financial Times*.

06/92."Korean dream in ashes." *Business Korea*.

12/05/94."Asian market profiles South Korea." *Electronic Media*.

01/03/95. "U.S. majors stake claim to South Korean turf." *Hollywood Reporter*, p. 11.

07/02/96. Untitled. *Media Daily*.

12/04/98. "Korean stars protest U.S. attempt to open South Korean film market." *Associated Press*.

10/04/2001. "More Asian women seek eyelid surgery." *Toronto Star*.

10/19/2002. "Fashionably Pale." *Korea Now: Biweekly Magazine*.

04/01/2006. "Mixed-race Korean welfare drive states." *Korea Times*.

08/31/2006. "Japanese women catch the 'Korean Wave.' " *Washington Post*.

Korean-Language Newspapers

12/07/1908. "Paengnam Sanin, Kungminhwak kwa mujirhak [Citizenship and materialism]." *Sŏbuk hakhoe wŏlbo*, p. 5.

12/18/29. "An article insulting Asians in US *Liberty* magazine." *Chosun Ilbo*, p. 2.

10/12/47. "Korean Americans' lives are wealthy." *Chosun Ilbo*, p. 2.

05/07/62. "Second-generation Korean Americans who don't know Korean." *Chosun Ilbo*, p. 2.

08/27/64. "What returning Korean Americans say, favorable comments." *Chosun Ilbo*, p. 4.

12/29/71. "Hardship for Korean Americans as U.S. economy declines." *Chosun Ilbo*, p. 4.

07/09/76. "Ko-mericans: Day and Night." *Chosun Ilbo*, p. 3.

01/26/78. "Ko-mericans in Hawaii. 75th year in US immigration." *Chosun Ilbo*, p. 6.

12/18/79. "Koreans have problems adapting to US society." *Chosun Ilbo*, p. 5.

02/06/81. "Korean American Sammy Lee denied TV commentator post because of discrimination." *Chosun Ilbo*, p. 8.

07/26/81. "Will racial discrimination always survive?" *Chosun Ilbo*, p. 5.

05/26/85. "Protestor on occupation of Seoul's U.S. Cultural Center." *Chosun Ilbo*, Society section.

11/05/85. "Korea's economy and racial sentiment." *Chosun Ilbo*, p. 2.

06/27/86. "Only a minority make up the recent anti-Americans movement." *Chosun Ilbo*, p. 2.

05/10/87. "Anti-Americanism in Korea, anti-Koreanism in the US." *Chosun Ilbo*, p. 3.

02/23/88. "Because he is Asian." *Chosun Ilbo*, p. 3.

07/29/88. "Korean Americans eager to volunteer as translators in '88 Olympics." *Chosun Ilbo*, p. 3.

09/17/90. "The viewpoint of anti-American college students." *Chosun Ilbo*, p. 14.

05/02/92. "Variety Store." *Chosun Ilbo*, p. 1.

05/03/92. "Why Koreans are the only ones attacked/lack of concern from other minorities." *Chosun Ilbo*, p. 18.

05/04/92. "Black and White inequality." *Chosun Ilbo*, p. 5.

05/05/92. "Koreans and Blacks, the way to co-exist." *Chosun Ilbo*, p. 5.

05/07/92. "US TV focuses too much on Korean-Black conflicts." *Chosun Ilbo*, p. 8.

02/19/93. "Crushed American dream/constant attacks." *Chosun Ilbo*, p. 23.

02/23/93. "Angry Korean Americans/US movie portrays Koreans as money-hungry." *Chosun Ilbo*, p. 30.

08/23/95. "Next year ~6,000 Koreans in US Seek to Naturalize." *Chosun Ilbo*, p. 39.

05/20/02. "Korean-American invitees to White House." *Chosun Ilbo*, p. 3.

01/09/03. "Media reps focus on anti-US feelings." *Hankook Ilbo*. http://www.koreatimes .co.kr/www/search/search_list.asp (retrieved December 22, 2007).

05/20/03. " 'Single race' and racial discrimination." *Chosun Ilbo*, p. 31.

04/19/06. "Fighter Kwak Sa-Jin's 'reason for standing in the ring': To end anti-biracial discrimination." *Chosun Ilbo*, p. 11.

03/02/07. "Do Koreans detest the Jewish?" *Hangyŭrae*, p. 21.

Korean-Language Internet Sites

http://kin.naver.com/db/detail.php?d1id=6&dir_id=61501&eid=/9Ji2eYJyPoaZGJwn +pLVYpljg2PhUfX&qb=x9GxubOywNo= (retrieved July 14, 2007).

www.daum.com. 2005. "The naturalized Koreans who know more about Koreans than Koreans do," May 5, 2005. http://k.daum.net/qna/file/view.html (retrieved July 14, 2007).

www.empas.com. 2006. "Are you criticizing me for loving Western men, not Korean men? Isn't that discrimination? You've got to be joking," February 15, 2006. http:// kdaq.empas.com/worry/view.html?n=215748&sq=%C7%D1%B1%B9%B3%B2%C0 %DA (retrieved July 14, 2007).

www.joara.com. 2007. "Why Korean men are considered to be stupid, from a logical standpoint," July 4, 2007.

www.joara.com/community/board/boardView.html?idx=103805&bbsid=board&sub _bbsid=board_mine (retrieved July 14, 2007).

www.naver.com. 2005. "Why do Korean women hate Korean men so much?" December 20, 2005.

Index

The letter *t* following a page number denotes a table. The letter *f* following a page number denotes a figure.

self-foreignizing and, 186–92; transnational feedback about, 233–35. *See also*
Los Angeles riots
Radio Korea, 183–84, 227
Rain, 68, 230
Reagan, Ronald, 72
Recognition: identities and, 150; political,
111–14, 164, 219, 243–44
Red Apple Boycotts (1990), 18
Reeves, Jimmie, 102
Research methods, 255–68; coding process in,
261; effort to better the world and,
267–68; ethnography in, 258–60; extended case method in, 260–61, 265–66,
281n5; focus groups and, 257–58;
grounded theory in, 265–66, 281n5; home
country context in, 255; interviews and,
255–58; logistics and analysis and, 261; in
Los Angeles county, 255–58, 260–61,
264–65; newspapers and, 260–61; participant observation and, 258–60; qualitative,
255, 267; questions in, 258; selection criteria and, 256; in Seoul, 257–61, 262–64;
subjectivity (insider/outsider) issues in,
261–65; theoretical lenses in, 261, 266
Rhee Syngman, 41
Robinson, Michael, 24
ROK (Republic of Korea): commodity racism
and, 88; politics and, 119–21; student
movements and, 72; U.S. military and,
49–50, 71, 113
Roman Holiday (film), 60–61
Roots (film), 98–99, 106, 147–48
Rudrappa, Sharmila, 196
Russell, John, 28, 31–32, 37, 89

Said, Edward, 56
Saika, Peggy, 152
Sararīman, 84
School shootings, South Korean views of,
61–62, 135
Scranton, Mary, 34–35
Segmented assimilation theories, 3–4, 168, 247
Segregation, in U.S. military, 93–94
Seoul, research in, 257–61, 262–64
Seoul Broadcasting System (SBS), 39
Sex workers, violence against, 72–73, 94
Sharpton, Al, 215
Shawshank Redemption, The (film), 106
Shopkeepers, tracking of buyers by, 87
Shorrock, Tim, 276n10

Similarity and difference, politics of, 186–92,
195, 247
Sin Chaeho, 24
Skylife (digital satellite service), 39
SKY (Seoul, Korea, and Yonsei Universities),
34
Small business ownership. *See* Entrepreneurship, ethnic
Social citizenship, 14–19, 139, 149, 165, 196, 219,
233, 243. *See also* Citizenship line
Social class: assimilation and, 4–5; Korean
Americans and, 141; Korean American
views of U.S., 122–23; limits of, 240; and
race in U.S., 140–43, 278n3
Social remittances: defined, 115–16; trans-
pacific, 134–37; from U.S. to South Korea,
223–41
Social Security, view of, 120
Socioeconomic status, 141–49, 378n3; ethnic
entrepreneurship and, 141–43, 186,
188–91, 279n9; of Korean American
sample, 256
SOFA. *See* U.S. Status of Forces Agreement
(SOFA)
Songtan land infractions, 71
South Koreans: Blacks and, 90–101, 112; discrimination and, 230–31; invisibility of,
78–82, 107–14; Latinos and, 8, 108–9,
275n11; partially present at "home,"
78–82; transnational feedback to, 223–41;
understanding of U.S. racial hierarchies
of, 236–39; White America and, 44–82;
White-Black America and, 83–114. *See
also* Racialization in South Korea
South Koreans, cultural system of, 23–43;
blood line purity and, 24–25, 100; collective authoritarian personality in, 85–86;
color hierarchy in, 27–33, 48, 84–85; early
encounters with White America and,
33–35; encounters with Euro-American
racism and, 36–40; ideologies in, 83–87;
Japanese influence on racial history of,
30–32, 84–85; migration and, 40–43; nation and ethnic nationalism and, 23–27;
"race" and, 27–33. *See also* Inferiority,
South Korean sense of
Spanish language, 163–65
Suburban and urban ethnic concentration,
143, 143t
Superior-high and inferior-low socioeconomic status, 141–49, 162